JUN 2 8 2007

V
t
III
at Urb

Public Opinion and Changing Identities in the Early Modern Netherlands

Studies in Medieval and Reformation Traditions

History, Culture, Religion, Ideas

Founded by
Heiko A. Oberman†

Edited by
Andrew Colin Gow, Edmonton, Alberta

In cooperation with
Thomas A. Brady, Jr., Berkeley, California
Johannes Fried, Frankfurt
Brad Gregory, University of Notre Dame, Indiana
Berndt Hamm, Erlangen
Susan C. Karant-Nunn, Tucson, Arizona
Jürgen Miethke, Heidelberg
M.E.H. Nicolette Mout, Leiden
Gustav Henningsen, Copenhagen

VOLUME CXXI

Alastair Duke

Public Opinion and Changing Identities in the Early Modern Netherlands

Essays in Honour of Alastair Duke

Edited by
Judith Pollmann
Andrew Spicer

BRILL

LEIDEN • BOSTON
2007

Cover illustration: Jan van Vliet. *De Liedjeszanger* (c. 1630), Atlas van Stolk, Rotterdam.

Brill has done its best to establish the rights to use the materials printed herein. Should any other party feel that its rights have been infringed, we would be glad to be in contact with them.

This book is printed on acid-free paper.

Library of Congress Cataloging-in-Publication Data

A C.I.P. record for this book is available from the Library of Congress.

ISSN   1573-4188
ISBN-13: 978-90-04-15527-5
ISBN-10: 90-04-15527-9

PRINTED IN THE NETHERLANDS

CONTENTS

LIST OF ILLUSTRATIONS

ABBREVIATIONS

AGN   *Algemene Geschiedenis der Nederlanden*, ed. D.P. Blok *et al.*
           (Weesp, 1977–83)
ARAB   Algemeen Rijksarchief Brussel
P. Benedict *et al.*, eds., *Reformation, Revolt and Civil War*
           P. Benedict *et al.*, eds., *Reformation, Revolt and Civil War in
           France and the Netherlands, 1555–1585*, Koninklijke Nederlandse
           Akademie van Wetenschappen Verhandelingen, Afd. Letter-
           kunde, Nieuwe Reeks 176 (Amsterdam, 1999)
BG   *Bijdragen tot de Geschiedenis*
BMGN   *Bijdragen en Mededelingen voor de Geschiedenis der Nederlanden*
BMHG   Bijdragen en Mededelingen van het Historisch Genootschap
Duke, 'From King and Country to King or Country?'
           A. Duke, 'From King and Country to King or Country?
           Loyalty and Treason in the Revolt of the Netherlands',
           Transactions of the Royal Historical Society, 5th ser., 32 (1982),
           113–135; repr. in *idem, Reformation and Revolt*
Duke, *Reformation and Revolt*
           A.C. Duke, *Reformation and Revolt in the Low Countries* (London
           and Ronceverte, 1990)
Duke, 'Dissident Propaganda'
           A. Duke, 'Dissident Propaganda and Political Organiza-
           tion at the Outbreak of the Revolt of the Netherlands',
           in P. Benedict *et al.*, eds., *Reformation, Revolt and Civil War*
Duke, 'Posters, Pamphlets and Prints'
           A. Duke, 'Posters, Pamphlets and Prints. The Ways and
           Means of Disseminating Dissident Opinion on the Eve of
           the Dutch Revolt', *Dutch Crossing* 27 (2003), 23–44
Duke, 'The Elusive Netherlands'
           A.C. Duke, 'The Elusive Netherlands. The Question of
           National Identity in the Early Modern Low Countries on
           the Eve of the Revolt', *BMGN* 119 (2004), 10–38
Duke and Tamse, eds., *Clio's Mirror*
           A.C. Duke and C.A. Tamse, eds., *Clio's Mirror. Historiography
           in Britain and the Netherlands*, Britain and the Netherlands 8
           (Zutphen, 1985)

ILE   *Iusti Lipsi Epistolae*
Israel, *Dutch Republic*
              J.I. Israel, *The Dutch Republic. Its Rise, Greatness and Fall*
              1477–1806 (Oxford, 1995)
NAK   *Nederlands Archief voor Kerkgeschiedenis*
SAA   Stadsarchief Antwerpen
SCJ   *The Sixteenth Century Journal*
TvG   *Tijdschrift voor Geschiedenis*

NOTES ON CONTRIBUTORS

HUGH DUNTHORNE is Senior Lecturer in History at the University of Wales, Swansea. His publications include *The Maritime Power. A Study of Anglo-Dutch Relations in the Age of Walpole* (1987) and *The Enlightenment* (1991). He is at present completing a book on the Revolt of the Netherlands and its impact on seventeenth-century Britain.

RAINGARD ESSER is Senior Lecturer in History at The University of the West of England, Bristol. Her recent publications include *Die Tudors und die Stuarts* (2004); 'Schwierige Vergangenheit. Amsterdamer Stadtgeschichten des 17. Jahrhunderts', *Zeitschrift für Historische Forschung* 30 (2003); *Kulturmetropolen – Metropolenkultur. Die Stadt als Kommunikationsraum im 18. Jahrhundert*, with Thomas Fuchs (2002); *Niederländische Exulanten im England des späten 16. und frühen 17. Jahrhunderts* (1996).

JONATHAN ISRAEL was Professor of Dutch History at UCL from 1985 to 2000 and since January 2001 has been Professor of Modern European History at the Institute for Advanced Study, Princeton. He is the author of *Radical Enlightenment. Philosophy and the Making of Modernity (1650–1750)* which was published in 2001.

GUSTAAF JANSSENS is the Director of the Archives of the Royal Palace in Brussels and Associate Professor in 'Archival Science' at the Catholic University of Louvain and the Free University of Brussels. He is the author of *Brabant in 't Verweer. Loyale Oppositie tegen Spanje's Bewind in de Nederlanden van Alva tot Farnese, 1567–1578*, Standen en Landen 39 (Kortijk-Heule, 1989) and of numerous articles on the sixteenth-century Netherlands, archival studies and the political history of Belgium and the Belgian monarchy since 1831.

GUIDO MARNEF is Professor of Early Modern History at the University of Antwerp. He is the author of *Antwerp in the Age of Reformation. Underground Protestantism in a Commercial Metropolis 1550–1577* (Baltimore, 1996), and of numerous articles dealing with Reformation and Revolt in the Low Countries.

M.E.H. NICOLETTE MOUT is Professor of Modern History and Professor of Central European Studies at the University of Leiden. She has published widely on Dutch and Central European history, mainly during the early modern period. Amongst her recent publications are *Die Kultur des Humanismus. Reden, Briefe, Traktate, Gespräche von Petrarca bis Kepler*, ed. Nicolette Mout (Munich, 1998) and 'Pia curiositas. Desiderius Erasmus and Heiko Augustinus Oberman in between Late Middle Ages and Reformation', in T.A. Brady *et al.*, eds., *The Work of Heiko A. Oberman. Papers from the Symposium on His Seventieth Birthday*. Kerkhistorische Bijdragen 20 (Leiden-Boston, 2003), 147–162.

HENK VAN NIEROP is Professor of Early Modern History at the University of Amsterdam, and Academic Director of the Amsterdam Centre for the Study of the Golden Age. He has published on the social, political and religious history of the Revolt of the Netherlands and the Dutch Golden Age. Among his books are: *The Nobility of Holland: from Knights to Regents* (1993); *Het verraad van het Noorderkwartier. Oorlog, terreur en recht in de Nederlandse Opstand* (1999); and with R. Po-Chia Hsia, eds., *Calvinism and Religious Toleration in the Dutch Golden Age* (2002).

ANDREW PETTEGREE is Head of the School of History at the University of St Andrews and founding Director of the St Andrews Reformation Studies Institute. His latest book, *Reformation and the Culture of Persuasion*, was published by Cambridge University Press in 2005.

JUDITH POLLMANN is Senior Lecturer in Early Modern Dutch history at the University of Leiden. She is the author of *Religious Choice in the Dutch Republic. The Reformation of Arnoldus Buchelius (1565–1641)* (1999) and of numerous articles on the religious history of the early modern Netherlands. She is currently working on a book on Catholic identity and religious change in the Habsburg Netherlands, 1520–1635.

*PAUL REGAN completed his Ph.D. thesis on 'The Construction of Patriotic Sentiment in the Sixteenth-Century Low Countries: Cartography, Calvinism and Rebel Propaganda' at the University of Southampton in 1995. He is now an Anglican parish priest serving in the diocese of Lichfield, England.

*ANDREW SAWYER completed his Ph.D. thesis on 'Pictures, Power and the Polity: a Vision of the Political Images of the Early Dutch Republic' at the University of Southampton in 2000. He has published several articles on political iconography as well as on history and computing.

JOKE SPAANS is Reader in the History of Christianity in the Subfaculty of Theology at Utrecht University. Her main publications are *Haarlem na de Reformatie. Stedelijke cultuur en kerkelijk leven 1577–1620*, Hollandse historische reeks 11 (The Hague, 1989); *Armenzorg in Friesland, 1500–1800. Publieke zorg en particuliere liefdadigheid in zes Friese steden. Leeuwarden, Bolsward, Franeker, Sneek, Dokkum en Harlingen* (Hilversum, 1998). She edited *Een golf van beroering. De omstreden opwekking in de Republiek in het midden van de achttiende eeuw* (Hilversum, 2001).

*ANDREW SPICER is Senior Lecturer in Early Modern European History at Oxford Brookes University. His *The French-Speaking Reformed Community and their Church in Southampton, 1567–c. 1620* (1997) was based on his University of Southampton doctoral thesis. He has co-edited *Society and Culture in the Huguenot World* (2002), *Sacred Space in Early Modern Europe* (2005), *Defining the Holy. Sacred Space in Medieval and Early Modern Europe* (2006) and his monograph *Calvinist Churches in Early Modern Europe* will be published in 2007.

JULIAAN WOLTJER is Professor Emeritus in Dutch history at the University of Leiden. His publications include *Friesland in hervormingstijd* (1960), *Recent Verleden. De geschiedenis van Nederland in de Twintigste Eeuw* (1992) and *Tussen vrijheidsstrijd en burgeroorlog. Over de Nederlandse Opstand, 1555–1580* (1994). He is currently completing *De escalatie van een conflict. Over de voorgeschiedenis en de eerste stadia van de Nederlandse Opstand* that will appear with Balans in Amsterdam.

* Supervised by Alastair Duke.

INTRODUCTION

Judith Pollmann and Andrew Spicer

In his *The Structural Transformation of the Public Sphere*, Jürgen Habermas argued in 1962 that the early eighteenth century had witnessed the emergence of a 'public sphere' or *Öffentlichkeit*.[1] In the bourgeois milieu of the London coffee houses, Parisian salons and the German table societies, literary debate and criticism flourished and developed into more fundamental debates on political and economic issues. Habermas argued that this was a new and fundamental shift in European culture, that laid the foundations for the development of modern politics in the West. Prior to the eighteenth century, he argued, the state had been the embodiment of the public sphere, its exclusivity and dominance represented in the rituals of the Church and the Court.

In recent years, a growing number of early modern historians have begun to challenge this periodization, offering arguments for the importance of 'public opinion' and perhaps even the existence of a 'public sphere' in sixteenth- and seventeenth-century Europe, well before the advent of coffee houses or the emergence of newspapers as a forum for debate.[2] Indeed, so obvious does this challenge now seem, that we may wonder why it has taken historians so long to do so. Of course, the reception of Habermas's work in the English-speaking world was much delayed until the appearance of an English translation in 1989, but he was widely read elsewhere.

---

[1] J. Habermas, *Strukturwandel der Öffentlichkeit. Untersuchungen zu einer Kategorie der bürgerlichen Gesellschaft* (Berlin, 1982).

[2] E.g. D. Zaret, 'Religion, Science and Printing in the Public Spheres in Seventeenth-Century England', in C. Calhoun, ed., *Habermas and the Public Sphere* (Cambridge, Mass., 1992); A. Fox, 'Rumour, News and Popular Political Opinion in Elizabethan and Early Stuart England', *The Historical Journal* 40 (1997), 597–620; J. van Horn Melton, 'Introduction', in J. van Horn Melton, ed., *Cultures of Communication from Reformation to Enlightenment. Constructing Publics in Early Modern German Lands* (Aldershot, 2002); B. Dooley and S. Baron, eds., *The Politics of Information in Early Modern Europe* (London, 2001); A. Pettegree, *Reformation and the Culture of Persuasion* (Cambridge, 2005); J.W. Koopmans, ed., *News and Politics in Early Modern Europe, 1500–1800* (Louvain, 2005).

One possible explanation may be that for historians of early modern Germany, Habermas's theory seemed to chime so beautifully with the 'confessionialization' theory that the historians Wolfgang Reinhardt and Heinz Schilling developed in the 1970s. This, too, was predicated on the great, and ever-increasing power of the early modern state, and on a notion that the state had been strengthening its grip on culture and religion at the expense of the voice of their subjects. It was perhaps only once attention had shifted towards the gap between the theory and the practice of absolute claims to power, and the *de facto* need for rulers to accommodate public opinion, that Habermas's periodization became less satisfactory.[3] A second factor may be that Habermas's bourgeois public sphere was very much a 'secular' phenomenon, while in the sixteenth and seventeenth centuries the most obvious, and best-studied, examples of engagement of large groups of subjects and citizens with public affairs were concerned with religion.[4] This was evident in pamphlet wars that erupted in the Germany of the 1520s, in France and the Netherlands in the 1560s, or in England between 1630 and 1660. It was a new emphasis on the fundamentally religious nature of political debate (and the political nature of religion), that made Habermas's distinction between the realms of the secular and the religious seem less appropriate. Recent scholarship on the eighteenth century, too, has emphasized the ongoing importance of religion in political thought and discourse.

Yet the speed with which historians of the sixteenth and seventeenth centuries are now building a case for the importance of 'public opinion' can only be understood if we realize that their arguments are based less on the presentation of brand new evidence than on marshalling the findings of existing research into popular culture and media. Historians of the sixteenth and seventeenth centuries have for decades been expending enormous energy on the study of early modern methods of communication. The original trigger for this was

---

[3] For a summary and assessment, see H.R. Schmidt, *Konfessionalisierung im 16. Jahrhundert* (Munich, 1992) and R. Po-Chia Hsia, *Social Discipline in the Reformation.Central Europe, 1550–1750* (London and New York, 1989). The importance of local compromise and public opinion is emphasized, for instance, in M. Forster, *The Counter-Reformation in the Villages. Religion and Reform in the Bishopric of Speyer, 1560–1720* (Ithaca, NY, 1992). Changing ideas on state power are discussed, for instance, in J. Miller, ed., *Absolutism in Seventeenth-Century Europe* (Basingstoke, 1990).

[4] As emphasized by Zaret, 'Religion, Science and Printing'.

probably the very influential idea that there had been a widening gap between popular and elite culture in early modern Europe.[5] In the course of re-examining this idea, and its eventual discarding, historians were forced to consider how semi-literate societies engaged with new knowledge and information, and with the wider political community beyond their own towns and villages. The result has been a much richer and more varied image of the early modern world. Historians discovered that there were a number of ways of participating in the literate world, and many ways of being a reader.[6] Under the influence of anthropological ideas and semiology, scholars have studied the political importance of public ritual and its inversion.[7] Others have focused on the role of sermons and images, songs and rumour in the shaping of public opinion.[8] Print has been the subject of careful scrutiny; and many now stress the continuing importance of script after the invention of printing – for instance for the newsletters that predated the newspaper, but also to circumvent censorship.[9] In some ways, then, the discovery of a public sphere in early modern Europe is more about a realignment of historiographical traditions than about a seismic shift of direction in early modern historiography.

The work of Alastair Duke illustrates this phenomenon very well. Long before sixteenth-century specialists thought about Habermas, Duke made it his business to explore how Netherlanders of the sixteenth century, and especially Netherlandish dissenters, came to think as they did: of religion and persecution, of their princes and their communities and their churches, of themselves and of their enemies. Much of what we know about the shaping and shaking of public

---

[5] E.g. K.V. Thomas, *Religion and the Decline of Magic. Studies in Popular Beliefs in Sixteenth- and Seventeenth-Century England* (Harmondsworth, 1973); P. Burke, *Popular Culture in Early Modern Europe* (London, 1978); R. Muchembled, *L'Invention de l'homme moderne. Sensibilités, moeurs et comportements collectifs sous l'Ancien Régime* (Paris, 1988).

[6] E.g. M. Spufford, *Small Books and Pleasant Histories: Popular Fiction and its Readership in Seventeenth-Century England* (Cambridge, 1981); T. Watt, *Cheap Print and Popular Piety, 1550–1640* (Cambridge, 1991).

[7] N.Z. Davis, 'The Rites of Violence. Religious Riot in 16th-Century France', *Past and Present* 22 (1973), 51–91. E. Le Roy Ladurie, *Le Carnaval de Romans. De la Chandeleur au mercredi des Cendres, 1579–1580* (Paris, 1979).

[8] R.W. Scribner, *For the Sake of Simple Folk. Popular Propaganda for the German Reformation* (Oxford, 1981); A. Fox, *Oral and Literate Culture in England, 1500–1700* (Oxford, 2000). Much of this also discussed in Pettegree, *Reformation*.

[9] E.g. J. Crick and A. Walsham, eds., *The Uses of Script and Print, 1300–1700* (Cambridge, 2004).

opinion in the Low Countries we owe to Duke, and much of what
we thought we knew, his gentle but thorough scrutiny of an enormous range of evidence has persuaded us to revise. He has explored
the logistics of print, and the making of myths, the role of posters
and images; the gathering of conventicles and the distribution of
pamphlets; the changing meaning of terms like 'treason', 'inquisition'
and 'discipline'.[10]

Duke has emphasized that to understand this early modern 'culture of communication' is particularly crucial in a Netherlandish context. The 'Elusive Netherlands' – the title of Alastair Duke's most
recent article – captures much of what scholars have to say about
that troubled and prosperous part of early modern Europe, that contemporaries could not even agree on what to call.[11] The Low Countries
were a 'composite state' within a composite state, a hotchpotch of
territories, linguistically, politically, and economically divided, that
had been acquired through freak patterns of inheritance and recent
conquests, artificially joined into a 'perpetual' unit in 1548. Yet whilst
the only common heritage of these lands was one of warfare with
one another, and a fierce attachment to local, urban and provincial
'privileges', they also contrived to stage one of the few (partially) successful revolts of the sixteenth century, and uniquely, to forge a new
republic of remarkable staying power. Memories of the Revolt shaped
much of the identity of the Dutch state, as well as its reputation
abroad. Especially in the late eighteenth and nineteenth centuries,
as Hugh Dunthorne demonstrates in his opening essay, memories of
the Revolt were appropriated by a host of writers and artists throughout Europe who used it to bolster their own protests against contemporary tyranny.

As the essays in this volume show, there can be little doubt that
public opinion played a crucial role in determining the destiny and
future shape of the Low Countries. It made the Netherlands the
stage as well as the subject for intellectual debate, and for a 'culture of communication' that was, increasingly, to shape the future
of Europe as it had done that of the Netherlands. The liveliness and
intensity of public debate in the Netherlands was enabled by the

---

[10] See his collected essays in Duke, *Reformation and Revolt in the Low Countries* and
idem, Politics, Print and Piety in the Sixteenth-Century Netherlands (forthcoming, 2008).
[11] Duke, 'The Elusive Netherlands'.

geography of these lands that made communication easy, by high literacy rates, by the degree of urbanization and by commerce and their position as 'bookshop of the world'. This enabled the frequent contact between what Andrew Pettegree calls 'news communities', which discussed, published and circulated selections of news that were of importance to the local community. Thus, as Pettegree shows, the citizens of Rouen were offered frequent updates on the progress of the Habsburg-Valois wars and developments in the Low Countries: all most relevant for merchants who needed to assess risks and markets.

The Habsburgs had always appreciated the importance of political display, and consciously deployed a range of techniques to cajole their subjects into support of and submission to the regime.[12] Their efforts to centralize the Netherlands found some expression in a new sense of 'Netherlandishness'; maps and chorographies of the Low Countries, as Paul Regan shows in his essay, began to reflect a fledgling sense of spatial and political unity. Yet the Habsburg rulers underestimated the growing disaffection in their Netherlandish possessions; despite fierce legislation against discussing heresy, printing heretical books and other forms of subversiveness, public opinion was turning against the crown. When this debate moved to the streets in the mid-1560s, and began the sequence of chaotic events that we know of as the Dutch Revolt, it was accompanied by a torrent of pamphlets. But this was not just a revolution created by print. As Henk van Nierop shows, rumour was equally important in fuelling events. Rumours about the impending introduction of the Spanish inquisition lent urgency to the campaign against the heresy legislation of 1565–66, and did much to undermine the authority of the church. Once war broke rumours were often the only source for news about the latest military and political developments.

Juliaan Woltjer's contribution presents evidence for the equally important prehistory of this protest, and the disquiet that developed among the members of the local elite in the 1550s and early 1560. He demonstrates how many local officials in different parts of the Low Countries obstructed the laws against heresy, while the Crown struggled to find an adequate response to the dissatisfaction among

---

[12] E.g. H. Soly, 'Plechtige intochten in de steden van de Zuidelijke Nederlanden tijdens de overgang van Middeleeuwen naar Nieuwe tijd. Communicatie, propaganda, spektakel', *TvG* 97 (1984), 341–361.

its subjects. When the duke of Alba arrived to re-enforce the authority of the Crown, he did little to try and improve the standing of the regime; the government relied on two very traditional tools for communicating its views: it was mainly through 'the theatre of suffering' and repeated calls for general processions that it offered some sort of interpretation of current events to its subjects. The General Pardon of 1570 was one of the few occasions at which they offered some positive news, yet Gustaaf Janssens shows that even in Bishop Richardot's robust defense of royal authority in his sermon on that occasion, it is possible to discern dismay about the violence of Alba's measures. By now this anxiety and alarm was also fuelled by new issues. Alba's centralist approach had increased existing fears about the disregard for the ancient privileges that were enjoyed by the cities and provinces of the Low Countries, a factor that contributed to the new eruption of Revolt in 1572. As Guido Marnef reminds us when charting the influence of the Charter of Kortenberg, the language of privileges played a crucial role in the justifications for the rebellion.

Yet to rebel was one thing, to know what to do next was another. The Netherlandish rebellion turned into a civil war, in which both sides needed to persuade the 'middle groups' in the population to join their sides. To do so both sides deployed a range of media, and appealed to different value systems, constantly shaping and reshaping definitions of what it was to be loyal and patriotic, what it was to be Netherlandish and un-Netherlandish. Both in the Northern and the Southern provinces, notions of Netherlandishness blended with religious views in shaping national discourses, first, about war and peace; later, about regional and national identities.

Nicolette Mout's essay discusses one of those Netherlanders who found themselves caught in the middle of the political conflict. The scholar Justus Lipsius was very fearful of the war and all it entailed, and his return to the Southern Netherlands and his reconciliation with Rome in 1591 were largely motivated by a desire for peace and quiet. Even so, the war was enough of a concern for him to feel he should at times intervene in public debate. In a public letter, later widely used in the North to discredit Spanish offers of truce, he advised the king to seek an accommodation with the Republic, so as to win time in which to regain hearts, minds and souls among the Dutch population, which would then eventually support a reconciliation with Rome and Madrid.

One of the interesting features of Lipsius's letter is that he recognizes and acknowledges the importance of influencing public opinion. In the Southern Netherlands, the 1590s at last witnessed serious efforts to try and generate public support for the Crown, fusing religious and political messages in a manner that was to prove extremely effective, while publicists, and especially the Jesuits, were doing much to catch up with the rebel propaganda. But catching up it was; it was not just in polemical writing, but also through a rich array of images that publicists for the Revolt had sought to influence the public before the loyalists began to follow suit. The extent to which the messages of political prints matched those of pamphlet literature is investigated by Andrew Sawyer, whose essay highlights some important differences that invite us to reflect on the ways in which different media operated.

In spite of all the evidence of lively public debate in the Netherlands, Joke Spaans reminds us that contemporaries were not inclined to consider this as a virtue of their society. In her analysis of the plays performed at a drama and poetry competition in Vlaardingen in 1616, she highlights how much the participating rhetoricians emphasized the need for unity, consensus and harmony in their society, and deplored the disagreements and conflicts over matters of religion and peace that were rocking the Dutch Republic during the years of the Truce. The debate over war and peace that erupted in the first decade of the seventeenth century, and that continued during the Truce years, was so vital not only because it exposed important faultlines within the Republic itself, but also because it inaugurated a new phase in the development of Netherlandish identities. One of the interesting side-effects of the Revolt had been a growing sense of 'Netherlandishness'; the sense of nation, that historians once believed was the *raison d'être* of the Revolt, was in fact a product of it.[13] As the war continued, neither side could afford to discard it. The need to reunite 'Ons Nederlant' was used by the authorities to urge for continuation of the war, and to appeal to the taxpayers' willingness

---

[13] S. Groenveld, 'Natie en nationaal gevoel in de zestiende-eeuwse Nederlanden', in C. van de Kieft, ed., *Scrinium et Scriptura. Opstellen over Nederlandse geschiedenis aangeboden aan Prof. Dr. J.L. van der Gouw* (Groningen, 1980); M.E.H.N. Mout, 'Van arm vaderland tot eendrachtige Republiek. De rol van politieke theorieën in de Opstand', *BMGN* 101 (1986).

to fund it. In the propaganda war, however, both camps were simultaneously developing enemy images that undermined the sense of
one common Netherlandish identity. In her essay on the Spanish
Brabanter, a play from 1617, Judith Pollmann shows how writers in
the Republic, many of them of southern descent, used anti-Spanish
imagery and memories of the Revolt to literally 'alienate' their former brethren in the south.

Within the Republic, too, notions of Netherlandish identity changed.
Culturally, it was not easy to see how notions of one Republic could
reach a cultural equilibrium with the proud particularism that many
had sought to defend in the Revolt. In a study of two provincial
histories, Raingard Esser shows how subtly this was done, by com-
bining an emphasis on the uniqueness of the local past with a commitment to the Union as a whole. Andrew Spicer's piece demonstrates
a quite similar mechanism; the towns, while set on emphasizing their
own superiority and identity, often in economic and political competition with one another, used gifts of stained glass to each other's
churches and those of villages in their area to emphasize bonds of
friendship and so to affirm a common identity as well as their own.

At the same time, there was only so much difference that could
be absorbed, even in the Dutch Republic. Jonathan Israel shows
that many in the Huguenot refuge found themselves torn by dilemmas very similar to that of Dutch society as a whole. If one's existence was predicated on a call for religious toleration, what, then,
was one to do with those whose ideas seemed beyond the pale? Far
from being among friends in a welcome liberal haven, Pierre Bayle
found himself under fierce attack from his coreligionists, and fellow-
sufferers of religious intolerance. It is a debate that has a peculiarly
contemporary resonance in the current Kingdom of the Netherlands,
where politicians are once more talking of preaching bans and censorship, and where society is struggling to redefine its notions of
Netherlandishness.

Jo Spaans is right to point out that Netherlanders of the early
modern period would have preferred to live in a world in which
'unity' and 'harmony' made public debate redundant. While six-
teenth- and seventeenth-century specialists and scholars do well to
emphasize the role of news and public opinion, they should probably bear in mind that some fundamental shifts in the conceptual-
ization of politics had to wait until the eighteenth century. Yet what
the essays in this book show is that even those who most deplored

divisions and debate, and who sought to silence dissenting voices, from the late sixteenth century onwards found themselves virtually forced to make their case in what had become a highly public arena of opinion and debate, that exercised a profound influence on the culture and self-image of the Netherlands.

CHAPTER ONE

DRAMATIZING THE DUTCH REVOLT. ROMANTIC HISTORY AND ITS SIXTEENTH-CENTURY ANTECEDENTS

Hugh Dunthorne

'The nineteenth century', it has been said, 'was the great age of sixteenth-century studies, both in Holland and Belgium.' It was then, following the establishment of the Kingdom of the Netherlands in 1813 and the Belgian Revolution of 1830 that Dutch and Belgian scholars went back to the Revolt of the Netherlands in order to rewrite its history from a new, national perspective.[1] It was then, too, that the great printed collections of correspondence and other sources, on which today's students of the Revolt still rely, were transcribed from the archives and published. But the Revolt was not only studied and interpreted afresh by professional historians and archivists. It was also popularized and romanticized – recreated and brought back to life in the theatre, in the visual arts, in historical novels as well as histories. This popularizing process was by no means confined to the Low Countries.[2] Across Europe and North America the Revolt came to be seen as a crucial episode in world history, 'one of the cardinal chapters in the development of modern liberty'.[3] Moreover, the modern process of popularization began not with a Belgian or Dutch writer but with two German dramatists: with Schiller, whose *Don Carlos* was first performed at Hamburg in 1787,

---

[1] J.W. Smit, 'The Present Position of Studies regarding the Revolt of the Netherlands', in J.S. Bromley and E.H. Kossmann, eds., *Britain and the Netherlands. Papers Delivered to the Oxford-Netherlands Historical Conference* (London, 1960), 12–17, quotation at 12; P.B.M. Blaas, 'The Touchiness of a Small Nation with a Great Past. The Approach of Fruin and Blok to the Writing of the History of the Netherlands', in Duke and Tamse, eds., *Clio's Mirror*, 135–137, 143–144, 147–150.

[2] Nor, of course, was it confined to the history of the Dutch Revolt. For the romanticization of history more generally, see H.R. Trevor-Roper, *The Romantic Movement and the Study of History* (London, 1969).

[3] G.P. Gooch, *History and Historians in the Nineteenth Century* (3rd ed.; London, 1920), 417.

and with Goethe whose tragedy *Egmont* was premiered two years
later in Mainz. Twin pillars of German classicism yet also profoundly
influential on the wider romantic movement, Goethe and Schiller
inspired composers like Beethoven and Verdi to add music to their
dramatic theme. Like Sir Walter Scott, who revered their writing
and was among the first to translate it into English, they inspired
painters and novelists to look to sixteenth- and seventeenth-century
history for their subject-matter. And they inspired historians – none
more than the Boston Unitarian, John Lothrop Motley, whose *Rise
of the Dutch Republic*, first published in London in 1855, was one of
the great international best-sellers of the age.

The historical evocations of the Dutch Revolt which began to
appear in various forms from the later eighteenth century onwards
were not, of course, the first to be devoted to this subject. During
the period of the Revolt itself and from quite an early date in its
progress, observers of events and those directly caught up in the
troubles had written accounts of what was happening. Some were
composed in Latin for a more or less learned readership. But a surprising number were written in, or translated into, one or other of
the vernacular languages of western Europe and were thus aimed at
what for the time could be considered a popular audience. Like all
contemporary histories, these early narratives were generally far from
impartial. Most were produced in order to bolster the efforts of one
or other side in the conflict, to justify their actions in taking up arms
and to trumpet their successes. And to begin with the Netherlanders
and their sympathizers in neighbouring countries had the field largely
to themselves. The earliest accounts came from outside the Low
Countries – from Basel, where both Adam Henricpetri, a Swiss jurist,
and the Huguenot Richard Dinoth published their accounts of the
'Belgic civil wars' in 1575 and 1586 respectively; and from Cologne
where the Austrian Michael von Aitzing's chronicle, *De leone Belgico*,
was printed and reprinted during the 1580s, its sober narrative
enlivened by the vivid and strongly pro-Netherlands engravings of
Frans Hogenberg.[4] During the next decade the initiative passed to

---

[4] Adam Henricpetri, *Niderlendischer erster Kriegen* (Basel, 1575; 2nd ed. 1577); Richard
Dinoth, *De bello civili Belgico libri VI* (Basel, 1586); Michael von Aitzing, *De leone
Belgico* (Cologne, 1583; later eds. 1585, 1588). Henricpetri's account was subsequently
translated and published in Dutch (1579), French (1582) and English (1583), Aitzing's
in German (1584).

Dutch writers – lawyers and office-holders such as Pieter Bor, Emanuel van Meteren and Jean-François Le Petit – whose solid documentary histories were widely read by contemporaries and are still of value today.[5] But it was not until the second quarter of the seventeenth century that accounts of the Revolt which were more sympathetic to the Spanish regime began to make their mark, with the appearance of *De Bello Belgico* by the Jesuit Famiano Strada and of Cardinal Guido Bentivoglio's *Della Guerra di Fiandra*. These works, too, circulated widely. First printed in Latin in 1632, Strada's history was quickly translated into no fewer than five vernacular languages, including Dutch and English, while Bentivoglio's account, also much reissued, was praised by Grotius and Clarendon – and indeed provided Clarendon with the model for his *History of the Rebellion and Civil Wars in England*.[6]

With the Peace of Münster and the end of the Netherlands' long war against Spain, the writing of histories of the Dutch Revolt came to an end – for the time being, at any rate. Of course, the Revolt could not be ignored altogether. When the English diplomat Sir William Temple wrote his famous *Observations upon the United Provinces of the Netherlands* in 1673, he included a narrative of the country's rebellion against Spain in his lengthy first chapter. But the Revolt was not what really interested him. The heart of his book lay in the chapters which followed, especially those concerned with government, religion and trade. Temple sought to anatomize the Dutch state in order to explain why, in an age of monarchy, this upstart republic was so effectively and justly governed. In an age of enforced religious uniformity, he wanted to explain how men and women of

---

[5] Pieter Christiaensz Bor, *Oorsprongk, begin ende vervolg der Nederlantscher oorlogen*, 2 vols. (Utrecht, 1595–1601; later eds. 1603, 1621–26, 1671–84); Emmanuel van Meteren, *Belgische ofte Nederlandtsche historie* (Delft, 1599; later eds. 1605, 1608, 1614); Jean–François Le Petit, *La Grande Chronique ancienne et moderne de Hollande*, 2 vols. (Dordrecht, 1601). Van Meteren's account also appeared in Latin (1598, 1600(?), 1670), in French (1618) and, combined with Le Petit's, in English (1608, 1609, 1627).

[6] Famiano Strada, *De bello Belgico*, 2 vols. (Rome 1632, 1647); Guido Bentivoglio, *Della Guerra di Fiandra*, 3 vols. (Cologne, 1632–39). Both works ran through many later editions and translations. The English edition of Strada (vol. I only) appeared in 1650 and of Bentivoglio in 1654 (reprinted in 1678). Grotius's high opinion of Bentivoglio's account is quoted by Henry Earl of Monmouth in his English translation: *The Compleat History of the Warres of Flanders* (London, 1654), fol. A4. Clarendon's judgement of the book is in his *Essays Moral and Entertaining*, ed. J.S. Clarke, 2 vols. (London, 1815), I, 245–246.

different religious beliefs were able to live harmoniously together in the Netherlands, 'like citizens of the world'. And, in common with many other writers on trade, he tried to explain how a country which lacked many natural resources of its own could nevertheless enjoy such an astonishing level of material prosperity.[7] Temple has been called a 'political scientist', a man of the early Enlightenment. Analytical rather than narrative in approach, he was concerned with questions of political structure, of economic growth and intellectual progress.[8] Moreover, these were the questions which continued to interest the 'philosophical historians' and others who wrote about the Netherlands over the next hundred years. Even the question of Dutch economic and political decline which increasingly preoccupied them – the question of whether and for what reasons the Republic had 'passed its meridian and begun sensibly to decay' and of how such decay could be avoided by other states – even that was a theme which Temple had already touched on.[9] Thus for a century or more the history of the Dutch Revolt, if not ignored altogether, was at any rate pushed into the shadows by matters of more immediate concern.

How, then, was the Revolt gradually brought back into the spotlight in the later eighteenth century, first as an object of scholarly enquiry and ultimately as one of popular enthusiasm? In the Dutch Republic itself the revival of interest seems to have happened, or at least to have begun, as a by-product of the growth of political journalism and of the public debates which followed the restoration of the stadholderate in 1747. Jan Wagenaar, who devoted almost a third of his multi-volume *Vaderlandsche Historie* to the Revolt and the Eighty Years' War, had first made his mark in the 1740s as an Amsterdam pamphleteer. And though his *Historie* famously claimed to be impartial, it was at heart a moderate defence of the rule of provincial states and urban magistrates, just as Pieter Paulus's later

---

[7] William Temple, *Observations upon the United Provinces of the Netherlands* (1673), ed. Sir G. Clark (Oxford, 1972), chapters 1, 2, 5 and 6, quotation at 106.

[8] C.B. Macpherson, 'Sir William Temple, Political Scientist', *Canadian Journal of Economics and Political Science* 9 (1943), 39–54.

[9] Temple, *Observations*, 122–126, quotation at 122. Eighteenth-century writing about the Netherlands is surveyed by G.J. Schutte, '"A Subject of Admiration and Encomium". The History of the Dutch Republic as Interpreted by Non-Dutch Authors in the Second Half of the Eighteenth Century', in Duke and Tamse, eds., *Clio's Mirror*.

study of the Union of Utrecht was a moderate defence of the house of Orange.[10] In the southern Netherlands, meanwhile, a new *Histoire des Troubles des Pays-Bas* was circulating in manuscript. Its author was a member of the Council of Flanders, Luc Jean Joseph van der Vynckt, who had been given access to the state archives through the patronage of the *philosophe* (and Imperial ambassador) Count Charles of Cobenzl.[11] And outside the Low Countries, too, philosophical historians were being drawn to the Dutch Revolt as a subject. Following the success of his *History of Scotland during the Reigns of Queen Mary and James VI* (1759), William Robertson (soon to be Principal of Edinburgh University) embarked on a *History of the Reign of Charles V* in order to examine the European context of Scotland's Reformation. Published in 1769 and widely praised, the book encouraged others to continue the story beyond 1555. A new French translation of Bentivoglio's *War of Flanders* appeared in Paris in 1769 and 1770 to coincide with the French edition of Robertson's *Charles V* which came out the following year.[12] Later in the decade Robertson's younger contemporary, Robert Watson, published a *History of the Reign of Philip II, King of Spain*, in which the Dutch Revolt loomed large. (When the book appeared in German translation its first volume was actually entitled *Geschichte der Entstehung der Republik der Vereinigten Niederlande*).[13] And Watson's work in turn prompted a sequel from William Lothian, son of the minister of the Scots church at Rotterdam, whose *History of the United Provinces of the Netherlands* carried the narrative on from Philip II's death to the Truce of 1609.[14]

---

[10] Jan Wagenaar, *Vaderlandsche Historie*, 21 vols. (Amsterdam, 1749–59), vols. VI–XI; Pieter Paulus, *Verklaring der Unie van Utrecht*, 4 vols. (Utrecht, 1775–78); I.L. Leeb, *The Ideological Origins of the Batavian Revolution* (The Hague, 1973), 75–86, 113–121.

[11] After its initial circulation in manuscript, van der Vynckt's *Histoire* was first printed in German translation (Zürich, 1793). It was not published in its original French until 1822.

[12] Guido Bentivoglio, *Histoire des Guerres de Flandre*, 4 vols. (Paris, 1769; Brussels, 1770). Work on the French translation of Robertson's *Charles V* had begun in 1768, even before the publication of the first English edition: S.J. Brown, ed., *William Robertson and the Expansion of Empire* (Cambridge, 1997), 151–152, 181–184.

[13] Robert Watson, *The History of the Reign of Philip the Second, King of Spain*, 2 vols. (London, 1777). A French translation appeared at Amsterdam also in 1777 and the German edition at Lübeck in 1782.

[14] William Lothian, *The History of the United Provinces of the Netherlands from the Death of Philip II, King of Spain, to the Truce made with Albert and Isabella* (London, 1780).

These books, not to mention the various reprints, translations and abridgements which they spawned, helped to bring the Dutch Revolt firmly back into the public eye.[15] But so also did a more dramatic event: the outbreak in 1776 of the rebellion of Britain's thirteen north-American colonies. Like all rebels, the colonists needed precedents to justify their action in taking up arms. They found them, naturally enough, in English law and history. But, as their ambassador John Adams explained to the Dutch States General in 1781, they found them also in the principles exemplified by 'the Helvetic and Batavian revolutions' – in other words in the legendary uprising of the Swiss cantons against their Habsburg overlords in 1307 and the Revolt of the Netherlands more than two and a half centuries later. Not much was known about the Swiss rebellion. Aegidius Tschudi's sixteenth-century *Chronicon Helveticum*, the main source of the story of William Tell and the peasant uprising, had been published in the mid-1730s; but it was not until 1788 that a modern account of the origins of the Swiss Confederation appeared.[16] The Dutch Revolt, on the other hand, was both more familiar as an event and far better documented in its history. So it was this more recent war in defence of liberty that became, in Benjamin Franklin's phrase, 'our great example' – 'a proper and seasonable mirror for the present Americans'.[17] Like the Netherlanders, the Americans had been subjected to unconstitutional taxation and an occupying army. King George III was thus seen as a new Philip II, governor Thomas Hutchinson of Massachusetts as a new Cardinal Granvelle, General Thomas Gage as a new duke of Alba; while George Washington, seeking to unite the colonies in the face of British tyranny and misgovernment, was the new William of Orange. If the Americans, moreover, were engaged in what seemed a hopelessly unequal struggle

---

[15] Wagenaar's *Historie*, for example, was reprinted in Dutch in 1770 and 1790, translated into German (1756–67) and French (1757–70), and condensed into several one- or two-volume abridgements: Schutte, '"A Subject of Admiration"', 117–119.

[16] J. Müller, *Geschichten Schweizerischer Eidgenossenschaft* (Leipzig, 1788).

[17] For Adams's address to the States General and other points of comparison mentioned in this paragraph, see G.C. Gibbs, 'The Dutch Revolt and the American Revolution', in R. Oresko *et al.*, eds., *Royal and Republican Sovereignty in Early Modern Europe* (Cambridge, 1997), 610. Franklin is quoted by Schutte, '"A Subject of Admiration"', 126, note 47; cf. B. Romans, *Annals of the Troubles in the Netherlands from the Accession of Charles V . . . a Proper and Seasonable Mirror for the Present Americans*, 2 vols. (Hartford, Conn., 1778–82).

against the most powerful empire in the world, they could take heart from the outcome of the no less unequal struggle of Holland and Zeeland against Spain two centuries before. As the dissenting minister Richard Price observed in 1776, when 'determined men [are] fighting on their own ground, within sight of their houses and families and for that sacred blessing of liberty, . . . all history proves' – and not least the history of the Dutch Revolt – 'that in such a situation a handful is a match for millions'.[18]

By recalling earlier rebellions in Europe, the American Revolution helped to breathe new life and immediacy into their history. And it was a history of obvious significance to Europeans like Goethe and Schiller who still lived under absolutist regimes and had experienced the arrogance and authoritarianism of princely power at first hand. In Schiller's case the experience had come early. In 1773, against his own and his parents' wishes, he had been forcibly enrolled in the Duke of Württemberg's Academy, an institution organized along rigidly military lines for the purpose of turning out loyal army officers and civil servants. In this 'slave plantation', as a contemporary journalist called it, the fourteen-year-old was to be trained in jurisprudence and, when that failed, in medicine. But if his state education compelled him, for a brief period, to work as a regimental doctor in the duke's army, it also made him a lifelong rebel. From his earliest drama, *The Robbers* (1782), performed in the teeth of official disapproval and published with the words 'Against Tyrants' on the title-page, to his last, *William Tell* (1804), 'the first drama of romantic nationalism', almost all Schiller's plays are indictments of despotism, obsessively returning to the theme of freedom's struggle against tyranny. His first scholarly project, conceived in 1786 though never completed, was to edit a series of studies on *The history of the most remarkable rebellions and conspiracies*; and it was for his defiant stand against political oppression that the French National Convention in 1792 made him an honorary French citizen[19] (he did not return the compliment, condemning the revolutionary leadership during the Terror as 'a depraved generation').[20] By comparison, Goethe's relations

---

[18] Price, *Observations on . . . the War with America* (1776), quoted in Schutte, '"A Subject of Admiration"', 113.

[19] T.J. Reed, *Schiller* (Oxford, 1991), 11, 18, 22, 39–40, 51, 84, quotation on 97.

[20] Quoted in L. Sharpe, *Friedrich Schiller. Drama, Thought and Politics* (Cambridge, 1991), 148.

with political authority were much less embattled, on the surface at
least. The son of a counsellor in the free Imperial city of Frankfurt-
am-Main, he spent most of his life after 1775 in the service of the
enlightened Duke Carl August of Saxe-Weimar in Thuringia. But
his involvement with the ducal court was not without tensions and
doubts. On the eve of his appointment he had visited the Swiss
Republic, where he considered settling and whose free people ('a
noble race, not wholly unworthy of their forefathers') he admired.[21]
It was after this visit, and while awaiting the call from Weimar, that
he first took up Egmont as a subject. The play was written – intermittently – over the next twelve years, a time when Goethe was
becoming increasingly disillusioned with his administrative duties at
Weimar and with German absolutism generally.[22] Nor is it accidental that it was written at a time of revolution. As the flames of revolt
spread from America to Europe, a new time of troubles was brew-
ing in the Netherlands. Dutch Patriots opposed the Prince of Orange,
in the Austrian Netherlands Brabanters obstructed the Emperor Joseph
II; and both in their rhetoric looked to the historic struggles of the
sixteenth century.

These were the circumstances, private as well as public, in which
Goethe and Schiller worked on their dramas about the Dutch Revolt.
But though they had origins in common, the two plays introduced
their subject in quite different ways. Schiller's tragedy, as he told the
director of the Mannheim theatre in 1784, was to be 'a family portrait in a royal household'.[23] Everything that happens on stage, from
private intrigues to political confrontations, does so within the formal world of the Spanish court near Madrid; and 'the rebellion in
Brabant' (II.ii.1164), looming in the background, is reported and
argued over but never seen.[24] In *Egmont*, by contrast, we are in the
Netherlands, indeed in Brussels, throughout. Constantly shifting from
street scenes (written in colloquial dialect) to the high politics of the

    [21] Quoted in N. Boyle, *Goethe. The Poet and the Age*, 2 vols. (Oxford, 1991–2000),
I, 207.
    [22] Boyle, *Goethe*, I, 251–256, 297, 300–301, 380–381, 480–481.
    [23] Quoted in Sharpe, *Schiller*, 81.
    [24] In this paragraph and subsequently, quotations from *Don Carlos* are identified
by act, scene and line and refer to the 1805 version, printed in Friedrich Schiller,
Sämtliche Werke, Berliner Ausgabe, ed. H.-G. Thalheim, 5 vols. (Berlin, 1980–90),
III. References to *Egmont* (1788), which is in prose, are identified simply by act and
scene.

regent's palace and then to the domestic life of Egmont and his mistress, the play offers a Shakespearean panorama of the city at the
beginning of Alba's governorship.[25] Of course, it is a play of ideas
too, as *Don Carlos* is. Blithely, almost unthinkingly attached to the
old freedoms and old ways of life, both his own as a great nobleman and those of the Netherlands people, Egmont is confronted first
by the more calculating and politically realistic outlook of the Prince
of Orange (II.ii) and ultimately by Alba, the implacable embodiment
of Spanish absolutism (IV.ii). He is a medieval nobleman caught in
a modern age, whose ruthlessness destroys him. In *Don Carlos*, on
the other hand, the authoritarianism of Spain's church and state is
measured not against older notions of freedom, but against those of
Schiller's own day. Rodrigo Marquis of Posa, who pleads the cause of
the persecuted Netherlands before Philip II in the audience scene –
the great set piece of the play – does so as a 'citizen of the world'
(III.x.3008), a man of the Enlightenment. His famous appeal to the
king for 'the freedom to think and speak' (III.x.3216–3217) reflects
Schiller's experience as a young author silenced in his own country;
and Posa's vision of a better kind of government, of constitutional
monarchy and republican virtue, echoes the ideas of Montesquieu,
Rousseau and the American Revolution.[26]

The progressive principles voiced in Schiller's tragedy resonated
through the nineteenth century and beyond. Advocates of reform in
1848 reiterated Posa's demands, just as theatre audiences under
Nazism applauded him. But there were other, more purely dramatic
ways in which *Don Carlos* and *Egmont* left their mark on the romantic generations that saw and read these plays. As an Enlightenment
thinker in sixteenth-century Spain, Posa may be an anachronism,
but he is a believable, full-blooded human being, not an intellectual
abstraction. So is Egmont: a man, like Goethe himself in the 1780s,
torn between public duties and private life (III.ii). The villains of the
plot – Alba and Philip II – are larger than life, but they are not
crude or one-dimensional. It was Philip II – isolated, vulnerable, a
victim of his own system and ultimately of the Inquisition – who

---

[25] On the Shakespearean elements in the play, see H.M. Waidson's introduction
to his edition of Johann Wolfgang von Goethe, *Egmont* (Oxford, 1960), v–vi.
[26] A.G. Blunden, 'Nature and Politics in Schiller's *Don Carlos*', *Deutsche Vierteljahrsschrift*
52 (1978), 241–256.

would most 'move people', Schiller believed, as the tragedy unfolded.[27]
[fig. 1.1] Moreover, just as the characters in both plays are vivid in
themselves, they play out their roles against backdrops rich in local
colour, from the gardens of Aranjuez and the gloomy Habsburg
court to the streets and squares of Brussels. They face one another
in dramatic set-piece encounters, as in the leave-taking of Orange
and Egmont (II.ii) or the chilling final scene between king and car-
dinal-inquisitor which seals the fate of Carlos (V.x). Consciously or
not, moreover, they are caught up in the broader sweep of historical progress.[28] For although both tragedies end with the death of
those who have sought to defend the freedom of the Netherlands,
they also convey hope for better times and a sense that the future
lies with the dead rather than the living. In prison on the eve of his
execution, Egmont dreams of the provinces' coming liberation (V.vi),
just as Posa, 'a citizen of ages yet to come', envisages a time when
'states will no longer squander their own children' through persecution and oppression (III.x.3081 and 3155). For all his power, Philip
II cannot slow 'the rapid wheel of destiny' (III.x.3168–70) – nor, it
is implied, can the petty tyrants still ruling in Schiller's own day.

Given the universality of their politics – the struggle of freedom
against tyranny – and their effectiveness as drama, it is not surprising that the *Don Carlos* and *Egmont* should have retained their currency during Europe's age of revolutions, nor that they should have
attracted artists of all kinds to the history of the Dutch Revolt as a
subject. When in 1809 Beethoven was invited by the Burgtheater in
Vienna to compose incidental music for a new production of *Egmont*,
he took the commission up partly because the theme of the play
was close to that of his own *Fidelio* (1805), 'the first great political
opera', and to the recent experience of his adopted city under French
military occupation. His music unifies and intensifies Goethe's tragedy,
particularly in the 'melodrama' which accompanies Egmont's dream;
and its first performance in 1810 had the additional effect of restoring Goethe's five-act text to the theatre, after a period of more than

---

[27] Quoted in Lesley Sharpe's introduction to Schiller, *Don Carlos and Mary Stuart*,
Eng. trs. H. Collier Sy-Quia (Oxford, 1996), xii.
[28] Derived from Kant, Schiller's notion of the 'grand design' of history, and of
the historian's duty to understand and promote that design, was most fully set out
in the inaugural lecture which he gave as Professor of History at Jena in 1789: the
lecture is printed in English translation as 'The Nature and Value of Universal
History', *History and Theory* 11 (1972), 321–334.

Fig. 1.1. Ivan Kyncl, Derek Jacobi as king Philip II in Schiller's *Don Carlos*, Sheffield and London (2005).

a decade when the play had been given in a shortened version made by Schiller.[29] *Don Carlos* had to wait longer to find a suitably committed composer; but when it did, in the mid-1860s, it was in similar circumstances. For Verdi, like Beethoven, admired the writing of the first German Romantics (he had already, in the 1840s, turned three of Schiller's plays into operas) and, even more than the composer of *Fidelio*, he was fired by his compatriots' struggle for unity and freedom. Following the Italian uprisings of 1848 his opera *La Battaglia di Legnano* (about the defeat of the Emperor Frederick Barbarossa by Milan and the Lombard League in 1157) had been premiered to wild enthusiasm in republican Rome. Banned by the Austrian authorities during the 1850s, the piece was revived in Milan in 1861 as *L'Assedio di Arlem* [The Siege of Haarlem], with its medieval Germans and Italians improbably transformed into sixteenth-century Spanish and Dutch. Thus in 1866, when Italy was again at war with Austria and Garibaldi preparing the march on Rome, Verdi was ready to return once more to his revolutionary theme. The result was *Don Carlo*, the last and finest of his Schiller operas and, in its treatment of political questions, his most mature work. While differing from Schiller's tragedy in details, Verdi's score enriches the characterization of the original – notably that of Philip II – and gives greater prominence to the Netherlands cause.[30] What is more, although Verdi's is certainly the most accomplished opera on this subject to be written in the nineteenth century, it is far from being the only one. From the 1830s onwards Europe's unflagging opera industry repeatedly found inspiration in the Dutch Revolt, as it did in so many other areas of sixteenth-century history. French grand opera about William the Silent, *tragédie lyrique* about Egmont, Italian *opere serie* on Alba and on the siege of Leiden, German *Singspiel* and Dutch *zangspel* about the *gueux*, semi-Wagnerian lyric drama on the Pacification of Ghent – all these and more had their hour on the stage.[31]

---

[29] Goethe, *Egmont*, ed. Waidson, x–xiii. The allusion to *Fidelio* as the first great political opera is quoted from Sir Isaiah Berlin's essay on Verdi in his *Against the Current. Essays in the History of Ideas* (London, 1979), 290.

[30] For an illuminating discussion of both *Legnano* and *Don Carlos*, see C. Osborne, *The Complete Operas of Verdi* (London, 1969), 189–193, 351–368.

[31] L.C. Mézeray, *Guillaume de Nassau*, first performed at The Hague in 1832; G. Salvayre, *Egmont* (after Goethe) (Paris, 1886); G. Pacini, *Il Duca d'Alba* (Venice, 1842); E. Petrella, *L'Assedio di Leida* (Milan, 1856); C. Decker, *Die Gueusen in Breda*

Most of these operas are now forgotten – or, like Donizetti's *Duca d'Alba*, only remembered for a couple of arias. But with romantic paintings and prints of the Dutch Revolt we are on firmer footing: these, at least, survive in town halls and museums or in illustrated texts. And we are on home ground, too, for they are largely the work of Dutch and Belgian artists. The revival of interest among artists in depicting events from the national past seems to have occurred partly in belated response to the resurgence of history-writing in the Netherlands during the second half of the eighteenth century. In 1803 the enlightened Felix Meritis Society of Amsterdam offered a prize for the best new painting of a historical subject from the early seventeenth century, and a similar competition formed part of the first 'exhibition of living masters' organized on the initiative of Louis Napoleon in 1808.[32] But it was with the establishment of the independent Kingdom of the Netherlands between 1813 and 1815 that historical genre painting really took off. From the Antwerp artist, Mathieu-Ignace van Brée, the new king William I commissioned in 1817 a large-scale canvas of *The Self-Sacrifice of Burgomaster van der Werff at the Siege of Leiden* and then – as a gesture of reassurance to his Belgian subjects – a painting of his ancestor *William of Orange Interceding in 1578 for Catholic Prisoners Arrested and Detained in Defiance of the Pacification*. This latter subject was evidently chosen to show that the aim of the king's religious policy was not to protestantize the Catholic south but to liberalize it. And limited though the political impact of the picture may have been (it did little or nothing to stem the conservative opposition of the Belgian clergy to the government's measures), it was widely admired as a painting. Indeed, the success of both these works prompted Van Brée to urge his pupils and fellow-artists to follow his example. Rather than relying on well-worn themes from scripture and mythology, they should seek inspiration 'by retracing the history of our country'.[33] And many

(Halle, 1838); M.A. van 't Kruis, *Les Gueux de Mer* (Netherlands [The Hague?], 1861); P. Benoit, *De Pacificatie van Gent* (Antwerp, 1879). For these and other examples, see F. Clément and P. Larousse, eds., *Dictionnaire des opéras*, 2 vols. (Paris, 1905; repr., New York, 1969); S. Sadie, ed., *The New Grove Dictionary of Opera*, 4 vols. (London, 1992); J. Towers, *Dictionary-Catalogue of Operas and Operettas*, 2 vols. (Morgantown, W. Va., 1910).
[32] P.J.J. van Thiel, ed., *Het vaderlandsch gevoel. Vergeten negentiende-eeuwse schilderijen van onze geschiedenis* (Amsterdam, 1978), 16, 23.
[33] Van Brée, *Discours aux Membres ... de l'Institut Royal des Pays-Bas* (1821), quoted

did – especially after the political split of the Low Countries in 1830
and the consequent emergence of distinct nationalist movements in
north and south.[34] For a generation, the production of patriotic historical genre pictures flourished. The abdication speech of Charles
V, the departure from the Netherlands of Philip II, the parting of
Orange and Egmont in 1567 (one of several subjects echoing Goethe's
tragedy) – these and other 'significant moments' from the national
past were displayed in annual salons or exhibitions of living masters
and reproduced as book illustrations or in prints to pin up in school
classrooms.[35] With their sometimes stagey composition and over-elab-
orate detail, such pictures can seem cluttered and melodramatic. But
at their best – as in the muted emotion of Louis Gallait's *Last Honours
Rendered to Counts Egmont and Hornes* (1851) [fig. 1.2] – they still have
a powerful impact.[36]

If artists were influenced by the growth of national feeling in both
parts of the Low Countries, so also (as was mentioned at the start
of this essay) was the emerging Dutch and Belgian historical pro-
fession. Yet professional historians were much less influenced by
romanticism. It has been suggested, indeed, that the Netherlands in
the nineteenth century 'had no tradition of romantic historiography'.[37]
The romance of the past was left to historical novelists like Jacob
van Lennep and Henri Conscience, writing from the 1830s onwards
in the wake of Sir Walter Scott; and Robert Fruin, professor of

in D. Coekelberghs and P. Loze, eds., *1770–1830. Autour du Néo-Classicisme en Belgique*
(Brussels, 1985), 152. Van Brée's two pictures are now displayed, respectively, in
the Stedelijk Museum at Leiden and in Ghent Town Hall. For William I's religious and educational policy and the clerical opposition which it provoked in Belgium,
see E.H. Kossmann, *The Low Countries 1780–1940* (Oxford, 1978), 124–129.

[34] Van Thiel, ed., *Vaderlandsch gevoel*, 19–22; S. Le Bailly de Tilleghem, *Louis
Gallait (1810–1887). La Gloire d'un romantique* (Tournai, 1987), 172.

[35] Van Thiel, ed., *Vaderlandsch gevoel*, 30, 34–35, 273, 281. The idea that the artist
should fix on an historically significant 'moment' which is suggestive of both past
and succeeding events derived from Lessing's influential essay *Laokoon oder über die
Grenzen der Mahlerey und Poesie* (Berlin, 1766; French trs., Paris, 1802), chapters 16
and 18. For evidence of the impact of Lessing's theory in the Netherlands, see C.W.
Opzoomer, *Het wezen en de grenzen der kunst* (Leiden, 1875).

[36] Contemporary comments on Gallait's picture, pointing out its comparative
restraint, are quoted in Le Bailly de Tilleghem, *Gallait*, 198–199. The painting made
its mark again in 2005 when it was shown in Brussels as part of a major exhibition, *Le Romantisme en Belgique*, marking the 175th anniversary of the modern Belgian
state.

[37] Blaas, 'The Touchiness of a Small Nation', 133–135, 142. Only in the writing of Groen van Prinsterer does Blaas find 'some sign of romantic influence'.

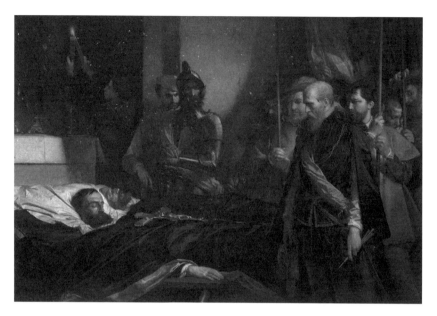

Fig. 1.2. Louis Gallait, *Last Honours Rendered to Counts Egmont and Hornes* (1851), Musée des Beaux-Arts, Tournai.

Dutch history at Leiden, disapproved even of the use of modern illustrations in works of history.[38] The one thorough-going romantic who wrote about the history of the Revolt of the Netherlands at this time was not a professional scholar at all but an amateur. And he was not Dutch or Belgian, but American. The New Englander, John Lothrop Motley, was drawn to the subject in part by his Protestant upbringing and ancestry, but more immediately through his early discovery of the German romantics. As a precocious student at Harvard he had written a graduation essay on Goethe, before going on (in 1832, when he was just eighteen) to study for his doctorate at Göttingen. There and in Berlin he read Schiller's unfinished *History of the Revolt of the United Netherlands against Spanish Rule* (1788), a work written soon after *Don Carlos*; and it was that book together with its sequel, *The History of the Thirty Years' War* (1792), that fired Motley's lifelong interest in Dutch and European history of the sixteenth and

---

[38] H. Vissink, *Scott and his Influence on Dutch Literature* (Zwolle, 1922); Kossmann, *Low Countries*, 172. The first novels of Scott to appear in Dutch translation were published in 1824. Fruin's views are quoted in Van Thiel, ed., *Vaderlandsch gevoel*, 27–28.

early seventeenth centuries.[39] Later, in 1851, he would return to
Europe. Then and in subsequent years he would visit and revisit the
cities of the Netherlands, acquiring the sense of locality which is such
a feature of his *Rise of the Dutch Republic*.[40] He would be welcomed
and assisted by state archivists – by Gachard in Brussels and at The
Hague by Groen van Prinsterer and by Bakhuizen van den Brink,
who annotated his *Dutch Republic* and *History of the United Netherlands*
when they were published in Dutch translation during the 1860s.
And further afield, as a diplomat representing his country in St.
Petersburg, Vienna and finally London, he would witness international power politics at first hand, using the experience to enliven
his writing about statesmen of the past, not least in his work on
Oldenbarnevelt.[41] Yet underlying all this later experience was what
Motley had absorbed from his early study of Schiller. The structure
and even the phraseology of Schiller's *Revolt* are reflected in *The Rise
of the Dutch Republic*.[42] The sense in Schiller that ordinary people as
much as political leaders are the protagonists in the Dutch struggle;
the polarity between Philip II, embodying 'despotism, feudalism, hierarchy, intolerance', and Orange, standing for 'freedom, democracy,
integrity'; the significance of the Revolt in the broader sweep of historical progress, where the Dutch and German peoples are united
in striving for freedom – all these themes were to be taken up by
Motley, and in the last case elaborated into a full-blown racial
theory.[43] Above all, perhaps, Motley took up Schiller's insistence as
a dramatist and scholar that history should be readable and that it

---

[39] Schiller had planned to write a six-volume history of the Dutch Revolt, though
in the event only the first volume (down to 1567) was completed. The introduction to the book, however, surveys the whole period of the Revolt to 1609.

[40] See, for example, the description of Antwerp Cathedral on the eve of the iconoclastic riots of 1566 in J.L. Motley, *The Rise of the Dutch Republic*, 3 vols. (1855;
Everyman Edition, London, 1906), I, 457–461.

[41] O.D. Edwards, 'John Lothrop Motley and the Netherlands', in J.W. Schulte
Nordholt and R.P. Swierenga, eds., *A Bilateral Bicentennial. A History of Dutch-American
Relations 1782–1982* (Amsterdam, 1982), 183–186.

[42] Compare the passage on Claudius Civilis which occurs both in Schiller's
'Historical Introduction' and in Motley's. *History of the Revolt of the United Netherlands*
see Schiller's *Works*, trs. A.J.W. Morrison, 4 vols. (London, 1846–49), I, 361–362;
Motley, *Dutch Republic*, I, 23–24. Many other examples could be cited.

[43] Schiller, *Revolt*, I, 350–351; D. Regin, *Freedom and Dignity. The Historical and
Philosophical Thought of Schiller* (The Hague, 1965), 78–79, 96–97; D. Levin, *History
as Romantic Art. Bancroft, Prescott, Motley and Parkman* (Stanford, Ca., 1959), 49, 73,
78, 87, 90; Edwards, 'Motley', 187–188.

could legitimately 'borrow' from the 'cognate art' of 'romance'.[44] The long popular success of *The Dutch Republic* owed much to its author's feeling for drama – comparable to Carlyle's, a reviewer said – and to his skill as a story-teller. It was a skill learned as much from Scott as from Schiller; and when on one occasion a young reader told him that his history was 'just like a novel', Motley took the remark as a compliment.[45]

Readable as he undoubtedly is, Motley is little read today. If he is discussed at all, it is in terms of the criticisms made of his work, first in the 1860s by Fruin and then later and more influentially by Geyl. He has been faulted for his Protestant bias, for his tendency to moralize and over-dramatize, to see history as a clash between good and evil with the good destined ultimately to prevail, and for his eagerness to project onto sixteenth-century Netherlanders the mind-set of modern liberalism.[46] Such faults are not Motley's alone of course. To a greater or lesser extent, they are typical of the whole romantic approach to history. As the examples collected in this essay show, romantic writers and artists of all kinds saw the past in polarized terms: freedom against constraint, progress against inertia. On the stage and in the picture gallery, they emphasized its moments of confrontation, reshaping or inventing historical characters to enhance the drama. And they interpreted history with an eye to modernity. To resuscitate history, to make the past live so that it could speak to the present, they imbued it with modern ideas and modern characters. Count Egmont's mistress Clara, the bourgeois woman who embodies Dutch freedom, is as much a figure of Goethe's own time (and of eighteenth-century middle-class drama) as the Marquis of Posa is of Schiller's – and both are entirely the playwright's invention.[47]

Characterized in this way and judged by the conventions of today's historical scholarship, the romantic vision of the past that was so popular in the nineteenth century seems crude and anachronistic.

---

[44] Schiller, *Revolt*, I, 349.

[45] Quoted in Levin, *History as Romantic Art*, 235, note 40. The comparison with Carlyle was made by J.A. Froude in the *Westminster Review* (April 1856), quoted Gooch, *History and Historians*, 416–417.

[46] Pieter Geyl, 'Motley and his "Rise of the Dutch Republic"' [1956], in Geyl's *Encounters in History* (London, 1963), 107–114; Edwards, 'Motley', 173–178, 187–188.

[47] *Egmont*, ed. Waidson, xxvi, xxviii–xxix.

Yet it was not unscholarly or uninformed; nor, in its own terms,
was it unhistorical. In writing *Don Carlos* Schiller relied initially on
a late seventeenth-century anecdotal novel by the Abbé de Saint-
Réal and a recent French play about Philip II by Sébastien de
Mercier. But he was soon 'busily reading Watson' on the same subject (Watson's *Philip II* had been available in German since 1782),
and from that work he was drawn into more prolonged and serious
study of the period. Reading history, he believed, would fill the gaps
still left in his education and provide a 'warehouse' of 'topics on
which to practise my pen and sometimes my mind'.[48] His *Revolt of
the United Netherlands*, the work which led to his appointment in 1789
as Professor of History at Jena, drew not only on recent studies like
Robertson's *Charles V* and Wagenaar's *Historie* (both of which were
similarly now available in German translation) but on more than a
dozen sixteenth- and early seventeenth-century histories from Dinoth
and Van Meteren to Bentivoglio and Grotius's *Annales et Historiae de
Rebus Belgicis*.[49] Goethe's sources for *Egmont* were admittedly fewer:
he is said to have used only Van Meteren and Strada. But from the
text of the play it is evident that he also knew the songs of the
Netherlands – the Calvinists' metrical psalms (I.i) and the *geuzen-
liederen* of the rebels (I.iii) – and that he had examined sixteenth-century engravings (I.iii).[50] Old engravings were studied by artists too,
both as a source of historical portraiture and as a guide to sixteenth-
century costume. Some Dutch and Belgian painters, indeed, went to
considerable lengths to ensure that their pictures of episodes from
the Revolt of the Netherlands were historically accurate. They sought
advice from scholars, read Wagenaar and other more recent historians and visited archives and libraries to consult the many accounts
written by contemporary observers and chroniclers. While working
on his *William of Orange* in 1818, Van Brée even arranged for Michiel
van Mierevelt's portrait of the prince to be brought from Delft to
Antwerp so that he could study it at first hand. And, in the next

---

[48] Quoted in Sharpe, *Schiller*, 85; Regin, *Freedom and Dignity*, 48.

[49] See the notes by Richard Fester on the sources of Schiller's *Revolt* in Schiller,
Sämtliche Werke, Säkular-Ausgabe, ed. E. van der Hellen, 16 vols. (Stuttgart, 1904–05),
XIV, 418–419; Sharpe, *Schiller*, 109–110.

[50] Goethe, *Egmont*, ed. Waidson, viii (historical sources), xi–xii (Goethe's interest
in music). For an example of the 'songs in Egmont's honour' mentioned by Clara
in the play, see E.T. Kuiper and P. Leendertz, eds., *Het Geuzenliedboek*, 2 vols.
(Zutphen, 1924–25), I, no. 31.

generation of history painters, Gallait went a step further. In the interests of greater realism and to supplement his documentary researches for The *Last Honours Rendered to Counts Egmont and Hornes*, he had the severed head of an executed criminal brought straight from the guillotine to his studio in Brussels. Rapidly copied in an oil sketch – the surviving canvas is marked 'Remi Bomal, ½ heure après l'execution, 15 Avril 1851' – it provided the model for the head of Egmont in the finished picture.[51]

Motley, too, drew on the old masters of Netherlands art, most obviously in the many pen-portraits which introduce the protagonists of his story as they appear on the scene.[52] But it was naturally the written record of Low Countries history which formed the main foundation of his work. At first, in *The Rise of the Dutch Republic*, he relied largely (though by no means exclusively) on printed material: on all the main contemporary chroniclers, on eighteenth-century historians like Wagenaar and Van der Vynckt and on the recently published (though as yet incomplete) correspondence of Philip II, William the Silent and other leading participants.[53] Later, for the *History of the United Netherlands*, he would turn increasingly to archive sources, 'prying and eavesdropping' on the 'secret councils' of European diplomacy; and he would do so again in his final study, on the Netherlands and Europe after the Truce of 1609, which was based on the unpublished and hitherto largely neglected papers of Oldenbarnevelt.[54] By any standards, the volume of documentation in Motley's histories is impressive. As an accomplished linguist, he drew on material in half a dozen European languages, besides Latin. And he had the

[51] Van Thiel, ed., *Vaderlandsch Gevoel*, 44–47, 88; Le Bailly de Tilleghem, *Gallait*, 119–120, 124–127, 156, 200. Direct studies of the dead and dying are not unusual in the work of romantic artists: Géricault made preparatory drawings in Paris morgues and hospitals when he was working on *The Raft of the Medusa* for the salon of 1819.

[52] See, for example, *Dutch Republic*, I, 96 (and note 3), 101 (and note 4); and on the portrait as a characteristic feature of romantic historiography, Levin, *History as Romantic Art*, 12–13, 197–201.

[53] Gachard gave Motley prior access to his continuing work on the correspondence of Philip II and of William the Silent.

[54] Hence the book's title: J.L. Motley, *Life and Death of John of Barneveld*, 2 vols. (London, 1874), though it is actually less a biography than a study of international diplomacy. It was intended as an introduction to the Thirty Years' War whose history, emulating Schiller, Motley still planned to write. The quotation about state secrets uncovered in the archives is from the *History of the United Netherlands*, 4 vols. (New York, 1860–67), I, 54–55.

linguist's ability to evoke in his own writing the tone and cadence of sixteenth-century prose. Some of his most vivid phrases, including the poetic last line of *The Dutch Republic*, are derived almost word for word from his sources.[55]

Like his whole view of Netherlands history – 'that prolonged tragedy of eighty years' which 'established the independence of Holland'[56] – Motley's prose style is famously vivid and dramatic. Nor is it unique in that. To a greater or lesser extent, a sense of drama is present in all the romantic representations of Low Countries history discussed in this essay – in Belgian and Dutch historical genre painting as much as in the writings of Goethe and Schiller and the operas derived from them. But, as Motley's evocative prose constantly reminds us, a similar sense of drama was already present in the very sources on which he and his fellow-romantics relied, those accounts and representations of the Dutch Revolt which were published or produced while the Eighty Years' War was still going on. For almost from the beginning the Revolt had been dramatized in contemporary songs, pamphlets and histories. It was presented as a conflict between good and evil, godly and heathen, with Orange cast in the role of Moses or David and Alba or Philip II as Pharaoh or 'that proud Philistine' Goliath.[57] Many of the early histories were constructed like dramas, moving from one set-piece tableau to the next and playing up instances of Spanish cruelty and intolerance[58] – much as Verdi and his librettists were to do when, in adapting *Don Carlos* for the operatic stage, they introduced a grand scene of *auto-da-fé*. The Revolt had been dramatized pictorially as well – in the numerous 'history prints' of Hogenberg and his followers as well as in paintings like Velázquez's *Surrender of Breda* (1635). If that picture

---

[55] 'As long as he lived, he was the guiding-star of a brave nation, and when he died the little children cried in the streets'. The latter part of this sentence is a quotation from a report of Cornelis van Aerssen, griffier of the States General, written a day after the assassination of William of Orange in July 1584: *Dutch Republic*, III, 456 and note 1. See also Levin, *History as Romantic Art*, 20–21, 199, 206.

[56] *Barneveld*, I, preface.

[57] *A Brief and True Rehersall of the Noble Victory . . . of Holland . . . against the Duke of Alba* (pamphlet trs. from Dutch; London, 1573), fol. A2v. On the imagery of the Beggar songs, see G. Groenhuis, 'Calvinism and National Consciousness. The Dutch Republic as the New Israel', in A.C. Duke and C.A. Tamse, eds., *Church and State since the Reformation*, Britain and the Netherlands 7 (The Hague, 1981), 119–120.

[58] S. Schama, *The Embarrassment of Riches. An Interpretation of Dutch Culture in the Golden Age* (New York, 1987), 82–87.

now stands out from many that were painted of the Low Countries wars by artists who lived through these events, it is not just because of its dramatic qualities – it draws on a play by Calderón, *El Sitio de Bredá*, performed at court in 1625 – but because it transcends conventional theatre, making the ritual of surrender seem at once historic and entirely lifelike.[59] As in Calderón's Spain, moreover, in the Netherlands too the Revolt was dramatized in the literal sense of being re-enacted on the stage. From as early as the 1580s and '90s, local amateur *rederijkers* or rhetoricians had been writing and performing plays about Egmont, about Alba's tyranny, about the siege of St. Geertruidenberg and the relief of Leiden, about the life and death of William of Orange.[60] And once England had joined the Dutch struggle in 1585, Elizabethan playwrights and professional actors followed suit. New plays on subjects like the sack of Antwerp and the battle of Turnhout were added to the repertoire of London theatres, and continued to be added in the 1620s and '30s when the war with Spain was resumed.[61]

In the end, then, the romantic view of Netherlands history which became popular in the nineteenth century may not have been so anachronistic after all. Unashamedly theatrical, often melodramatic and richly coloured, it was a view very much of its time, as all imaginative representations of the past are. Yet it did not lack solid historical foundations, nor was it without precedents. In songs and pictures, in the spoken as well as the printed word, the romantics revived and elaborated a way of representing the Dutch Revolt as a human drama which had already emerged and become popular before the end of the sixteenth century.

---

[59] J. Brown and J.H. Elliott, *A Palace for a King: the Buen Retiro and the Court of Philip IV* (New Haven, Conn., 1980), 178–182.

[60] H. van Nuffel, *Lamoraal van Egmont in de geschiedenis, literatuur, beeldende kunst en legende* (Leuven, 1968), 32–34; D. Kunzle, *From Criminal to Courtier. The Soldier in Netherlandish Art 1550–1672* (Leiden, 2002), 243–244; F. Moryson, *Shakespeare's Europe*, ed. C. Hughes (London, 1903), 373, 376, 386; G.W. Brandt and W. Hogendorp, *German and Dutch Theatre 1600–1848* (Cambridge, 1993), 369–371, 394–396.

[61] *A Larum for London or the Siedge of Antwerpe* (London, 1602); A. Collins, ed., *Sidney Papers*, 2 vols. (London, 1746), II, 136; G.E. Bentley, *The Jacobean and Caroline Stage*, 7 vols. (Oxford, 1941–68), III, 76–77, 350–351, 415–417; J. Limon, *Dangerous Matter. English Drama and Politics in 1623–24* (Cambridge, 1986), 62–88; M. Butler, *Theatre and Crisis 1632–42* (Cambridge, 1984), 234–235.

CHAPTER TWO

A PROVINCIAL NEWS COMMUNITY IN SIXTEENTH-CENTURY EUROPE

Andrew Pettegree

In recent years scholars have devoted increasing attention to the nature – or even the viability – of public opinion in sixteenth-century Europe. The received opinion that the operation of public opinion would necessarily await the emergence of a Habermasian 'public sphere' in the eighteenth century looks increasingly threadbare.[1] The thirst for information long pre-dated the invention of the coffee shop in Georgian England, and nowhere more so than in the thriving, bustling cities of Italy, Germany, France and the Netherlands.

In Europe's centres of commerce and trade, information was at a premium for quite obvious reasons. Merchants had to know whether roads were safe, and whether changes in the ruling personnel of lands near or distant threatened carefully nurtured business relationships. But the appetite for news clearly went beyond this. Not only was marketplace opinion informed, it clearly occurred to those in power that they had to devote care and attention to shaping this opinion. In this way a news community shaded into what can truly be regarded as nascent public opinion.

Two aspects of this phenomenon have particularly interested scholars in several disciplines. The first is the way in which the articulation of information on current affairs helped shape a changing sense of identity. Early modern societies inherited a sense of identity that was profoundly local. Citizens might feel a generalized sense of themselves as part of larger national communities, particularly in time of war, but their primary points of identification were more specific: to kin, to their lord, to their parish or guild, to their city. One of

---

[1] J. Habermas, *Strukturwandel der Öffentlichkeit. Untersuchungen zu einer Kategorie der bürgerlichen Gesellschaft* (Darmstadt, 1986); translated into English as *The Structural Transformation of the Public Sphere. An Inquiry into a Category of Bourgeois Society* (Cambridge, 1989).

Alastair Duke's most influential essays has been his discussion of the extent to which the Dutch Revolt involved a complex process of negotiation with pre-existing senses of identity before a notion of nationhood could coalesce around an independent northern state.[2] In the Netherlands, as elsewhere, a sense of national identity had also to compete with new, super-national identities in a religiously divided Europe. In a Europe of Catholics and Protestants, with whom did one enjoy true kinship?

For the rulers of these complex societies it was especially important to be seen as a personification or incarnation of an emerging national identity. Yet regality had also to respect the complexity of allegiance. This was true of a ruler's relationship with his cities as with his leading nobles. In the urban context the greatest contemporary expression of this complex relationship was the *joyeuse entrée*, a ceremonial event at which a ruler took symbolic possession of the city, while simultaneously promising to respect its liberties.[3] The essence of kingship was encapsulated in these dignified events: the assertion and acknowledgement of might and theoretically untrammelled power, balanced by recognition that effective rule was always necessarily co-operative. Citizens had simultaneously to be awed and persuaded. A community of interest was an active, participatory community, even if expressed in a rhetoric of deference and power.

In sixteenth-century societies the exercise of power was always persuasive; agreement must be cultivated, even where duty was formally commanded. In this context, a number of scholars, including Alastair Duke, have recently begun to pay particular attention to the role of print in shaping an active, politically aware and co-operative public: and the consequences for the body public when this co-operation began to break down.[4] The development of such a literature of persuasion and dissent is all the more striking because in the sixteenth century print was not necessarily the primary mechanism for the circulation of official information. Laws, regulations and ordinances would traditionally be relayed by word of mouth, and this process continued into the sixteenth century. In France the oral publication of official edicts took on an increasingly ritualized character. In Paris

---

[2] Duke, 'From King and Country to King or Country?'.
[3] J. Blanchard, 'Les Spectacles du rite. Les Entrées royales', *Revue historique* 305 (2003), 475–519, has a full bibliography on this subject.
[4] Duke, 'Dissident Propaganda', and his 'Posters, Pamphlets and Prints'.

edicts were first registered in the Parlement of Paris and then declaimed by the official crier at designated cross-roads and public places. The crier was accompanied by the royal trumpeter; for edicts of special importance several trumpeters were decreed.[5] From Paris edicts radiated out into the provinces, to Lyon, Orléans, and eventually Toulouse and Bordeaux, to be first received and digested by the town council, before a modest replica of the Paris ceremony was enacted for the local public.

Such official edicts lay at the heart of royal administration and one can chart the increased ambition of government – both in terms of scope of government activity and its reach into the provinces – through the printed versions that followed the oral proclamation. The right to print edicts was a privilege much prized in the publishing industry, because the profits were both swift and sure.[6] Edicts were purchased, individually or in collections, in large numbers, no doubt largely by lawyers and merchants who needed for professional and economic reasons to be precisely aware of their provisions. Yet even in this era the authorities' use of print went far beyond the exploitation of the new medium solely for the publication of official orders. Governments were concerned also to shape the way in which current events were discussed and interpreted. Nowhere was this more the case than in the volatile and independently-minded towns of France and the Netherlands. Here, even in the last decades of the fifteenth century, one can witness a precocious battle to command public sympathy, as the French and Burgundian regimes promoted conflicting visions of current events.[7]

---

[5] In an edict of 1556 the places in which an edict would be proclaimed (accompanied by the royal trumpeters) were listed as follows: 'devant la principale porte du Palais; a l'apport de Paris devant Chastelet; a la croix du Trehoir aux Halles; a l'apport Baudoyer; place de Greve devant l'hostel de la ville au Carrefour sainct severin; a la place Maubert pres la crois des Carmes; au carrefor du mont saincte Geneviefve pres le puis; rue sainct Jacques devant les Jacobins, & au bout du pont sainct Michel'. Ordonnance du Roy & de sa || Court des Monnoyes, contenant les || prix & poix, tant des monnoyes de Fran || ce qu'estrangeres, d'Or & d'Argent, aus- || quelles ledict Seigneur à dõné cours || en son royaume, pays, terres & || seigneuries de son o- || beissance [Lyon, du Rosne, 1556]. Avignon BM: 8o 14528.

[6] In France the right to print royal edicts was held by a sequence of respected figures in the publishing industry, including Guillaume Nyverd and Federic Morel, both of whom proclaimed their privileged status by styling themselves 'imprimeur ordinaire du roy' on the title page of royal edicts.

[7] J.-P. Seguin, 'L'Information à la fin du XVe siècle en France. Pièces d'actualité

These are books that emanated quite clearly from close to the
seat of power. In their physical appearance they appropriate the
confident quarto format of the official edicts of the day; biblio-
graphically they are neat, assured and technically sophisticated work,
often published by printers whose more usual stock in trade were
large and expensive books. They were intended to be read by people
who were among the shapers of opinion in the towns of France and
the Netherlands: this was cheap print for men who were the habitual
purchasers of more expensive books. Yet thus far no-one has been
able to document the existence of an equivalent provincial news community, beyond the routine (if still influential) publication and proclamation of official edicts.

That must now change with the investigation of a remarkable survival, recently rediscovered in the collections of the Bibliothèque
Municipale (the Bibliothèque Méjanes) of Aix-en-Provence.[8] The
Bibliothèque Méjanes is one of the great libraries of provincial France,
a collection of vernacular and learned literature assembled in the
eighteenth century, but reaching back into the first age of printing.
Although it contains very many magnificent books, its greatest strength
lies in the thousands of items of printed ephemera, mostly pamphlets
from the French Wars of Religion and even, as we shall now see,
from an earlier era.

On a recent research trip I had occasion to examine one item,
ostensibly a group of three small pamphlets. In fact the *recueil* contained some thirty-three items, two thirds of them books published
in Rouen in the early 1540s. Many were previously totally unknown:
more than half represent the only surviving copy of the book in
question.

There are good reasons why these books should previously have
escaped the attention of bibliographers. The largest survey of French
provincial printing, the *Répertoire Bibliographique*, was constructed by
delegating individual volumes, devoted each to a single printing
centre or group of towns within a region, to local specialists.[9] The

---

imprimées sous le règne de Charles VIII', *Arts et traditions populaires* 4 (1956), 309–330,
and 5 (1957), 46–74, and his, *L'Information en France de Louis XII à Henri II* (Geneva,
1961).

  [8] Aix-en-Provence, Bibliothèque Méjanes, Rés. S 25.
  [9] *Répertoire Bibliographique des livres imprimés en France au seizième siècle*, 30 vols. (Baden-

individual volumes vary in quality, but by and large the editors concentrated their searches on a survey of the major Paris collections and libraries in their own vicinity. Books printed in one part of France but presently located in another distant provincial collection could quite easily slip through the net, as was the case with the Rouen books in this volume in Aix. A number of the titles listed were at least known to the greatest twentieth-century expert on ephemeral news publications, Jean-Pierre Seguin, but based as he was in the Bibliothèque Nationale in Paris he too was clearly unaware of the collection in Aix.[10] The present article therefore represents the first systematic examination of this unique body of material.

The Aix *recueil* contains thirty-three items, around two thirds of which were printed in Rouen in a short eight year period between 1537 and 1544. Even on a most cursory examination it is clear that they are very different in character from the confident, relatively fine work of the Parisian and Netherlandish news sheets of the incunabula age. The Rouen books are small octavos of around 12 centimetres, mostly four or eight leaves long (that is eight or sixteen printed pages). The Rouen items in the collection are almost all unpaginated, and lack even the customary bibliographic signature in the bottom margin. They are all printed in a simple black letter type with a single and equally crude title-page woodcut by way of decoration. These illustrative woodcuts are mostly of battle or tournament scenes and are extremely crudely drawn; several are reused more than once in the pamphlet sequence.

These then are the most ephemeral of ephemeral books. Seldom more than one printed sheet in length, they could have been dashed out and on sale in less than two days. They required no great expertise to produce, and could indeed have been the work of an artisan printer relatively new to the trade – as seems indeed to have been the case. They served a specific purpose in a specific community at a time of peculiarly heightened awareness of public affairs.

Baden, 1968–80). Rouen and Caen were reserved for a separate set of subsidia volumes (also incomplete). P. Aquilon & A.R. Girard, *Bibliographie normande. Bibliographie des ouvrages imprimés à Caen et à Rouen au seizième siècle* (Baden-Baden, 1992).

[10] Seguin, *L'Information en France*, nos. 152, 154, 155, 156a, 159, 160–163, 166, 170, 172, 177, 180, 187–188, 192, 193, 195, 204, 211, 215, 218.

Rouen in the 1540s was a bustling, mercantile city of around 70,000 inhabitants.[11] Despite the growth of Lyon in the first half of the century, it could still with justice defend its long-standing claim to be the second city of the kingdom. In the prosperous and populous province of Normandy it jealously defended its role as provincial metropolis; Rouen was the seat of both the local Parlement and the home of the local royal administration. This defined its civic life, but its commercial life was also shaped by its relative proximity to Paris. Although Rouen was one of the greatest cities of the kingdom, its book world was largely a satellite of the capital. The local printing industry was small compared, for instance, to the magnificence of Lyon's well-established publishing houses, a crucial two hundred kilometres more distant from the magnetic pull of the capital.[12]

In consequence the indigenous printing industry of Rouen was small and provincial, concentrating on repeated editions of the most popular books, mostly school books and church primers. If Rouen had developed a specialism it was to service a lively export market for standard church texts (Books of Hours and Breviaries) destined for England.[13] To meet the requirements of more aspirational and wealthy local customers Rouen booksellers turned to the great centres of print in northern and southern Europe: most obviously Paris, but also Antwerp, Venice and Basel. The market for vernacular books seems to have been too small to justify any local reprints of popular French recreational literature, such as the farces and romances that were already steady sellers for many Parisian printers. Still less was there a demand for local editions of edicts or news pamphlets,

---

[11] For Rouen, see P. Benedict, *Rouen during the Wars of Religion* (Cambridge, 1981); S. Carroll, *Noble Power during the French Wars of Religion. The Guise Affinity and the Catholic Cause in Normandy* (Cambridge, 1998).

[12] For Lyon printing see H.-L. Baudrier and J. Baudrier, *Bibliographie lyonnaise. Recherches sur les imprimeurs, libraires, reliers et fondeurs de lettres de Lyon au XVIe siècle*, 12 vols. (Lyon, 1895–1921). The latest survey of Lyon printing, however, conducted as part of the St Andrews French book project, adds something like a further 30% of items not known to Baudrier to the corpus of Lyon print. M. Hall, 'Lyon Publishing in the Age of Catholic Revival, 1565–1600', unpublished Ph.D. thesis (St Andrews University, 2005). On the role of printing in the Lyon economy, see R. Gascon, *Grand Commerce et vie urbaine au XVIe siècle. Lyon et ses marchands* (Paris, 1971).

[13] Aquilon and Girard, *Bibliographie normande*. M. Lane Ford, 'Importation of Printed Books into England and Scotland', in L. Hellinga and J.B. Trapp, eds., *The Cambridge History of the Book in Britain*, vol. III, *1400–1557* (Cambridge, 1999).

a market that once again could be fully supplied from Paris, one day's journey up river.

This seems to have changed very suddenly in the years between 1538 and 1544. These, it must be remembered, were exceptionally turbulent times in European politics, and especially in the complex triangular relationship between France, England, and the rulers of the Habsburg lands.[14] The resumption of the seemingly inevitable conflict between Francis I and the Emperor Charles V in 1536 followed a period of febrile, at times frantic, search for diplomatic advantage. At one time in the mid 1530s French ambassadors pursued the search for allies simultaneously in England, with the Lutheran Protestant princes in Germany, and, more scandalously, at the court of Barbarossa, the corsair Prince of Tunis. This last overture would result, in 1536, in the first formal treaty between France and the Ottoman Sultan in Constantinople. Despite this wide-ranging search for allies, when Francis renewed the conflict with a thrust into Piedmont and Savoy, France found itself relatively isolated, and Imperial forces soon turned the tables with incursions onto French soil from both north and south. The emperor's armies were eventually obliged to withdraw, but only after the depredations of the armies had caused great hardship to the local populations. After two seasons of indecisive campaigning both sides were happy to accept an offer of the pope, Paul III, to preside in person over negotiations between the quarrelling parties at Nice, and a peace was duly concluded. A month later, on 14 July 1538, Charles and Francis were personally reconciled at a meeting at Aigues-Mortes. When, the following year, the emperor needed to return to the Netherlands to deal with the aftermath of the rebellion at Ghent, he sought and obtained from Francis permission to travel across French territory.

The emperor's progress across French territory and lavish reception at Paris were regarded with astonishment in other European capitals, yet the reconciliation between Europe's two premier monarchs proved to be of short duration. The new amity with Charles inevitably caused the greatest suspicions elsewhere in Europe; to

---

[14] The best account of these events is to be found in *Les Memoires de messire Martin du Bellay, Seigneur de Langey* (Abel L'Angelier: Paris, 1586). See also Ernest Lavisse, *Histoire de France*, 9 vols. (Paris, 1900–11), V: Henry Lemonnier, *La Lutte contre la maison d'Autriche. La France sous Henri II (1519–1559)* (Paris, 1904). R.J. Knecht, *Francis I* (Cambridge, 1982).

insulate France against a possible deterioration of relations with other former allies diplomatic emissaries embarked on a new round of embassies to Venice and the Ottoman Turk. Meanwhile the marital adventures of Henry VIII of England briefly raised the possibility of a new French bride for the English king. But it was the imperial rivalry over Italy which would precipitate a new round of fighting, sparked by the mysterious assassination of a French diplomat, apparently at the hands of imperial troops. War was declared on 12 July 1542, but Francis was unable to find a strategically coherent means to carry the fight to the enemy. When in 1543 the Emperor concluded an offensive alliance with a revitalized Henry of England, it was clear that the major theatre of conflict would be in the north, and the fighting on French soil.

For the inhabitants of Normandy there was a pressing need to keep abreast of these events, many being played out close to its shores, or in areas crucial to the trade and prosperity of Rouen's merchant traders. This provided an opportunity to a venturesome individual previously unknown to the publishing trade, Jean L'Homme. Little is known of L'Homme beyond his responsibility for the works that bear his name; he had no apparent history or family connection in Rouen's book world, and his period of activity was exceptionally short. But in this short period he developed a valuable, and clearly exceptionally valued, specialism. In the six years between 1538 and 1544 he turned out at least forty news pamphlets, almost all of which are known from only one surviving copy. This of course raises the possibility that there may have been many others, now completely lost.

The items in the Aix *recueil* offer a fairly representative sample of his work. The earliest date from the period 1538–40, and relate the curious history of the meetings between Francis, the emperor and the pope at the time of the Treaty of Nice, and of the emperor's subsequent progress through France.[15] Charles's route took him to Paris from Bordeaux and via Poitiers; after taking leave of his royal host he travelled on through Chantilly and Soissons, before passing

---

[15] ¶ Le tri~uphant || departement de nostre sainct pere le || Pape/ Du treschrestien Roy de Frã= || ce/ & de Lempereur de Romme/ auec || les grans dons & presens ~q le~d empe= || reur a faict a la Royne de France/ et || aux aultres dames & damoyselles. || ¶ Cum gratia & priuilegio. [Rouen, L'Homme, 1538]. Aix, Méjanes: Rés. S 25 (23).

on to imperial territory at Valenciennes. These events certainly piqued the interest of France's reading public. The entries into Orléans and Paris were the subject of several accounts published in the capital, and the main Paris entry even found its echo in the publications of another modest provincial press in far away Toulouse.[16] The fact that L'Homme chose to publish an account of the emperor's entry into Valenciennes rather than the more sensational events in Paris may support the view that there were other accounts of the Emperor's journey, now lost.[17] But the Valenciennes entry was also a significant moment. It was the point at which Charles took leave of his honour guard, which included Francis I's two sons; it was also at Valenciennes that Charles first met a delegation from the uneasily repentant Ghent rebels. L'Homme's relation of these events is one of the few works in the Aix *recueil* that survives in more than one copy; but on closer inspection, the two copies turn out to be quite separate editions. The Aix copy notes in the colophon that it was published on 15 March; the only other surviving copy, in the Bibliothèque Nationale in Paris, was published five days later, on 20 March.[18] Nothing illustrates the thirst for information more eloquently than the fact that Jean L'Homme's first edition apparently sold out within a week.

---

[16] *La double et copie dunes letters envoyees d'Orleans contenant a la verite le triumphe faict a lentree et reception de lempereur* [Paris, Corrozet, 1540]; *La magnificque et triumphante entrée du tres illustre et sacre Empereur faicte en la excellent ville et cite de Paris*. *Inventaire chronologique des editions parisiennes du XVI* siècle. V, 1536–1540* (Paris, 2004), nos. 1722–1725. For the Toulouse work see Jean d'Abundance, *Prosopopeïe de la France à l'empereur Charles le Quint sur al nouuelle entrée faite à Paris*. [Toulouse, Nicolas Viellard, 1540]. This book is known only from an entry in the bibliography of du Verdier. See *Répertoire bibliographique*, XX, Vieillard no. 53. See also Claude Chappuys, *La complainte de Mars sur la venue de l'empereur en France* [Paris, 1540], *Inventaire*, V. 1634.

[17] ¶ La triumpha= || te & magnificque entree de Lempereur || Charles tousiours Auguste cin= || quiesme de ce nom/ acompai= || gne de messeigneurs le Daul || phin de France & duc Dor || leans/ en sa ville de || Valentiennes [three dots] || M. D. XXXIX. || [Rouen, L'Homme, 1540]. C4v: ¶ Jmprime a Rouen par Jehan lhomme. || Le quinztesme iour de Mars Mil cinq c~es. || trente neuf. Aix, Méjanes: Rés. S 25 (24).

[18] ¶ La triumphã= || te & magnificque entree de Lempereur || Charles tousiours Auguste cin= || quiesme de ce nom/ acompai= || gne de messeigneurs le Daul || phin de France & duc Dor || leans/ en sa ville de || Valenciennes.: || M. D. xxxix. || [Rouen, L'Homme, 1540]. C4v: ¶ Jmprime a Rouen par Jehan lhomme. || Le vingtiesme iour de Mars Mil cinq c~es. || trente neuf. Paris BN: Rés. Lk7 10038.

The appetite for news in Rouen was such that Jean L'Homme could not hope to monopolize the production of these short news pamphlets. The most substantial competition came from Guillaume de La Motte, who in 1537 had published a short and rather more conventional pamphlet, a lamentation by Gilles Corrozet of the passing of Madeleine de France, first wife of James V of Scotland.[19] La Motte also published his own contribution to the literature generated by Charles V's French progress, a celebratory oration of the Court author Claude Chappuys.[20] But it was L'Homme who secured the prestigious task of publishing the official declaration of war in 1542. This was one of the frequently issued works in the Aix *recueil*. It was published first in Paris by Poncet Le Preux, and then in at least three other locations around France: at Troyes, Lyon (in at least two editions) and at Rouen.[21] Once again L'Homme published at least two separate editions. The Aix copy notes in the colophon that it was published on 4 August (almost four weeks after the king's declaration at Ligny).[22] The copy that survives in the Musée Condé in Chantilly, on the other hand, was printed on 10 August.[23]

The complex events of the war of 1543–44 stimulated the most active period in the lifetime of L'Homme's Rouen press. Hostilities began with a formal declaration of war by Henry of England and

---

[19] Deplora || tion sur le trespas de tres || noble Pr~icesse ma dame || Magdaleine de France || Royne Descoce. || [Rouen, Guillaume de La Motte, 1537]. Aix, Méjanes: Rés. S 25 (27).

[20] La complaincte de || Mars sur la venue de Lempereur en France. || ¶ Au treshault/ trespuissant: tresvertueux & tres= || chrestian [sic] Roy Francoys premier de ce nom/ || Claude Chappuys son treshumble || & tresobeissant Libraire: & varlet || de chambre ordinaire. [Rouen, for La Motte and Burges, 1540]. Aix, Méjanes: Rés. S 25 (25).

[21] *Cry de la guerre ouverte entre le roy de France et l'Empereur roy des Hespaignes* [Paris, Le Preux, 1542], Paris BN: Rés. Lb 30 86; *Cry de la guerre* [Lyon, Dolet, 1542], Paris BN: Rothschild IV 4 49; *Cry de la guerre* [Lyon, s.n., 1542], London BL: C 33 h 10; *Cry de la Guerre* [Troyes, Paris, 1542], Paris BN: Rés. Lb 30 224. Seguin, *L'Information*, nos. 167–9.

[22] ¶ La desclara= || ration [sic] de la Guerre. Faicte par || le treschrestian [sic] Roy de France || Contre Lempereur et tous ces || subiectz: tãt par mer ~q ~p terre. || [hand] Cum p. iuilegio [sic] || [Rouen, L'Homme, 1544]. [ ]4v: Jmprime par Jehan Lhomme. Le quattriesme iour daoust Lã de grace || Mil cinq centz quarantedeux. Aix, Méjanes: Rés. S 25 (11).

[23] La desclara= || ration [sic] de la Guerre. Faicte par || le treschrestian Roy de France || contre Lempereur et tous ces || subiectz: tãt par mer ~q ~p terre. || Cum priuilegio. || [Rouen, L'Homme, 1542]. [ ]4v: Jmprime par Jehan Lhomme. Le || dixiesme iour daoust Lã de grace || Mil cinq centz quarantedeux. Chantilly, Musée Condé: IV B 72.

this was faithfully republished in Rouen – it would presumably have been particularly important to Rouen's merchant community to know the precise terms of the conflict with the northern neighbour.[24] Throughout the two years of relatively intense fighting that followed, events in this northern theatre naturally dominated the output of the Rouen press. Local readers were kept abreast of the frustration of an English naval attack on Harfleur;[25] the defence of Landrecies in Picardy against Imperial forces in September; and the successful campaign of the Duc de Vendôme in Artois.[26] The Rouen presses also celebrated the French triumph in retaking Luxembourg in September 1543, a signal reverse for the unfortunate William of Cleves, France's former ally forced by Charles earlier in the year to make a humiliating separate peace.[27] In the southern theatre the highpoint of French success was the capture from the Duc de Savoye of the port town of Nice by the Duc d'Enghien, working in close co-operation with the fleet of Barbarossa, and these events too merited a pamphlet from L'Homme's press. In this case good news travelled reasonably swiftly: the town fell on 22 August, yet Rouen readers were able to read an account of these events scarcely three weeks later.[28]

---

[24] ¶ Declaration || de la guerre enuers le Roy de || france de par le roy den-gleter= || re et de par les subiectz la di= || cte declaration faicte a monsei= || gueur [sic] lembassadeur de france || estant pour lors a la court du || grant conseil dengleterre. || ¶ Publie a Rouen a son de trõ || pe parmy la ville et carfourgs || dudict lieu. Le cin~qesme iour || de Juillet. Mil cinq cens qua || rãtetrys. Cõtre les~d angloys. [Rouen, L'Homme, 1543]. Aix, Méjanes: Rés. S 25 (9).

[25] ¶ La prinse et || de faicte des Angloys par les || Bretons deuãt la Ville de bar || fleu pres la hogue au pays de || cost~etin duche de Normendie || Le. xxii. iour de Juillet mil c~iq || cens Quarante troys. || [woodcut]. Aix, Méjanes: Rés. S 25 (6). For two Paris editions of this work see Seguin, L'Information, nos. 182 and 183.

[26] ¶ La deffaicte || des Bourguignons et Henouyers/ || faicte par monsieur de Vendosme || et le prince de Melphes: en || la conte Dartoys. || pres Landrecy. || [Rouen, L'Homme, 1543]. [ ]4r: ¶ Jmprime par Jehan Lhomme || imprimeur: ce mardy xxix. || iour Daoust cinq cens || Quarante trois. Aix, Méjanes: Rés. S 25 (4); La grande prinse et deconfiture des Espagnols et Bourguignons et Anglais devant la ville et chateau de Landrecy [Rouen, La Motte, 1543]. Seguin, L'Information, no. 193.

[27] La deffaicte et || destrousse du conte Guillau || me deuant Luxembourg/ || faicte par les Frãcoys ioux || te la teneur des letres cy a= || pres declarees. Auec la chã || son nouuelle. || Nouuellement imprime. [Rouen, 1543]. Aix, Méjanes: Rés. S 25 (22).

[28] ¶ La prinse de || Nice en sauoye. Par ung g~etil || hõme du pais. Auec vne lettre || enuoyee par le Roy d~enemarc: || au treschrestien roy de France. || [Rouen, L'Homme, 1543]. [ ]4v: ¶ Jmprime par J. Lhõme || Le. xi. iour de Septembre. Aix Méjanes: Rés. S 25 (10).

A noticeable trend of these news pamphlets was their patriotic
tone. They record almost exclusively military successes, rather than
the evident reverses that left France at the beginning of 1544 still
perilously poised. But before fighting resumed the French nation
could at least celebrate a more joyful event, when on 20 January
1544 Catherine de Medici, wife of the Dauphin Henry, at last, after
ten years of marriage, gave birth to a son. The event was greeted
with ecstatic celebrations at court, and eagerly hymned by the court
poets; Rouen's printers hastened to carry the good news to an eager
populace.[29]

On the war front 1544 dawned with a significant victory in the
Italian theatre, where in January Enghien, Lieutenant General of
Piedmont, had laid siege of Carignano. An imperial relieving force
was defeated at the battle of Cerisole on 14 April, allowing Enghien
to complete the conquest of Carignano. These events were widely
celebrated in France, not least in Rouen.[30] The northern theatre presented a more ominous prospect. In May imperial forces recaptured
Luxembourg and advanced into France; by July the emperor himself was engaged in the siege of St.-Dizier, and imperial troops roamed
through Champagne. Through all of this the Rouen pamphlets keep
up a remarkably optimistic aspect, recording notable Imperial reverses,
such as the death of the prince of Orange, killed in the imperial
assault on St.-Dizier,[31] and a further triumph for Antoine de Bourbon,
Duc de Vendôme, better known by his later title of King of Navarre,
but at this point leader of the armies of Francis I in Picardy.[32] But
in truth the prospects for French forces were bleak; perhaps a hint

---

[29] ¶ De la triumphante || et heureuse Natiuite de mõseigneur Le duc filz ||
premier de monseigneur le Daulphin. [Rouen, 1544]. Aix, Méjanes: Rés. S 25 (15).

[30] ¶ La prinse et assault || de la ville de carignen faicte par monsieur ||
Danguyen le xx. iour Dapuril. || [Rouen, Jehan Le Prest, 1544] || Aix, Méjanes: Rés. S 25
(13).

[31] ¶ La deffaicte || du prince Dorenge auec sa gendar= || merie. Ensemble la
v~egeance de || la mort du duc de Cleues fai= || cte par le duc de Cassonne
|| son oncle [three dots] || [Rouen, L'Homme, 1544]: Jmprime nouuellement par
Jehan || lhomme le nenfie [sic] iour du moys || Daoust mil cinq cens qua= ||
rante quatre. Aix, Méjanes: Rés. S 25 (30).

[32] ¶ La deffaicte || des Angloys & Bourguignons faicte || par le treshault sieur
et prince mõsieur || de Vandosme/ auec le nombre des pri= || sonniers enseignes
& guydõs/ & aultres || victoires obtenues du depuys par ledit || sieur/ comme
plus amplement vous est || declaire. [Rouen, L'Homme, 1544]: Jmprime par Jehan
lhomme le huict= || iesme iour Daoust/ mil cinq centz qua= || rante quatre.
Aix, Méjanes: Rés. S 25 (32).

of this predicament came with a pamphlet recording, in more sober style, the order of battle arrayed for the defence of France's vulnerable frontiers.[33] In fact, the enemy had progressed far beyond the frontiers of France, and there was general relief when the emperor, himself over-extended and running short of funds, agreed to make peace. The Peace of Crépy, signed on 18 September and published in Paris two days later, was hardly expected to endure, but there was no hint of this as its terms were published and studied through the kingdom – not least in Rouen, where Jean L'Homme brought news of the treaty to his local audience.[34]

The peace with Charles, however fragile, did not itself end the war, since parallel peace talks with England had made little headway. In the summer of 1545 a reinvigorated Francis I conceived a bold plan to carry the fight to the English, and a large naval fleet was assembled in Le Havre. This time it was Guillaume de La Motte who published for the benefit of Rouen readers a list of the ships assembled for the proposed invasion.[35] The French fleet did indeed set sail, and troops were briefly landed on the Isle of Wight; but a major naval engagement was averted when a gale blew the French fleet back towards their ports.

This last indecisive engagement also marks an end to the period of activity of the two Rouen presses. La Motte's account of the French naval forces is almost his last known publication, though a Robert La Motte is briefly recorded as active in Rouen a decade

---

[33] Lordre de lar= || mee du Roy nostre sire: pour la gar || de des frontieres de France: contre || le camp de Lempereur: et celuy des || Angloys noz ennemys. || [Rouen, L'Homme, 1544]: Nouuellement Jmprime par Jehan lhomme le c~iquiesme || iour du moys Daoust là || de grace mil c~iq centz || Quarãtequatre. Aix, Méjanes: Rés. S 25 (31).

[34] La Publication du || traicte de la Paix faicte & accordee entre tres= || haultz & trespuissans princes Francoys par la || grace de Dieu Roy de France treschrestien/ et || Charles Empereur & Roy des Espaignes. || Publie a Paris le samedy. xx. iour de Sept~e= || bre. Lan de grace mil cinq c~es quarãte quatre. || ¶ Auec priuilege. || [Rouen, 1544]. Aix, Méjanes: Rés. S 25 (3).

[35] ¶ Lordre triu= || phant et grand nombre des Nauyres es= || quipez pour le faict de la Guerre par mer || a lencontre du Roy Dengleterre. Ordõ= || nez par le commandemene [sic] du Roy nostre || syre & ses lieutenans en ce faict & regard || Auec les nõs des gentilzhõmes & autres || deleguez & cõmis cappitaines des~d nauy= || res. Aussi les noms des pillotes & cõdu= || cteurs du~d esquipage le tout selõ lordõnã || ce & voulloir du~d seigneur. Auec la nou= || uelle reformation de la Paix faicte entre || Lempereur & le Roy. || [Rouen, La Motte, 1545]. Aix, Méjanes: Rés. S 25 (12).

later. Jean L'Homme also prints a small number of books in the
year 1545, including a rare royal edict, but is not heard of again.
A decade later a Martin L'Homme surfaces briefly in Rouen before
moving to Paris, where he prints small tracts in much the same style
as the earlier Rouen publishing firm. But for the moment, the presses
of Rouen are stilled; the news market in Normandy would await the
turbulent events of the French Wars of Religion before the level of
printing activity witnessed in the 1540s would be attained once more.

The short history of the L'Homme press in Rouen raises many
interesting questions. There is no doubt that the small, rudimentary
pamphlets turned out by L'Homme found an eager readership in
Rouen. Given the number of these works, and the demand for instant
reprints, are we justified in describing this as a news community?
Only, one might suggest, in some respects. It is clear, in the first
instance, that the events shared with Rouen's reading public are
extremely carefully chosen. L'Homme's pamphlets carry news only
of French success: Rouen's merchants, anxious for their cargoes and
consignments, will learn of French reverses only by word of mouth.
No French press, in Paris or the provinces, would provide a written
account.

In this context it is legitimate to ask what lay behind the establishment of L'Homme's press, and the other small ventures that
flourished in Rouen during these years. Are we dealing here with a
market for news, or a conscious attempt to shape opinion? It is clear
that L'Homme's press was officially sanctioned. A number of his
books include on the title-page an explicit reference to a privilege,
presumably one granted by the local Rouen authorities. A number
of the colophons contain a more explicit reference to the local power,
noting a book was published 'par commandement de Justice' or 'de
lauctorite & consentement de iustice'.[36] Edicts, and official documents
such as the declaration of war in 1542, are accompanied by a crude
woodcut representation of the royal coat of arms: a normal appur-
tenance of such edicts, but a clear visual signal that the work was
printed with authority. In the light of this evidence we should at

---

[36] Combat faict en= || tre les Angloys/ Et la Guer || nison de Therouenne
[three dots] || [woodcut] || ¶ Par cõmandem~et de Justice [Rouen, Jacques Gentil,
1543]. Aix, Méjanes: Rés. S 25 (29).

least consider the possibility that L'Homme's publications were not only officially authorized, but formally commissioned, and perhaps even wholly paid for by the local council. In this case they may have been intended for distribution to the local citizenry, rather than for commercial sale.

Printers would be fully familiar with such commissions. When a local ordinance, or royal decree, was to be published locally, normally as a broadsheet poster, the work would be commissioned from a local jobbing printer, and the whole consignment delivered to the local authorities.[37] The fact that such broadsheets rarely survive has completely disguised the importance of such commissions to the economics of the provincial print industry.[38] But larger pamphlets could also be commissioned for distribution, rather than sale. Alastair Duke provides us with a specific example of a treatise in defence of indulgences, ordered to be published by the cathedral chapter at Utrecht, in the wake of Luther's criticisms.[39] Presumably here the chapter was acting to defend their economic interests, and the pamphlet (an edition of five hundred copies) might well have been given away free.

It is not implausible that the production of pamphlets in Rouen reflects a similar conscious effort by the Rouen authorities to bolster morale. One notes in this connection that the output of optimistic bulletins from the military theatres reaches its peak in August 1544, in truth the moment of greatest jeopardy for France. One could well imagine the Rouen authorities taking action to stem the panic that was close to seizing Paris; but there again there would equally have been a lively commercial market for news in these perilous times. In the absence of corroborative sources these are questions that cannot satisfactorily be resolved. What is certain is that

---

[37] Contracts for such payments are recorded in several volumes of the *Répertoire bibliographique*, extracted from local archival records. Often this enrolled record of the payment to a local printer is the only surviving indication that the broadsheet ever existed. See, by way of illustration, the seven ordonnances and proclamations commissioned by the town council of Bourges for printing by Jacques Garnier between 1562 and 1563. *Répertoire bibliographique*, vol. XIII, 28.

[38] A notable exception is the wonderful collection of locally printed broadsheets, printed on the instructions of the municipality of Troyes, preserved in the library of Troyes, Archives Municipales (now deposited in the Bibliothèque Municipale of Troyes). *Répertoire Bibliographique*, vol. XII, Jean Moreau, nos. 1, 7, 18, 24, 71, 74.

[39] Duke, 'Posters, Pamphlets and Prints', 30.

the conjunction of a strong desire on the part of the authorities to promote reassurance, and a thirst for news among Rouen's commercial classes, created a happy business climate for the fortunate Jean L'Homme.

During the crisis of the sixteenth century books would be published in over one hundred towns and cities around France. Yet most of these places would establish their printing presses only in the last two or three decades of the century, and even then only intermittently. In these smaller local publishing houses pamphlets often formed a large part of the stock in trade, if not the sole rationale for the establishment of a local printing press. In this way the burning issues of the day were carried to a whole multitude of increasingly politicized citizen readers, who were able to judge the competing claims first of Catholic and Protestants, then of Leaguers and Royalists. Sometimes these books were reprints of Paris or Lyon works, sometimes published in two local towns that had chosen competing loyalties.[40] Citizens of these towns were thus able to follow the play of events, both near and far: accounts of battles and sieges from the French wars, but also events from elsewhere in Europe that abutted on French affairs: the campaigns of the duke of Parma against the insurgent Dutch, the defeat of the Spanish Armada, the subsequent feats and calamities of foreign forces on French and Netherlandish soil.[41]

The brief career of Jean L'Homme offers a precocious window on this world of anxiety and debate from a period not normally associated with the proliferation of a popular news literature. The exigencies of the moment created what was, in the context of 1540s Normandy, a new demand and a new niche market in Rouen's book world. One only wonders what other small worlds of print may be encompassed in the still uncatalogued volumes of so many European libraries.

---

[40] See, for instance, the contrasting loyalties of printers in the two principal cities of Britanny, Rennes and Nantes, in the last decade of the century. *Répertoire bibliogaphique*, vol. XIX.

[41] On this Franco/Netherlandish news market see now Andrew Pettegree, 'France and the Netherlands. The Interlocking of Two Religious Cultures in Print during the Era of the Religious Wars', *Dutch Review of Church History* 84 (2004), 318–337.

CHAPTER THREE

CARTOGRAPHY, CHOROGRAPHY AND PATRIOTIC SENTIMENT IN THE SIXTEENTH-CENTURY LOW COUNTRIES[1]

Paul Regan

The oldest surviving map of the Low Countries produced by a native Netherlander is Hieronymus Cock's map of 1557 [fig. 3.1]. Along the edge of the map itself, Cock explained the reasons for producing this representation of the Low Countries. 'Studying, dear reader,' he wrote, 'some descriptions of the Netherlands which have been published, I realized that none of these is as complete as this country deserves'. He expressed the hope that the map and the additional information presented in the margins would encourage the viewer to love his *patria* or *vaderland*.[2]

In recent decades, historians have drawn attention to the way in which, throughout the sixteenth and seventeenth centuries, maps and chorographies were used to express and to encourage a love of the *patria*.[3] During the early modern period, maps began to be drawn more accurately and came to be recognized as having a more wideranging purpose and significance. The development of the printing press meant not only large scale production of books but also that

---

[1] This article draws upon chapter 4 of my, 'The Construction of Patriotic Sentiment in the Sixteenth-Century Low Countries: Cartography, Calvinism and Rebel Propaganda', unpublished Ph.D. thesis (Southampton, 1995), which was supervised by Alastair Duke.

[2] H.A.M. van der Heijden, *The Oldest Maps of the Netherlands* (Utrecht, 1987), 55, 57. The English translations are by Van der Heijden.

[3] For sixteenth-century Germany, see G. Strauss, *Sixteenth-Century Germany. Its Topography and Topographers* (Madison, Wisc., 1959) and his article, 'The Image of Germany in the Sixteenth Century', *The Germanic Review* 34 (1959), 223–234; for France, H. Ballon, *The Paris of Henri IV. Architecture and Urbanism* (Cambridge, Mass., 1991), 213–214, 220–249; and for England, V. Morgan, 'The Cartographic Image of "The Country" in Early Modern England', *Transactions of the Royal Historical Society*, 5th series, 29 (1979), 129–154.

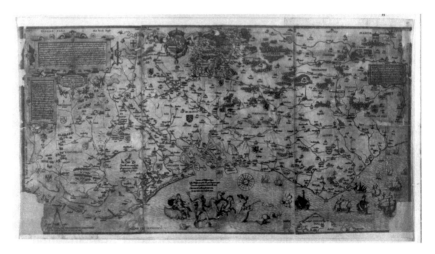

Fig 3.1. Map of the Netherlands (1557) (Untitled), Hieronymus Cock. (By kind permission of the Biblioteca Nazionale Centrale, Firenze: Lafrery, volume I, 75)

illustrations, including maps, could be reproduced in significant numbers. As governments began to realize how valuable maps could be for governance and in war, they encouraged the technological developments which made the production of scale maps possible.[4] Maps ceased to be just one-off productions designed to resolve specific problems and became objects of beauty and more general utility for ever wider audiences. It is the conviction of a growing number of historians that, as well as bringing pleasure, many of these maps expressed and stimulated a sense of pride in cities, regions and countries by providing visual displays of the viewer's homeland.

Some historians have tried to link this development with the political events of the period. Richard Helgerson has argued that, in England, maps and chorographies played 'their part in the long, slow movement of thought and action that brought the king's enemies to the field . . . Maps let them [sixteenth-century Englishmen] see in a

---

[4] See D. Buisseret, ed., *Monarchs, Ministers and Maps* (Chicago, 1992); P.D.A. Harvey, *The History of Topographical Maps. Symbols, Pictures and Surveys* (London, 1980); J.B. Harley and D. Woodward, eds., *The History of Cartography*, I (Chicago, 1987). Morgan, 'The Cartographic Image', 141–142, draws this point out well.

way never before possible the country – both county and nation – to which they belonged and at the same time showed royal authority – or at least its insignia – to be a merely ornamental adjunct to that country. Maps thus opened a conceptual gap between the land and its ruler, a gap that would eventually span battlefields'.[5] The contribution of chorographies, or *written* descriptions of the geography of an area, to the formation of identities may seem less obvious. However, as Gerald Strauss has demonstrated in the case of Germany, chorographical books fostered pride in a homeland by providing the reader with a wealth of details about the history, prosperity and glory of that land. Like maps, chorographical works put the *patria* on display but they did so through words rather than an image.[6]

It is striking that the Low Countries have not been considered in the surveys of geographical works for indications of the beginnings of a territorial identity. This absence is surprising, because from the mid-sixteenth century to the mid-seventeenth century, the Low Countries were the European centre of cartographic production.[7] The economic prosperity of the Habsburg Netherlands and later the Dutch Republic meant that the domestic market for geographic works was probably greater there than anywhere else in Europe. The region was also one of the major centres of publishing and printing houses.[8] Second, this period of economic supremacy and cartographic dominance coincided with a time when identities in the Low Countries were complex and fluid in character. The Netherlandish region had always been marked by strong civic and provincial

---

[5] R. Helgerson, 'The Land Speaks: Cartography, Chorography, and Subversion in Renaissance England', *Representations* 16 (1986), 51–85, there 52, 56.

[6] On chorographies in the Netherlands, see Raingard Esser's essay in this volume.

[7] R.V. Tooley, *Maps and Map-Makers* (7th ed.; New York, 1987), 29–35; L. Bagrow, *History of Cartography*, ed. and transl. R.A. Skelton (1st German ed., 1951; London, 1964), 180–185; A.G. Hodgkiss, *Understanding Maps. A Systematic History of their Use and Development* (Folkestone, 1981), 95; C. Koeman, ed., *Atlantes Neerlandici. Bibliography of Terrestrial, Maritime and Celestial Atlases and Pilot Books, Published in the Netherlands up to 1880*, 5 vols. (Amsterdam, 1967–71), I, v.

[8] K.H.D. Haley, *The Dutch in the Seventeenth Century* (London, 1972), 120–124; C.R. Boxer, *The Dutch Seaborne Empire 1600–1800* (London, 1965), 161–162; and L. Voet, *The Golden Compasses. A History and Evaluation of the Printing and Publishing Activities of the Officina Plantiniana at Antwerp*, 2 vols. (Amsterdam, 1969–72).

identities and these continued through the sixteenth and seventeenth
centuries. For most Netherlanders, the '*patria*' remained the village,
the city and the province. As well as these more ancient loyalties,
the sixteenth and seventeenth centuries saw the development within
the Low Countries of not one but three different 'national' or supra-
provincial identities: a general pan-Netherlandish identity in the second half of the sixteenth century and, following the division between
the Northern and Southern Netherlands, a 'Dutch' identity in the
north and a Southern Netherlandish identity in the south. The nov-
elty of these supra-provincial identities in this period should not
be overlooked. The Low Countries, roughly in the form in which
it is understood today, was the creation of the Valois dukes of
Burgundy and the Habsburgs, whose state-building was not complete until the 1540s. The very idea of a Netherlandish state, then,
increasingly distinct *within* and *from* both the Holy Roman Empire
of the German nation and the kingdom of France was still novel in
the mid-sixteenth century when map production began in earnest.

The fluid character of Netherlandish supra-provincial identity, the
strong economy and the production of maps and other geographical works all suggest that the Low Countries would be a significant
region for examining the hypothesis that geographic works both
expressed and stimulated 'national' and regional identities. This can
be questioned in two main ways. Firstly, is there any evidence that
maps and chorographical works expressed the different forms of identity which existed in the sixteenth-century Low Countries? What
influence would these works have had upon those who collected and
viewed them? Secondly, what was the market for these works? Were
the maps and chorographies meant just for the educated elites? How
many such works were produced? Without answers to this second
group of questions, it will prove difficult to estimate the degree of
influence of geographic works upon public opinion and the formation of identity in the Low Countries.

Initially maps in the Low Countries were produced by the state
but this changed in the mid-sixteenth century with the expansion of
commercial production centred on Antwerp. Gerard de Jode, who
went on to produce an atlas in the 1570s, and Hieronymus Cock
both published maps during the 1550s. Links with foreign markets
and centres of production had also been established by this date:
both Cock and De Jode had connections with Italian mapmakers
and Abraham Ortelius, the future creator of the first atlas, was

already collecting maps at the Frankfurt Fair in 1556.[9] Antwerp's ascendancy in the cartographic trade, really came about when Christopher Plantin started publishing maps in 1558. Plantin had established his printing press in Antwerp in 1555, publishing ten works in his first year. He expanded at such a rate thereafter that his company became the largest printing press in Europe, using, at its peak in January 1574, 16 presses.[10] When Plantin began to publish maps in 1558, his main trading network had already been established, so he was able to purchase and to sell maps and other geographical works at a number of European trading centres such as Paris, London, Augsburg and Frankfurt almost immediately. He had business contacts with merchants from Italy, Lyon, Cologne and Spain.[11] Something of the scale and European breadth of Plantin's trade in maps can be gained by considering what happened to the 686 copies of maps Gerard Mercator sold to Plantin between 1566 and 1576. In the Low Countries, 312 maps were sold: 44 in Plantin's Antwerp shop; 205 to booksellers in Antwerp and Mechelen specializing in cartographical production; 14 to ordinary booksellers and 49 to private customers. Another 247 maps were sent to France, all but ten of these to Paris. 127 maps went to four other countries: 51 to Germany; 30 to England; 24 to Spain; and 22 to Italy.[12]

Some idea of the number of maps being sold in Antwerp at this time can be obtained from an examination by Jan Denucé of extracts relating to cartographical and topographical works from the accounts of the House of Plantin. The extracts record the purchase, delivery and sale of seven to eight thousand maps in the years 1555–99 of

[9] J. Keuning, 'XVIth-Century Cartography in the Netherlands (Mainly in the Northern Provinces)', *Imago Mundi* 9 (1952), 35–63, there 51–52 (for Cock and De Jode); J. Denucé, *Oud-nederlandsche kaartmakers in betrekking met Plantijn*, 2 vols. (Antwerp, 1912–13; repr. Amsterdam, 1964), I, 118–119 (for Cock), II, 3 (for Ortelius); H.E. Wauvermans, *Histoire de l'école cartographique belge et anversoise du XVIᵉ siècle*, 2 vols. (Antwerp, 1895), II, 35 (for Cock); M. Destombes, 'A Panorama of the Sack of Rome by Pieter Brueghel the Elder', in idem, *Selected Contributions to the History of Cartography and Scientific Instruments* (Utrecht, 1987), 107, 112 (for Cock).

[10] Voet, *The Golden Compasses*, I, 31–33, 81. To put the figure of 16 presses into perspective, Voet notes that four presses was a high figure in the sixteenth and seventeenth centuries. Another famous sixteenth-century firm, Estienne in Geneva, never had more than four presses.

[11] Voet, *The Golden Compasses*, I, 32, and Denucé, *Oud-nederlandsche kaartmakers*, I, 17. Voet, *The Golden Compasses*, II, 395–398, 400–401.

[12] Voet, *The Golden Compasses*, II, 421.

which an unknown proportion appear more than once in the accounts. The most cautious estimate of the total number of maps passing through Plantin's printing house, based upon the assumption that each map was recorded twice in the accounts, would be 3500. Since Plantin was only one of the many establishments in the Low Countries selling maps, albeit by far the most important, it becomes clear that thousands of maps must have been produced and sold during the second half of the sixteenth century.[13]

The abundance of cartographic and geographic material in the 1560s and 1570s is also shown by the emergence of a new format, atlases, from 1570 onwards, which developed so that new small scale maps could be organized and presented in a systematic manner. The first such atlas to conform to the definition of 'a systematic and comprehensive collection of maps of uniform size' was Abraham Ortelius's *Theatrum Orbis Terrarum* of 1570.[14] Seventy maps appeared in the first edition of the *Theatrum* and the number rose with the subsequent editions so that by 1584, the *Theatrum* contained 114 maps.[15] The *Theatrum* was followed in the Low Countries by another two major atlases, Gerard de Jode's *Speculum Orbis Terrarum* (1578) and Gerard Mercator's *Atlas* (1585–95).[16] Of these three atlases, Ortelius's *Theatrum* was by far the most successful. From 1570 to 1598 Ortelius supplied Plantin in Antwerp with nearly 2000 copies of the *Theatrum*, 900 of these between the years 1570 and 1576.[17] This figure and the extracts from the Plantin archives show that the total number of atlases produced during the last thirty years of the sixteenth century must have been at least several thousand.[18] Although Antwerp

---

[13] Denucé, *Oud-nederlandsche kaartmakers*, I and II, *passim*.

[14] Bagrow, *History*, 139, 176–185; Hodgkiss, *Understanding Maps*, 93; C. Koeman, *The History of Abraham Ortelius and his Theatrum Orbis Terrarum* (New York, 1964), 25, 47, 49; L.A. Brown, *The Story of Maps* (London, 1951), 164–168.

[15] Koeman, *The History of Abraham Ortelius*, 27–34, 42–44.

[16] For Gerard de Jode, see Wauvermans, *Histoire de l'école cartographique belge*, II, 165–168; F. van Ortroy, *L'Oeuvre géographique de Gerard et Corneille de Jode* (Ghent, 1914; repr. Amsterdam, 1963); Denucé, *Oud-nederlandsche kaartmakers*, I, 163–201. For Mercator see J. Keuning, 'The History of an Atlas. Mercator-Hondius', *Imago Mundi* 4 (1947), 37–62.

[17] Koeman, *The History of Abraham Ortelius*, 39, 41–42, 44–45.

[18] The extracts in Denucé, *Oud-nederlandsche kaartmakers*, I and II, record the purchase and sale of just over 4000 atlases in the years from 1565 to 1601. The following were included in the category of atlas: the *Theatrum Orbis Terrarum* with the

developed as a major centre for the production and marketing of maps and atlases, the Low Countries were less well supplied with chorographical works. The fame attached to Lodovico Guicciardini's *Description of All the Low Countries*, first published in 1567, has obscured the scarcity of native Netherlandish chorographical works in the six-teenth century.[19] In fact, there appear to have been only four other chorographical works on the Low Countries published in this period, two of which were unfinished.[20] Their relative scarcity was largely due to the remarkable success of Guicciardini's *Description* which pro-vided a full description of the Low Countries, and effectively cor-nered the market for chorographical works.

The *Description* followed much the same pattern as the German 'topographical-historical' works and cosmographies of this period. Guicciardini introduced the work with comments of a general nature on the names accorded to the region, the number of towns, great rivers and its countryside, the customs of the people and political matters. He then described each province in turn, paying particular attention to Brabant and, especially, Antwerp. The work also appeared with a map of all the Low Countries and a series of maps of most of the provinces.[21] Guicciardini's work proved to be a great com-mercial success; three Italian and two French editions of the book appeared in the sixteenth century, followed in the seventeenth cen-tury by a series of French, Dutch and Latin editions. It was not

---

Addimenta and *Supplementa*, Mercator's *Atlas*, the *Speculum Orbis Terrarum* and the *Spieghel der Werelt* or *Epitome*.

[19] The first edition was published in Italian in Antwerp. I used the French edi-tion, Ludovico Guicciardini, *Description de tout les Pais Bas autrement dict la Germanie Inferieure ou Basse Allemaigne. Messire Lodovico Guicciardini Patritio Florentino* (Antwerp, 1567). On Guicciardini, see Denucé, *Oud-nederlandsche kaartmakers*, and H. De la Fontaine Verwey, 'The History of Guicciardini's Description of the Low Countries', *Quærendo* 12 (1981), 22–51.

[20] Strauss, *Sixteenth-Century Germany*, 61. The four works were the first volume of Johannes Goropius Becanus, *Origines Antwerpianae* (1569), the little known *Itinerarium Belgicum* of 1587 and two works relating to the province of Holland and the sur-rounding area. See B.A. Vermaseren, 'Het ontstaan van Hadrianus Junius' *Batavia* (1588)', in M. Nijhoff, ed., *Huldeboek Pater Dr Bonaventura Kruitwagen* (The Hague, 1949), 417; P.H. Meurer, 'Gerhard Stempel, Georg Braun en het *Itinerarium Belgicum* (Keulen, 1587)', *Caert Thresoor* 3 (1984), 3–8; and for the unfinished works, E.O.G. Haitsma Mulier, 'Grotius, Hooft and the Writing of History in the Dutch Republic', in Duke and Tamse, eds., *Clio's Mirror*, 55–56.

[21] Guicciardini, *Description*, *passim*.

until 1649–51 that any serious attempt was made to replace the work and reprints continued to appear until 1662.[22]

The main market for all these maps, atlases and Guicciardini's *Description* was the more well-to-do and educated elements of Netherlandish society. This was especially the case with the atlases and the *Description*. The first edition of the *Theatrum* (1570) contained 53 map sheets and 70 maps in total. Ortelius sold to Plantin the 'afgeset' or coloured copies 'op groot papier' (large format and wide margins) at a price of 16 guilders each, the uncoloured copies, 'op klein papier' (smaller format), at just five guilders and ten stuivers. Later editions with the inclusion of more maps were sold by Ortelius for steadily higher prices: in the years 1584–90, when the atlas contained 100 map sheets and 114 maps, the *Theatrum* fetched 16 guilders for an uncoloured copy and 26 guilders for a coloured copy; and from 1595 the uncoloured copy, containing 147 maps, cost 23 guilders.[23] The other major atlases and Guicciardini's work were in much the same price range.

The cost of these atlases was beyond the means of even the skilled workers employed by Plantin as the master printers and compositors, who in 1580 received 105 and 165 guilders a year respectively.[24] A slightly more affordable shorter atlas with a compilation of 70 maps based upon those in Ortelius's *Theatrum* was published by Plantin in 1577. Entitled *Spieghel der Werelt gestelt in Ryme* ('Mirror of the World set to Verse'), the atlas was priced at one guilder and two stuivers thus putting it within reach of a wider public. The atlas proved to be a success, selling so well that by 1583 at least 1100 copies had been delivered to Plantin and within 22 years five Dutch editions and six French editions had been produced.[25]

The cheapest of all the geographical works, the loose-leaf maps, were also available to a wider market. At one end of the scale were the great wall maps which could cost as much as a guilder. Philip Galle's wall map of the Low Countries, produced in 1578, cost 18–25

---

[22] De la Fontaine Verwey, 'The History of Guicciardini's Description', 49–50.
[23] Van der Heijden, *The Oldest Maps*, 90–91.
[24] Voet, *The Golden Compasses*, II, 309–356; Koeman, *The History of Abraham Ortelius*, 39; C. Clair, *Christopher Plantin* (London, 1960), 284–285. These workers were master craftsmen, not apprentices.
[25] M.P. Heyns, *Spieghel der werelt, ghestelt in ryme* (Antwerp, 1577). For details of sales see Koeman, *The History of Abraham Ortelius*, 27. The French edition was entitled *Le Miroir du monde*. The work is often referred to as the *Epitome*.

stuivers when coloured, six to eight stuivers when untouched.[26] Poorer quality maps could also be purchased for as little as one stuiver.[27] For Plantin's workers, such as the printers and compositors whose monthly wages came to 175 and 275 stuivers respectively, the cheaper maps were evidently affordable.

Some indication of the spread of maps can be obtained from probate inventories during this period. Based on the published collections of inventories, which need to be treated with caution, it would seem that by the late 1560s only a small minority of people possessed a map and that, with the exception of the nobility, they did not have great quantities of maps. However, the inventories do indicate that people from various walks of life and from different parts of the Low Countries were buying maps and some of the maps which they possessed were maps of the Low Countries. The buyers included the nobility, brewers, burgomasters and priests.[28]

During the second half of the sixteenth century, not only was there increasing production and sales of geographical works, including

---

[26] Van der Heijden, *The Oldest Maps*, 84–87.

[27] The plates used in Plantin's edition of the *Description* in the early 1580s could be bought separately at one stuiver each. Koeman, *The History of Abraham Ortelius*, 50. By way of comparison, the average price of the pamphlets sold by Plantin to the States General in the years 1578–82 was 1.25 stuivers; see C.E. Harline, *Pamphlets, Printing, and Political Culture in the Early Dutch Republic* (Dordrecht, 1987), 63–64.

[28] H.A. Enno van Gelder, *Gegevens betreffend roerend en onroerend bezit in de Nederlanden in de zestiende eeuw*, Rijks geschiedkundige publicatiën, Grote Serie 140 and 141 (The Hague, 1972–73), *passim*. An analysis has been made of over two hundred and fifty inventories drawn from both volumes, excluding those which only contain details about income and law contracts, and including numbers 121A–121C in vol. 140, v–vii. Other published inventories appear in J. Scheerder, 'Documenten in verband met confiscatie van roerende goederen van hervormingsgezinden te Gent (1567–1568)', *Bulletin de la Commission Royale d'Histoire* 157 (1991), 125–242, and A. Hallema, 'Inventarissen van Franeker burgers en boeren omstreeks 1550', *BMHG* 46 (1925), 53–89, and his, 'Nogmaals een drietal inventarissen van Franeker burgers en boeren kort na 1550', *BMHG* 49 (1928), 270–340. Some of the inventories in Enno van Gelder's sample appear also in Scheerder's article. The published collections of these inventories need to be treated with some caution because there is no means of knowing how representative these inventories are. The inventories, for example, which Enno van Gelder edited for the Rijks Geschiedkundige Publicatiën provide only a sample of all the inventories in the archives. Furthermore, most of the published inventories collected by Enno van Gelder and others relate to individuals cited before the Council of Troubles in 1567–69. This group, composed mainly of Protestant sympathisers and those who were active against the central government in 1565–67, may well be unrepresentative of the market. The fact that the majority of the published inventories concern individuals cited before the Council of Troubles also means that there are only a few published inventories from the years *after* 1570.

expensive atlases and chorographies as well as cheaper loose-leaf maps, there was a gradual change in the depiction of the Netherlands. Before 1550, only two maps of the entire Netherlands appear to have been made; in the second half of the century, 47 different cartographic representations of the Low Countries are known to have been produced.[29] In other words, before 1550, maps of the Low Countries barely existed but, by 1600, maps of the Low Countries were common. This suggests that there was a growing market to support their production and an increasing interest in the location and geography of the Netherlands. This growth was undoubtedly stimulated by the Eighty Years' War, but Hieronymus Cock's assertion, in 1557, that he had produced his map of the Low Countries in order that people might love the *patria* shows that patriotic pride was another influence.

This is also apparent in the two most successful geographic works of the sixteenth-century Low Countries: Ortelius's *Theatrum* and Guicciardini's *Description*. In his preface to the *Theatrum*, Ortelius explained why he thought maps were so important. He argued that a knowledge of geography generally, and maps in particular, was essential in the study of history and current affairs. He acknowledged the pleasure which people found in maps. Finally, perhaps anticipating future criticism of his work, Ortelius asked his readers to send in further details and maps of their native land if they considered that their country was not covered adequately by the atlas: 'some there are peradventure', he wrote

> which will looke to finde in this our Theater more descriptions of particular Countreys, (for the every man naturally, for the love that he beareth to his native soile, would, I doubt not, wish that it were here severally described amongst the rest). . . .[30]

Ortelius assumed that people wanted to see maps of their own homeland, whether that was a city, a province or a large state.

He himself was not exempt from this desire to see maps of his own land. In 1584, he produced an antiquarian map of the Low

---

[29] Van der Heijden, *The Oldest Maps, passim*. The first modern map of the entire Low Countries did not appear until 1547.

[30] The quotation is taken from the preface in the English edition: Abraham Ortelius, *The Theatre of the Whole World: Set Forth by that Excellent Geographer Abraham Ortelius* (London, 1606). This preface is based upon the prefaces in the original Latin (1570) and Dutch (1571) editions.

Countries and in the dedication wrote 'with pleasure the citizen Abraham Ortelius dedicates this map of his native country as it was in Roman times to the senate and people of Antwerp. S.P.Q.A. = Senatui Populoque Antwerpiensi'. In one of the cartouches, Ortelius was praised for his scholarly endeavours: 'Studying books on ancient history, Ortelius disclosed the antique monuments of the Roman Netherlands. Glean, reader, the first grains of your native soil and learn from which ancestors you are the offspring.'[31]

Similar expressions of a supra-provincial sentiment appear in Guicciardini's *Description*. As Guicciardini was an Italian, the *Description* may be thought to be an inappropriate place to look for expressions of Netherlandish patriotism. The work is prefaced, though, by a series of poems in five languages, Latin, Greek, Italian, French and Dutch, praising Guicciardini for his achievement in showing the world the glories of the Netherlands. In the only Dutch poem which appears in the series, the poet uses the device of an allegory, in which the Netherlands appears as a woman called 'Belgica'. The poet calls upon 'Belgica', 'schoon edel' bloeme' ('beautiful, noble flower'), to stop sitting in a dejected manner between her rivers, because Guicciardini had come to take her down to Italy. Belgica's beauty would, at last, receive the dues it deserved and her progress down to Italy would display her wonders to all. The poet concludes by bidding 'Belgica' farewell as she sets out on her tour through the world and calls upon her to reward her workman for his labours. Lucas d'Heere, a poet and painter from Ghent, produced a sonnet in French, in which he tells the reader that, through the book, he would come to an understanding:

> Of our beautiful lands and of its qualities/
> Of our towns, cities and their properties/
> Peoples, arts, industry and their magnificence/
> Which Guicciardini describes par excellence.[32]

The comments which appear on the maps produced by Cock and Ortelius and in the prefatory poems to Guicciardini's *Description* show clearly that the humanist patriotic motif which featured in maps and

---

[31] Van der Heijden, *The Oldest Maps*, 161–163.

[32] 'De nostre beau païs & de ses qualitez,/ De noz villes, Citéz, & leurs proprietez,/ Peuples, arts, industrie, & leur magnificence;/ Lesquels GUICCIARDIN descrit par excellence.' Guicciardini, *Description*. The Dutch poem begins 'Belgica ontwaect . . .'.

chorographical works elsewhere in sixteenth-century Europe was also present in the Low Countries during this period. Like their counterparts elsewhere, Netherlandish humanists, like Cock, Ortelius and d'Heere, expressed a sense of pride in their country through maps and chorographical works. They also clearly believed that their creations could deepen feelings for the homeland, whether that was understood to be a city, a province or the entire Netherlands.[33]

Although the principal means by which Cock and Ortelius hoped to influence viewers was by putting the country on 'display', it is possible that other features of the maps, atlases, and Guicciardini's *Description*, also helped construct an identity which saw the Netherlands as a unified political body distinct from both Germany and France. One of the less obvious features of the maps was the frontier. In 1551–52, the Antwerp civic authorities purchased from Jacob van Deventer a large wall map of the Low Countries which was described in the accounts as '. . . a map of all the lands over here, also with all the frontiers of those lands'.[34] This description reminds us that with the advent of scale maps, the idea of territorial frontiers gradually began to take hold in Europe. Although some early modern maps depicted boundaries with reasonable accuracy, it was, generally, not until the eighteenth century that the frontiers of most areas were delineated clearly and accurately on maps, and diplomats and governments began to take serious account of geographical frontiers in negotiations leading up to treaties.[35] The frontiers that appear on

---

[33] For more evidence that humanism deepened patriotic sentiment and brought about a greater expressiveness in patriotic sentiment, see L. van den Branden, *Het streven naar verheerlijking, zuivering en opbouw van het Nederlands in de 16de eeuw* (Ghent, 1956), on the campaign to purify and glorify the Dutch language. There are a lot of works on humanist interest in the ancient past. See, for example, K. Tilmans, *Aurelius en de Divisiekroniek van 1517. Historiografie en humanisme in Holland in de tijd van Erasmus* (Hilversum, 1988); and I. Schöffer, 'The Batavian Myth during the Sixteenth and Seventeenth Centuries', in J.S. Bromley and E.H. Kossmann, eds., *Some Political Mythologies. Papers Delivered to the 5th Anglo-Dutch Historical Conference*, Britain and the Netherlands 5 (The Hague, 1975).

[34] Denucé, *Oud-nederlandsche kaartmakers*, I, 60–61: '. . . een caerte van alle de landen van herwaerts over, met oock alle de frontieren van dezelve landen'. The map probably gave more attention to the frontiers of the provinces than to the frontiers of the Low Countries.

[35] D. Buisseret, 'The Cartographic Definition of France's Eastern Boundary in the Early Seventeenth Century', *Imago Mundi* 36 (1984), 72–80. J.W. Konvitz, *Cartography in France 1660–1848. Science, Engineering and Statecraft* (Chicago, 1987), 32–33. See also, D. Buisseret, 'Cartography and Power in the Seventeenth Century',

the sixteenth-century maps of the Low Countries, then, including the map purchased by the Antwerp magistrates, should not be taken as a precise rendering of borders on the ground but as rather generalized frontiers.

What is important about the frontiers, though, was not so much their accuracy, or lack of it, as the fact that mapmakers choose to represent a frontier at all. Unlike France, for example, the Low Countries had only recently become a 'country' as opposed to a mere region; unlike France, there was no longstanding sense of a 'Netherlands'. Anything, then, which served to distinguish the Low Countries from the surrounding countries would tend to establish the notion of a Netherlandish state and the frontiers which appear on the maps, marking the Low Countries off from France and Germany, were one such distinguishing agent.

A cautionary note must be added, though. Lines or dots indicating *provincial* frontiers also appear on most of the sixteenth-century maps of the Low Countries but the lines distinguishing the Low Countries as a whole from the surrounding areas appear clearly in only a few maps.[36] The map of the Low Countries which appeared in Ortelius's *Theatrum* illustrates this point well [fig. 3.2]. The map contains not only a confusing number of frontiers, but the lines that distinguish the provinces from each other are also no different from those separating the Netherlands from France and Germany.[37] It is true that when maps were painted, as an unknown proportion of them were, frontiers were usually outlined but provincial boundaries were as likely to be emphasized as 'national' frontiers.[38]

Proceedings of the 10th Annual Meeting of the Western Society for French History 10 (1984), 103–105, and, more generally, J. Ancel, 'L'Évolution de la notion de frontière', *Bulletin of the International Committee of Historical Sciences* 5 (1933), 538–554.

[36] See the following maps in Van der Heijden, *The Oldest Maps*, 10, 23, 27, 29, 34, 45, 46 and 48.

[37] Given the high sales of the *Theatrum*, Ortelius's map of the Low Countries was probably seen by more people than any other map of the Low Countries. Its only rival would have been the map of the Low Countries which appeared in Guicciardini's *Description*.

[38] See the copy of Ortelius's map of 1570 in Van der Heijden, *The Oldest Maps*, 133, where the province of Brabant has been highlighted by the map-colourer. The possible importance of colouring and frontiers was noted by Brown, *The Story of Maps*, 176: 'It could make a map beautiful to look at, and it could be used more effectively than any other device *to set off or differentiate adjacent political areas*, land forms and bodies of water . . .' (my italics).

Fig. 3.2. *Descriptio Germaniae Inferioris* (1570), Abraham Ortelius; Frans Hogenberg
(?), engraver. The map appears in the 1581 French edition of the Theatrum Orbis
Terrarum, entitled Theatre de l'Univers (British Library, Maps C.2.c. 16)

A second distinguishing agent was the focus of the map. The practise of orientating the map to the north was introduced in the late
Middle Ages via the portolano charts but it did not become cartographic convention until much later.[39] Mapmakers in the sixteenth
century, therefore, still had scope for arranging the material in such
a way as to emphasize or marginalize different aspects of the subject. Jacob van Deventer, the creator of the first scale map of the
Low Countries [fig. 3.3], stuck to the principle of orientation to the
north. When presented in this way, the Low Countries appears less
as a subject in a portrait and much more as a stretch of the coast-
line in northwest Europe. In other works, the map is orientated so
as to emphasize the Netherlands and to exclude from view most or

---

[39] E. Raisz, *General Cartography* (London and New York, 1938), 80.

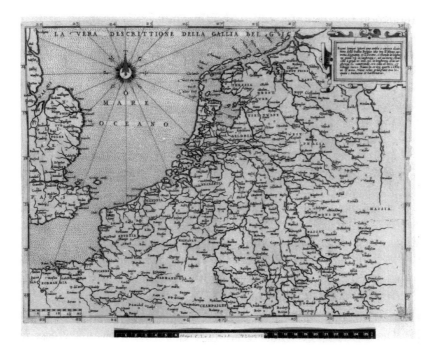

Fig. 3.3. *La Vera Descrittione Della Gallia Belgica* (1560/65). This map, engraved by Paolo Forlani, is probably a copy of Jacob Van Deventer's original map of the Low Countries. [See Van der Heijden, *The Oldest Maps*, 37–52] (British Library: Maps C.7.e.1)

all of England and much of the adjoining French and German lands. This was the case, for example, with Ortelius's map of 1570 [fig. 3.2] and Hieronymus Cock's map of 1557 [fig. 3.1].[40]

One thing which can be stated with certainty about the sixteenth-century maps of the Low Countries is that the adoption of a common nomenclature for the area was hastened by the spread of the Netherlandish maps. Van Deventer's wall map of 1551–52 was described in the Antwerp accounts as a map of 'de landen van her-waerts over' ('the lands over there'). Such an imprecise designation was obviously unsuitable when the commercial expansion of map

---

[40] On the orientation of maps of the Low Countries see Van der Heijden, *The Oldest Maps*, 59, 92–95.

production began in the mid-sixteenth century. Accordingly the maps of the Low Countries quickly acquired terms that specifically denoted the Netherlands. The Dutch term *Nederlanden*, the Latin words *Gallia Belgica* and *Inferior Germania* and the French *Pays Bas* appears on maps of the Low Countries from 1557, *Belgica* without the attendant *Gallia* from 1567, the German *Niderlendt* from at the latest 1579.[41]

While these terms all specifically refer to the Low Countries, their variety shows that confusion about the nature and status of the Low Countries continued in the second half of the sixteenth century: Netherlanders and other Europeans were still unsure about whether to classify the Low Countries as Germanic, French, a mix of the two or as something standing by itself.[42] In Guicciardini's work and the first two atlases of 1570 and 1578, the association with Germany remained strong. Guicciardini entitled his work *Description de Tout le Pais Bas* and added *autrement dict La Germanie inferieure ou Basse Allemaigne* ('otherwise called Low Germany'). Ortelius placed the Netherlands clearly within Germany writing,

> But Germanie as it is now taken, we do confine by the German or Dutch tongue; . . . wherfore all those countries which at this day use the same language, we comprehend under the name of Germany, And so the greatest length thereof stretcheth from Calais on the West to the river Vistula or Wixel Eastward . . . The names of the severall regions are there, Flanders (the most Westerly), Brabant, Zeland, Holland, Frisland, Denmarke, Mecklenburgh, Pomerland, Prussia. . . .[43]

The *Spieghel der werelt* followed the same lines as the *Theatrum*, emphasizing the linguistic understanding of 'Germania'.[44] In the 1578 *Speculum Orbis Terrarum*, the Netherlands is classified as '*Inferior Germania*'; indeed, the whole of the first edition is dedicated to Germany.[45] The

---

[41] *Gallia Belgicae* and *Inferioris Germaniae* appear on one of Arnout Nicolai's two maps of the Low Countries produced in 1557. *Gallia Belgica, Germania Inferior, Pays Bas* and *Nederlanden* appear on Hieronymus Cock's map of 1557. *Belgica* first appears on the map of the Netherlands from 1567, attributed to Cornelis d'Hooghe, and *Niderlendt* on Frans Hogenberg's map of the Low Countries produced in the second half of the 1570s. Van der Heijden, *The Oldest Maps*, 108–110, 121–123, 137–139, and Denucé, *Oud-nederlandsche kaartmakers*, I, 49. Any of these names might have appeared on Van Deventer's early maps of the Low Countries from the late 1540s and early 1550s.

[42] On the confusing nature of Netherlandish nomenclature, see Duke, 'The Elusive Netherlands', there 11–22.

[43] Ortelius, *The Theatre*, section 33.

[44] Heyns, *Spieghel der werelt, ghestelt in ryme*.

[45] Van Ortroy, *L'Oeuvre géographique*, 33–82.

last of the three great atlases, Mercator's work of 1585, was the first to break with the practice of including the Low Countries under Germany and also the first to accord a separate, distinct section to the maps of the Netherlands. However, the Low Countries was instead considered as part of France ('*Belgii inferioris*').[46]

Both the frontiers, names and the focus of the maps of the Low Countries and the way in which the Netherlands was categorized in the atlases and Guicciardini's work, demonstrate that the extent to which these geographical sources influenced the population was complex. On the one hand, the works indicate the survival of the older political associations; on the other, the emergence of a distinct political entity, deserving of attention in itself and not just as part of a larger association. In spite of this mixed message, though, the maps, atlases and the *Description* must have tended to strengthen the notion of a common Netherlands because the Low Countries was, generally, presented as a distinct and unified area of which the provinces formed but parts.

That these works always emphasized the unity of the provinces rather than their distinctiveness from each other is evident in a number of ways. It is often forgotten that a concern for objectivity or neutrality was implicit in the development of scale maps. The idea of a uniform scale militated against deliberate misrepresentations of the size of provinces or countries. At the same time the old pictorial representations of towns, cities, rivers and mountains were replaced by a set of uniform symbols. To borrow a phrase from the map historian J.B. Harley, all areas were treated alike and appeared alike. Accordingly, the provincial differences that beset the Low Countries were not represented on maps of the entire area. The provinces nearly always appeared on the maps but they did so as equal parts of one whole.[47] This is also true of the three atlases: the maps of the provinces always appear after the map of the Low Countries and as part of the Low Countries. It cannot be said, however, that Guicciardini treated all parts of the Low Countries equally in his *Description*. Of the 399 pages on the Low Countries, 88 are devoted to the city of Antwerp, and the three main provinces of Brabant, Flanders and Holland account for 229 pages (57.3% of the whole

---

[46] Keuning, 'The History of an Atlas', 38, 40–41.
[47] J.B. Harley, 'Silences and Secrecy: The Hidden Agenda of Cartography, and Subversion in Renaissance England', *Imago Mundi* 40 (1989), 57–76, there 65–66.

book). In the part of the book which deals with the description of
the provinces, 66.4% relates to these three key provinces. Whilst
making allowance for the particular features of provinces, though,
Guicciardini still groups them all together under the title of the Low
Countries. The singularity of the provinces is confirmed, but so too
is their association together.[48]

The unity of the provinces is also emphasized in the short descriptions of the Low Countries which appeared alongside the cartographic representations. The columns of instructive facts and popular
beliefs about the Netherlands were intended to serve as a didactic
complement to the cartographic image. In some cases, the com-
mentaries perpetuate the older association of names and cultural and
political ties,[49] but the general effect of these little descriptions must
have been to help strengthen the notion of a Netherlandish identity.
One such description, from Johannes van Deutecum's map of 1594,
provides a useful illustration of this genre:

> It is a striking, splendid, beautiful country adorned with many big,
> prosperous, populous towns; some of the 208 fortified and moated
> towns can be reckoned among the finest of Europe . . . It has many
> fine inland rivers of which the Rhine, Moselle, and Scheldt are the
> most important and an incredible quantity of big and small ships . . . It
> has beautiful forests, too, full of game; and because of the healthy air,
> in some parts people live to a greater age than in other countries.[50]

Van Deutecum's summary, which in substance was much the same
as all the other anecdotal accounts which accompanied these maps,
assumed that the lands and people so described, however diverse
they may have appeared, were united. In this respect, Van Deutecum's
description, like the neutral quality of most maps of the Low Countries,
served to foster and spread a general Netherlandish identity.

There was one map which more than any other produced in the
sixteenth century would have tended to promote a sense of Netherlandish distinctiveness and unity: the *Leo Belgicus*. The map was pub-

---

[48] Guicciardini, *Description, passim.*
[49] In one of the cartouches for his map of 1566, Gerard de Jode comments,
'. . . In our day the Netherlands include Burgundy, Lorraine, the duchy of
Luxemberg . . .'. Van Deutecum, in his map of 1594, states: 'Rightly these Dutch
provinces have always been considered as German, since the greater part of their
inhabitants are held to be Germans both in origin and speech . . .'. Van der Heijden,
The Oldest Maps, 118–120, 191–195.
[50] Van der Heijden, *The Oldest Maps*, 191–195.

lished by an Austrian nobleman, Michael von Aitzing, and appeared in 1583 as part of a history of the Netherlands, covering the years 1559–83. The idea of a map of the Netherlands in the shape of a lion was derived from the lions present in the coat-of-arms of most of the provinces. This map, the first in a long line of Belgian and later Holland lions, drew together many of the cartographic and political strands of the sixteenth-century Netherlands. The idea of a Netherlandish territorial entity and indeed of the notion of a territorial frontier had, by the 1580s, become so widely accepted that the Netherlands could be symbolized in a form defined by its frontiers. In this proclamation of the peculiar character of the country, the map also emphasized, unlike many maps of the Low Countries, the separation of the Netherlands from both France and Germany and, at the same time, the unity of the provinces within a greater Netherlandish body.[51]

There is no evidence that Von Aitzing thought of the map as a symbol of Netherlandish patriotism. From the emphasis on impartiality in the introduction it is clear that the Austrian's principal concern was to ensure that the map reached as wide a public as possible. The map was a commercial item: the metamorphosis into a lion was a gimmick. However, such was the potential of the map that it soon became a patriotic emblem. In an anti-Spanish pamphlet of 1598, for example, the Netherlands appeared as a wounded lion, its forepaw wrapped in a bandage. The state of the lion and the accompanying text of the great charter known as the *Joyeuse Entrée* were meant to represent the suffering which the tyrannical Spanish had inflicted upon the Low Countries. The woodcut map with the lion was clearly based upon the various Belgian lions which appeared after 1583.[52]

Conclusion

Richard Helgerson's thesis that maps and chorographies played a small part in the development of anti-royalist thought in sixteenth-

---

[51] M. Von Eytzinger, *De leone Belgico, eius que topographica atque historica descriptione liber* (Cologne, 1583); W. Bonacker, 'Le Baron Michael von Eitzing (1530–98)', *Revue Belge de Philologie et d'Histoire* 37, part 2 (1959), 950–966; R.V. Tooley, 'Leo Belgicus. An Illustrated List', *Map Collector's Circle. Map Collector's Series* 7 (1963), 4–16, plus plates; and Van der Heijden, *The Oldest Maps*, 158–160, 164–165, 209–210.
[52] Van der Heijden, *The Oldest Maps*, 218–219.

and seventeenth-century England could not equally be applied to the early modern Low Countries. A trade in maps and other geographical works did develop from the mid-sixteenth century onwards, with material on the Netherlands forming a significant part of this trade. However, maps in general, let alone maps of the Low Countries, were too few in number to have exercised much influence political influence. The market for geographical works was still in its infancy during the first crucial stages of the Revolt of the Netherlands between 1560 and 1580. In the longer term, thought, these works influenced opinion and identity by giving graphic and written substance to that which, hitherto, had been vague and insubstantial; namely, the notion of a 'country'. What made this development in the Low Countries particularly important was the fact that a Netherlandish 'country' had only recently taken shape. The importance of the maps, atlases, and the *Description*, then, should be recognized in two ways. They helped to spread and consolidate the notion of a Netherlandish country distinct from both France and Germany, while, within the Low Countries, they facilitated the development of a Netherlandish patriotic sentiment.[53]

---

[53] In the seventeenth century, the maps and the *Description* also helped maintain a common Netherlandish identity. Guicciardini's *Description* continued to be published until 1662 and maps of the whole of the Netherlands remained more popular than separate maps of the two parts of the Netherlands until the second half of the seventeenth century. See H.A.M. van der Heijden, 'De oudste kaarten van Nederland en de opkomst van het nationaliteitsbesef', *Spieghel Historiael* 21 (1986), 547–555.

CHAPTER FOUR

'AND YE SHALL HEAR OF WARS AND RUMOURS OF WARS'. RUMOUR AND THE REVOLT OF THE NETHERLANDS

Henk van Nierop

Friday, 19 September 1572, was a day like any other for Wouter Jacobsz, with some good, and mostly bad news.[1] Yet the proposition that *any* day could be rated as 'normal' in Holland since the outbreak of the Revolt is one Wouter would have angrily rejected. Until the summer of 1572 Wouter Jacobsz had led an uneventful life as prior of a convent of Augustinian canons at Gouda. Yet after his hometown had surrendered to the Orangist rebels in June 1572, he had fled and found asylum in Amsterdam, the only major town in Holland that remained loyal to Church and King during the rebellion of 1572. During his unsolicited exile he kept a diary, in which practically every day from August 1572 to July 1578, he jotted down the facts he observed, the rumours he heard, as well as his private reflections, increasingly gloomy and pessimistic, about the civil war.

On this particular day Wouter admitted he could not well describe the diversity of the tidings (*nyemaren*) people recounted. The good news was that there had been talk of the Prince of Orange losing five or six thousand men (during the failed relief of Mons in Hainaut, 5–12 September 1572). But was it true? 'These tidings continued among the common people', he wrote, 'yet so far no authentic letter to the Stadholder has confirmed them'. The bad news was that others said that the rebels at Brill, Enkhuizen and Hoorn were fitting out a great fleet of men of war to set upon either the King's ships or the town of Amsterdam. There were also tidings that the Danish Sound had been closed for (rebel) ships from Waterland in North

---

[1] Wouter Jacobsz, *Dagboek van Broeder Wouter Jacobsz (Gualtherus Jacobi Masius) Prior van Stein. Amsterdam 1572–1578 en Montfoort 1578–1579*, ed. I.H. van Eeghen, 2 vols. (Groningen, 1959–60), 17–18.

Holland, and that war had broken out between France and England. In the evening, new grief arose from talk that sixteen hundred rebels were pouring into Enkhuizen from Bremen and Hamburg; people also said that no less than six hundred rebels were being lodged at 's-Gravezande (the site of a monastery related to Wouter's own) and other villages around Delft. 'In sum', Wouter concluded,

> it was said that anxiety had overwhelmed the country, forcing every-body to despair were it not for the exhortation of the Lord, saying: 'and when ye shall hear of wars and rumours of wars, be ye not trou-bled: for such things must needs be; but the end shall not be yet'.[2]

Historians have investigated the role played by pamphlets, plays, and prints in the shaping of public opinion during the Revolt of the Netherlands.[3] Yet it becomes immediately clear, when reading Wouter Jacobsz's diary, that written information – let alone printed infor-mation – played only a limited role in the daily provision of infor-mation for the inhabitants of the Low Countries during the Revolt. This chapter explores the theme of 'rumour' in three big cities, Antwerp, Ghent and Amsterdam, in the western commercial and urbanized 'core-provinces' during the first dozen years of the Revolt. The main sources, partly overlapping in time, are Wouter Jacobsz's diary (Amsterdam 1572–78) and two of the greatest chronicles of the Revolt, those by Godevaert van Haecht (Antwerp 1565–74) and Marcus van Vaernewijck (Ghent 1566–68).[4]

All three texts abound with references to rumour as a key source of information. Early modern chroniclers, like modern professional historians, were highly sensitive to the sources of their information. A small scrap of paper, preserved by chance in the manuscript of Godevaert van Haecht's chronicle in the Antwerp archives, sheds light on how van Haecht gathered and recorded news items:

---

[2] Mark 13, 7; cf. Matthew 24, 6; Wouter Jacobsz, *Dagboek*, 18.

[3] Duke, 'Dissident Propaganda'; C.E. Harline, *Pamphlets, Printing and Political Culture in the Early Dutch Republic* (Dordrecht, 1987); D. Horst, *De Opstand in zwart-wit. Propagandaprenten uit de Nederlandse Opstand 1566–1584* (Zutphen, 2003); P.A.M. Geurts, *De Nederlandse Opstand in pamfletten 1566–1584* (Nijmegen 1956, repr. Utrecht 1978).

[4] Marcus van Vaernewijck, *Van die beroerlicke tijden in die Nederlanden en voornamelijk in Ghendt 1566–1568*, ed. F. Vanderhaeghen, 5 vols. (Ghent, 1872–81); Godevaert van Haecht, *De Kroniek van Godevaert van Haecht over de troebelen van 1565 tot 1574 te Antwerpen en elders*, ed. R. van Roosbroeck, 2 vols. (Antwerp, 1930).

16 tiding 36 ships evaded flood to Holland
16 hear Middelburg magistrates being captured etc.
17 hear Swiss in country 3 regiments
18 rumour all becomes peace[5]

Striking is not only the scrupulousness with which Van Haecht recorded the nature of his sources (tiding, hearing, rumour), but also that these were in all cases *oral* sources. Word of mouth remained, even in the highly literate Low Countries, the most important of the sources of information. Only a small elite had access to the burgeoning trickle of hand-written newsletters (*avvisi, relaciones*), written by professional hack writers, while the first printed newspapers (*courantos*) in the Netherlands only started to appear in the early seventeenth century.[6] Even when accounts of major events, such as the capture or the relief of a town or the conclusion of a peace treaty, were published in pamphlet format, the process of writing, printing and distributing the texts would inevitably take some time, causing the pamphlet to appear days, or sometimes weeks, after the event, long after an oral narrative had spread. A pamphlet about the siege of Haarlem professed it wished to tell the truth about the events, 'otherwise, you would hear it from the mouth of the common people'. Without doubt, this was what already had happened by the time the pamphlet appeared on the market.[7]

Chroniclers of the Revolt like Godevaert van Haecht and Marcus van Vaernewijck composed their works some time after the events they describe had taken place. This implies they had ample time to verify their sources, throwing out such bits of information based on rumour as had proven false, while presenting as rock-solid facts oral information that in due course had turned out to be accurate. They would only discuss 'rumour' itself when the frenzied circulation of stories and gossip became a fact worthy of attention in its own right. Godevaert van Haecht, for example, noted in July 1567 that

---

[5] Van Haecht, *De kroniek*, I, xviii. I have not been able to locate matching entries in the chronicle.

[6] M. Schneider, *De Nederlandse krant. Van 'nieuwstijdinge' tot dagblad* (Amsterdam, 1943), 21–28, 43–49; M. Infelise, *Prima dei giornali. Alle origini della pubblica informazione (secoli XVI e XVII)* (Rome and Bari, 2002); F. de Vivo, 'Paolo Sarpi and the Uses of Information in Seventeenth-Century Venice', *Media History* 11 (2005), 37–51.

[7] Harline, *Pamphlets*, 12.

there was more rumour of war than I [can] write; it was rumoured
that the fugitive princes and lords, like a fog suddenly descending,
would assault these lands. One ought not to write this down before
the event occurs; yet it must be recounted because of the magnitude
of the rumour.[8]

Wouter Jacobsz, by contrast, never had the opportunity to edit his
daily notes. He probably intended to prepare his diary for publication as some sort of chronicle at a later date – there are numerous
instances where he addresses an imaginary 'reader'. Yet the author,
after six years of meticulous diary keeping, for some unknown reason, became separated from his manuscript. His unedited manuscript
therefore allows us a unique glimpse into his thinking and reveals
much about the way he turned the daily stream of information into
journal entries.

Reading Wouter's diary is like being plunged into an oral world.
The text makes it abundantly clear that ordinary people in Amsterdam,
clerical or lay, who wished to be informed about the war had to
rely almost completely on hearsay. To be sure, for Wouter, a cleric
and a diary-keeper to boot, the world of scripture was all-important;
yet pamphlets or other printed material were simply never his sources
of information. It is striking how Wouter, like Godevaert van Haecht,
meticulously accounts for the origins of his material. He distinguishes
between four forms of communication. To begin with, there are
events in or near Amsterdam he has witnessed in person. Such entries
are often prefixed by sentences such as 'we saw . . .' or even 'I saw
with my own eyes . . .'.[9] Only in such instances does Wouter frequently fail to mention any source at all, since it is evident that the
account of these events must be based on his own observation. The
reliability of this type of information is unquestionable. Secondly,
Wouter recorded events related by reliable witnesses, usually people
well known to him. He frequently writes how friends, relatives, and
fellow-clerics came to visit him in Amsterdam and how he never
failed to question them in detail about events in their hometowns.
There was also a constant flow of letters, although correspondence
between Amsterdam and the rebel cities was strictly forbidden. In
general, Wouter tended to regard such news, whether it came orally
or by letter as being reliable when he was acquainted with the mes-

---

[8] Van Haecht, *De kroniek*, I, 228.
[9] Wouter Jacobsz, *Dagboek*, I, 124.

senger. Yet he also often writes how 'letters' are being read, apparently in public, in which certain items of news are being related. Such letters, written by correspondents unknown to him, he treats with suspicion. Finally, Wouter found out about the great majority of events by word of mouth or 'rumour'. Such news items are announced as 'people say that . . .', 'rumour has it that . . .', 'it is rumoured that . . .', or 'there is talk of . . .'. Wouter is extremely cautious about the truthfulness of such rumours.

Rumour is an elusive medium. Like other oral information, it has ceased to exist by the time contemporaries recorded it. Historians can only have access to rumour by way of accounts written by contemporaries, who are often equally wary as to their veracity as present-day historians. Early modern authors were by definition part of a script culture, distrustful towards the oral world of the common people. Cesare Ripa, in his widely-read allegorical design-book *Iconologia* (1593), described the personification of 'Rumour' as a woman with two large wings, her entire body covered with feathers, eyes, mouths, and ears, holding a trumpet in her right hand.[10] Ripa had borrowed the image from Virgil, who in Book IV of the *Aeneis* had described Rumour as 'a horrendous monster',

> . . . Her carcase huge
> Is feathered, and at the root of every plume
> A peering eye abides; and, strange to tell,
> An equal number of vociferous tongues,
> Foul, whispering, lips, and ears, that catch at all.[11]

Yet in spite of their awareness of the unreliability of rumour, contemporaries at the same time were almost completely dependent on hearsay for their supply of news, just as much as the rest of the population. Historians have argued for rumour as an alternative circuit of information for the powerless, a medium through which the common people can collectively create their own discourse as an alternative for government-controlled information. In reality rumours frequently interacted in multiple ways with various forms of script culture, certainly in the highly literate urban Netherlands.[12]

---

[10] Cf. the Dutch translation, Dirck Pietersz Pers, *Iconologia of uytbeeldinghen des verstants* (Amsterdam, 1644), 160.

[11] Translated by T.C. Williams, quoted in G.W. Allport and L. Postman, *The Psychology of Rumor* (New York, 1947), ii; cf. Virgil, *Aeneis*, Bk. IV, lines 173–176.

[12] R. Darnton, 'An Early Information Society: News and the Media in Eighteenth-Century Paris', *American Historical Review* 105 (2000), 1–35.

Rumour is a medium or channel through which we receive news, or 'stories about events'.[13] Yet whilst other media (e.g., letters, pamphlets, broadsheets, prints, or printed edicts and proclamations) present a bounded, final version of events, rumour is flexible, and never finished. It is continually being processed interactively, shaped and adapted by an infinite number of anonymous participants. It never reaches a final form, and it can exist in any number of versions at the same time. Some modern scholars have equated rumours with *false* rumours. Yet a rumour may be either a false or a true account of certain facts.[14] It is precisely the uncertainty about the truth of rumours that made them so difficult for Wouter Jacobsz and his contemporaries to come to terms with.

Verification was therefore essential. The period of time a rumour remained in circulation was generally regarded a good measure for its veracity. 'The tidings continued among the common people', was Wouter Jacobsz's comment, in September 1572, on the rumours about the Prince of Orange's losses. In January 1574 a rumour was spread that the prince had died; but people did not believe it, says Wouter, *although* the rumour ran as many as three or four days.[15] Marcus van Vaernewijck, the assiduous Ghent chronicler, relates a buzz about a murderous assault on the *gueux* leader Hendrik van Brederode in Antwerp in June 1566, with clerics having allegedly incited the two perpetrators. 'Yet this rumour did not continue for long and it must therefore be considered doubtful', was his critical comment.[16] During the iconoclastic riots at Ghent in August 1566 many 'lies' circulated that were nevertheless given credence by some people; yet van Vaernewijck found them fallacious because they 'did not continue but evaporated like smoke'.[17]

Chroniclers and diarists, like modern historians, tried as much as possible to check their information against other, independent sources. Wouter Jacobsz relates how in January 1574 a man and a woman, separately from each other, arrived at Amsterdam; both told the

---

[13] Cf. E.H. Shagan, 'Rumours and Popular Politics in the Reign of Henry VIII', in T. Harris, ed., *The Politics of the Excluded, c. 1500–1850* (Basingstoke, 2001); Darnton, 'An Early Information Society', 1.

[14] J.-N. Kapferer, *Rumors. Uses, Interpretations, and Images*, trs. Bruce Fink (New Brunswick and London, 1990), 2–3.

[15] Wouter Jacobsz, *Dagboek*, I, 17, 358.

[16] Van Vaernewijck, *Van de beroerlicke tijden*, I, 18.

[17] *Ibid.*, I, 180; cf. II, 119.

latest news from Gouda, 'with similar voices, although they did not know it from each other'.[18] That should guarantee their information was trustworthy.

Another way of checking rumours was asking for information from others who might be witnesses or simply better informed. This was not an easy procedure for ordinary townspeople lacking a nation-wide network of correspondents. Van Vaernewijck writes about an incident in Antwerp he regarded a 'downright lie'; he nonetheless relates it so as to expose the vile mentality of those who had spread the rumour. He then goes on to write he has no access to the ser-vices of a trusted friend or relative (*familiaer*) or a secretary who could inform him about current events.[19]

That was a good point. The correspondence of a great aristocrat like William of Orange is full of requests for verification of rumours. In 1556 for example, the prince's father William of Nassau asked him to confirm or deny rumours that he was recruiting troops; while two years later William of Hesse warned the prince not to believe rumours about an assault on his person. In 1564 William of Jülich-Kleve wrote to Orange that a rumour that Elector August of Saxony had suffered a lethal hunting accident was false; and on 10 July 1573 the prince found it necessary to write a letter to the States of Holland about his failed attempt to relieve the town of Haarlem in order to prevent false rumours from circulating.[20]

The best way of verifying a rumour remained to check it against a letter or similar solid, trustworthy *written* piece of evidence. Thus, as we have seen, Wouter Jacobsz complained in September 1572 that 'no authentic letter to the Stadtholder' had confirmed the great losses allegedly incurred by the Prince of Orange. Yet to his great relief three weeks later the sheriff (*schout*) of Amsterdam sent a ser-vant to Wouter with the message that he had received just such a letter. Earlier, the Stadholder had sent a servant to Amsterdam with

---

[18] Wouter Jacobsz, *Dagboek*, I, 363.
[19] Van Vaernewijk, *Van de beroerlicke tijden*, II, 43.
[20] William of Nassau to William of Orange, 26 March 1565. The correspon-dence of William of Orange, no. 11872, 26 March 1556, at www.inghist.nl/Onderzoek/Projecten/WVO; William of Hesse to Orange, 28 March 1558, no. 1053; William of Jülich-Kleve to Orange, 25 August 1564, no. 5587; Orange to August of Saxony, 16 September 1564, no. 126; Orange to William of Hesse, 18 September 1564, no. 1109; William of Hesse to Orange, 5 February 1565, no. 1117; Orange to the States of Holland, 10 July 1573, no. 3383.

another letter written by the duke of Alba, stating that the town of
Mons had been captured; this message was validated (*in waerden
genomen*) by the sounding of bells throughout Amsterdam and a procession carrying the Holy Sacrament through the streets; the religious, including Wouter Jacobsz himself, on this occasion celebrated
Mass and sung a festive *Te Deum*. What better proof could one wish?[21]

If the writers of diaries and chronicles were suspicious about
unverified rumours, so were those in power. Persistent rumours, true
or false, often lead to public unrest, violence, and rebellion. The
authorities sometimes tried to suppress rumours, but apparently with
little result. When news reached the Low Countries in April 1568
that William of Orange's rebel forces were marching along the Rhine,
the Antwerp magistrates forbade spreading it on the penalty of
flogging and the loss of citizen's rights, 'unless one can prove it is
true'.[22] The authorities never succeeded in having a monopoly on
the spreading of news, but they made sure that official announce-
ments had proper markers that separated them from mere rumour.
Official proclamations were always preceded by the sounding of trumpets (*trompetslag*). They were announced from public places such as
the steps of the town hall, or printed and pasted on public places
such as the doors of churches and town halls. The magistrates of
Ghent, for example, in April 1567 had an edict banning the Reformed
religion first publicly read from the town hall and then posted 'at
the usual places', on both occasions with the flourish of trumpets.
The preamble to the edict included a narrative of the events over
the past few months; the form of publication made it clear to the
burghers of Ghent that this was not mere rumour but an official,
and therefore supposedly truthful, rendering of affairs.[23]

One reason for being suspicious towards rumours was that they
were seldom believed to be a neutral medium of information.
Rumours – specifically false rumours – were widely regarded as being
dispersed by one's opponents. The correspondence of Cardinal
Granvelle is full of hints that Granvelle's opponents are 'sowing'
rumours about the introduction of the Inquisition with the aim of

[21] Wouter Jacobsz, *Dagboek*, I, 17, 19, 27.
[22] Van Vaernewijk, *Van de beroerlicke tijden*, IV, 57–58; Van Haecht, *De kroniek*, II,
21, 92.
[23] Van Vaernewijk, *Van de beroerlicke tijden*, II, 156–157.

discrediting Granvelle and inciting the common people to sedition.[24] Chroniclers and diarists, too, were convinced that rumours were commonly biased. 'The rebels are planting rumours so as to deprive the Catholics of courage', thought Wouter Jacobsz in April 1573, 'by dispersing rumours among the common people that they have many soldiers and allies, whilst diminishing the King's army to naught'.[25] Rumours, apparently false, about pro-Spanish sentiments at Leiden, were being 'continually renewed, but with some changes, so as to appear novel'.[26] Godevaert van Haecht thought in November 1566 that the Antwerp clergy hoped to persuade the craft-guilds to re-establish their altars and re-open their chapels, by publicly preaching that the King was on his way to the Netherlands at the head of an army.[27] Similarly the clergy of Ghent, according to van Vaernewijck, 'opened their entire bag of invented fallacious rumours' (*gedichte leugenmaren*): preparations were allegedly being made to receive King Philip with his army; the Queen of England had converted to Catholicism; masses were being secretly celebrated in her palace; she wanted the clergy to observe the seven hours; she had told the leaders of the Dutch Reformed Church in London to become Catholic, or leave. All of this was only intended to frighten the *gueux*, but, van Vaernewijck thought, the common people did not believe such 'priestly lies' (*papenlueghenen*).[28]

If rumour were manipulated, it could easily degenerate into slander. The Catholics at Ghent tried to discredit the Calvinist preacher Hermannus Moded: he had run away with a married woman, kept three wives, and had syphilis. The Protestants reciprocated by tainting the Dominican Jan Vanderhaghen as a carouser and a drunkard, whose belly was his God; he used to have sexual intercourse with beguines and married women 'under the guise of hearing confession' and had sired a child with a married young lady.[29] There was, of course, nothing new with discrediting the Catholic clergy, and especially the mendicants, with allegations of lasciviousness and

---

[24] *Correspondance du Cardinal de Granvelle (1565–1586)*, ed. E. Poullet and C. Piot, 12 vols. (Brussels, 1877–96), I, 51, 72, 86.
[25] Wouter Jacobsz, *Dagboek*, I, 222.
[26] *Ibid.*, I, 1.
[27] Van Haecht, *De kroniek*, I, 123.
[28] Van Vaernewijk, *Van de beroerlicke tijden*, II, 61–62.
[29] *Ibid.*, II, 11; on Vanderhaeghen, cf. *ibid.*, II, 122.

sexual abuses. It was rumoured, when the convent of the Antwerp Franciscans had burned down in February 1567, that the monks used to make good cheer, eating meat at Lent in the company of married women; but van Vaernewijck later found out that the rumour had been planted by the *gueux*, who wished all monasteries torched.[30]

Some rumours were simply too fantastic to be believed. Yet they were in circulation, particularly in frenzied times like the 'Wonder year' 1566. The Spanish, according to one story, had built a secret pit hidden under a handsome room in the state goal at Vilvoorde Castle, full of sharp knives, spears, and spikes; a group of captured *gueux*, as they were led in, tumbled into the upturned knives. Van Vaernewijck does not believe this story because 'tyrannical' Spanish soldiers, 'who might, perhaps, have liked the scenario', were the source of the rumour.[31] Around the same time, in June 1568, when the Prince of Orange's brothers were leading a successful campaign in Groningen, the *gueux* planted 'many strange rumours'. Two or three armies were said to operate in Friesland, with six thousand horses; each horseman was equipped with three or four guns, each an arm's length, fitted with leather straps against recoil, spitting bullets the size of a small tennis ball that would bring down a man and his horse. More wondrous still, the horsemen wore harnesses with a frontal edge so sharp as to deflect incoming fire.[32]

From the miraculous to the supernatural was only a small step. At Antwerp the birth of Siamese twins triggered the rumour that 1566 would be 'a very marvellous year'. At Ghent, it had been prophesied several years earlier that a huge bird would hang itself from the church spire, and that a crippled cobbler would then come to live in the small house next to the church, 'jumping with two crutches'. Both prognostications had been fulfilled, causing people to say that this year would be wondrous.[33] The burghers of Antwerp in July 1567 saw two suns shining in the sky and shadows on the ground of horsemen and soldiers.[34] At Paris in December 1572, people saw a sword hovering in the firmament 'as if God threatened them because of the [Bartholomew] massacre'; and one year later

---

[30] *Ibid.*, II, 126.
[31] *Ibid.*, IV, 1.
[32] *Ibid.*, IV, 128.
[33] Van Haecht, *De kroniek*, I, 48.
[34] *Ibid.*, I, 228.

it was said that massive swarms of storks had been fighting in the
sky over Zurich and that it had rained blood.[35]

One reason why rumour played a key role in the diffusion of
information during the 1572–76 crisis in Holland was that both
parties in the conflict made corresponding with the enemy a pun-
ishable offence.[36] Wouter often complains about the dangers of communication with his friends and relatives in enemy territory. In
September 1572 he writes how the *procuratrix* of the nuns of St. Agnes
in Gouda ran into trouble after he had sent her a letter. Months
later he was to learn from a fellow-exile from Gouda that his letters had compromised the Gouda convents to such an extent that
soldiers had been billeted there. Wouter decided to stop writing to
his native town altogether after hearing the rumour, possibly fallacious, that two girls had been hanged for delivering mail.[37]

Despite these difficulties, however, letters remained an important
source of information. Wouter Jacobsz's diary is full of references to
letters as the source of various tidings. Despite great difficulties he
succeeded in maintaining a network of correspondents who provided
him with news. From Utrecht, Anna Zandersdr, a fugitive nun from
the Gouda St. Agnes Convent, and possibly a relative of Wouter's,
wrote that she had found a messenger going to Gouda, whose services she invited Wouter to share. Wouter immediately wrote two
letters for Gouda and sent them back to Anna, who duly forwarded
them.[38] Not only did he glean information from letters sent directly
to him in person, but also from correspondence sent to other inhabitants of Amsterdam. There are numerous entries where he states
that 'a letter was shown' or 'we heard a letter being read' containing certain pieces of information. Apparently, letters were widely
shared and read aloud in smaller or larger gatherings.[39]

Letters, in their turn, could also be sources of rumour. A buzz
would go round that a letter had been received containing certain
information. The reference to a written piece of evidence apparently

---

[35] *Ibid.*, II, 225, 275.
[36] Wouter Jacobsz, *Dagboek*, I, 114; Orange to the *eerste deurwaarder* (first bailiff)
of the Hof van Holland, 29 November 1572; Correspondence William of Orange,
no. 6893.
[37] Wouter Jacobsz, *Dagboek*, I, 4–5, 116.
[38] *Ibid.*, I, 43, 45.
[39] *Ibid.*, I, 28, 47–48, 66, 112, 125, 226, and many other examples.

served to increase the credibility of the rumour, yet chroniclers and
diarists remained cautious if they had not actually seen the letter in
question. This was the case in March 1575, when the whole country was humming with hopeful rumours about a peace treaty being
concluded at Breda between the rebels and the Brussels government.
'We hear good tidings', Wouter wrote, but he added pessimistically
that 'these seldom offer comfort, for such tidings are rarely true'.[40]
Nevertheless, people spoke of a letter written by one of the rebel
deputies to a priest at Haarlem, asserting all went well. 'Various letters' moreover affirmed that parties had reached agreement on essential points. Better still, a man who had been in jail at Woerden
arrived in Amsterdam; he said he had been released without paying ransom, because 'letters had been received' at Woerden declar-
ing that peace had been concluded. And on 27 March even the
burgomasters of Amsterdam propagated the news that they had
received letters professing that peace had been concluded the previous day.[41] Yet Wouter had reason to be sceptical: soon afterwards
rumours began to spread, this time true, that the Breda peace talks
had floundered.

Letters, then, played an important role, both as sources of rumour
and as means of verification. There was constant interaction between
written and spoken information; chroniclers and diarists consequently
had to be familiar both with the written and the oral world. A given
piece of information could go through various phases, written and
oral; a writer of news tidings in, say, Venice, might pick up a piece
of gossip, write about it in his *avviso*, which he then sent off to
France, the Empire, and the Netherlands; here, people would talk
about the contents of the newsletter, moulding and transforming the
text according to their own needs; the news item might end up in
a printed pamphlet; and a diarist or chronicler might write about
the news, the gossip, or the pamphlet.

It is difficult to point out which rumours had their origins in manuscript news tidings, for most *avvisi* are no longer extant. Yet it is
likely that the numerous instances where van Haecht, van Vaernewijck
or Wouter Jacobsz discuss foreign news, and particularly matters of
grand policy, manuscript news tidings were their sources, or rather

---

[40] *Ibid.*, I, 478.
[41] *Ibid.*, I, 478, 482, 484.

the sources of the rumours they relate. One may surmise, for example, that many news items about the war against the Ottomans in the Mediterranean found their origins in handwritten newsletters. Godevaert van Haecht relates how at the end of October 1565 the news came 'everywhere' that two months previously a great armada from Italy and Spain had chased the Ottomans from Malta; and that 'one heard', in January 1568, about the 'unspeakable mortality' that had afflicted Constantinople by the end of the previous year, daily killing off up to 2,000 people, and preventing the Ottomans from attacking Italy.[42] Several times van Haecht pinpoints the arrival of the mail from Spain as the source of such rumours: in June 1567, for example, the mail (*een poste*) arrived from Spain 'with eight horses', resulting in a rumour that the king was preparing to come to the Netherlands with his son.[43] No one had read these letters but the mere arrival of the mail was sufficient for fresh rumours to arise. Similarly, Wouter Jacobsz reports on Ottoman offensives in the Mediterranean in 1574 and 1575: on 3 November 1574, that they had taken La Goleta, and two weeks later, in a rare mood of optimism, that the loss of that fortress had moved the King of Spain towards peace in the Low Countries.[44] It is difficult to think of other sources for such rumours than written newsletters, but much research remains to be done to bear this out.

The constant ebb and flow of news tidings and rumours, some miraculous, some hopeful, many of them foreboding yet more suffering, did not fail to have a deep psychological impact on the war-weary population. Nowhere is this more visible than in Wouter Jacobsz's diary, who regarded the uncertainty and pain inflicted by the ever-changing and often contradictory tidings as an additional punishment imposed by God. When he heard, on 1 May 1573, another spurious report that Haarlem had surrendered to the Spanish, his comment was: 'we heard it, we wished it, and hoped that it be true; yet we feigned we were unconcerned. We desired very much to question someone about it, but when [a witness] appeared, we eschewed to address him, being afraid to hear the contrary'.[45] And at the occasion of another canard stating that Gouda and Leiden were on the

---

[42] Van Haecht, *De kroniek*, I, 13; II, 6.
[43] *Ibid.*, I, 225.
[44] Wouter Jacobsz, *Dagboek*, 453, 456.
[45] *Ibid.*, I, 244.

brink of reverting to the king's obedience, he felt compelled to give an account of 'the reason I have written all this without however having certainty':

> Thus never a day passed without something special being related as news, even if it often happened that we heard messages contrary to each another. And I have always written them down exactly as we received them so as to move the reader to compassion with all such diverse anxiety as we suffered through this. Because it has often happened that we, being somewhat gladdened by good tidings, received a message that grieved us to death. Nonetheless, we always hoped that the good news we heard – even if it was often untrue – would one day become real.[46]

We have so far discussed rumour as a medium, a channel through which news – true stories, false stories, dubious stories – was being transmitted. Yet rumours, once a sufficient number of people gave them credence and participated in their reproduction, adjustment, and diffusion, could became a solid historical fact, a constituent part of the public opinion they helped to shape; and a powerful agent that mobilized the inhabitants of the Low Countries and their rulers into action. The historian Georges Lefebvre is the author of a classic account of the mass panic that gripped the French countryside in 1789, when the rumour was spread that vagrants and beggars, bribed by reactionary noblemen, were about to set fire to the peasants' farmhouses.[47] This *grande peur* caused a wave of peasant rebellions aimed against noble manor houses and their inhabitants; while rural unrest, in its turn, persuaded the newly constituted National Assembly in Versailles to abolish all 'feudal' rights and thereby effectively put an end to the ancien régime in France. During the outbreak of the Revolt of the Netherlands, too, mere rumour at several occasions galvanized the people into action.

The persistent and ever-mounting stream of rumours about the imminent introduction of the 'Spanish inquisition' into the Netherlands during the early and mid-1560s brought about a frenzied atmosphere. It was this fear that prompted the confederate nobles to present their petition to Margaret of Parma in April 1566, which set in motion the chain of events that triggered the Revolt: moderation

---

[46] *Ibid.*, I, 138.
[47] G. Lefebvre, *La Grande Peur de 1789* (Paris, 1932).

of the *placards*, Calvinist open-air preaching, iconoclastic riots, repression, a wave of Protestant exiles, and military conflict.

Historians have persuasively argued that neither the king, nor his Brussels government, ever considered introducing the 'Spanish' inquisition into the Netherlands, and that the whole affair was therefore a 'myth', part of what later became known as the 'Black Legend'.[48] Nor was there any need to import foreign institutions: the apparatus of repression in the Low Countries was, according to Philip, *'plus impitoyable'* than the Spanish one.[49] Yet the point was that the population widely believed that the introduction of the 'Spanish' inquisition was imminent, while the government failed to persuade them this was not the case. Rumours started in 1559, triggered by the planned institution of fourteen new bishoprics, which were expected to be more efficient in coping with the problem of heresy. By May 1562 rumours had been circulating for over a year, well before pamphlets and handbills started to play a role in the forming of public opinion.[50] The fall of Granvelle in 1564 gave rise to hope that the placards would be moderated; yet Philip's letters from the Segovia Woods, widely known by November 1565, cranked the rumour engine back to life. Godevaert van Haecht aptly summarizes the situation: by the end of 1565 the country was full of 'ugly rumours and troubles' about the introduction of the Spanish inquisition; special inquisitors were to be forced upon the cities and scrutinize the religious faith of the hapless citizens; an anonymous denunciation would suffice to send a person to the stake, without due process of law.[51] It was not the introduction of any Spanish institutions that upset the common people, but the subversion of legal procedures that traditionally guaranteed the burghers of the Low Countries' towns a certain measure of protection under the law. The term 'Spanish inquisition' merely served as convenient shorthand for the subversion of legal prerogatives embedded in the cherished 'privileges' of the Low Countries.

By the end of March 1566, Antwerp was full of rumours about the imminent introduction of the Spanish inquisition. The people

---

[48] W. Thomas, 'De mythe van de Spaanse inquisitie in de Nederlanden van de zestiende eeuw', *BMGN* 105 (1990), 325–353.
[49] *Ibid.*, 336.
[50] *Ibid.*, 341.
[51] Van Haecht, *De kroniek*, I, 17, cf. Duke, *Reformation and Revolt*, 170.

said the king wrote 'daily' that the inquisition ought to be introduced into the towns of the Netherlands. Ships with soldiers were
said to be ploughing their way from Spain to the Low Countries,
but thanks to the grace of God, all the soldiers had drowned. As a
result of such rumours, all Spaniards became suspect. Vagrant jour-
neymen from the border area of Spain and Gascony, in search of
a job, were expelled from Antwerp because people feared they were
soldiers. People said that a Spaniard, a resident of Antwerp for twenty
years, had been an inquisitor in Spain and was to resume his old
trade here. Another Spaniard had built a large house in Brussels
'so as to be an inquisitor', but fearing the confederate nobles, had
fled back to Spain. The activities of Duke Erich of Brunswick, who
was in the Empire levying troops for the government, were regarded
with suspicion: there was a rumour that he was prepared to launch
an attack on Antwerp and massacre all those who opposed the
inquisition.[52]

By the end of July talk about the Spanish inquisition abated, partly
because William of Orange proclaimed at Antwerp that the inquisition and heresy placards had been abolished forever, but also
because soon afterwards the iconoclastic riots held everyone's attention.[53] Historians have charted how image breaking moved from one
area to another, starting in Southwest Flanders and ending in the
remote town of Groningen.[54] In its initial phases, roving bands of
iconoclasts, trekking from one town to another, provided the mechanism for its propagation. At Ghent, iconoclasm began with grain
riots, when many people, 'in particular insolent women', spread the
rumour that a grain merchant was hoarding grain so as to raise
prices. Often the news of iconoclasm in one town prompted the
destruction of the images in the next one. At 's-Hertogenbosch, on
22 August, the image breaking was set off by the news that at
Antwerp all the churches and chapels had been demolished two days
before.[55] The next day, the rumour reached Amsterdam, where merchants showed fragments of marble and alabaster from altars and

---

[52] Van Haecht, *De kroniek*, I, 26–30.
[53] *Ibid.*, I, 105.
[54] J. Scheerder, *De beeldenstorm* (Bussum, 1974).
[55] *Kroniek eener kloosterzuster van het voormalig Bosscher klooster 'Mariënburg' over de troebelen te 's-Hertogenbosch e.e. in de jaaren 1566–1575*, ed. H. van Alfen ('s-Hertogenbosch, 1931), 2.

images smashed at Antwerp, thus providing instant verification; the result was another round of iconoclasm.[56]

Alastair Duke has described how the iconoclasm in the county of Holland took place amidst a series of alarming rumours: the Spanish inquisition was on the verge of being introduced, troops were being raised in the Empire, the Catholic clergy was going to be massacred, and the Protestants wiped out. In many Holland towns it was said that the Grey Friars had compiled a 'certain alleged blood-book' with the names of Protestants and lukewarm Catholics, either with a view to confiscating their property, or worse.[57]

Such chilling rumours focused the attention of the iconoclasts on the convents of the mendicants, who were widely believed to be actively involved in the persecution of Protestants.[58] Wild stories continued to circulate after their convents had been gutted. At Antwerp, it was said that the iconoclasts had found half a dozen Minorites locked up in deep windowless pits, where they had spent the last five or ten years, wallowing in their own excrement, 'because they had taught the Gospel'.[59] The people of Ghent, before the onset of the iconoclasm, used to shoot guns at the Dominican House; they tarnished its inhabitants as 'inquisitors, tyrants and persecutors, who like cannibals relished at eating roasted human flesh', an unmistakable reference to their role in bringing Protestants to the stake.[60] 'Master Hans', the public hangman, said he had often been called to the Dominicans' convent to chop off the heads of as many as seven or eight friars; three or four torture racks had been discovered at their convent, and one friar had been found incarcerated in an oubliette. More astounding stories were told 'by the common folk and women' after the iconoclasts had done their work:

> they had found small chests under the altars containing scraps of parchment with strange, illegible texts, bones and white powder, granulated like raisins, and other marvellous things. They believed that this referred

---

[56] Laurens Jacobsz Reael, 'Uittreksel uit de Amsterdamsche gedenkschriften van Laurens Jacobsz. Reael, 1542–1567', ed. J.C. Breen, *BMHG* 17 (1896), 23.

[57] Duke, *Reformation and Revolt*, 131.

[58] Reael, 'Uittreksel', 36; Van Haecht, *De kroniek*, I, 47.

[59] Van Haecht, *De kroniek*, I, 101; cf. Van Vaernewijk, *Van de beroerlicke tijden*, I, 181: a monk had allegedly been found at the Franciscan monastery who had been locked up for thirty-six years; Van Vaernewijck considers this 'a downright lie, although many people said they had seen him'.

[60] Van Vaernewijk, *Van de beroerlicke tijden*, I, 88–89.

to witchcraft and that this was why the priests made so many signs of the cross above the altar.[61]

And as if this were not enough, people said a rat-trap had been unearthed with consecrated wafers as bait.[62]

The writers of diaries and chronicles of the Revolt would have been familiar with the appraisal of Dame Rumour in Virgil's *Aeneis*, 'who begins small, but in movement (. . .) grows mighty'. They would have shared the poet's suspicion of news tidings orally transmitted and they would have much preferred to base their accounts on solid written sources. Yet their predicament was that they were almost entirely dependent on word of mouth. They therefore assiduously dedicated themselves to the task of processing the daily stream of rumours into solid, trustworthy history. They did so by seeking verification, gauging how long a rumour continued to circulate, checking it against other sources, oral and written, looking for biases by deconstructing the interests of those who had planted the rumour, dismissing some stories because they were simply too fantastic, whilst preserving others; because they recognized that rumours, however deceptive they might be, mobilized people to action, and were, for that reason, part and parcel of the history of the Revolt.

---

[61] *Ibid.*, I, 177–178.
[62] *Ibid.*, I, 180.

CHAPTER FIVE

PUBLIC OPINION AND THE PERSECUTION OF HERETICS IN THE NETHERLANDS, 1550-59[1]

Juliaan Woltjer

When a few hundred nobles marched into the palace of Margaret of Parma in April 1566, and presented her with a petition to end the persecution of heretics, they knew they could count on widespread sympathy from the population of the Netherlands – amongst the burghers and officials, Catholics and Protestants, there was no support for the royal policy. Yet what was a public secret on the streets of the Netherlands somehow came as an unpleasant and unexpected surprise to the king. Of course, Philip knew that there was opposition to his policies. Although by this date he had been in Madrid for several years, in the 1550s he had spent time in the Netherlands, and he had had plenty of opportunity to get to know the situation on the ground. Even so, the king was distinctly overoptimistic about the extent to which 'good Catholics' were prepared to support his policies. This article will suggest that the gap between the strict laws against heresy and their actual implementation on the ground was accompanied by a conspiracy of silence among Philip's officials, that left the king very much under-informed about the real state of public opinion around this issue in the Netherlands.

Charles V and Philip II considered it their sacred duty to defend the old traditions and the old Church against all innovations, and all those whom they regarded as heretics. Precisely because they thought in terms of heresy, they found it difficult to compromise. When legislation did not work, their remedy was to make the 'placards' even harsher. The legislation against heresy culminated in the

---

[1] This article is a reworked version of a chapter of my forthcoming book, *De escalatie van een conflict. Over de voorgeschiedenis en de eerste stadia van de Nederlandse Opstand*, that will be published by Balans in Amsterdam. I am grateful for Balans's gracious permission to publish this English version ahead of the book.

notorious placard of 1550, that was confirmed by Philip II immediately after he succeeded his father. Their disapproval of heresy was
so intense that they decreed the death penalty even for those heretics
who were prepared to abjure their convictions, so as to prevent any
chance of a 'relapse' of the convict or the 'contamination' of others.

   The five case studies presented in this chapter will demonstrate
how far removed this ideology was from actual practice. It concerns
a number of exceptional instances, such as the actions of the Inquisitor
Titelmans; the open air sermons or *prêches* outside Antwerp in 1558;
two major conflicts, one in Amsterdam, the other in Friesland, and
finally a remarkable appointment in Groningen, where such conflicts
were avoided. In all five cases, persecution and government stric-
tures met with resistance from relevant officials. The cases do not
reflect the overall situation, in some instances persecution still produced many victims. Yet these extraordinary cases illustrate well how
very small the social support base for persecution really was.

Titelmans and the Council of Flanders

Pieter Titelmans had been inquisitor of Flanders since 1545. He was
convinced that heresy was spreading fast, and that it should be met
with force. Given the urgency of the situation, the inquisitor thought
he should not be hindered by civic legislation or urban privileges;
thus he did not consider himself bound to the rule that a citizen
could only be arrested with the assistance of two *schepenen*, local
judges. When the Catholic queen, Mary Tudor, succeeded to the
throne in England in 1553–54, and many Protestant refugees returned
to the Netherlands, there was every reason to be on full alert. Even
so, in some respects Titelmans was more moderate than Charles V
and Philip II. He did not follow imperial edicts but abided by canon
law, so that a heretic who was prepared to abjure could expect, at
worst, life imprisonment. The Council of Flanders agreed with him
in this matter; soon after the placard of 1550 this body had successfully requested permission to modify the penalties for penitent
heretics, and it was to make frequent use of this option.[2] Nevertheless,
the relationship between the Council of Flanders and the inquisitor

---

[2] J. Decavele, *De dageraad van de Reformatie in Vlaanderen (1520–1565)*, 2 vols.
(Brussels, 1975), I, 34.

was fraught with difficulties.[3] The Council was not impressed with the proactive approach of the inquisitor, that met with major resentment among the population so that when Titelmans made arrests, he often felt threatened by the amassing crowds. Yet while he thought he should be able to count on the assistance of the councillors of Flanders, of bailiffs and lower ranking judicial officials, when making arrests and conducting trials, he refused to give the secular judges access to his information. In response, the Council refused any direct cooperation by any of its members (although their subordinates, like bailiffs, were instructed to assist him). Only Titelmans's actions against the Anabaptists got more support from secular judges.

Titelmans's jurisdiction extended to Walloon Flanders – the *kasselrijen* of Lille, Douai and Orchies – and the Tournaisis. Initially, he spent much time in Tournai and frequently visited Lille; later he focused especially on Flanders. Tournai witnessed five executions in 1552–54, and no more until the Calvinist provocations in 1561. In that year *chanteries*, psalm-singing demonstrations of Reformed strength, shook the town; it became painfully evident that, for all Titelmans's pressure, the Calvinist movement in the city had prospered. In Lille and its surrounding areas, Guy de Bray was active as leader of the Calvinist community. Through a tip-off Titelmans received intelligence of these conventicles, and on 6 March 1555 organized a raid; De Bray escaped, but the ensuing prosecutions resulted in seven death sentences, four of which were against members of the same family. This was the nadir of Lille's 'church under the cross'; even though De Bray was returned for a visit in 1559, the inquisitor had achieved a limited success. Yet one gets the impression that even if Titelmans made many victims and sometimes caused a panic – many fled to Antwerp or elsewhere – he received so little cooperation that he could not really stop the tide of heresy.

Prêches *outside Antwerp in 1558*

The gap between the theory and practice of persecution can also be illustrated at Antwerp through some peculiar incidents in 1558 which

---

[3] Decavele, *Dageraad*, 16–26, and cf. also 103 and 342; J. van der Wiele, 'De inquisitierechtbank van Pieter Titelmans in de zestiende eeuw in Vlaanderen', *BMGN* 97 (1982), 19–63.

shed light on the attitude of the various authorities in the city.
Antwerp was an exceptional place. As the biggest city in the Low
Countries, where people could live in relative anonymity, it attracted
many Anabaptists and Calvinists. Apart from the Walloons, there
was also a Flemish speaking group, which Gaspar van der Heyden
from 1555 moulded into a Calvinist church gathering.

Van der Heyden preferred to draw his lines clear and sharp; members of the community were no longer to be involved with 'Roman
abominations and superstitions', not even for the purpose of baptism, marriages and funerals.[4] That was a serious issue, since marriages were considered invalid without an ecclesiastical ceremony, so
that any children born from such a relationship were illegitimate.
Burying the dead without involving the church was impossible, since
clandestine burials led to suspicions of homicide. No wonder, then,
that not everyone accepted Van der Heyden's strict approach, and
soon he also acquired a colleague who saw things differently. Adriaan
van Haemstede, a former priest and a graduate from Louvain,
preached not only for Van der Heyden's community but also taught
elsewhere, in the circles of 'protestantizing' Catholics – sometimes
without telling the consistory that he was doing so. This caused
resentment because the consistory believed that persecution necessi-
tated 'a separation between the children of God and those of the
World, [a separation] which rests mostly in the confessing of faith
and in placing oneself under the discipline of Christ'.[5] But there were
other reasons for the controversy, too; these Catholics were of higher
standing than the humble community that Van der Heyden had
gathered together. Feelings ran so high that it was necessary to consult the Emden consistory for advice in the matter.[6]

Unlike Van der Heyden, Van Haemstede was prepared to appeal
to the authorities. Perhaps he was strengthened in this conviction
when an ordinance of 1 March 1558 banned 'clandestine and secret
gatherings and conventicles', because these would lead to sedition
and conspiracies.[7] Apparently, he hoped that public sermons would

---

[4] Van der Heyden to the Emden consistory in E. Meiners, *Oostvrieslandts kerke-
lycke geschiedenisse*, 2 vols. (Groningen, 1738–39), I, 365–370.
[5] *Brieven uit onderscheiden kerkelijke archieven*, ed. H.Q. Janssen and J.J. van Toorenbergen,
Werken der Marnix-Vereeniging, 3rd series, 2 (Utrecht, 1878), 72; A.J. Jelsma,
Adriaen van Haemstede en zijn martelarenboek (The Hague, 1970), 22–28.
[6] *Brieven*, ed. Janssen and Van Toorenbergen, 50–88.
[7] *Antwerpsch archievenblad* 2 (1865), 343.

be allowed instead; when he was proved wrong, and some in his audience were imprisoned, tortured and executed, their relatives argued that it was not their kinsmen who should be called to account by the court but Van Haemstede himself, who had led their kin astray with his reassurances.[8] Van Haemstede then turned to one of the burgomasters, presumably *binnenburgemeester* Nicolaas Rockox, and asked him to put an end to the persecutions. In the lengthy discussion that ensued, the burgomaster asked him: 'if your faith is truly orthodox and apostolic, why then are you gathering in secret, and why don't you preach openly in the churches?' When Van Haemstede gave the obvious reply that he and his followers did not have a church at their disposal, the burgomaster had to admit that the magistrates did not have the authority to grant them the use of a church.

The reaction of the burgomaster is astonishing. Did he not know that the emperor's legislation forced all modernizers to operate underground? Did the placard of 1550 not play any role in his thinking? Apparently he did not consider that for some decades Europeans had been deeply divided over the question which opinions were orthodox and apostolic, and which ones were not. Had he never considered ecclesiastical issues before? It certainly looks like it. Even so, at the time, it seems that the burgomaster's response made sense. The Protestants grew in courage; according to the dean and chapter of Antwerp, they were even considering petitioning Philip II, when the latter visited Antwerp in late May, to request permission to preach publicly. Upon reflection, they decided not to do so, but soon afterwards Van Haemstede began to preach publicly outside the city.[9] On Corpus Christi, 9 June 1558, he even provocatively did so within the city, positioning himself on the Meir bridge and preaching while the Corpus Christi procession passed. As far as we know, this episode did not have any consequences for him.

Things went quite differently with the clandestine gatherings. On 18 June, just ten days after the sermon on the Meir bridge, there

---

[8] W.G. Goeters, 'Documenten van Adriaan van Haemstede', *NAK*, new series 5 (1908), 1–67, there 12–13 and 61–62; G. Marnef, 'Publiek versus geheim. Adriaan van Haemstede en zijn streven naar een publieke kerk in Antwerpen in 1558', in J. de Zutter, L. Charles and A. Capiteyn, eds., *Qui valet ingenio. Liber amicorum aangeboden aan Dr. Johan Decavele bij gelegenheid van zijn 25-jarig ambtsjubileum als stadsarchivaris van Gent* (Ghent, 1996), 373–383. These victims cannot be retraced in the *Antwerpsch archievenblad* but it is very unlikely that Van Haemstede would have made them up.

[9] Marnef, 'Publiek versus geheim', 374.

was a raid on the house in which Van der Heyden had just distributed the Lord's Supper. Van der Heyden himself escaped, but his host was arrested, and since a list with names of elders and deacons fell into the hand of the sheriff, all these had to take flight. Van der Heyden, too, went into exile; soon afterwards he was in Frankfurt. In these circumstances, the members of Van der Heyden's community questioned whether holding conventicles was tenable; they consulted Dathenus in Frankfurt, who, in a letter of 20 September 1558, asked for Calvin's advice.[10] A reply is not extant; it may have been overtaken by events.

Van Haemstede, in the meantime, continued to preach openly in the woods and the fields outside Antwerp. It beggars belief that there should have been public *prêches* outside the city, while Philip II was still in the country. Yet, even though not all details are clear, Protestant and Catholic sources complement each other so well on the main issues that the matter is beyond doubt. He also preached in the city, in town houses and at (wedding?) banquets; the Protestant community first rented a house, but soon moved to larger premises. At the city mill, the preacher celebrated the Lord's Supper in the presence of around 200 attendants, some of them Walloons. The Anabaptists, too, were publicly baptizing a number of adults.[11]

While the magistrates turned a blind eye, monks and priests were protesting vigorously, both from the pulpit and at Philip II's court, and by December, there were fears in Antwerp that the government in Brussels would send commissioners to put an end to the *prêches*. Many curious people now sought to seize their last opportunity to hear a Calvinist sermon; the sermons on 8 and 11 December attracted audiences that were larger than ever and on Sunday 12 December there were two thousand or, according to some, even three to four thousand, listeners. At last, the city government intervened; on 13 December it banned the sermons and prohibited attendance at them, and the civic militia companies were called upon to enforce the ban and guard the gates, so as to prevent Van Haemstede from preaching outside the city. When he persisted, the city government set a price of no less than three hundred *carolusguldens* on his head, and

---

[10] Dathenus to Calvin, Johannes Calvinus, *Johannes Calvini Opera quae supersunt omnia*, ed. G. Baum, E. Cunitz and E. Reuss, 59 vols. (Braunschweig and Berlin, 1863–1900), XVII, 345–346.

[11] 'Vertoog van de Antwerpse clerus', in Marnef, 'Publiek versus geheim', 373–380.

that of two Anabaptist leaders, and of fifty guilders on those of the elders and deacons.[12]

In the meantime, the Antwerp pensionary Jan Gillis had departed for Brussels to try and prevent the sending of commissioners. His efforts were in vain; Governor Emmanuel-Philibert of Savoy decided on 16 December to send the prosecutor general and a member of the Council of Brabant to Antwerp. The Antwerp clergy, especially the Dean and the chapter, had high hopes of the commissioner and compiled a report to inform them of the Antwerp situation.[13]

Once the governor received the commissioner's report he ordered the sheriff to proceed with the necessary arrests and executions; as early as 12 January Anton Verdickt, an elder of the Antwerp community, was burned at the stake in Brussels, a week later two executions followed in Antwerp – another two were conducted some time later.[14] Seven Antwerp Calvinists in total were executed in 1558–59; on 20 December 1558, 36 people who had already fled were summoned. Such penalties were, apparently, the minimum required to sustain some credibility with the authorities in Brussels.

The freedom that Van Haemstede and his followers had enjoyed for six months in 1558 was a one-off. Still, the episode clearly demonstrates how little support there was amongst Antwerp magistrates for the official religious policies of their Habsburg overlords. This did not mean they were against persecution per se, as is shown by the raid on Van der Heyden's conventicles and also by the treatment meted out to the Anabaptists, 22 of whom were executed in 1558 and another 17 of whom died the following year. In the years 1560–65, again, 34 Anabaptists died on the scaffold, but only another six Calvinists.[15] Particularly notable is the high number of aliens among the persecuted. Were those who had been known in the city since childhood more easily forgiven their dissenting ideas? Was it harder to convict citizens who had the protection of local urban privileges? It is worth noting, too, how often the trials were postponed, 'because of the small number of *schepenen* present'.

---

[12] *Antwerpsch archievenblad* 2 (1865), 353–355.
[13] Marnef, 'Publiek versus geheim', 378–380. The report was compiled after 11 December and can therefore not be the reason for the intervention from Brussels.
[14] Marnef, 'Publiek versus geheim', 375–376.
[15] G. Marnef, *Antwerpen in de tijd van de Reformatie. Ondergronds protestantisme in een handelsmetropool, 1550–1577* (Amsterdam and Antwerp, 1996), 120.

Amsterdam

Equally revealing is a series of court cases in 1550s Amsterdam. The
tensions that had gripped the city during the 1530s, when Anabaptist
agitation had almost led to a political coup, took a long while to
subside. Willem Bardes, sheriff since 1542, initially did not have any
qualms about the persecutions, which hit both the militant Batenburgers
and the pacifist Mennonite Anabaptists.[16] When Anabaptists who had
fled Antwerp were interrogated in 1549, they were asked repeatedly
whether they had any plans to conquer villages or cities. Yet their
denials, and refusal to condone such actions, may have sown the
first seeds of doubt about persecution among the judiciary.[17] In May
1552, the authorities received a tip-off about Anabaptist gatherings
in the home of Volckje Willemsdr. The nightwatch got itself a good
catch; eleven death sentences were the result, even if Volckje herself, who kept a lodging house, was cleared. During the interrogations many names were mentioned of heretics in Friesland, Hoorn,
Leiden and Antwerp; death sentences followed everywhere. Behind
the Amsterdam sentences, however, it was now no longer the sheriff
but burgomaster Hendrik Dirksz who was the driving force.[18] Between
1553 until the arrival of the duke of Alba, in 1567, no more heretics
were condemned to death in Amsterdam, and it is clear that after
his experiences in 1549 and 1552, Bardes no longer exerted himself
to obtain death sentences for heresy, a situation that was to result
in growing tensions between burgomaster Hendrik Dirksz and the
sheriff.

Nevertheless, it was not the burgomaster but the parish priest of
the Oude Kerk who confronted Bardes first. Floris Egbertsz, who
had a baccalaureate in theology from the University of Louvain, had
been rector of the Oude Kerk since 1550. In his previous post, in
Edam, he had been involved in various heresy trials; these had
promptly ceased when the rector left Edam for Amsterdam. Sir Floris

---

[16] J.J. Woltjer, 'Het conflict tussen Willem Bardes en Hendrick Dirckszoon', *BMGN*
86 (1971), 178–199. See, on Bardes's position, J.D. Tracy, 'Habsburg Grain Policy
and Amsterdam Politics. The Career of Sheriff Willem Dirkszoon Bardes, 1542–1566',
SCJ 14 (1983), 293–319.

[17] *Documenta Anabaptistica Neerlandica*, vol. II, *Amsterdam (1526–1578)*, ed. A.F. Mellink
(Leiden, 1980), 94, 110, 116, 117, 132, 137. Cf. G. Grosheide, *Bijdrage tot de geschiedenis der Anabaptisten in Amsterdam* (Hilversum, 1938), 231–232.

[18] Woltjer, 'Het conflict', 186–189.

was very suspicious of Willem Bardes; he was minded to believe rumours that Bardes had been involved with Anabaptists in the 1530s, and was seeking evidence to prove it. Thus, he sought the help of one of his parishioners, Sophie Harmansdr. from Zwolle, who because of her bilious appearance was known as Yellow Fye. She was a pitiable creature, who had difficulty in supporting herself, and regularly received alms from Sir Floris. Her father, Harman van Zwol, had been executed on 28 July 1535 as an Anabaptist, so she was presumed to know quite a bit about Anabaptist circles; it was her tip-off that had triggered the trials of 1552. It seems that Floris now probed her for tales about the sheriff, and got exactly what he wanted. He heard that the sheriff and his wife had received adult baptism before the Anabaptist turmoil of 1535. The rector duly contacted head inquisitor Ruard Tapper, and around Christmas 1553, the public prosecutor of the Court of Holland came to Amsterdam to investigate, followed by a member of the Privy Council. Yet extensive interrogations did not produce a clear outcome, and eventually created doubts about the accusation. In May 1556 it was not Bardes, but Yellow Fye and Volckje, the landlady of the victims of 1552, who were arrested and taken to The Hague, and in March 1558, they were joined by the rector and burgomaster Hendrik Dirksz, who were both suspected of interfering with the witnesses, and of putting pressure on Volckje and especially on Fye.

It became a complex and lengthy trial, in which the Privy Council and the Great Council became involved. The Court of Holland considered Fye, Volckje and a third witness, Cornelis Maartensz, to be 'very lascivious and sordid persons' and refused to base a judgment on their testimonies while there was no corroborating evidence. Volckje died after eighteen months of imprisonment; Fye was kept in custody for another three years, until sentence was finally passed on her on 3 March 1562. On the scaffold her tongue, with which she had borne false witness, was cut out, after which she was burned; as often befell those who bore false witness, she was herself given the penalty that was normally reserved for the crimes of which she had accused others. The Court did not get permission to torture the rector, so that he got off lightly, even though he had to declare that he had accused Fye, the sheriff and his wife 'erroneously, indiscreetly and being poorly informed'. He was exiled from Amsterdam, was banned from any further involvement with the inquisition, and had to pay the costs of his own imprisonment. The burgomaster was

released, and immediately began a law suit against Bardes. When
the troubles of 1566 began, the matter was still unresolved, and he
had, in the meantime, been reappointed as burgomaster in 1563.
Even so, in Amsterdam, the accused had clearly succeeded in turning the table on the accusers. The fate of Sir Floris set an ominous
example for other inquisitors.

Friesland

According to the reports of Hippolytus Persijn, president of the Court
in Leeuwarden since 1548, the ecclesiastical situation in Friesland
was alarming. Ignorance and abuses were rife among the clergy, and
there were many Anabaptists. In 1553 it was therefore agreed to
send Herman Letmatius, dean of the chapter of St. Marie in Utrecht,
and Franciscus Sonnius to Friesland, Overijssel, Groningen, and 'its
surrounding areas' so that they might exercise the role of inquisitor
and, above all, root out all Anabaptism.[19] Inquisitor Sonnius had
been very concerned about the placard of 1550 and refused to implement this to the letter;[20] soon after their arrival in Leeuwarden on
9 April 1554 the two clerics decided that there were simply too
many Anabaptists for them to be able to follow their instructions.
In defiance of both the letter and spirit of the placard, they proposed an amnesty for all those who were prepared to abjure within
fifty days. To bind such people more closely to the church they had
to comply with a series of other requirements, like weekly attendance
at mass under the eyes of the parish priest. About ninety people
took up the offer, but most of these had broken with the Anabaptists
previously and simply took advantage of this opportunity to reconcile themselves with the church; other Anabaptists did not come forward. The inquisitors now changed strategy, and organized a hunt
for Anabaptists. A mere eleven were caught, among whom were two
people who were mentally ill. Most Anabaptists had gone into hid-
ing or into exile, but there were three executions. On 15 October

---

[19] A.H.L. Hensen, 'Eene inquisitiereis door Friesland', *Archief voor de Geschiedenis van het Aartsbisdom Utrecht* 24 (1897), 215–245.
[20] P.E. Valvekens, *De inquisitie in de Nederlanden der zestiende eeuw* (Brussels, 1949), 270–271.

1554 the inquisitors departed for the south, without even having bothered visiting Groningen or Overijssel.

Even after the departure of Sonnius and Letmatius, the Frisian Court remained divided. The president, Persijn, favoured rigorous persecution but most of the councillors did not want to punish the Anabaptists at all, so long as they were not misbehaving and were simply misled in matters of faith.[21] Rather than deal with the dissenters, they wanted to address the abuses in the church, and so take the wind out of the sails of the heretics. Some even announced they would rather resign their posts than be party to death sentences for the Anabaptists; one of the councillors, Aggaeus van Albada, even acted on this threat, and in 1559 became *syndicus* of Groningen's Ommelanden instead.[22] Others swore an oath to enforce the strict placards, but still failed to implement them. It was only strong pressure from Brussels that induced them to condemn another three Walloon Anabaptists to death; Jacques D'Auchy, born near Arras, and two others who had fled Antwerp for Harlingen and who had, according to the Margrave of Antwerp, kept a French school there. They were arrested on orders from Brussels[23] in October 1557 but it took until 14 March 1559 before they received the death sentence.[24]

Sonnius

When he accepted the commission to go to Friesland, Sonnius had written to Viglius van Aytta, the president of the Council of State and the Privy Council, that the inquisition alone could not solve the problems, but that he hoped that the removal of abuses in the church and strict controls on the doctrinal and moral standards of the clergy would help to undermine the appeal of the heretics. After his Frisian experiences, he was more convinced than ever that persecuting simple folk was not the answer to dissent. For some time, he had been

---

[21] J.J. Woltjer, *Friesland in hervormingstijd* (Leiden, 1962), 116.
[22] F. Postma, *Viglius. De jaren met Granvelle 1549–1564* (Zutphen, 2000), 185.
[23] Margrave to Viglius, 4 October 1557, ARAB, Aud. 235 f. 5.
[24] *Documenta Anabaptistica Neerlandica*, vol. VII: *Friesland (1551–1601) and Groningen (1538–1601)*, ed. A.F. Mellink and S. Zijlstra (Leiden, 1995), nr. 67. Compare also his confession, there nr. 65.

pondering a plan to improve the administration of the church, by
dividing the very large dioceses into more manageable units, by
extending the number of bishops and by ensuring that the new
appointees were of the highest standard; both the bishops and most
of the canons of the new Cathedral chapters should hold doctorates
or licienciates in theology or canon law. He had drafted a first version of the scheme while attending the second session of the Council
of Trent, from May 1551 to April 1552. On 9 November 1553,
before his departure for Friesland, he had urged Viglius to receive
him, if only just for an hour, for a confidential conversation.[25]
Confidentiality was vital because the scheme would affect many vested
interests; those of the current bishops in the Netherlands, of the
German and French prelates whose jurisdiction extended within the
Netherlands, and of the noble families who would lose the opportunity to gain lucrative posts for their younger sons, who rarely took
degrees. If details of the plan leaked out prematurely, it was certain
to be attacked.

Sonnius' plan attracted the support of Viglius and of the chief
inquisitor Tapper, yet while the relationship between Charles V and
the pope was poor, there was no opportunity to see it realized until,
in March 1558, Sonnius at last went to Rome to lobby for the
scheme. Because of the infirmity of the elderly pontiff, there were
many delays but after the Peace of Cateau-Cambrésis the matter
could at last be settled; in May 1559 Sonnius received the papal
bull. Although all appointments needed to be approved by Rome,
Philip II was granted the right to appoint all bishops except those
of Mechelen and Antwerp, which the pope reserved for himself, just
as he also retained his traditional right to appoint the bishop of
Cambrai. Much still had to be decided, the diocesan boundaries
were still to be settled, as had the remuneration for the bishops.
This, again, took much time since the curia insisted on payment of
at least twelve thousand écus before it would commence the process –
money that the Brussels government did not have to hand.[26]

---

[25] F. Postma, 'Nieuw licht op een oude zaak. De oprichting van de nieuwe bis-
dommen in 1559', *TvG* 103 (1990), 10–27, there *passim* and 17; *idem, Viglius. De
jaren met Granvelle*, 147–149.

[26] Granvelle to Philip II, 5 January 1561, *Papiers d'état du cardinal de Granvelle d'après
les manuscrits de la Bibliothèque de Bésançon*, ed. C. Weiss, 9 vols. (Paris, 1841–52), VI,
246–247.

Lindanus

When it came to Friesland, the Brussels authorities had not been prepared to wait so long. After the departure of Letmatius and Sonnius, it was decided, as an advance on the new scheme, to send an ecclesiastical commissioner to Friesland. Viglius had chosen the theologian Willem Lindanus for this role.[27] Born in Dordrecht, this priest was a professor at the University of Dillingen, which the bishop of Augsburg had founded in 1551. In an attempt to avoid disputes about his jurisdiction, the bishop of Utrecht and the archdeacons who had authority in Friesland delegated their powers to him and he was given a seat in the Provincial Court. Even so, disputes proved inevitable; the bishops and archdeacons had been neglecting their duties in Friesland for so long that Frisians saw it as their customary right that they could ignore non-Frisian ecclesiastical authority. Of course Lindanus saw it as his duty to discipline priests who were not orthodox or who were married, but since the old customs had been guaranteed in a treaty of 1524, Frisians apparently considered themselves entitled to choose married or unorthodox priests. What Lindanus called 'abuses', the majority of Frisians found acceptable. A conflict with the provincial estates was inevitable and after Persijn's departure the Court (formally representing Philip II) and its new president, Karel van der Nitzen, actually supported the resistance to Lindanus. In May 1559, the latter began an investigation into the heterodox views of Steven Silvius, the priest of Oldenhove, the main church in Leeuwarden. There were good reasons indeed to question his orthodoxy. He denied the existence of purgatory and said that one should therefore not pray for the dead, that candles should not be offered to saints but used to spin by; that one should not travel to Rome or to Compostela but to one's poor fellow man; that everyone should look into his own heart, to see what he should do. He considered good works necessary, but did not believe these could be used to compensate for sins. He emphasized the need to believe in Christ and taught that one should not invoke the Saints but follow their example. He urged people to hear the word of God but not to attend mass, and he considered the eucharist as the seal and

---

[27] P.Th. van Beuningen, *Wilhelmus Lindanus als inquisiteur en bisschop. Bijdrage tot zijn biografie (1525–1576)* (Assen, 1966); Postma, *Viglius. De jaren met Granvelle*, 144–146.

confirmation of the forgiving of our sins at the cross, which should be revered because the Lord had left it to us. On the other hand, he had 'actively reproved' the Anabaptists, Zwinglians, Mennonites and David Jorists. In short, he was a man who did not fit into any category, but who charted his own path, and even had the courage to tell his audience that he himself did not always know the answers. Twice, he had said in a sermon that he could not know for certain whether the sacrament was the body of Christ. He had a wife – Lindanus called her a concubine – and several children. A vicar of Oldenhove, Hendrik Drolshagen, had similar ideas.[28] It is unsurprising that Lindanus was extremely concerned. Yet locally Silvius was much respected; in 1558 he had even become chairman of the committee of the States that led the resistance against Lindanus. To accommodate his views, he had been released from the obligation to say mass, and in support of his bid for a doctorate at Heidelberg he was given 'wonderful references'.[29] After Silvius's departure Lindanus persisted for another year, but in 1560 he left the province, worn out and defeated. The Frisian church could continue in its old ways.

Groningen

When Lindanus began his investigation in May 1559, Silvius had already left Leeuwarden for the University of Heidelberg, where the adherents of various Protestant groups were teaching. In spite of objections from the strict Lutheran Heshusius he was awarded a doctorate there on 8 March 1559 and by 29 March he was already in Groningen to receive the eight jugs of wine that were customarily granted to the newly elected priest of the Church of St. Maarten. The dates show that he had gone to Heidelberg with a view to his expected appointment in Groningen; it was stipulated that the rector of St. Maarten should have a doctorate.[30] In Groningen, too, he

---

[28] Woltjer, *Friesland*, 91–92 and for more examples, there, 90–96.
[29] *Ibid.*, 100.
[30] E. van Dijk, 'Dr. Johannes Eelts, *ca.* 1528–1588, *persona* te Groningen, en de tegenstelling katholicisme/protestantisme in zijn tijd', *Groningse volksalmanak* (1970–71), 16–48, there 25.

never said mass.[31] It would have been interesting to see how he responded in the 1560s, but he died as early as 1561. His appointment indicates that the city and region of Groningen were an ecclesiastical anomaly. The three eldest priests and the two senior burgomasters chose the priest of the Church of St. Maarten.[32] In 1557, the magistrate had banned appeals to the bishop of Utrecht. Any issues should be presented to the dean, and if necessary to the *ambtman* of the Gorecht, and in the last instance to the Council of Groningen. Authorities from outside the region were denied any say, and none of the bishops had much power. Only the city and the Gorecht fell under the authority of the bishop of Utrecht, its surrounding Ommelanden belonged to the diocese of Münster, while the area of Westerwolde came under Osnabruck.[33]

With Steven Silvius, the Groningers appointed a protestantizing priest to their most important ecclesiastical post, and they did so in full knowledge of what they were doing. The appointment was not an accident but seems representative of the religious climate in Groningen. From the start of the Reformation, attempts were made to paper over the divisions. Thus, the Anabaptist phase of the 1530s resulted in only one death sentence, against the leader of the attack on the Johannite convent in Warffum. The rector of the school of St. Maarten was Regnerus Praedinius, who was closely aligned with the Swiss theologians, Bullinger especially. During his period in office the school offered a nine-year course, which included Greek and which, in the two final years, covered much of the Arts syllabus of the Universities. Theological matters were not excluded, and pupils from the northern Netherlands and northwest Germany attended the school; of those who went on to study at University many went to Basel or Lausanne. Viglius called Praedinius 'of very suspect doctrine', but attempts to have him dismissed came to nought.[34] Perhaps pressure from Brussels would eventually have made his position

---

[31] J.J. Woltjer, '"De zuivering der leer". Over protestantiserende katholieken en protestanten in Groningen in 1556', *NAK* 78 (1995), 1–17, there 4, note 10.

[32] Van Dijk, 'Eelts', 21.

[33] J.J. Woltjer, 'De zuivering der leer', in W.J. Formsma, ed., *Historie van Groningen. Stad en Land* (Groningen, 1976), 207.

[34] F. Postma, 'Regnerus Praedinius (*c.* 1510–1559), seine Schule und sein Einfluss', in F. Akkerman, G.C. Huisman and A.J. Vanderjagt, eds., *Wessel Gansfort (1419–1489) and Northern Humanism* (Leiden, 1993), 312, note 87.

untenable, as many thought, but he died in 1559. Praedinius's coun-
terpart at the A-school, Gerlacus Verrutius, too, was not orthodox,
but more oriented towards spiritualism. Yet however much room
there was for protestantizing Catholics in Groningen, there was no
tolerance for secret Protestant conventicles. In 1558 attempts to form
a clearly Protestant but underground community were strictly prohibited; these, too, would have challenged the attempts of the magistrate to maintain unity, and would have escaped government control.[35]

Maarten van Naarden, since 1541 the lieutenant of the stadholder
of Groningen, and *de facto* representative of the Brussels government
in the province, had reported on the situation in Groningen to the
central government in 1544, 1548 and 1555.[36] However, he had not
managed to gain support for tougher action. There were probably
two reasons for the reticence of the Brussels officials. First, the emperor
had not a single soldier or stronghold in the area, while the city was
easily defensible. Despite Charles's victory over the German Protestants
in 1547, the defeat of the imperial troops at Drakenburg meant that
his position in northwestern Germany remained weak. It was crucial not to tempt Groningen to seek support in East Friesland or
Bremen. From 1552 it was, moreover, easy to argue that intervention should be postponed until the new bishops could take up their
posts and take action. On other issues, too, Van Naarden was opposed
by Groningen's burgomasters and the provincial estates.[37] In 1556
he asked to be relieved of his duties 'because of old age' (he had
been born around 1490), and the following year this request was
agreed. Soon afterwards he was appointed as a councillor in the
Court of Holland.[38] His successor in Groningen was yet another law
graduate, Johan de Mepsche. It was probably because he was citizen of Groningen, had good relations there, and knew local conditions that he was better able to defend the Habsburg interests than
the 'alien' Van Naarden had been.

---

[35] Postma, 'Praedinius', 316–318; Woltjer, '"De zuivering der leer"'.
[36] F. Postma, 'Vreemde heren. Opstand en reductie, 1536–1594', in P.Th.F.M.
Boekholt, ed., *Rondom de reductie. Vierhonderd jaar provincie Groningen, 1594–1994*, Groninger
Historische Reeks 10 (Assen, 1994), 67.
[37] *Ibid.*, 69.
[38] F. Postma, 'De mislukte missie van Mr. Maarten van Naarden als lieutenant-
stadhouder van Stad en Lande, 1541–57', *BMGN* 120 (2005), 1–27.

Conclusion

Flanders, Antwerp, Amsterdam, Friesland and Groningen tell five very different tales, but in many respects these shed a very similar light on the attitude of the authorities to the heresy issue. Each of them highlights that neither the Netherlandish authorities nor the population sympathized with the policy of fierce persecution of heresy that Charles V and Philip II promoted. Even many of the councillors at the centre did not support the Habsburg policies. The trial of Floris Egbertz was discussed at length by the Privy and Great Councils; Christiaen de Waerdt, public prosecutor in Holland between 1548 and 1558, and subsequently councillor in the High Court of Mechelen, knew the Amsterdam case inside out, while similarly, the divisions in the Frisian court were a topic of extensive discussion in Brussels, both in the Council of State and the Privy Council.[39] There is no doubt that both in Brussels and Mechelen, officials were well aware that Bardes in Amsterdam and the king's council in Friesland were turning as much of a blind eye to heresy as they possibly could. But how much of this got through to the king himself? Probably not much, and certainly not much detail – more likely he got a general notion that things were wrong but that it was difficult to pin them down. Acting on royal orders, some Spaniards in 1557 were busy looking for heretics in the Low Countries, most importantly Bartolomé Carranza, whom Philip was to appoint archbishop of Toledo in 1557. Yet he and his colleagues focused mostly on those Spaniards who had fled the Iberian peninsula for the faith, and on the booksellers who exported heretical books to Spain via Antwerp. To chart these commercial links, the Augustinian Lorenzo de Villavicencio attended the Frankfurt book fair incognito – having shed clerical dress for the occasion. They were also keeping a sharp eye on Spanish students in Louvain, who might be influenced by suspect fellow-students; their reports prompted Philip II in 1559 to ban Castilian students from pursuing their studies outside Spain and to force all those who were abroad to return home. It is likely that both the king and these Spaniards were hampered in their understanding of the situation in the Netherlands because they did not know enough French to be able to communicate easily with the Netherlanders, or to pick up

---

[39] Van Beuningen, *Lindanus*, 94–95.

enough of their conversations. As a consequence, they found it difficult to form a clear picture of the situation there, and ended up thinking in caricatures; Carranza reported to Philip that the Netherlands were doomed because heretics remained unpunished and heretical books were sold in the palace gates.[40] The pressure exerted by Philip and his Spanish surroundings was such that high officials in the Netherlands chose to hide the true state of affairs rather than openly to express their views to the king. Viglius, for instance, was as unhappy about the attitude of the Frisian councillors in their conflict with Lindanus as he had been about the placard of 1550. 'Are you Catholic councillors? If the King finds out, what would he say?', he is said to have exclaimed during a meeting.[41] But although he was the highest ranking public servant in the Netherlands, he did not tell the king! Apparently he worried about an ill-considered response. Was the king so impervious to dissenting views that it was better to leave him in ignorance than to engage him in discussion?

If many rejected the strict prosecution of heresy, what did they want in its stead? Generally, the moderates lacked a programme or a theoretical basis for defending toleration as a matter of principle. Yet if the opponents of persecution did not have very clear principles, they did have very strong feelings; sooner or later their sense of justice and fairness, their sense of proportion, was offended by the horrendous capital punishments for simple people who erred in the faith. Such an attitude did not rule out lighter penalties or disciplinary measures; quite the opposite. One senses that many of them came to the view that draconian laws were counterproductive.

In heresy trials the burden of proof was often problematic. Once a stubborn heretic was imprisoned, his culpability was often evident from his own confession, yet much more complex was the situation before arrests could be made, or when a prisoner denied the charges. By fighting for legal protection, and especially through their efforts to try and prevent spurious accusations, both the Court of Holland and the States hampered the struggle against heresy – sometimes accidentally, at other times quite consciously. Thus, a false charge like the one that had been levied against sheriff Bardes in Amsterdam

---

[40] I. Tellechea Idigoras, 'Bartolomé Carranza en Flandes. El clima religioso en los Países Bajos (1557–1558)', in E. Iserloh and K. Repgen, eds., *Reformata Reformanda. Festgabe für Hubert Jedin*, 2 vols. (Münster, 1965), II, *passim* and 325.
[41] Van Beuningen, *Lindanus*, 94–95.

in 1553 was made well-nigh impossible in Holland law in 1556. As one of its conditions for the granting of a tax in 1555, the States of Holland demanded that all witness statements supporting an accusation should from now on be public. An (undated) gloss on this law commented this would benefit the 'various people of honour who have been accused of heresy or other crimes', as had been shown in Friesland, Utrecht, Antwerp and other places where this was customary – unfortunately we do not know which 'people of honour' the writer had in mind.[42] Of course Philip was not enthusiastic, but he urgently needed money for the war against France and he therefore conceded to this demand in two stages, in December 1556 and March 1557, when he gave orders that all witness statements offered to the Court of Holland should be made public.[43] Effective prosecution became difficult if much of the evidence had to be presented before an arrest could be made, and when accusers openly had to face public disapproval.

Yet such examples of resistance against strict persecution should not let us forget that there were also officials who were principled supporters of the persecution of heretics, and who did take action against them. What for some people was evidence that persecution was counterproductive, for others, like Titelmans, it seemed to prove how necessary it was to maintain a hard line. For that reason, there continued to be many victims, while many others had to flee their country, kinsmen and familiar surroundings for fear of persecution.

What Philip thought of the matter became evident once again just before his departure to Spain, when he sent a letter about the struggle against heresy to the Great Council in Mechelen and the provincial courts and councils.[44] In the text for the Great Council he referred to a speech he recently had given to this body, and the contents of which he was now confirming in writing. Just as his father had done, he blamed the spread of heresy on the laxity of officials who had failed to implement the strict placards, either because they did not show enough zeal for the faith, or even because they

---

[42] ARAB, Aud. 1440/4 no. 3.

[43] *Archieven van de Staten van Holland en de hen opvolgende gewestelijke besturen*, ed. P.A. Meilink (The Hague, 1929), nos. 606, 631, 635.

[44] *Collection des documents inédits concernant l'histoire de la Belgique*, ed. L.P. Gachard, 2 vols. (Brussels, 1833–45), I, 332–339. See also *Recueil des ordonnances des Pays-Bas, 1506–1700*, 2nd series, 7 vols. (Brussels, 1893–1957), VII, 507–511.

were favouring the heretics. This situation was unacceptable; through the many trade contacts with the neighbouring countries and during the recent wars, heresy had spread further every day. Now peace had come at last, he wanted to root out heresy – as far as possible, he added carefully. The placard should not just be used against the Anabaptists but also against Lutherans and 'Sacramentarians'. The strictness of the placards could not be a pretext for modifying them. Judges should apply the law, not judge it. They should not have any scruples, since it was not they but the Prince who was responsible for the content of the placards. And one should not just punish those who acted in breach of the placards, but also those in the judiciary who failed to implement them. The message was clear, but also very far removed from actual practice. What would the officials who were discussed in this paper have made of these commands? I do not know of a single example of action being taken against 'negligent' judges. But neither, as far as we can tell, did they offer any protest against this policy. They probably knew there was no hope of changing the king's mind.

Behind all the polite phrases, Philip's messages at his parting from the Low Countries had made it painfully clear that the problems were enormous. The Netherlanders listened to his commands about the persecution of heretics, but the majority had no intention of putting them into practice. The king, on his part, was never going to give in. In the years he had spent in the Netherlands, Philip had developed a very simple and negative view of the Low Countries, that he ruled without understanding the forces at work there. He thought in black and white terms, in which there was no room for the attitude of the majority of the Netherlandish population, his officials included. From his father he inherited a climate in which no one dared to contradict him – at least where heresy was concerned – and his officials continued to operate as they had done in Charles's time. The king never got to know their nuanced views and the realities on the ground. For this reason, what was a matter of common knowledge and increasing public consent in the Low Countries, could simultaneously remain completely hidden from the royal view. Within a few years, it was to become evident what price there was to pay.

CHAPTER SIX

'SUPEREXCELLAT AUTEM MISERICORDIA IUDICIUM'. THE HOMILY OF FRANÇOIS RICHARDOT ON THE OCCASION OF THE SOLEMN ANNOUNCEMENT OF THE GENERAL PARDON IN THE NETHERLANDS (ANTWERP, 16 JULY 1570)

Gustaaf Janssens

After a debate lasting four years, and constant delays, Fernando Alvarez de Toledo, the duke of Alba and governor of the Netherlands, announced a long-expected royal pardon in Antwerp on 16 July 1570. This kind of sovereign grace, which granted an amnesty under certain conditions to a group of people who had committed crimes against the state, was traditionally seen as a measure to bring peace to the country and establish the king's power and reputation.[1] The public announcement of this magnanimous royal favour was an opportunity *par excellence* for the king to make a public display of his clemency and for his subjects to confirm their loyalty to the king. This rite took the form of a religious and civil ceremony. Just as the public ceremonies were intended as a means of communication, the publication of the speeches made during the ceremony gave permanence to the event that had taken place.[2] This essay will focus on one of these addresses, the homily delivered by François Richardot on 16 July 1570 on the announcement of the pardon in Antwerp Cathedral.

---

[1] V. Soen, 'C'estoit comme songe et mocquerie de parler de pardon. Obstructie bij een pacificatiemaatregel (1566–1567)', *BMGN* 119 (2004), 309–328, there 309, 311–313. On the general political context of the General Pardon, see G. Janssens, *'Brabant in het verweer'. Loyale oppositie tegen Spanje's bewind in de Nederlanden van Alva tot Farnese. 1567–1578*, Standen en landen – Anciens Pays et Assemblées d'États 89 (Kortrijk–Heule, 1989), 137–167. My thanks to Ms. Violet Soen (FWO-Vlaanderen, KU Leuven, Department of History) for making available the manuscript of, 'De koning en de pastoor als Goede Herder. De reconciliatie van "ketters" in de zestiende-eeuwse Nederlanden (1520–1590)', *Trajecta* 14 (2005), 337–362.

After the abdication of his father Charles V in October 1555, Philip II had remained in the Netherlands for some time. He continued the struggle against France and his victory at Saint-Quentin (10 August 1557) allowed him to avenge his father's defeat at Metz four years previously. The king could now leave for Spain with his head held high.[3]

To replace the king, a governor from the 'blood royal' was sought to rule in the Netherlands, which Philip II entrusted to his half-sister Margaret of Parma.[4] During her administration from 1559 to 1567, there was great unrest in the Netherlands, with opposition to a number of centralizing policies in government. The nobility and the clergy found common cause in their opposition to the formation of new dioceses. Despite the pronouncements on heresy, the protestants gained a constant stream of new adherents and in 1565 a large number of mostly minor Protestant nobility formed an association and in April 1566 submitted their grievances to the governor.[5]

A proposal to use a collective pardon – 'Grâce et pardon' – to 'pacify' the dissident nobility, as suggested by Charles de Brimeux, the count of Megen, at a meeting of the Council of State in mid-March 1566, was greeted without enthusiasm in both Brussels and Madrid. The king preferred to grant grace on an individual basis to those who admitted they had 'been misled' and sought reconcilia-

---

[2] R.J. López, 'Ceremonia y poder en el Antiguo Régimen. Algunas reflexiones sobre fuentes y perspectivas de análisis', in A. Gonzalez Enciso and J.M. Usunariz Garayoa, eds., *Imagen del rey, imagen de los reinos. Las ceremonias públicas en la España Moderna (1500–1814)* (Pamplona, 1999), 45–46.

[3] M. Rodriguez Salgado, *Un imperio en transición. Carlos V, Felipe II y su mundo* (Barcelona, 1992), 256–270; H. Kamen, *Philip of Spain* (New Haven and London, 1997), 69–70; G. Parker, *The Grand Strategy of Philip II* (New Haven and London, 1998), 99.

[4] M. Herrero Sánchez, 'La monarquía hispánica y la cuestión de Flandes', in P. Sanz Camañes, ed., *La Monarquía Hispánica en tiempos del Quijote* (Madrid, 2005), 509. Calls for 'a governor of the blood' were often heard in the Netherlands after the governorship of Luis de Requesens (1573–76), see Janssens, '*Brabant in het verweer*', 275 and 346. On the myth of 'the royal blood', see J.J. Woltjer, 'De vredemakers', in S. Groenveld and H.L.Ph. Leeuwenberg, eds., *De Unie van Utrecht. Wording en werking van een verbondsacte*, Geschiedenis in veelvoud 6 (The Hague, 1979), 78.

[5] G. Parker, *The Dutch Revolt* (London, 1977), 55–70. Janssens, '*Brabant in het verweer*', 105–116. See also A. Goosens, *Le Comte Lamoral d'Egmont (1522–1568). Les Aléas du pouvoir de la haute noblesse à l'aube de la Révolte des Pays-Bas*, Analectes de l'histoire du Hainaut 8 (Hainin, 2003), 62–143. On Margaret of Parma, see G. Janssens, 'Margaretha of Parma', in H.J. Hillerbrand, ed., *The Oxford Encyclopedia of the Reformation*, 4 vols. (New York and Oxford, 1996), II, 6.

tion. He aimed to reserve a collective grace or General Pardon for his planned return to the Netherlands.[6] All salvation depended on his arrival, wrote Pedro del Castillo in June 1566 to Cardinal Granvelle.[7]

During the summer of 1566 religious tensions in the Netherlands escalated. Violent iconoclastic riots broke out and a trail of destruction extended northwards from the Western reaches of Flanders and Brabant. Monasteries were attacked and the contents of churches were destroyed.[8] This wave of iconoclasm and sacrilegious violence against all that was Catholic caused a huge shock.[9] From that time onwards it became clear that an ecclesiastical reconciliation would have to be a necessary foundation for any pardon that was to be granted by the king.[10] The Beggars protest had been transformed into heretical violence.[11]

In the autumn of 1566 Margaret of Parma attempted to bring the situation back under control. She had achieved some success when, in the spring of 1567, the duke of Alba arrived in the Netherlands with a large army and extensive political powers.[12] Meanwhile many people had set their hopes on the king's announced arrival. Philip of Saint Aldegonde, the lord of Noircarmes, wrote on 3 February 1567 to the count of Egmont that when the king came, he would have to announce a General Pardon.[13] Egmont himself

---

[6] Soen, 'C'estoit comme songe', 315–316.

[7] P. del Castillo to Cardinal Granvelle, 23 June 1566, Ms. Besançon, Bibliothèque municipale, *Collection Granvelle*, nr. 22, fol. 296.

[8] G. Marnef, 'The Dynamics of Reformed Religious Militancy in the Netherlands, 1566–1585', in P. Benedict *et al.*, eds., *Reformation, Revolt and Civil War*, 54–56. See also G. Janssens, 'Rapporten uit 1569 over herstelde schade aan kerken en kapellen in de Vlaamse Westhoek. Een bron voor de geschiedenis van de eerste fase van de Beeldenstorm in 1566', in J. De Zutter, L. Charles and A. Capiteyn, eds., *Qui valet ingenio. Liber amicorum aangeboden aan Dr. Johan Decavele ter gelegenheid van zijn 25-jarig ambtsjubileum als stadsarchivaris van Gent* (Ghent, 1996), 279–288.

[9] Janssens, *'Brabant in het verweer'*, 127.

[10] Soen, 'C'estoit comme songe', 319.

[11] Duke, 'Dissident Propaganda', 129.

[12] Janssens, *'Brabant in het verweer'*, 131, 133–134, 137–139. On Alba, W.S. Maltby, 'Alvarez de Toledo, Fernando', in Hillerbrand, ed., *The Oxford Encyclopedia of the Reformation*, I, 22–23.

[13] Noircarmes to Egmont, 2 February 1567, Archivo General de Simancas [AGS] *Secretaría de Estado* [*Estado*], legajo [leg.] n° 536, f° 38. On Philip of Saint Aldegonde, lord of Noircarmes, see M. Baelde, *De collaterale raden onder Karel V en Filips II (1537–1578)* (Brussels, 1965), 310–311. On Lamoral, count of Egmont, see B. De Troyer, 'Egmont', in J. Maton *et al.*, eds., *Nationaal Biografisch Woordenboek* (Brussels, 1964–), I, 431–61.

proposed a *status quo* until the king's arrival, and described that event as a necessary precondition for the restoration of order.[14] Margaret of Parma was convinced that Philip II should come to the Netherlands as a clement and benevolent sovereign.[15] Juan de Albornoz, secretary to the duke of Alba, pointed out that it was necessary for the king to return as a 'merciful and good sovereign'.[16] Meanwhile the duke of Alba, entirely in accordance with his instructions, was in favour of repression. He set up an extraordinary court, the Council of Troubles, to punish those responsible for the unrest of 1566.[17] Severe penalties were meted out. A number of high-ranking noblemen, including the counts of Egmont and Hornes, were accused of high treason, sentenced to death and beheaded.[18] Others escaped punishment by leaving the country in time. The duke of Alba was instructed to pacify the land and announce a pardon; thus repression was to come first, and a possible act of mercy could only follow later.[19] He was to undertake 'the dirty work' so that the king could come and bestow his grace under conditions of peace and good order.[20] On his arrival he therefore demanded loyal assistance from the Privy Council while awaiting the coming of the king.[21] It was entirely in accordance with views of the time that a possible pardon could only be announced after the king's authority had been forcibly restored.[22]

---

[14] Egmont to the king, 26 June 1567, AGS, *Estado*, leg. n° 536, fol. 85, summarized in *Correspondance de Philippe II sur les affaires des Pays-Bas*, ed. L.P. Gachard (Brussels, 1848), I, 547.

[15] Margaret of Parma to the king, 6 and 17 June 1567, AGS, *Estado*, leg. n° 536, fol. 72 and fol. 61.

[16] J. de Albornoz to Gabriel de Zayas, 31 October 1567, AGS, *Estado*, leg. n° 535, fol. 92.

[17] G. Marnef and H. de Schepper, 'Conseil des Troubles (1567–1576)', in E. Aerts *et al.*, eds., *Les Institutions du gouvernement central des Pays-Bas Habsbourgeois (1482–1795)* (Brussels, 1995), 470–478, and A. Goosens, *Les Inquisitions modernes dans les Pays-Bas méridionaux 1520–1633*, 2 vols. (Brussels, 1997), I, 159–164. In a letter to the king on 6 July 1568 the duke of Alba spoke of the 'Consejo de la rebellión', in M. Fernandez Navarrete, S. Salva and P. Sainz de Baranda, eds., *Colección de documentos inéditos para la história de España*, 113 vols. (Madrid, 1842–95), XXXVII, 297.

[18] Goosens, *Le Comte Lamoral d'Egmont*, 167–204. On the counts of Egmont and Hornes and their significance in the collective historical consciousness in the Low Countries, see G. Janssens, *Les Comtes d'Egmont et de Hornes, victimes de la répression politique aux Pays-Bas espagnols*, Historia Bruxellae 2 (Brussels, 2003).

[19] Soen, 'C'estoit comme songe', 322–323.

[20] Janssens, '*Brabant in het verweer*', 133–134 and 401–402.

[21] Alba to the Private Council, 31 August 1567, Brussels. General State Archives [ARAB]. *Papers of State and Audience [Aud.]*, n° 249/1, fol. 1.

[22] M. de Waele, 'Un Modèle de clémence. Le Duc d'Albe, lieutenant-gouverneur

Following this period of repression, there was a demand for and expectation of an act of mercy, even in 1565–67. This was nothing new and a royal pardon was generally seen in the Netherlands as a means of pacification, because the amnesty would be able to restore peace to the country and re-establish the authority of the absent monarch.[23] It is tempting to speculate about what would have happened if Philip II had actually come to the Netherlands in 1567–68 and announced a general pardon. In the autumn of 1567, however, the king announced that he would not be coming at that time and in the end Philip II never returned to the Netherlands. Instead of dying out, resistance and rebellion continued to smoulder and flared up regularly.[24]

Cardinal Granvelle, who had been forced to leave the Netherlands in 1564 but was kept closely informed about the evolution of the political situation by his Vicar-General Maximilien Morillon, meanwhile became more and more convinced that violent action in the Netherlands would not resolve anything. In mid-1568 he considered that a royal act of mercy with a carefully chosen form of words would certainly be a success.[25] He, along with many other leading loyal figures in the Netherlands, would now press for the pardon to be announced swiftly.[26]

The duke of Alba had arrived in the Netherlands with some 10,000 soldiers. To supply and maintain these troops was expensive and so

---

des Pays-Bas, 1567–1573', *Cahiers d'histoire. La Revue du département d'histoire de l'Université de Montréal* 16 (1996), 21–32, there 28. With thanks to Ms. Violet Soen, who referred me to this study.

[23] Janssens, '*Brabant in het verweer*', 128.

[24] On the reasons why the king ultimately did not come to the Netherlands, see G. Parker, 'The End of the Dutch Revolt?', in A. Crespo Solana and M. Herrero Sánchez, eds., *España y las 17 provincias de los Países Bajos. Una revisión historiográfica (XVI–XVIII)* (Cordoba, 2002), I, 269–290.

[25] Janssens, '*Brabant in het verweer*', 164, and G. Janssens, 'Cardinal Granvelle and the Revolt in the Netherlands. The Evolution of his Thought on a Desirable Political Approach to the Problem, 1567–1578', in K. De Jonge and G. Janssens, eds., *Les Granvelle et les anciens Pays-Bas* (Louvain, 2000), 140. Violet Soen ('C'estoit comme songe', 324, note 100) rightly points out that the cardinal was not always in favour of a General Pardon.

[26] V. Soen, 'Geen pardon zonder paus! Studie over de complementariteit van het pauselijk en het koninklijk pardon (1570–1574) en pauselijk inquisiteur-generaal Michael Baius (1560–1576)', unpublished M.Phil. dissertation, Department of History (Catholic University of Louvain, 2003), 89–111. This highly interesting study was awarded the Mgr. De Clercq Prize for Religious History 2004 by the 'Koninklijke Vlaamse Academie van België' (Royal Flemish Academy of Belgium for Science and the Arts). It will soon be appearing in the 'Verhandelingen' series of the Academy's 'Klasse der Menswetenschappen'.

as to avoid being dependent on the often unreliable shipments of
money from Spain, a plan was worked out to ensure that the
Netherlands would finance the cost of the war itself through new
and permanent taxes.[27] The governor probably intended to announce
the pardon in 1569 before proposing the tax.[28] Ultimately this did
not happen and the new taxes were proposed to the States-General
by the duke on 20 and 21 March 1569. Tough resistance followed,
led mainly by Flanders and Brabant, and in 1572 this ultimately
succeeded in defeating the proposal for the Tenth and Twentieth
Pennies.[29]

Calls for a pardon had increased during 1568–69, and were finally
heeded in the summer of 1570. The ecclesiastical and civil ceremonies both took place in Antwerp on 16 July 1570.[30] It is not
immediately clear why Antwerp was chosen, although the governor
may have organized the ceremony there because it was where there
had been a significant Protestant presence and the iconoclastic riots
had been at their most furious in August 1566. The new 'Spaniards'
Castle', the military bastion intended to keep the city in order, was
also virtually complete. With the announcement of the pardon in
Antwerp the duke would finally be able to finish his task in the
Netherlands.[31] The ceremony in the antwerp cathedral was possibly
meant to make the populace forget the iconoclastic fury.

Responsibilty for delivering the homily on this occasion fell to François
Richardot, bishop of Arras.[32] He was relatively well-known, having
preached the sermon at the funeral service of Charles V in 1558.[33]

---

[27] These were the well-known Tenth and Twentieth Pennies, see F.H.M.
Grapperhaus, *Alva en de tiende penning* (Zutphen, 1982).
[28] Janssens, 'Brabant in het verweer', 165.
[29] *Ibid.*, 147–159.
[30] Soen, 'Geen pardon zonder paus!', 120–125. See also 'Relación de lo que
sucedido en la publicación del Perdón General en la villa de Amberes a 16 julio
1570', anonymous report intended for the duke of Alba, Madrid. Palacio de Liria.
Archivo de los Duques de Alba, *Caja* 69, n° 10.
[31] Soen, 'Geen pardon zonder paus!', 100 and 115–116. On the Iconoclasm in
Antwerp, which 'purified' the cathedral on 20 August 1566, see G. Marnef, *Antwerp
in the Age of Reformation. Underground Protestantism in a Commercial Metropolis, 1550–1577*
(Baltimore and London, 1996), 89–90.
[32] Soen, 'Geen pardon zonder paus!', 116.
[33] G. Janssens, 'El sermón fúnebre predicado por François Richardot en Bruselas
ante Felipe II con ocasión de la muerte del emperador Carlos V', in J. Martínez
Millán, ed., *Carlos V y la quiebra del humanismo político en Europa (1530–1558). Actas*

Born in 1507 at Morey in Franche Comté, after his graduation Richardot joined the Augustinian hermits at Champlitte. He had studied philosphy and theology in Paris where he received his doctorate. In 1529 he travelled first to Tournai before returning to Paris as professor of theology. Later he was discharged from his monastic vows and spent some time in Rome as a secular priest; subsequently he lived at the ducal court of the d'Estes at Ferrara. François Richardot was noticed by the Granvelle family; he became a teacher at the college of Besançon and was involved in the administration of the local diocese. It is clear that an ecclesiastical career was awaiting him under the protection of the Granvelle family. In 1554 he was ordained titular bishop of Nicopolis. In 1556 Antoine Perrenot de Granvelle, who had been bishop of Arras since 1538, called Richardot to assist him as a suffragan bishop. He was to devote the rest of his life to pastoral work in the Netherlands.[34]

François Richardot was one of the many lawyers and clergymen from Franche Comté who made their careers in the Netherlands under the protection of Antoine Perrenot de Granvelle.[35] When Antoine Perrenot de Granvelle was appointed archbishop of Mechelen in 1560, François Richardot succeeded him in 1561 in the diocese of Arras. As a bishop, Richardot engaged in a great deal of pastoral work. He also played an important part in the foundation of Douai University. In the political domain he clearly belonged to the 'loyal central group'. He pleaded for mercy on behalf of the count of Egmont and was in favour of a royal pardon.[36] François Richardot died in his diocesan city of Arras on 26 July 1574.

---

del Congreso internacional, I (Madrid, 2001), 349–362. See also P. Van Peteghem, 'Une Oraison funèbre pas comme les autres: celle de François Richardot pour Charles V. Les pompes funèbres de Bruxelles (29 et 30 décembre 1558)', in J. Paviot, ed., Liber amicorum Raphaël De Smedt, Miscellanea neerlandica 25, 3 vols. (Louvain, 2001), III, 259–287. These two articles were produced independently and complement one another.

[34] On F. Richardot (1507–1574), see R. Muchembled, 'Richardot, François', in Hillerbrand, ed., The Oxford Encyclopedia of the Reformation, III, 431, and L. Duflot, Un Orateur du XVIe siècle. François Richardot, évêque d'Arras (Arras, 1898).

[35] Duflot, Un Orateur, 1–77. See also J. Vanhoutte, 'Van robins tot très grands nobles. Carrièreplanning en huwelijksstrategie bij het geslacht Richardot in de Zuidelijke Nederlanden (1540–1701)', in G. Marnef and R. Vermeir, eds., Adel en macht. Politiek, cultuur, economie (Maastricht, 2004), 19–23.

[36] Duflot, Un Orateur, 159–160. On the loyal central group at the time of resistance and rebellion in the Netherlands, see J.J. Woltjer, 'Political Moderates and Religious Moderates in the Revolt of the Netherlands', in P. Benedict et al., eds., Reformation, Revolt and Civil War.

Bishop Richardot was a pastorally motivated pulpit orator. He often preached on Sundays and gave the homily on 11 November 1563, at the opening session of the 24th session of the Council of Trent.[37] Besides preaching at the emperor's funeral, Richardot spoke at other public religious ceremonies and, unusually, even during his lifetime a number of his sermons were published.[38]

In the homily given by François Richardot at the announcement of the General Pardon, the 'clemency' and 'mercy' of the king and the concern for ecclesiastical unity were his central themes.[39] The entire sermon had a strong biblical basis, with quotations from and references to passages from Old and New Testaments. In particular there are quotations from the Psalms, but also from the prophet Isaiah and the letters of Paul.[40] Richardot was particularly familiar with the Pauline epistles.[41]

In his introductory thoughts Richardot states that 'of all the virtues, clemency ('la clémence') is the one that produces the most glory and honour for princes and adds the greatest lustre to their crown'. That is because this benevolence allows princes to resemble most closely the Divine Majesty of Whom they are the image and likeness, as the Psalmist writes: 'This is my sentence: gods you may be, sons all of you of a High God' (Ps. 82 (81),6).[42] This benevolence tempers the severity of legal judgements and leaves room for grace, 'just as the mercy of God always exceeds the severity of his judgement'. Here the preacher is referring to verse 13 from the second chapter of the letter of James: 'mercy triumphs over judgement'.[43] This quotation sets the tone: God spares evil doers out of respect for the

---

[37] H. Jedin, *Geschichte des Konzils von Trient*, 4 vols. (Freiburg, 1975), IV, 2, 159–160.

[38] A catalogue of these printed works in: Duflot, *Un Orateur*, 284–292.

[39] F. Richardot, *Sermon, faict en l'eglise cathedralle d'Anvers, en présence de l'excellence de monseigneur le Duc d'Alve, le iour de la publication des pardons de leurs Saincteté et Maiesté Royalle Catholique* (Antwerp, 1570). It was published by the Plantin press. I have used the copy kept in the library of the Plantin-Moretus Museum in Antwerp. This, alongside two copies in the Royal Library (Brussels) and one in the library of Postel Abbey, is one of the four known copies, see L. Voet, *The Plantin Press (1555–1589)* (Amsterdam, 1982), V, no. 2145.

[40] For the Latin quotations I have used the *Nova vulgata Bibliorum Sacrorum editio* (Vatican City, 1979). English Bible quotations are from *The New English Bible. The Old Testament* (Cambridge, 1970) and *The New English Bible. The New Testament* (2nd. ed.; Cambridge, 1970).

[41] Richardot had taught the letters of Paul in Paris, see Duflot, *Un Orateur*, 10.

[42] Richardot, *Sermon*, 3: 'Ego dixi: "Dii estis, et filii Excelsi omnes"'.

[43] *Ibid.*, 5: 'superexcellat autem misericordia iudicium'.

good and therefore princes may sometimes, to save the just, suspend vengeance against the wicked, because 'it is not fitting that the judges of this earth should condemn the innocent together with the sinner'.[44] In a compassionate judgement 'love and fidelity have come together; justice and peace join hands' (Ps. 85 (84),11).[45] Therefore, continues Richardot, 'every good prince must moderate justice in such a way that it contains nothing of cruelty and administer benevolence in such a way that it does not become a cause of gross and great injustice'.[46] Certainly, he continues, 'en ceste province Belgique' [in this province of the Netherlands] many dreadful things have taken place. Violence has been done to churches, holy things have been profaned, priests have been subjected to cruelty, religion has been attacked, there has been confusion everywhere and numerous excesses. As the prophet Isaiah says, 'the Lord has poured upon you a spirit of deep stupor; he has closed your eyes' (Is. 29, 10). This has been followed by 'a long and sad spectacle of cruelty', but after every storm comes a calm and so, Richardot says, both the grace of the pope and the royal Pardon will bring calm. Richardot finds examples from church history of merciful and just reincorporation of heretics into the church community. He mentions St. Martin, St. Augustine and Pope Leo the Great.[47] This is a good thing, and he cries out with Paul: 'how welcome are the feet of the messengers of good news!' (Rom. 10, 15) People may therefore rejoice and say 'Hark! Shouts of deliverance in the camp of the victors' (Ps. 118 (117), 15).[48]

Richardot demonstrates how a good king who is faithful to God will act, using the example of the Old Testament King Hezekiah. He was the son of idolatrous King Ahaz – the bad king *par excellence* – but shows loyalty to the true faith. He listens to the advice of the prophet Isaiah, reopens the temple and sets the Israelites back on the right path.[49] In this way Richardot makes the link to his second

---

[44] *Ibid.*, 4–5. Cf. Gen. 17, 23–25.

[45] *Ibid.*, 5: 'misericordia et veritas obviaverunt sibi, iustitia et pax osculatae sunt'.

[46] *Ibid.*, 6: 'Doibt en tous bons princes la iustice estre tellement modérée, qu'elle n'ayt aucune espece de cruaulté et la clémence tellement reiglée, qu'elle ne soit cause d'un licencieux desbordement de toute iniquitée'.

[47] *Ibid.*, 10–11.

[48] *Ibid.*, 7–9.

[49] *Ibid.*, 11–12. On Ezechia: J.E. Burns, 'Ezechia (Hezekiah), King of Juda', in William J. McDonald *et al.*, eds., *New Catholic Encyclopedia*, 17 vols. (New York and Sidney, 1967–79), V, 774–775.

theme: concern for the Catholic church. Richardot compares the
attacks that the church is facing in his time to the attacks on the
temple of Jerusalem. This is because the church is the true temple
of God. The pastors (priests, bishops and deacons) keep the lamp
of the true Catholic religion burning in the midst of the temple.
This is because it is the task of the clergy to preserve good morals
and to banish all vice, scandal and indecency from their midst, for
'If salt becomes tasteless, how is its saltness to be restored?' (Math.
5, 13).[50]

Richardot then turns to the king. He praises him because he has
allowed the decrees of the Council to be implemented and points
out that God is calling upon him to be a defender of the temple
and preserve calm and public order. Richardot also points to the
history of the Jewish people, and specifically to the period when
Jeroboam rebelled against Robiam, the son of Solomon. He praises
Philip II for his struggle against the apostates; the king sees with his
own eyes the ruins of God's temple and he can also see the destruction and plundering of church buildings.[51] He will therefore understand that clemency is necessary to bring about the unity and
agreement among Christians. According to Richardot, the temple
(the church community) has three doors: the door by which one
enters (baptism), the door by which one leaves (excommunication)
and the door by which one can return. Richardot appeals for this
door to become a great open gateway, so that the trumpet can sound
'to proclaim a year of the Lord's favour' (Is. 61, 2).[52]

Richardot then turns very specifically to those who wish to be reconciled. He extends an emotive plea to them to be reunited 'because
the gate stands open'.[53] He also calls upon the duke of Alba to do
whatever is necessary to allow as many people as possible to reap
the fruits of the royal pardon.[54]

Richardot ends his sermon with a prayer in which he asks that
God would ensure that the gracious act 'would be glorious for the
King, fruitful for all penitents and a source of happiness and joy for

---

[50] Richardot, *Sermon*, 14–20.
[51] *Ibid.*, 21–38. On king Jeroboam: B. McGrath, 'Jeroboam I, King of Israel', in
MacDonald, ed., *New Catholic Encyclopedia*, VII, 871.
[52] Richardot, *Sermon*, 39–48.
[53] *Ibid.*, 48.
[54] *Ibid.*, 50.

the fatherland'. If the pardon is fruitful for the penitents, this will 'create a sound basis for real faith, for the authority of the church, for obedience to the King, for respect towards the magistrates and for public calm and peace'. So those who have not yet been persuaded by the severe action of the law will now at length be persuaded by grace and mercy ('*miséricorde*') and so come to repentance. The joy and happiness of those who repent will ensure 'that, in this land, virtue, love and fear of God, honour given to the church and the respect due to His Majesty and all his good ministers, will grow and blossom'.[55]

The homily given by François Richardot is, just like the homily given on the occasion of the funeral service of Charles V in 1558, built according to the principles set out in the various *artes praedicandi* that were in circulation in the early sixteenth century. In terms of its structure and content these also show a large degree of continuity with texts from earlier centuries.[56]

The bishop, who received his religious training from the Augustinians, no doubt knew that according to political Augustinianism the State receives a religious mission, whereby the Good Shepherd King is an emanation of the Divine Majesty for his subjects.[57] It therefore emphasized the divine characteristics of the monarch. For early sixteenth-century authors like Antonio de Guevara, the king is 'a good and just ruler', 'a good shepherd', 'the representative of God on earth' (*vicarius Dei*), 'similar to God'.[58] This idea of the Divine

---

[55] Richardot, *Sermon*, 51–53: 'Les vertuz, l'amour et craincte de Dieu, l'honneur de lEglise, et le respect deu à Sa Majesté, et à tous ses bons ministres'.

[56] A. Redondo, *Antonio de Guevara (1480?–1545) et l'espace de son temps. De la Carrière officielle aux oeuvres politico-morales*, Travaux d'Humanisme et de Renaissance 48 (Geneva, 1976), 161–168.

[57] P.F. Moreau, 'La Paix de Dieu', in F. Châtelet *et al.*, eds., *Histoire des idéologies*, 2 vols. (Paris, 1978), II, 120–124.

[58] Redondo, *Antonio de Guevara*, 226–238, 597–598 and 691. See also J.A. Maravall, *Estado moderno y mentalidad social (Siglos XVI–XVII)*, 2 vols. (Madrid, 1972), I, 242–243 and 260–622, and his *Utopia y reformismo en la España de los Austrias* (Madrid, 1982), 353. For a bibliography on A. de Guevara, see E. Blanco, 'Bibliografía de Fray Antonio de Guevara, O.F.M. (1480?–1545)', *El Basilisco* 26 (1999) <http://www.filosofia.org/cla/gue/1999blan.htm> (consulted on 27 June 2005). See also G. Janssens, 'Barmhartig en rechtvaardig. Visies van L. de Villavicencio en J. Hopperus op de taak van de Koning', in W.P. Blockmans and H. van Nuffel, eds., *Staat en religie in de 15e en 16e eeuw. Handelingen van het colloquium te Brussel van 9 tot 12 oktober 1984* (Brussels, 1986), 25–42.

Majesty emanating to the king is already seen in Rupert of Deutz as early as the twelfth century, but it was mainly developed by John of Salisbury.[59] It was an understanding of kingship which remained widespread in early modern Spain.[60]

Clementia and *misericordia* are characteristics *par excellence* of the good and just prince, who is obliged to ensure the peace during his reign. This involved an active effort for peace and justice, for the honour of the kingdom, the integrity of its territory and the defence of the faith. Kingship is kingship by God's grace. As the representative of God on earth, the king's mission is to reign so that everyone can live well and so that peace and justice, prosperity and welfare are assured for all.[61] With the reference to Psalm 85 (84), verse 11 ('Love and fidelity have come together; justice and peace join hands'), Richardot was clearly creating a link to an image that was very current in the medieval theology of peace: true peace comes through mercy and truth, through justice and peace. Early on, even Augustine places the emphasis on justice as a condition for peace.[62]

Justice is the hallmark of the good monarch;[63] he is the just and peace-making king. Peace is not possible without justice, as can also be gleaned from medieval peace treaties.[64] Writing with the intention of restoring the sovereign's prestige after the problems raised by the Castilian Comunidades rebellion, sixteenth-century authors like Sebastián Fox Morcillo and Felipe de la Torre had emphasized that the Good King is a sovereign who brings peace;[65] although these

---

[59] M.L. Arduini, *Rupert von Deutz (1076–1129) und der 'status Christianitatis' seiner Zeit. Symbolisch-prophetische Deutung der Geschichte*, Beihefte zum Archiv für Kulturgeschichte 25 (Colone, 1987), 187.

[60] C. Lisón Tolosana, *La imagen del Rey. Monarquía, realeza y poder ritual en la Casa de los Austrias* (Madrid, 1991), 62 and 100–103.

[61] *Ibid.*, 31, 89–90, 94–95.

[62] K. Schreiner, 'Gerechtigkeit und Frieden haben sich geküßt (Ps. 84, 11). Friedensstiftung durch symbolisches Handelen', in J. Fried, ed., *Träger und Instrumentarien des Friedens im hohen und späten Mittelalter*, Vorträge und Forschungen herausgegeben vom Konstanzer Arbeitskreis für mittelalterliche Geschichte 43 (Sigmaringen, 1996), 43–46.

[63] Maravall, *Estado moderno*, II, 230; P. Molas Ribalta, *Consejos y audiencias durante el reino de Felipe II* (Valladolid, 1984), 81.

[64] Schreiner, 'Gerechtigkeit und Frieden haben sich geküßt', 45.

[65] S. Fox Morcillo, *De Regni regisque institutione libri III* (Antwerp, 1556); F. de la Torre, *Institución de un rey christiano, colegida principalmente de la santa Escritura, y de sagrados Doctores* (Antwerp, 1556). On these authors, see R.W. Truman, *Spanish Treatises on Government, Society and Religion in the Time of Philip II* (Leiden, 1999), 39–88.

Spaniards, such as Joachim Hopperus, and also François Richardot, see the announcement of the royal general pardon as a means of re-establishing the authority of the king and strengthening the Catholic religion. Through the pardon the painful episode of profanation and iconoclasm can be brought to a close. The law has acted and justice has been done; now peace has another chance. The theme of '*iustitia et pax*' appears in the same context and with reference to the text of the same psalm in *Seduardus, sive de vera iurisprudentia* by Joachim Hopperus.[66] This is an indication that the views of Richardot and Hopperus on justice and peace and on the mission of the king run in parallel. It is significant to point out here that Hopperus played an important part in the writing of various draft texts for the General Pardon and that he was clearly convinced that justice, mercy and peace always coincide.[67]

To explain that, for the sake of the just, vengeance against wicked men is sometimes suspended, Richardot refers to verse 13 from the second letter of James: 'mercy triumphs over judgement'.[68] In the reference to Psalm 85 (84), verse 11 ('*misericordia et veritas obviaverunt sibi, iustitia et pax osculatae sunt*') an echo can also be heard of the end of the prologue of the gospel of John (Jn. 1, 17: 'for while the Law was given through Moses, grace and truth came through Jesus Christ') and verse 14 of the sixth chapter of Paul's letter to the Romans (Rom. 6, 14: 'for sin shall no longer be your master, because you are no longer under law, but under the grace of God'). So the grace of God transcends the law. Grace and compassion bring peace. In the General Pardon all this becomes a reality.

In his sermon, François Richardot emphasized that the sovereign must take care of the temple. Here, as in the eulogy for Charles V, the comparison with King Solomon is never far away. In his 1558 homily Richardot names King Solomon, son of David, in the same breath as King Philip II, son of Charles V. This is because both kings are to continue and finish their father's work. In 1558 Richardot

---

[66] J. Hopperus, *Seduardus, sive de vera iurisprudentia, ad regem, libri XII* (Antwerp, 1590), 21 and 336, cited in G. Janssens, 'Doctrina y oficio del rey según el consejero Hoppero (J. Hopperus)', *Lias. Sources and Documents Relating to the Early Modern History of Ideas* 9 (1982), 137–161, there 138 and 141. On Hopperus, G. Janssens, 'Hopperus, Joachim', in Hillerbrand, ed., *The Oxford Encyclopedia of the Reformation*, II, 254–255.

[67] On the role of Hopperus, see Soen, 'Geen pardon zonder paus!', 107.

[68] Richardot, *Sermon*, 4–5: 'superexcellat autem misericordia iudicium'.

urges the young Philip II to 'use his power and property' to support 'the ruins of the true temple of God, which is the church'. This is, in his opinion, 'urgently needed, in view of the events of the present time'.[69] The king is thus the defender of the temple, the protector of peace and unity, and able to act as a good and learned physician, namely 'driving out the bad humours from the body and preserving the good', in other words 'banishing and driving out the defects from society and preserving virtue in it'.[70] Here Richardot is establishing a link to the common and well-known image of the king-physician.[71]

With his image of the three doors of the 'temple' Richardot is probably taking his inspiration from John 10, 9 ('I am the door; anyone who comes into the fold through me shall be safe'). Later come the words 'I am the good shepherd' (Jn. 10, 11). This connects with the image of the Good Shepherd. The mission of the king was to preserve the church community and the true religion and ensuring that the door by which the reconciled can re-enter is held fully open. Philip II is firmly convinced of this. He wrote to the duke of Alba that 'To take care of religion is the most important task that I have'.[72]

There was also a message for the duke of Alba, the representative of law and order, by advocating a less repressive approach. Richardot's strong emphasis on clemency meant that, in his opinion, it was necessary to extend the principle of clemency beyond the pardon itself and for it to be applied more generally in Alba's government in the Netherlands. This opinion was shared by Viglius, president of the Council of State, who commented in a letter to Hopperus that the most clement version of the pardon was not pub-

---

[69] Janssens, 'El sermón fúnebre', 354; P. Van Peteghem, 'Une Oraison funèbre', 278–283.

[70] 'Expulser les maulvaises humeurs et conserver les bonnes: c'est à dire, comme dit Platon, de bannir et chasser les vices de la republicque, et y maintenir la vertu', see Richardot, Sermon, 21.

[71] Janssens, 'Brabant in het verweer', 121–122, with reference to D. Lagomarsino, 'Furió Ceriol y sus Avisos acerca de los Estados Bajos', Bulletin Hispanique 80 (1978), 88–107, there 98–99.

[72] 'La religión, es el principal cuydado que yo tengo', Philip II to the duke of Alba, s.d. [1570?], AGS, Estado, leg. n° 544, fol. 154. On the 'Good Shepherd King', see Janssens, 'Brabant in het verweer', 386–418 and Truman, Spanish Treatises, 82, 85–86.

lished.[73] Later, in May 1573, Richardot, together with Bishop Martin Rythovius from Ypres and Abbot Jean Lantailleur from the Benedictine Abbey of Anchin, expressed his concerns in a letter to the king on the political events taking place in the Netherlands. In their letter these three prelates also expressly criticize the policy of the duke of Alba.[74] Like a number of other loyal people and groups – among them the theological faculty of Louvain[75] – François Richardot did not hesitate to criticize the policy of the governor, when the welfare of the Netherlands and the future of the monarchy are in jeopardy.[76]

It is unclear whether Richardot knew the writings of his older contemporary Antonio de Guevara or whether he even understood Spanish. There were various editions of the works of this Spanish Friar Minor circulating at the time, both in the *Libro aureo de Marco Aurelio* – including one edition published in 1529 in Antwerp by Joannes Graphaeus – and in the *Relóx de Príncipes*. In 1540 a French translation of the latter work by Estienne Caveiller also appeared in Paris.[77] It is also not certain whether Richardot was familiar with the works by Fadrique Furió Ceriol (1559), Sebastián Fox Morcillo (1556) and Felipe de la Torre (1556), that were published in Antwerp. He was no doubt aware of the ideas of the 'Mirrors of Princes', written in the tradition of Giles of Rome and John of Salisbury.[78]

---

[73] Viglius to Hopperus, 22 August 1570 in *Analecta Belgica in sex partes divisa*, ed. C.P. Hoynck van Papendrecht, 3 vols. (The Hague, 1743), II, ii, 574. On Viglius, see D. Doyle, 'Viglius, Joachim van Aytta van Zuychem', in Hillerbrand, ed., *The Oxford Encyclopedia of the Reformation*, IV, 235–236.

[74] Janssens, '*Brabant in het verweer*', 198.

[75] The theological faculty of the University of Louvain to Alba, 18 May 1573, see F.X. de Ram, 'Les Docteurs de la faculté de théologie de Louvain et le duc d'Albe', *Bulletin de l'Académie Royale des Sciences, des Lettres et des Beaux-Arts de Belgique*, 1st series, 22 (1855), 183–190.

[76] On loyal resistance in the Netherlands, see G. Janssens, 'El oficio del Rey y la oposición leal en Flandes contra Felipe II', in J. Martínez Millán, ed., *Felipe II (1527–1598). Europa y la Monarquía Católica*, 4 vols. (Madrid, 1998), I, i.

[77] Redondo, *Antonio de Guevara*, 758–759.

[78] On Giles of Rome [Aegidius Romanus], see D. Guttierez, 'Gilles de Rome', in M. Viller *et al.*, eds., *Dictionnaire de spiritualité*, 17 vols. (Paris, 1932–95), VI, 385–390, and Ch.F. Briggs, *Giles of Rome's* De regimine principum. *Reading and Writing Politics at Court and University, c. 1275–c. 1525*, Cambridge Studies in Paleography and Codicology 5 (Cambridge, 1999), 9–19. On John of Salisbury, see D.E. Luscombe, 'Jean de Salisbury', in Viller *et al.*, ed., *Dictionnaire de spiritualité* (Paris, 1974), VIII, 716–721.

His earlier homily in 1558 suggests that one possible influence on Richardot were the theological and exegetical writings of Rupert of Deutz,[79] a number of whose works were printed in Cologne during the first half of the sixteenth century.[80] Deutz had argued that Bible preaching was a task for every priest and above all for prelates.[81] Richardot had been the author of guidelines concerning the exercise of the priestly office and specifically on the administration of the sacraments.[82] In his sermon on the occasion of the pardon, he specifically emphasized the pastoral duty of priests, which may reflect the influence of Rupert of Deutz.[83] This is a tentative suggestion, but it is certainly true that Rupert of Deutz emphasized God's mercy by referring to the scriptural texts which are also referred to in Richardot's homily. Hence in *Liber de divinis officiis*, when Rupert is speaking about baptism, he expressly quotes from Psalm 85 (84), verse 11 ('*misericordia et veritas obviaverunt sibi, iustitia et pax osculatae sunt*'). In this way Rupert is emphasizing that in baptism God's mercy and peace become a reality for mankind.[84] Also in Rupert's *De sancta trinitate et operibus eius*, he comments on both this verse from the Psalm and verse 13 from the second chapter of the letter of James ('*superexcellat autem misericordia iudicium*').[85]

Although Richardot's sermon was a response to the field preaching of 1566, its contents represented the logical continuation of the principles expressed in the sermon delivered in 1558 concerning the

[79] As I argued in my study of the homily for the funerary oration of Charles V in 1558, see Janssens, 'El sermón fúnebre', 356–357.

[80] In the Stiftsbibliothek of Xanten there are two editions (1526 and 1549) of *De divinis officiis*, see *Katalog der Stiftsbibliothek Xanten*, ed. H. Föhl and A. Benger (Kevelaer, 1986), 292. The library of the theological faculty of the KU Leuven owns an edition of *De operibus Sanctae Trinitatis* (1539). See *Early Sixteenth Century Printed Books 1501–1540 in the Library of the Leuwen Faculty of Theology. Supplement. Ten years of Acquisitions 1994–2004*, ed. F. Gistelinck and L. Knapen (Louvain, 2004), 77.

[81] J.H. van Engen, *Rupert of Deutz*, Publications of the UCLA Center for Medieval and Renaissance Studies 18 (Berkeley, 1983), 271.

[82] F. Richardot, *Ordonnances faictes aux curez et recteurs . . . du diocese d'Arras, touchant plusieurs choses concernant leur office. Et principalement sur l'administration des saincts Sacremens* (Antwerp, 1562). See also Duflot, *Un Orateur*, 115–117.

[83] Richardot, *Sermon*, 40.

[84] Rupertus Tuitiensis, *Liber de divinis oficiis*, ed. H. Haacke, Corpus Christianorum. Continuatio Mediaevalis 7 (Turnhout, 1967), 224.

[85] Rupertus Tuitiensis, *De sancta trinitate et operibus eius*, ed. H. Haacke, Corpus Christianorum. Continuatio Mediaevalis 21 and 23 (Turnhout, 1971–72), I, 408 and II, 1623.

divine origin of the king's power. In his homily Richardot addresses his listeners directly. First of all the sermon is intended for those who want to reconcile themselves with the Church and the king. They are emphatically urged to take this step and told that they will be able to rely upon the mercy of the king and the Catholic church. In 1566, Protestant preachers instigated their audience to abolish all images and to turn away from the Roman Catholic Church. Now dissidents are invited by the bishop to come back to this church. It is hard to know how influential the sermon was, but in the city of Antwerp 14,128 reconciliations took place, which is remarkable considering the many excluded, e.g. Protestant preachers, elders, consistory members and iconoclasts.[86] The homily was only one aspect of the carefully directed ceremony surrounding the publication of the pardon which served to demonstrate the mercy of the king. By rejecting merciless repression, Richardot highlighted the virtues of the king and made it clear that, for him, Philip II was the Good Shepherd.

---

[86] Janssens, '*Brabant in het verweer*', 166–167.

CHAPTER SEVEN

RESISTANCE AND THE CELEBRATION OF PRIVILEGES
IN SIXTEENTH-CENTURY BRABANT

Guido Marnef

Although the violation of privileges through the repressive heresy
legislation of Philip II is regarded as a key factor in the outbreak of
the Revolt of the Netherlands, the rights and autonomy of the urban
elites had gradually been eroded during the first half of the sixteenth
century by the centralizing policies and state formation undertaken
by Charles V. The establishment of new central institutions and of
an extensive standing army, necessary for the Emperor's many wars,
presented a real threat to the cities. The outbreak of urban protest
and revolt – usually as a result of particular vested interests – and
the subsequent repression by the emperor led to a reduction of the
political influence of the guilds and to a loss of urban autonomy in
general.[1] At the same time, Charles V and his central government
still needed the consent of the Estates when he asked for an (extraordinary) subsidy, which resulted in time-consuming consultations
and bargaining.[2]

Charles V went further and sought to alter the privileges enjoyed
by the towns which were enshrined in the terms of the *Joyeuse Entrée*.
On 23 May 1549 the States of Brabant assembled in the presence
of Charles V and the regent Mary of Hungary. Philip was prepared
to swear to uphold the terms of the *Joyeuse Entrée* as future heir, but
Charles V made it clear that there were some points which were
not workable and others which did not further the welfare and the
tranquility of the country. Therefore, he asked the States to start a

---

[1] G. Marnef, 'The Towns and the Revolt', in G. Darby, ed., *The Origins and Development of the Dutch Revolt* (London and New York, 2001), 89–90, with further literature, where, for Brabant, I am discussing the revolts and collective actions in 's-Hertogenbosch (1525) and Brussels (1528 and 1532). I am preparing an article on the subject of collective actions in sixteenth-century Brussels.

[2] See for interesting examples P. Gorissen, *De prelaten van Brabant onder Karel V (1515–1544). Hun confederatie (1534–1544)*, Standen en Landen 6 (Leuven, 1953).

process of consultation in order to revise the *Joyeuse Entrée*.[3] Eventually, the States revised several articles, principally to the advantage of the prince.[4]

By the early 1570s, the political climate had dramatically changed as a result of the events of 1566–67, the subsequent repression of the Netherlands under the duke of Alba and the seizure of Den Briel and Vlissingen, followed by many of the towns of Holland and Zeeland, by the Sea Beggars and the forces of William of Orange in 1572. In these circumstances, it was possible for the urban authorities to reassert their privileges and re-evaluate their constitutional relationship with their prince. The debate over privileges that took place during this period and in particular within the province of Brabant – one of the key provinces in the Low Countries – did much to shape the political culture of the Dutch Revolt and the eventual identity of the emergent Republic.

During 1574 the States of Brabant became particularly politically active, especially the members of the third estate, represented by the four provincial cities of Antwerp, Brussels, Louvain and 's-Hertogenbosch, which formulated various complaints and demands. They regarded the timing as propitious, following the departure from the Low Countries of the duke of Alba at the end of 1573. His vigorous policy was associated with many evils: a harsh repression of political and religious dissidents, an unsparing war, new taxes, and a profound disrespect for ancient privileges and customs. The political leaders of the Brabantine cities hoped that the new governor, Luis de Requesens, would be able to meet their demands.[5] Being faced with important Dutch military successes from the very beginning, Requesens had to face a difficult situation. Middelburg, the last royalist stronghold at Walcheren, was captured by the rebels on 18 February 1574 and to make matters worse the underpaid Spanish

---

[3] L. Galesloot, 'Charles-Quint et les États de Brabant en 1549', *Bulletin de la Commission Royale d'Histoire*, 4th series, 10 (1882), 145–158.

[4] J. Mennes, 'De Staten van Brabant en de Blijde Inkomst van kroonprins Filips in 1549', *Standen en Landen* 18 (1959), 49–165, who presents a text edition of the *Joyeuse Entrée*, giving the text of the Entry of 1515 and the opinion of the nobility and the towns.

[5] See for the political situation in Brabant under Alba and Requesens, G. Janssens, '*Brabant in het verweer*'. *Loyale oppositie tegen Spanje's bewind in de Nederlanden van Alva tot Farnese 1567–1578* (Kortrijk-Heule, 1989), chapters 2–3.

army started to mutiny. In Antwerp, the soldiers at the citadel demanded immediate payment and at the end of April the city government was forced to grant a loan of 400,000 guilders.[6] Requesens realized that the huge amount of money needed to finance the war could not merely come from Spain and asked the States to grant a new subsidy of two million guilders.[7]

The States of Brabant were prepared to consider Requesens's request but they immediately used the occasion as an opportunity to articulate their political agenda. Already in January 1574 they sent the regent a remonstrance in which they deplored the violation of the privileges, such as the *Joyeuse Entrée*, and asked for the restoration of the old situation.[8] The Antwerp city government refused to join this remonstrance because they had their own particular complaints and requests.[9] Antwerp had, indeed, suffered more than any other from the duke of Alba's programme of repression and political reform. In 1571, Alba had appointed a governor who not only commanded the Spanish garrison but also possessed far-reaching judicial and administrative power. At the same time, he created two new institutions: a Treasury that controlled the Antwerp city finances and a Council of Justice, competent in all criminal cases and in civil matters involving more than 200 guilders. Both institutions were dominated by those loyal to Alba.[10]

---

[6] G. Parker, *The Dutch Revolt* (2nd ed.; Harmondsworth, 1985), 164–165, and his, *El ejército de Flandes y el Camino Español 1567–1659* (Madrid, 1986), 236–237; J.L. Motley, *The Rise of the Dutch Republic. A History* (London, 1882), 562–565; F. Prims, *Geschiedenis van Antwerpen*, 8 vols. (Brussels, 1982), VI.A, 77–78.

[7] H. Pirenne, *Histoire de Belgique*, 7 vols. (Brussels, 1900–32), IV, 51; H.G. Koenigsberger, *Monarchies, States Generals and Parliaments. The Netherlands in the Fifteenth and Sixteenth Centuries* (Cambridge, 2001), 237; Claude de Mondoucet to the king of France, 12 February 1574, in *Lettres et négociations de Claude de Mondoucet résident de France aux Pays-Bas (1571–1574)*, ed. L. Didier, 2 vols. (Paris and Reims, 1892), II, 114; Stadsarchief Antwerpen (henceforth: SAA), *Privilegiekamer*, 2359, undated memorandum by the States of Brabant. It is remarkable that the traditional histories of the Dutch Revolt do not pay attention to Requesens dealings with the States of the loyal provinces.

[8] The submission of the *remonstrance* is mentioned in the letter of the Antwerp magistracy to the deputies in Brussel, 18 January 1574, in SAA, *Privilegiekamer*, 2409.

[9] Antwerp magistracy to the deputies in Brussel, 4 February 1574, in SAA, *Privilegiekamer*, 2409.

[10] G. Marnef, *Antwerp in the Age of Reformation. Underground Protestantism in a Commercial Metropolis, 1550–1577* (Baltimore and London, 1996), 116–117. Frédéric Perrenot, lord of Champagney and younger brother of Cardinal Granvelle was appointed governor of Antwerp.

As a consequence, the Antwerp city fathers did their utmost to turn back the clock and regain their former power. Two aldermen and a pensionary resided almost permanently in Brussels, where they lobbied Requesens at court and through central government.[11] While these deputies were active in Brussels, the magistracy commissioned two other aldermen and a town secretary or a clerk (*griffier*) with the explicit charge to search and record 'the contraventions of the old rights, privileges, costumes, and usages of the Land of Brabant'. Furthermore, they were asked to make an inventory of the looting and other offences committed by Spanish soldiers.[12] At the same time, the Brussels city government turned to their archives, examining old charters and privileges. In particular it was the representatives known as the Nine Nations who were most active. The Nine Nations united the deans and sworn men of the craft guilds and the hundred men of the civic militia.[13] They constituted the third member of the Broad Council and had a fixed number of places in the town magistracy. In the wake of the 1477 revolts, the Nine Nations had succeeded in strengthening their position in the city government, but only a few years later, in 1480, Maximilian of Austria and Mary of Burgundy had restored the privileged place of the traditional patrician families.[14] Charles V continued the process of 'aristocratization' within the Brussels city government.[15] Yet, the Nine Nations always tried to maintain a critical voice in the Broad Council, for instance when the regent asked the States of Brabant to grant a subsidy.[16]

Against this background, it is hardly surprising that the States of Brabant, including the Antwerp city government and the Nine Nations,

---

[11] See their correspondence in SAA, *Privilegiekamer*, 2409, and SAA, *Privilegiekamer*, 551, fol. 70r° (commission for two aldermen and pensionary Engelbert Maes, 15 April 1574).

[12] Antwerp magistracy to the deputies in Brussel, 18 January 1574, in SAA, *Privilegiekamer*, 2409.

[13] A study of the social profile of the representatives of the Nine Nations in the 1570s is still needed in order to put their ideas in an adequate social context.

[14] F. Favresse, ed., 'Documents relatifs à l'histoire politique intérieure de Bruxelles de 1477–1480', *Bulletin de la Commission Royale d'Histoire* 98 (1934), 51–75. R. van Uytven, '1477 in Brabant', in W.P. Blockmans, ed., *1477. Le Privilège general et les privilèges régionaux de Marie de Bourgogne pour les Pays-Bas* (Kortrijk, 1985), 253–258.

[15] Cf. for instance the regulations of 18 June 1528 imposed by Charles V, printed in *Den luyster ende glorie van het hertoghdom van Brabant* (Brussels, 1699), 111–118. These regulations reduced the influence of the Nine Nations to the advantage of the seven patrician lineages (*geslachten*).

[16] See for an excellent exemple A. Louant, 'Les Nations de Bruxelles et les États de Brabant de 1556–1557', *Bulletin de la Commission Royale d'Histoire* 99 (1935), 223–250.

tried to profit from Requesens's relative weakness. Their investigations into the ancient rights and privileges of Brabant reveal one of the fundamental characteristics of the Brabantine political culture: the use of the elaborate constitutional tradition as a vehicle for the preservation of the power of the representative bodies. Within this system, power was exercised through a carefully determined institutional framework enshrined in the specific charters and privileges that were the cornerstone of their strong constitutional tradition. It was especially during times of political crises – for instance when there was a succession problem within the ducal dynasty – that there was bargaining with the prince and which in a number of cases led to the granting of charters favorable to the whole duchy or to specific States or towns.[17] The representatives of the Antwerp and Brussels city government focused on these moments in Brabantine history in which the States, and especially the towns, succeeded in limiting the power of the Lord, the duke of Brabant. This is very clear in an extensive resolution drawn up by the Nine Nations of Brussels in 1574.[18]

First of all, they emphasized the great suffering, calamities and violence that had taken place in the Land of Brabant for almost seven years – in other words since the arrival of the duke of Alba. They then went on to look at particular periods in the Brabantine constitutional tradition. It is interesting to present here a brief survey of these phases because this reveals the arguments and priorities of the Nine Nations:

– 27 September 1312, Duke John II granted the Charter of Kortenberg promising that his subjects were free from service and obedience while he did not remedy the failings and shortcomings in the Land of Brabant.[19]

---

[17] H.A. Lloyd, 'Constitutionalism', in J.H. Burns and M. Goldie, eds., *The Cambridge History of Political Thought 1450–1700* (Cambridge, 1991), and for developments in Brabant in a crucial period P. Avonds, *Brabant tijdens de regering van Hertog Jan III (1312–1356)* I, *De grote politieke krisissen* (Brussels, 1984), and II, *Land en instellingen* (Brussels, 1991).

[18] SAA, Pk., 2359, undated. The document is headed 'States General 1574' which seems to indicate that the *memorandum* was compiled for the States General assembled in Brussels on 4 June 1574.

[19] See the text of this charter in J. van der Straeten, *Het Charter en de Raad van Kortenberg*, 2 vols. (Leuven, 1952), II, 12*–19*.

- 12 July 1314, the Walloon Charter confirmed that privileges and charters of abbots, towns and Land of Brabant would be 'permanent and steadfast'.[20]
- 17 August 1332, Duke John III confirmed the Charter of Kortenberg for the whole duchy so that the Land of Brabant would be treated with justice and truth.[21]
- 6 November 1362, Duke Wenceslas and his wife Johanna promised that they would not ask their subjects for a subsidy or services, except in very specific cases.
- 8 March 1355, the towns and liberties of Brabant made an agreement 'in honour and to the profit of the duke', promising to maintain each others' charters, privileges and customs. This agreement was renewed on 28 February 1372 when Duke Wenceslas and Johanna promised justice for the towns and liberties and to maintain charters and privileges, particularly the Charter of Kortenberg and the Walloon Charter.
- At the *Joyeuse Entrée* of Wenceslas and Johanna in 1356, the Charter of Kortenberg and the Walloon Charter were explicitly confirmed, together with all privileges, charters and usages.[22] If the duke or one of his ministers contravened these agreements, they were no longer due service or obedience.
- 17 September 1372, Duke Wenceslas and Johanna confirmed the Charter of Kortenberg and the Walloon Charter.[23] No service or obedience was needed should the duke contravene one of these charters.
- 4 November 1415, the three States of Brabant promised to maintain and further each others' privileges and rights.
- 14 May 1421, an edict of Duke John IV stated that some members of the Council of Kortenberg were publicly disciplined in Leuven because they had contributed to the duke's alienation of his subjects, whereupon the States of Brabant elected a '*ruwaard*' or governor. In this edict, John IV confirmed that in case of non-observance of the edicts 'the three States with most of their

---

[20] Not in 1313 as mentioned in the document of the Nine Nations.
[21] The text in Van der Straeten, *Het Charter en de Raad van Kortenberg*, II, 27*–29*.
[22] Cf. article 34 of the *Joyeuse Entrée* of 1356, in R. van Braght, *De Blijde Inkomst van de hertogen van Brabant Johanna en Wenceslas (3 januari 1356)*, Standen en Landen 13 (Louvain, 1956), 105.
[23] The text in Van der Straeten, *Het Charter en de Raad van Kortenberg*, II, 32*–42*.

followers – which are the Nine Nations – are entitled to elect a *Rouwaert* [...] to the better welfare and profit of our common Land of Brabant'.[24] The *ruwaard* would have as much power as a prince or lord of the country.

– The Nine Nations claimed that they did not owe the lord any service or subsidy and that these are suspended as in old times – more precisely as happened on 13 and 16 June 1479 – until his Majesty and his lords will have repaired the damage and suffering of the country committed by the soldiers. Furthermore, they added that they would not consult [in the meetings of the Broad Council] as long as the situation was not remedied. They would rather die than act against reason and justice.

This survey may seem long and repetitive but it clearly shows the direction of the Nine Nations' reasoning. First of all, they selected specific charters and precise moments in Brabantine constitutional history. It was not by accident that the Charter of Kortenberg (1312) and the Walloon Charter (1314) – and their later confirmations – figure so prominently in this document. The Charter of Kortenberg was a constitutional contract in which the duke promised the States to observe a set of obligations. Of utmost importance was the creation of a new institution, the Council of Kortenberg. This council comprised fourteen councillors – four from the nobility and ten from the towns. Louvain and Brussels each had three representatives; Antwerp, 's-Hertogenbosch, Tienen and Zoutleeuw one each. Thus the towns had a majority in the new council, so that it could be argued that the duke and his council were placed in the hands of the towns.[25] Nonetheless, we are poorly informed about how the Council of Kortenberg really functioned. There are indications that the representatives of the towns and the nobility did not meet together as one body – so that the nobles were by definition outnumbered – but that they assembled separately and then formulated their opinion.[26]

---

[24] 'Ende dat die drie Staten metten meesten gevolghe van hen dwelck zijn de natien dan souden mogen kiesen een Rouwaert die hen gelieft ende tot hunnen goetduncken tot meeste oirbaer, welvaert ende profijt ons gemeyn Landts van Brabant'.

[25] R. van Uytven, ed., *Geschiedenis van het hertogdom Brabant tot heden* (Leuven and Zwolle, 2004), 105, 118–119.

[26] P. Avonds, *Koning Artur in Brabant (12de–14de eeuw). Studies over riddercultuur en vorstenideologie* (Brussels, 1999), 111–117. I thank my Antwerp colleague Piet Avonds for this and other suggestions.

But even if we take this distinction into account, it is clear that, in
the sixteenth century, the Nine Nations regarded the Charter of
Kortenberg as a basis for urban power.

The Walloon Charter also corresponds with this pattern of urban
ascendancy. It was in the first place an answer to the financial crisis
of the duchy and placed the ducal finances and the appointment of
judicial and fiscal officers under the supervision of the States. As a
result of both charters, the towns dominated the administration of
the duchy until 1320. In fact, the towns regarded themselves as advocates of the 'common good'.[27] It is not difficult to see a parallel
between the situation of the duchy in the early fourteenth century
and the financial problems caused by the war in the 1570s.

Another obvious feature is the frequent reference to the different
confirmations of the Charter of Kortenberg and the Walloon Charter.
In contrast, the famous *Joyeuse Entrée* of 1356 is mentioned sparingly.
The Nine Nations even regarded this charter primarily as a confirmation of the Kortenberg and Walloon Charter. Joseph van der
Straeten, the author of a study on the Charter and the Council of
Kortenberg, remarks when dealing with the confirmation of 1372
that the fourteenth-century Brabanters had a clear predilection for
the Charter of Kortenberg and the Walloon Charter which they saw
as the guarantees *par excellence* for their privileges.[28] This statement
applied, of course, initially to the influential towns of Brabant.

The States of Brabant, and particularly the towns, also promised
mutual assistance in order to maintain the acquired privileges (cf.
the agreements of 1355, 1372 and 1415). The practice of mutual
assistance and of urban alliances was an old one in Brabant, going
back to 1262. It strengthened the position of the towns within the
duchy and may have contributed to the development of a 'national'
Brabantine feeling, although one should add that the many towns
were not always in harmony.[29] The Nine Nations limited the assis-

---

[27] Avonds, *Brabant tijdens de regering van Hertog Jan III*, 51–54, and for the concept
of the 'common weal' in Brabant, *idem*, '"Ghemeyn oirbaer": volkssoevereiniteit en
politieke ethiek in Brabant in de veertiende eeuw', in Joris Reynaert, ed., *Wat is
wijsheid? Lekenethiek in de Middelnederlandse letterkunde* (Amsterdam, 1994), 164–180.

[28] Van der Straeten, *Het Charter en de Raad van Kortenberg*, I, 94–95, 288–289.

[29] J. van Gerven, 'De Brabantse steden: één groep? Belangentegenstellingen en –
conflicten tussen de steden onderling van de dertiende eeuw tot de vijftiende eeuw',
BG 81 (1998), 385–406; G. Boland, 'Les Deux Versions du pacte d'alliance des
villes brabançonnes de 1261–1262', *Belgisch tijdschrift voor filologie en geschiedenis* 23
(1944), 281–289.

tance to the level of the province of Brabant and did not mention forms of inter-provincial collaboration. In this context, it is remarkable that the Nations did not refer to the old alliance between Brabant and Flanders concluded in 1339 and renewed by rebellious Brussels and Ghent in 1578.[30]

Another element prominent in the document of the Nine Nations is the idea that service and obedience were no longer due when the duke did not observe the granted charters and privileges. There was, in other words, a kind of contract theory: prince and subjects were bound by mutual rights and duties. Infringement of these rules could lead to the temporary or permanent deposition of the lord. Should this occur, there was the obvious question how to fill the gap. When referring to the edict issued by Duke John IV in May 1421, the Nine Nations explicitly mentioned the right to appoint a *ruwaard* or governor in case the duke or his ministers did not respect the laws and customs of the Land of Brabant. It is not by chance that the Nine Nations did so, since they had belonged to the most active *dramatis personae* in the turbulent 1420s. A number of nobles and towns had joined forces in 1420 and declared Duke John IV temporarily deposed and chose the duke's younger brother, Philip of Saint-Pol, as *ruwaard*. When John IV invaded the duchy with foreign troops and returned to Brussels, the craft guilds rebelled and arrested several partisans of the duke. Philip of Saint-Pol acknowledged the efforts of the Brussels craft guilds and granted them a number of places in the Brussels city government. It was also at the beginning of 1421 that the craft guilds united into Nine Nations.[31] Therefore, it is not surprising that in 1574 the events of 1421 still belonged to the 'collective memory' of the Nine Nations. The argument for the deposition of the Lord and the appointment – by the States – of a *ruwaard* was of course an option in 1574, although at

---

[30] A.C. De Schrevel, 'Le Traité d'alliance conclu en 1339 entre le Flandre et le Brabant renouvelé en 1578', in A. Cauchie *et al.*, eds., *Mélanges d'histoire offerts à Charles Moeller*, 2 vols. (Leuven and Paris, 1914), II; P. Avonds, 'Beschouwingen over het ontstaan en de evolutie van het samenhorigheidsbesef in de Nederlanden (14de–19de eeuw)', in R. van Uytven, ed., *Cultuurgeschiedenis in de Nederlanden van de Renaissance naar de Romantiek* (Leuven and Amersfoort, 1986), 45–58.

[31] Jean Baerten, 'De politieke evolutie te Brussel in de 15de eeuw', *Tijdschrift voor Brusselse Geschiedenis* 2 (1985), 111–122, esp. 112–114; F. Favresse, 'Esquisse de l'évolution constitutionelle de Bruxelles depuis le XII siècle jusqu'en 1477', in *idem*, *Études sur les métiers bruxellois au moyen âge* (Brussels, 1961), 230 ff.; Van Uytven, ed., *Geschiedenis van Brabant*, 166.

that moment a radical one.[32] The idea gained currency and there were advocates in December 1574 for a *ruwaard* to be appointed and Antwerp placed in the hands of William of Orange. The key figure in this conspiracy was Maarten Neyen, a Calvinist and clerk at the Antwerp city administration. He was accused of organizing rebellious meetings in which he enunciated the Spanish tyranny, and complained that the Spaniards 'did not observe the privileges of Brabant, pretending that there was one privilege that authorized them to nominate a '*ruwaard*' or governor. And for that function, they wanted to appoint in Antwerp William of Orange'.[33]

One might regard the ideas articulated within the Nine Nations as quite radical and it is perhaps not surprising that some of the other members of the States of Brabant, particularly the abbots and the nobility, did not fully endorse the Brussels memorandum in 1574. Yet, on other points and problems, the different members of the States of Brabant reached a consensus. They compiled, for instance, an extensive remonstrance, containing no less than 89 articles, in which they focused on the judicial administration of the duchy of Brabant. Here too, the States supported their arguments by referring to old privileges, going back to the *Joyeuse Entrée* of Philip the Good in 1430. They particularly insisted on the competence and the composition of the Council of Brabant – the provincial court of justice – and pleaded for a judicial system that did not harm the welfare of the country.[34] The claims put forward by the members of the States of Brabant and the charters and privileges they obtained had been part of a concrete process of state formation and as a consequence subjected to changing power relations. Already in the 1960s Raymond van Uytven emphasized that the impact of the Brabantine charters can not be overestimated. They were, indeed, important milestones in the development of a strong constitutional tradition, but they could be revoked or neglected once the Lord regained power.[35]

---

[32] The possibility of appointing a *ruwaard* in 1574 was not further elaborated by the Nine Nations, although we must emphasize that archives related to the Nine Nations' activities and the States General of 1574 are not abundant.

[33] Luis de Requesens to Philip II, 13 March 1575, in L.P. Gachard, ed., *Correspondance de Philippe II*, III, 268–269. Neyen, who could escape, was banished on 16 April 1575: ARAB, *Papieren van Staat en Audiëntie*, 1683/1.

[34] Undated remonstrance [1574], SAA, *Privilegiekamer*, 2439.

[35] R. van Uytven, 'De rechtsgeldigheid van de Brabantse Blijde Inkomst van

How did Luis de Requesens deal with the propositions and requests put forward by the States of Brabant and their individual members? To some extent the Spanish regent was prepared to make concessions related to institutional reform. He abolished the Council of Troubles and restored the Antwerp city government to its pre-Alba position.[36] At the same time, he continued to complain about the Brabanters' stubborn attachment to their privileges.[37] Requesens did not give in on all of the points and so the States of Brabant decided to send a representative to the king. In August 1574 Dirk van Hille left for Spain with an extensive submission dealing with the privileges and the general political situation of the land.[38] But in Madrid Van Hille was kept waiting on the court and in the end his mission did not yield any results.[39]

Although the memorandum in 1574 had focused on the Brabantine charters, the political ideas and practices of the province, and in particular the *Joyeuse Entrée* had contributed to the wider political debate over privileges since the earliest stages of the Dutch Revolt. In fact, one of the key documents of the Brabantine political tradition, the *Joyeuse Entrée*, was published as a piece of political propaganda. In 1564, 1565 and 1566 Gottfried Hirtshorn, a printer active in Cologne, produced three editions of the *Joyeuse Entrée*. Hirtshorn had Brabantine origins; from time to time he appeared in Antwerp and in Cologne he used Philip van Wesenbeke, brother of the Antwerp pensionary Jacob, as his commercial agent. Everything seems to indicate that the copies of the *Joyeuse Entrée* were primarily destined for the Antwerp market.[40] In 1564–66 there was an increasing political

3 januari 1356', *TvG* 82 (1969), 39–48; R. van Uytven and W. Blockmans, 'Constitutions and their Application in the Netherlands during the Middle Ages', *Belgisch Tijdschrift voor Filologie en Geschiedenis* 48 (1969), 399–424, especially 402–410.

[36] Instructions for the reform and renewal of the Antwerp city government, undated [late 1574] in ARAB, *Papieren van Staat en Audiëntie*, 809/12.

[37] See for instance Requesens to Philip II, 28 June and 25 July 1574, in *Nueva colección de documentos inéditos para la historia de España y sus Indias*, ed. F. de Zabálburu and J. Sancho Rayon, 6 vols. (Madrid, 1892–96), III, 151–153, and IV, 112–114.

[38] Janssens, '*Brabant in het verweer*', 227–228.

[39] P.L. Muller, 'Stukken betreffende de zending van Dirk van Hille naar Spanje van wege de Staten van Brabant 1574–1575', *BMHG* 10 (1887), 1–35.

[40] H. de la Fontaine Verwey, 'De Blijde Inkomste en de Opstand tegen Philips II', in *idem, Uit de wereld van het boek*, 4 vols. (Amsterdam, 1975–97), I, 118–120; J. Benzing, *Die Buchdrucker des 16. und 17. Jahrhunderts im deutschen Sprachgebiet* (Wiesbaden, 1982), 236, 244; P. Valkema Blauw, *Typographia Batava 1541–1600. Repertorium van boeken gedrukt in Nederland tussen 1541 en 1600*, 2 vols. (Nieuwkoop, 1998), nos. 5943, 5955.

turmoil in the Low Countries and the king was openly criticized for his strict religious policy. In this context, the argument that a bad Lord, who violated the rights and customs of his country, should not be obeyed undoubtedly found a willing audience in dissident circles. In the 1570s there were at least three other editions of the *Joyeuse Entrée* published, one in Delft (1574) and two in Cologne (1577, 1578).[41]

It is certainly not a coincidence that a number of influential Calvinist propagandists, who used arguments from the *Joyeuse Entrée* and from the Brabantine constitutional tradition in general, were born or active in Brabant. Gilles le Clercq, a Calvinist leader and a go-between between consistories and confederate nobility, was from Tournai but during the *Wonderjaar* was mainly active in Antwerp. In a commentary on the Request of the nobility, he explicitly drew upon the *Joyeuse Entrée* and stated that the placards and the actions of the Inquisition were a violation of this famous charter.[42] Another Calvinist leader, friend of William of Orange and diligent publicist of the Revolt, was Marnix van Saint-Aldegonde; a Brabantine noble-man, he was also familiar with the *Joyeuse Entrée*. In his *Libellus supplex* (1570) he referred to the privileges of Brabant as a vehicle for dis-obedience and resistance.[43] One member of the Brabantine urban political elite was Jacob van Wesenbeke, the pensionary of Antwerp (1556–66), who was a key political figure in the city and in the province beyond. During the *Wonderjaar* he became William of Orange's secretary and in 1567 he followed his master into exile. As Martin van Gelderen amply demonstrated, Van Wesenbeke's works, mainly published in 1568–69, were of great importance for the political thought of the Dutch Revolt. He emphasized three crucial values which were closely connected and essential for the welfare of the country: liberty, privileges and the States. He too frequently invoked the *Joyeuse Entrée*'s clause concerning disobedience and referred to the Brabantine constitutional tradition.[44]

---

[41] De la Fontaine Verwey, 'De Blijde Inkomste', 121–123; Valkema Blauw, *Typographia Batava*, nos. 6111, 6143.

[42] P.A.M. Geurts, 'Het beroep op de Blijde Inkomste in de pamfletten uit de Tachtjarige Oorlog', *Standen en Landen* 16 (1958), 3–15, there 4–5; M. van Gelderen, *The Political Thought of the Dutch Revolt 1555–1590* (Cambridge, 1992), 112–113.

[43] Van Gelderen, *The Political Thought*, 123–126. A text edition of an English ver-sion (1571) of this *Libellus Supplex* in Martin van Gelderen, ed., *The Dutch Revolt*, Cambridge Texts in the History of Political Thought (Cambridge, 1993).

[44] A fine analysis in Van Gelderen, *The Political Thought*, 115–119.

The conception of the trinity of liberty, privileges, and States as the cornerstone of the political order was further elaborated in the 1570s. An important exponent of these ideas was Johan Junius the younger, governor of Veere in Zeeland, who also referred to Brabantine charters, such as the *Joyeuse Entrée*. Van Gelderen remarked that after 1572 Holland became the new centre of political propaganda, but at the same time, 'the arguments continued to be Brabantine in spirit'.[45] Nonetheless what he and most authors have overlooked was that Johan Junius was originally a citizen of Antwerp. In 1553 and 1555 he was an alderman but he had left the Antwerp city government because he could not bear the prosecution of innocent Protestants. In 1580, he returned from Heidelberg to Antwerp to become a burgomaster in his home city.[46]

The constitutional rights and the political debates that centred on the province of Brabant, therefore, played a prominent role in the emerging political culture of the Dutch Republic. This is particularly well demonstrated by the discussions and arguments put forward in 1574 by the representative bodies of Brabant. Conceptions of good governance were formulated and the importance of political rights and duties were emphasized. The lord of the country was not a supreme sovereign but bound by specific rules. The great medieval Brabantine charters, marks of a strong constitutional tradition, played a crucial role in this way of reasoning. The Nine Nations of Brussels advocated the most radical ideas and developed arguments which went beyond the terms of what one might call 'loyal opposition'. For the moment, all these ideas did not lead to spectacular results, but a few years later, in 1576, after the sudden death of Requesens, the States of Brabant intensified their actions and had a profound and far reaching influence on the political developments in the Netherlands.[47]

In the late 1570s and the early 1580s Brabant once again became the centre of political life. From 1577 to 1583 – the period of the so-called Calvinist Republics in Brabant and Flanders – William of

---

[45] *Ibid.*, 130–133.
[46] Floris Prims, *Beelden uit den Cultuurstrijd*, Antwerpiensia, 15th series (Antwerp, 1942), 523–534; J.P. Blaes and A. Henne, eds., *Mémoires anonymes sur les troubles des Pays Bas 1565–1580*, 5 vols. (Brussels, 1859–66), v. 26.
[47] Janssens, '*Brabant in het verweer*', chapters 4 and 5.

Orange, the regent, the States General and the central government institutions all resided in Brussels and Antwerp. It was in these years of political and religious radicalization that the political and institutional framework of the rebellious provinces took shape. The Brabantine tradition of representative assemblies and constitutional charters continued to have an influence in the ideological pamphlet literature, including that of a radical nature.[48] At the same time, the Brabantine political culture had a deep impact on actual political developments. On 8 December 1577, the States General accepted Archduke Matthias of Austria as governor and captain-general of the Netherlands. The long list of conditions made it clear that the young governor could not make important decisions without the permission and approval of the States General. Furthermore, he was obliged to restore all ancient privileges, usages and customs which had been violated or forcibly removed.[49] Such statements had a resonance in the political arguments articulated by the Nine Nations of Brussels and of the Brabantine constitutional tradition in general. A few years later, the Frisian lawyer Agge Albada, who played an important role at the peace conference of Cologne in 1579, explicitly linked the conditions imposed upon Matthias with the Brabantine privileges. In his *Acten van den vredehandel geschiet te Colen*, published in 1581, he commented that:

> In the privileges of Brabant it is explicitly stated that even if the prince himself (not to mention the prince's deputy) should break the laws and rights of the country, not only the States in general, but every one concerned of whatever rank he might be, is allowed to refuse him obedience and respect, for as long as the king fails to comply entirely with the statutes and privileges. But a person appointed by the prince to act as governor, who undertakes something against the statutes and privileges, is considered by such deeds to have immediately forfeited his office and must be regarded by the whole population as being dismissed.[50]

---

[48] See for instance the *Emanuel-Erneste. Dialogue de deux personnages sur l'estat des Païs Bas* (Antwerp, 1580) by Gerard Prouninck van Deventer, a former town secretary of 's-Hertogenbosch, analysed in Van Gelderen, *The Political Thought*, 146–147, and Geurts, 'Beroep op de Blijde Inkomste', 12–13. See also the excerpt in E.H. Kossmann and A.F. Mellink, eds., *Texts Concerning the Revolt of the Netherlands* (Cambridge, 1974), esp. 209–210.

[49] See the articles in *ibid.*, 141–144.

[50] Quoted in *ibid.*, 199. See on Albada, W. Bergsma, *Aggaeus van Albada (c. 1525–1587), schwenckfeldiaan, staatsman en strijder voor verdraagzaamheid* (n.p., 1983).

Furthermore, Albada referred to the deposition of Duke John IV in 1421 and the election of his brother Philip of Saint-Pol as *ruwaard*,[51] a political event that belonged to the collective memory of the Brussels Nine Nations. At the time Matthias of Austria was accepted, the Nine Nations, and the committee of Eighteen, chosen from the milieu of the Nations, exercised considerable political influence in Brussels and even put the States General under pressure.[52] The notion of a '*ruwaard*' was introduced once again and at the instigation of the Nine Nations William of Orange was elected by the States General as *ruwaard* or particular governor of Brabant.[53]

When in 1580 the States General started negotiations with François de Valois, duke of Anjou and brother of the French king, the Antwerp magistrates referred to the old family ties between the dukes of Brabant and – through the dukes of Burgundy – the French dynasty. At the same time, Philip II could be rejected because he was not inclined to peace and brought tyranny upon city and country. As a consequence, it was permissible to forsake the Spanish king, invoking the Brabantine privileges, such as the *Joyeuse Entrée*, and natural law.[54] It will be no surprise that in the Act of Abjuration and the *Plakkaat van Verlatinghe* the classical elements of liberty, privileges and the States, central to the Brabantine discourse, were still present.[55]

---

[51] Kossman and Mellink, eds., *Texts*, 199.

[52] G. Marnef, 'Het protestantisme te Brussel onder de "Calvinistische Republiek", ca. 1577–1585', in W.P. Blockmans and H. van Nuffel, eds., *Staat en religie in de 15ᵉ en 16ᵉ eeuw* (Brussels, 1986), 240, and 277, note 55.

[53] See the letters by the Antwerp deputies in Brussels to the magistracy, 6, 7 and 20 January 1578, in SAA, *Privilegiekamer*, 2398, and A.C. de Schrevel, ed., *Recueil de documents relatifs aux troubles religieux en Flandre, 1577–1584*, 3 vols. (Bruges, 1921–28), I, 176–177 (excerpts from the resolutions of the States General, 8 and 9 January 1578).

[54] Cf. the propositions and deliberations within the Antwerp Broad Council from May until July 1580, in SAA, *Privilegiekamer*, and State Archives Antwerp, *Fonds stad Antwerpen*. I will elaborate this point in a book on the Calvinist Republic in Antwerp.

[55] *Plakkaat van Verlatinge 1581. Inleiding, transcriptie en vertaling in hedendaags Nederlands*, ed., introd. and transl. M.E.H.N. Mout (The Hague, 1979), 53 ff. Politicians from Brabant had an active share in the preparation and the redaction of the *Plakkaat*.

CHAPTER EIGHT

JUSTUS LIPSIUS BETWEEN WAR AND PEACE. HIS PUBLIC LETTER ON SPANISH FOREIGN POLICY AND THE RESPECTIVE MERITS OF WAR, PEACE OR TRUCE (1595)*

Nicolette Mout

The state and its rulers called forth a great deal of discussion among humanists. They endlessly and eloquently wrote about a surprisingly unvarying series of topics: the nature of kingship and political power, the relationship between the ruler and the law, the ruler's duty to his subjects, the relationship between the ruler and his counsellors and/or the country's representative institutions, and the education of princes. In humanist political discourse political wisdom ('*prudentia*') was singled out among the virtues and usually contrasted with damaging irrational behaviour springing from sheer lust for power. In sixteenth-century humanist circles north of the Alps, moral philosophy and political advice often went hand in hand, producing such works as Erasmus's *The Education of a Christian Prince* (1516) and Jean Bodin's *Six livres de la république* (1576). However, humanists disseminated their ideas not just in books, but in a variety of ways, of which personal communication by letter was one. Political issues appeared frequently in their letters, albeit often in the guise of news items or short political statements only, and political advice was sometimes given in the form of a public letter. During the 1350s, for instance, Petrarch wrote a number of public letters to Emperor Charles IV, urging him to come to Rome for his imperial coronation, in the hope that the emperor would use the opportunity to put the affairs of Italy in order.[1] Such public letters on topical subjects came close to the genre of political orations, in which the speaker

* My heartfelt thanks to the editor of the *Iusti Lipsi Epistolae* VIII, Dr Jeanine de Landtsheer (Louvain), without whose help this article could not have been written.
[1] F.-R. Hausmann, 'Francesco Petrarcas Briefe an Kaiser Karl IV. als "Kunstprosa"', in F.J. Worstbrock, ed., *Der Brief im Zeitalter der Renaissance* (Weinheim, 1983).

dealt with comparable subject matters.[2] Political orations as well as
public letters on political topics, especially when they were uncalled
for by the ruler, were not without their dangers, as they exposed
the speaker's or writer's views, which might be judged improper by
the ruler. During the turbulent sixteenth century, therefore, most
humanists would take great care not to offend the authorities by giving a boldly controversial public speech or writing a public letter
that might give them offence. It is only too true that by the end of
the sixteenth century 'for the most part humanism had been tamed
into conformity to the needs of absolute monarchies and established
churches'.[3]

Why, then, would an illustrious scholar such as Justus Lipsius
(1547–1606) want to meddle in politics? Why, in the beginning of
the year 1595, did he write a long letter on Spanish foreign policy?
By that time Lipsius was firmly ensconced in academic life. His position as professor of History and Latin at Louvain University was
unassailable. He was basking in his well-deserved fame as a philol-
ogist, philosopher, and historian. Although his letter was sent as a
private missive to Francisco de San Víctores de la Portilla, a Spanish
nobleman and captain in the service of the Brussels government who
had married into an Antwerp family, its contents were very soon
divulged and even translated from the original Latin into French.
At first Lipsius denied being its author, stating that he would only
have written in Latin. To the influential Dutch politician Cornelis
Aerssens he conceded that he had written the letter in Latin, but
said that he addressed it only to one person, and had kept no copies.
The latter point was untrue because he was able to tell the Leiden
printer Franciscus Raphelengius Jr. that the French translation of
the letter was not correct. In fact Lipsius had encouraged the addressee
San Víctores to share the contents of the letter with others as he
saw fit. No wonder, then, that the letter lived on in the form of
manuscript copies as well as printed pamphlets in several languages

---

    [2] H. Hardt, 'Poggio Bracciolini und die Brieftheorie des fünfzehnten Jahrhunderts.
Zur Gattungsform des humanistischen Briefs', in Worstbrock, ed., *Der Brief im Zeitalter
der Renaissance*, 91–92; A. Grafton, 'Humanism and Political Theory', in J.H. Burns
and M. Goldie, eds., *The Cambridge History of Political Thought 1450–1700* (Cambridge,
1991), 9–10.
    [3] Ch.G. Nauert, Jr., *Humanism and the Culture of Renaissance Europe* (Cambridge,
1995), 195.

until *c.* 1621, the year that the Twelve Years' Truce between Spain and the Dutch Republic ended. Pieter Christiaansz Bor printed the full text in a Dutch translation in the fourth volume of his history of the Dutch Revolt, *Nederlandsche Oorlogen* (Amsterdam, 1621). Another important historian of the Revolt, Emanuel van Meteren, provided a summary in his *Historie der Neder-landscher [. . .] Oorlogen* (The Hague, 1614), naming Lipsius as the probable author.

The letter dealt with the current state of European politics as seen from the perspective of King Philip II of Spain. Should the king continue the current wars against his three enemies: the French, the English, and the Dutch rebels, or should he seek peace with them, or perhaps conclude a truce?[4] The 1590s were a time of economic and political crisis for the Spanish monarchy. Excessive taxation, shortage of capital, bad harvests, together with the government's excessive debts caused by its aggressive foreign policy and military involvement in the Old and New World alike led to economic recession and political unrest. Spanish support for the French Catholics meant a heavy drain on the treasury, for Philip II not only financed several costly military expeditions into France, but also paid for a number of Spanish garrisons and he directly subsidized the French Catholic League with substantial sums. At the same time Philip II found himself with a powerful enemy at sea. The English not only supported the Dutch rebels, but they regularly attacked the Indies and took many Spanish and Portuguese ships, thereby seriously impeding the monarchy's transatlantic trade. The Dutch, too, took many Hispanic prizes at sea and in 1591–92 their army, led by the young stadholder and gifted general Maurice of Nassau, succeeded in reconquering the greater parts of the Dutch eastern provinces Overijssel and Gelderland. The town of Groningen was successfully besieged in 1594: its capture meant that the northern provinces Friesland and Groningen were now completely incorporated into the budding Dutch Republic. For the Spanish king, victory over the rebels in the Northern Netherlands seemed further away than ever.

---

[4] Justus Lipsius, *ILE*, VIII: *1595*, ed. J. de Landtsheer [Brussels, 2004 (but actually published in 2005)], 95 01 02 S. For Francisco de San Víctores de Portilla, cf. *ILE*, VII: *1594*, ed. J. de Landtsheer (Brussels, 1997), 94 12 22 S. For the fate of the letter in 1595, cf. *ILE*, VIII, 95 08 09 BU; 95 08 29; 95 09 06; 95 09 11. Aerssens was clerk of the States General since 1584 and a close collaborator of Oldenbarnevelt.

To make it worse, tensions were rising at home, especially in Aragon. Rebellion broke out in Zaragoza in 1591, and although it was suppressed quickly and efficiently, Philip II was certainly frightened by the idea that he would have to deal with 'another Netherlands' within Spain itself.[5]

The Southern Netherlands, although securely under Spanish rule after the fall of Antwerp in 1585, went through a prolonged period of internal political unrest, if not crisis, after the death of their governor, Alexander Farnese, duke of Parma, in December 1592. The Spanish royal envoy Pedro Enriquez de Acevedo, count of Fuentes, surprised the Council of State by appointing, on the king's order, the army general Peter Ernst of Mansfeld as interim governor without even consulting the Council. It marked the beginning of the so-called 'Spanish Ministry' at the Brussels court: a group of Spanish advisers either sent by the king or summoned by the governors, who in due course came to dominate government consultations about foreign affairs and military matters. At first, however, the interventions of Fuentes and his colleague Esteban de Ibarra – appointed Secretary of State and War by Philip II – were not particularly successful, as the members of the Council of State tended to support Mansfeld against them. Only after the arrival of the new governor, Archduke Ernest of Austria, in January 1594, did Fuentes and Ibarra gain decisive influence on all important matters of state. Almost immediately Ibarra became the archduke's private secretary in charge of secret state correspondence and, subsequently, his political confidant. Together with other Spanish courtiers he and Fuentes succeeded in controlling the political agenda, to the exclusion of the Councils and often even of the governor himself. No wonder the Council of State and the indigenous nobility repeatedly protested against this overriding Spanish influence on the country's government. From time to time their objections even led to violent incidents involving the Spanish politicians. Finally, the general mood had become so bilious that even the politically inexperienced Archduke Ernest saw the need to appease public opinion and to come to a working agreement with the great and the good of the country. On the 2 January 1595 –

---

[5] J. Elliott, *Imperial Spain 1469–1716* (London, 1963), 279–295; G. Parker, *The Grand Strategy of Philip II* (New Haven and London, 1998), 274–275; A. Th. van Deursen, *Maurits van Nassau. De winnaar die faalde* (Amsterdam 2000), 117–140.

the very day Lipsius wrote his letter to Francisco de San Víctores –
Archduke Ernest summoned the provincial governors together with
several bishops, abbots, Knights of the Golden Fleece, members of
the Council of State and other notables to a conference in his Brussels
palace. The idea was to discuss the main problems with an open
mind, and to try and find solutions that would be acceptable to the
king as well as to the Brussels government and the population at
large. After more than two weeks of almost daily working sessions
the participants of the conference managed to set down their grievances in a document of nearly eighty pages, which was sent to King
Philip II. Predictably, the Spanish interference in what the inhabitants of the Southern Netherlands regarded as their country's internal affairs loomed largest in it. As this policy of intervention was the
result of the king's express orders, it was likely that complaints about
the 'Spanish Ministry' would fall on deaf ears. More effect could
perhaps be expected from the insistent pleas for peace in the document, as in 1594 the king himself had authorized Archduke Ernest
to offer the rebellious Dutch a peace proposal based on the Pacification
of Ghent. It was refused by Oldenbarnevelt because it would have
meant recognition of Philip II as Lord of the Netherlands – impossible after the Act of Abjuration of 1581 – and because recent attempts
on or conspiracies against the life of stadholder Maurice could
all be traced back to circles connected with the Brussels court.[6]
Nevertheless, the Brussels document of January 1595 is an eloquent
testimony to the sincere longing for peace prevalent in the war-weary
Southern Netherlands at the time, even if some realistic politicians
were, however, still counting on a prolonged war with the Dutch
rebels.[7]

---

[6] H. de Schepper, 'De katholieke Nederlanden van 1589 tot 1609', in D.P. Blok
et al., eds., Algemene Geschiedenis der Nederlanden, 15 vols. (Haarlem, 1979), VI, 280–282;
G. Parker, 'The Decision-Making Process in the Government of the Catholic
Netherlands under "the Archdukes", 1596–1621', in his Spain and the Netherlands
1559–1659. Ten Studies (London, 1979), 164–176; Van Deursen, Maurits van Nassau,
134–136; W.J.M. van Eysinga, De wording van het Twaalfjarig Bestand van 9 April 1609,
Verhandelingen der Koninklijke Nederlandse Akademie van Wetenschappen, Afd.
Letterkunde, new series, 66 no. 3 (Amsterdam, 1959), 13.
[7] The document was published as Résolutions des États généraux de 1600, ed. L.P.
Gachard (Brussels, 1849), 415–450. Cf. also L. van der Essen, 'Un "Cahier de
doléances" des principaux Conseils des Pays-Bas concernant la situation des "provinces
obéissantes" sous le gouvernement de l'archiduc Ernest', Bulletin de la Commission
Royale d'Histoire 88 (1924), 291–311.

The correspondence between Lipsius and Francisco de San Víctores about Spanish foreign policy must be considered against this background of crisis in Spain and trouble in Brussels. San Víctores, not Lipsius, took the initiative. On 22 December 1594 the Spanish nobleman wrote a letter to Lipsius about recent political developments concerning the Netherlands (and about the exceptionally severe winter weather). The good news was that Emperor Rudolf II was considering sending peace envoys to the prince-bishop of Liège and to stadholder Maurice of Nassau; the bad news was that King Henry IV of France was preparing for war against Spain and that French and English troops had taken the strategically important Spanish fortress near Brest and killed the garrison.[8] Víctores had enclosed a letter to Lipsius by Charles de Ligne, prince-count of Arenberg. This important politician had served the Brussels government as a soldier and diplomat before becoming in 1586 a Knight of the Golden Fleece and president of the Council of Finance. However, his contact with Lipsius had nothing to do with politics. Arenberg had a hobby: he had painted a number of herbs and plants, and now he wanted to organize this collection according to a botanical classification system. Maybe Lipsius could recommend a young man from Louvain who could help him with the job?[9] Unfortunately, Lipsius could not find such a person, but in his next letter to San Víctores, written on Christmas Day 1594 with frozen fingers because of the excessive winter cold, he expressed his opinion of recent political developments. The two branches of the Habsburg dynasty, in Austria and in Spain, were, according to him, favoured by the Almighty, but their rule was severely impeded by the system of government with its slow decision-making processes. Lipsius did not expect to see peace shortly, but a truce would be a good thing, and he wished that Henry IV of France would understand that peace, not war, would help him to strengthen his rule.[10] As San Víctores tells us in his reply to Lipsius, he received this letter just as he was having a political discussion with a guest, a high-ranking member of the Brussels court. He mentioned Lipsius's views, whereupon the (anonymous) guest, a nobleman who was an admirer of Lipsius, requested a fuller

---

[8] *ILE*, VII, 94 12 22 S.
[9] *Ibid.*, 94 12 21 A.
[10] *Ibid.*, 94 12 25 S.

treatment of the question: why did Lipsius prefer the conclusion of a truce to war or peace?[11]

On the following day, 2 January 1595, the nobleman's request was met. Lipsius wrote his long letter on Spanish foreign policy. Unfortunately, it is impossible to identify San Víctores's noble guest. It is suggested that it might have been the governor of Tournai, Philip de Croy, count of Solre, to whom Lipsius would address a letter in the summer of 1596 in which he dealt with similar problems. Philip de Croy was one of the politicians Archduke Ernest had summoned to his conference of January 1595. It might even have been Esteban de Ibarra, the powerful secretary of State and War, who, a fortnight later, actually discussed with Lipsius certain political problems which were related to the ones the latter had mentioned in his long letter of 2 January 1595 to San Víctores.[12]

Proof of such a discussion is to be found in another missive by Lipsius. Thanking Ibarra in a letter, written on 17 January 1595, for the enjoyable conversation and meal he had had with him the day before, Lipsius considered the question whether indifferent and slow reactions ('*frigus et tarditas*') were becoming for a prince.[13] It was not difficult to guess that Philip II was meant. The king had not visited the Netherlands since 1559. The business of governing the Netherlands and, moreover, fighting the Dutch rebels from Spain was fraught with difficulties, of which communication between the two countries was just one. Even if Philip had been quicker in his decisions, the distance between Madrid and Brussels would still have meant the slow implementation of royal policies. But the pressure of the king's official duties meant that he spent hours and hours at his desk, insisting on seeing every state paper, trusting no one except

---

[11] *ILE*, VIII, [95] 01 01.
[12] These suggestions are made by J. de Landtsheer, cf. *ILE*, VIII, [95] 01 01. Cf. also G. Tournoy, J. Papy and J. de Landtsheer, eds., *Lipsius en Leuven. Catalogus van de tentoonstelling in de Centrale Bibliotheek te Leuven, 18 september–17 oktober 1997*, Supplementa Humanistica Lovaniensia 13 (Louvain, 1997), 223–225. Perhaps the name of the prince-count of Arenberg might be added. He is mentioned by name in the letter, albeit in the completely different context of botanical studies, but he knew the addressee San Víctores well, and was a high-ranking courtier and politician in his own right. Diego de Ibarra, a brother of Esteban entrusted with a leading role in the reform of the Spanish army in the Southern Netherlands, received a complimentary copy of Lipsius's *De militia romana* in September 1595, cf. *ILE*, VIII, 95 09 02 M, 95 09 12 M.
[13] *ILE*, VIII, 95 01 17 I.

perhaps his secretaries. In the early nineties, his administrative tasks had become an almost intolerable burden now that his health was failing. At the Brussels court Philip was often criticized for being both slow in dealing with the country's problems as well as being indifferent to the country's fate.[14] Lipsius had to tread carefully in his letter to Ibarra, obviously not wanting to antagonize his host or the king himself. Quoting examples from Roman as well as contemporary history, he recommended, not surprisingly, well-considered actions over hasty ones. Sometimes slowness was acceptable, even necessary in politics; Lipsius quoted the king's father, Emperor Charles V, to reinforce this view. In the present situation, however, it seems that Lipsius considered too much slowness to be dangerous, as it could harm the prince's reputation. He approvingly quoted Girolamo Balbi, bishop and diplomat in the service of Ferdinand I, who in 1523 had urged Pope Adrian VI to take direct action by organizing a crusade against the Ottoman Turks, because in this case delay might mean the ruin of Europe.[15]

In his letter of 2 January 1595 Lipsius was much more outspoken than in his letter to Ibarra written a fortnight later. San Víctores received nothing less than a short treatise on Spanish foreign policy and its European consequences. Lipsius identified three enemies of the Spanish king: the French, the English, and the Dutch rebels, who were to be considered internal enemies. It would be advantageous to Philip II if he were at peace with the English and the French, because then he would be free to deal with the Ottoman threat as well as with the Dutch rebels. But unfortunately, according to Lipsius, there was hardly a chance that peace could be concluded either with Elizabeth I of England or Henry IV of France, although they were both short of money and not backed by public opinion, and even though their subjects were well aware of the fact that war damaged trade. Peace with the English queen would be the best option, as she was holding a few North Sea ports which were regarded as gateways to the Dutch rebel provinces. However, Elizabeth was inclined to continue the war for fear of Spanish

---

[14] *Ibid.*; cf. also G. Parker, *Philip II* (London, 1978), 24–37, 178–199; H. Kamen, *Philip of Spain* (New Haven and London, 1997), 211–241, 298–313.

[15] 'Beatissime pater, inquit [Girolamo Balbi], Fabius Maximus cunctando rem Romanam restituit; tu vide ne cunctando rem Romanam atque adeo Europam evertas': *ILE*, VIII, 95 01 17 I, 39–41.

supremacy. Henry IV had numerous troubles in his kingdom and might therefore be willing to conclude a peace, but Lipsius was not certain about Philip's views: maybe the Spanish king did not want peace with France. But it was always possible, in Lipsius's view, to conclude a truce with Henry IV. In the war against the Dutch rebels Philip II had been very unfortunate so far, and Lipsius saw no remedy there. The Dutch rebels were in possession of all the strategic fortresses, their military force was up to the mark, they had plenty of money, and their government functioned well enough, although there were internal tensions. Here, Lipsius saw a chance for psychological warfare. Sowing discord in the Northern Netherlands might result in the reconversion of a few hundred or even thousands of Dutchmen to Roman Catholicism and to re-acceptance of the King's rule. Since the Dutch, in Lipsius's view, had an extraordinary love of money and gain, he recommended to 'fish with this golden bait'. But if this kind of psychological warfare were to be effective, a truce must be concluded first. Lipsius himself preferred a proper peace with the Dutch, but he considered this an unrealistic proposal. The Northern Netherlands were prospering, their ruling elite was as wealthy and powerful as kings, a few neighbouring German princes had become their allies, and they had lost all respect for their natural lord, the king of Spain. The Spaniards, on the other hand, had no good soldiers or politicians. So a truce with the Dutch rebels would be the best option and Lipsius expected it would yield the same advantages as a proper peace. If the war would be continued, the Brussels government would not have the opportunity to reform its army, which was absolutely essential as mutiny was rife. The government itself suffered from disorderliness and other shortcomings; a truce would give the rulers of the Southern Netherlands the necessary break so that deficiencies could be remedied. Lipsius ended his letter with a *captatio benevolentiae*: if there was anything imprudent in it, it should be excused because of his love of the fatherland and of liberty, which was incumbent of a good counsellor.[16]

Set against the background of Lipsius's correspondence as a whole, the letter is highly unusual. According to his own theory of letter-writing explained in his treatise *Epistolica institutio* (Leiden, 1591), this letter belonged to the category of 'serious matters', which included

---

[16] *ILE*, VIII, 95 01 02 S.

consultations on the state of the commonwealth, including military or political matters, and, emphatically, also on peace.[17] Remarks on current politics or military developments do appear frequently in Lipsius's correspondence over the years, but never before had he written such a long and pertinent letter on the problems of the day, with the express aim of giving political advice. At first sight, this action is also contrary to Lipsius's image of himself, as contained in his well-known autobiographical letter to his favourite pupil Johannes Woverius, dated 1 October 1600, and published two years later by him in a volume of his collected correspondence.[18] There, he presented himself as a true humanist scholar, whose uneventful life is filled by reading, teaching and writing. His life was not to be compared to that of real great men, whose political or military deeds (*'res gestae'*) merit description.[19] He had kept away from politics, depicting his scholarly career as a succession of politically innocent travels to interesting places like Italy, Vienna and Jena, and then returning to his beloved fatherland for which he had really longed for all this time. His long stay at Leiden University (1578–91) he portrayed as a period spent in refuge while the civil war was raging in the Netherlands. In the end, he felt forced to return to his native country, the Southern Netherlands. He tells us in the autobiographical letter that this decision was mainly inspired by the religious condition of the rebellious provinces and by the attacks he had to suffer on his reputation (*'Religio et Fama'*).[20]

The political and military course of the rebels, Lipsius feared at the time, could only lead to disaster. William of Orange was murdered in 1584, and the subsequent actions of the earl of Leicester were deeply worrying for Lipsius, although at first he had welcomed the new governor and put his trust in him. Nor did he have any

---

[17] J. de Landtsheer, 'From Ultima Thule to Finisterra: Surfing on the Wide Web of Lipsius' Correspondence', in K. Enenkel and C. Heesakkers, eds., *Lipsius in Leiden. Studies in the Life and Works of a Great Humanist on the Occasion of his 450th Anniversary* (Voorthuizen, 1997), 48, 50.

[18] *ILE*, XIII, *1600*, ed. J. Papy (Brussels, 2000), 00 10 01.

[19] *Ibid.*, 7–8: 'Legere, docere, scribere et cetera tranquillum et ab actione remotum esse'.

[20] K. Enenkel, 'Humanismus, Primat des Privaten, Patriotismus und Niederländischer Aufstand. Selbstbildformung in Lipsius' Autobiographie', in Enenkel and Heesakkers, eds., *Lipsius in Leiden*, now corrects the interpretation of the autobiographical letter given by G. Oestreich, 'Justus Lipsius in sua re', in his, *Geist und Gestalt des frühmodernen Staates* (Berlin, 1969).

confidence in government by the Estates. On the contrary, he saw the rebellious provinces in the throes of political strife almost bordering on civil war. Dirck Volckertsz Coornhert's vehement attack on the ideas he had expressed in his *Politica* (1589) about the relations between Church and State and the problem of religious pluriformity greatly upset him. After his stay in Leiden he longed for a peaceful existence in his native country, untroubled by political and religious dissension.[21] In 1593 he wrote to his old friend Johannes Lernutius in Bruges that he considered the period spent amidst the troubles of the Northern Netherlands to have been a time spent in transition, rather than settled in a fixed abode. His return to the Southern Netherlands, he wrote, was motivated by religious and political considerations, and also by concern for his reputation, which was slandered in the North but respected in the South. In a letter written in December of the same year to another friend, Petrus Oranus in Liège, he confirmed this in the strongest possible terms. He confessed that living in Leiden had meant living with the enemy, thereby turning into an enemy himself; religious considerations and his loyalty to the king of Spain had been the reasons why he had gone back to his native country.[22] If anything, he was a victim of the manifold political troubles of his time, not an actor on the political stage.

At certain moments in his life before 1595, Lipsius had expressed a strong preference for a humanist *vita contemplativa* coupled with his distaste for involvement in politics. In a letter to his acquaintance Gerardus Falkenburgius for instance, written as early as 1575, Lipsius painted a picture of himself facing the troubles in the Netherlands

---

[21] M.E.H.N. Mout, 'In het schip: Justus Lipsius en de Nederlandse Opstand tot 1591', in S. Groenveld, M.E.H.N. Mout and I. Schöffer, eds., *Bestuurders en geleerden. Opstellen over onderwerpen uit de Nederlandse geschiedenis van de zestiende, zeventiende en achttiende eeuw, aangeboden aan Prof. dr. J.J. Woltjer bij zijn afscheid als hoogleraar van de Rijksuniversiteit te Leiden* (Amsterdam and Dieren, 1985), 54–64; J. de Landtsheer, 'Le Retour de Juste Lipse de Leyden à Louvain selon sa correspondance (1591–1594)', in C. Mouchel, ed., *Juste Lipse (1547–1606) en son temps. Actes du colloque de Strasbourg, 1994* (Paris, 1996); Justus Lipsius, *Politica. Six Books of Politics or Political Instruction*, ed. J. Waszink (Assen, 2004), 24–28.

[22] *ILE*, VI, ed. J. de Landtsheer (Brussels, 1994), 93 05 30 L: 'E Batavis quaeris quid me abduxerit? Melior ratio, nisi erro. Iamdiu hoc agito, et in communibus istis turbis stationem illam elegeram, non sedem'; 93 12 25 H, 26–29: 'Nam benigna mihi omnia apud Batavos fuisse, etiam hostis inter hostes debeo fateri. At revocavit me pietas et vinculum in meum Regum, quorum illam et hunc colam quamdiu terram hanc colam'.

in such a way as became a true Stoic. He stressed the value of his
retired life as a scholar and boasted of his spiritual strength resulting from his inner freedom. Taking ancient figures who had lived
through troubled times, too, as his example he advocated sensible
and dignified behaviour, such as had been shown by the Roman
statesman Marcus Aemilius Lepidus, whom Tacitus had praised for
his prudence and moderation. Lipsius wanted to practice constancy
in his own life, telling Falkenburgius that he held on to God and
virtue, taking care of himself, especially in relation to the politically
powerful; he was neither trying to flatter the rulers, nor to provoke
them. As long as the political and military situation in his homeland
did not improve, Lipsius intended to lie low and not expose himself.[23] As soon as he arrived in Leiden in 1578 in order to take up
his professorship of History and Law he told two of his best friends –
Johannes Lernutius and Victor Giselinus – that he did not aspire to
any high political office in the rebellious provinces, unlike some of
his countrymen. On the contrary, he intended to abide by his decision taken long ago not to meddle in politics in such a troubled
commonwealth. Anyway, he regarded his stay in the Northern
Netherlands as only temporary: it would last 'not longer than until
these tumults fall silent and the fury subsides'.[24]

Unfortunately, Lipsius was not in a position to escape politics as
long as he was in Leiden. He was elected vice-chancellor of Leiden
University in February 1579 and had to stay in office for two years.
It was the stadholder of the province of Holland, William of Orange
himself, who made the appointment, and this meant that the vice-
chancellorship was not an exclusively academic post, but also had a
political side to it. Whoever held the office had to cooperate with
the Estates of Holland and the stadholder, and serve their needs as
well.[25] When in 1580 a dispute broke out in the Leiden Reformed
Church in which the university also became involved, Lipsius tried

---

[23] *ILE*, I, *1564–1583*, ed. A. Gerlo, M.A. Nauwelaerts and H.D.L. Vervliet
(Brussels, 1978), 75 08 01.
[24] *Ibid.*, 78 04 01; cf. also 78 09 03. The quotation is from Plautus, *Miles gloriosus*.
[25] M.E.H.N. Mout, 'Justus Lipsius at Leiden University 1578–1591', in A. Gerlo,
ed., *Juste Lipse (1547–1606). Colloque international tenu en mars 1987*, Travaux de l'Institut
Interuniversitaire pour l'étude de la Renaissance et de l'Humanisme (Brussels, 1988);
R.-J. van den Hoorn, 'On Course for Quality: Justus Lipsius and Leiden University',
in Enenkel and Heesakkers, eds., *Lipsius in Leiden*.

to act as a calming influence. Two years later the problems were still not resolved, as the question of ecclesiastical discipline continued to divide the faithful. On Lipsius's advice the university Senate did not give way to the wish of the States of Holland to send an envoy to The Hague to discuss this problem with the government. Lipsius himself emphatically did not want to get involved: 'I do not want to be singed by those flames [i.e. religious disputes] which nowadays are encircling so many people', he wrote to his friend Jan van Hout, who happened to be Leiden's town secretary and in that capacity was embroiled in the heated discussions about ecclesiastical discipline.[26] Lipsius was re-elected vice-chancellor of the university in February 1587 and served for another two years, albeit very reluctantly. During that period the greatest trial of strength, for the university and Lipsius alike, was the sudden dismissal of the famous Law professor Hugo Donellus because of his political opinions. Donellus had criticized the States of Holland and, it was claimed, thereby gravely insulted the curators of the university and the burgomasters of Leiden who sided with the States against the earl of Leicester. Lipsius tried to intervene and defend Donellus, as was his duty as vice-chancellor, but all his efforts were in vain. Apart from the trouble concerning Donellus's dismissal, Lipsius became involved in a long drawn-out conflict about university jurisdiction between the university and the town on the one hand and the Court of Holland on the other. It is clear from his letters that from that time onwards, until his departure from Leiden in 1591, Lipsius lived in constant fear of new difficulties that might arise either within the university or concerning the wider political situation. Especially while vice-chancellor he had been confronted with problems which were directly connected with the still uncertain relationship between religion and political life in the rebellious provinces, and he had not liked this at all. The bitter controversy with Coornhert about toleration, fired by positions Lipsius had taken in his *Politica* (1589), did nothing to change this point of view.[27]

---

[26] *ILE*, I, 82 05 14 H. For the troubles in Leiden's Reformed Church, see C. Kooi, *Liberty and Religion. Church and State in Leiden's Reformation 1572–1620*, Studies in Medieval and Reformation Thought 82 (Leiden, 2000), 55–124.
[27] Mout, 'Justus Lipsius at Leiden University', 96–99.

Lipsius's departure from Leiden to his native Southern Netherlands and his reconversion to Roman Catholicism in 1591 were actions embued with political and religious meaning and were rightly appreciated as such at the time.[28] Once he had finally received his coveted professorship in History and Latin at Louvain University in the autumn of 1592, he made a point of clearly demonstrating his genuine piety and attachment to the Roman Catholic Church as well as his unswerving loyalty to the king of Spain. In a few letters, written around that time, one finds sentences such as 'I have left the places which are adverse to the religion and to the king, where I have stayed all too long', together with expressions of his desire to serve his fatherland, his hope for a Spanish victory and, implicitly or explicitly, his longing for peace.[29] On the other hand he praised a former Law student from Leiden, Adam Leemput, because he had retired from public life. According to Lipsius's appreciation of Stoic tenets, a man would only find peace by turning inward and concentrating on God and divine things.[30] He himself complained quite often about attacks on his person and writings. These he probably saw as the inevitable consequence of his scholarly fame, concomitant with his public role as an academic teacher and sometime administrator, as he had had the same problem in Leiden.[31] Also in those later years in Louvain he stressed the fact that the holding of any public office, which would inevitably involve him in politics, would greatly distress him.[32]

In order to understand Lipsius's sudden emergence as writer of a public letter on European politics in January 1595 it is important to be aware of his constant endeavours to be on good terms with the rulers of the Southern Netherlands as well as with the representatives of the Roman Catholic Church, and of his anxieties in this

---

[28] Mout, 'In het schip', 55–56, 61–62; De Landtsheer, 'Le Retour de Juste Lipse de Leyden à Louvain'.

[29] *ILE*, V, *1592*, ed. J. de Landtsheer and J. Kluyskens (Brussels, 1991), 92 01 05 A; 92 09 11, 4–5; 92 09 23; 92 11 03 V. Cf. also his dedicatory letter for his work *De Cruce* to the Estates of Brabant, 92 11 04; *ILE*, VI, 93 02 07; 93 12 25 H, are examples.

[30] *ILE*, VI, 93 01 11.

[31] *ILE*, II, *1584–1587*, ed. M.A. Nauwelaerts and S. Sué (Brussels, 1983), 87 05 05, 171–19: 'Sed rarum tamen aliquid in hac urbe, non solum Schola, cui Lipsii nomen non insertum vero sive falso'; *ILE*, VI, 93 01 29 T²; 93 02 10 B, *ILE*, VII, 94 09 11 H and many other letters from the early 1590s.

[32] *ILE*, VII, 94 09 28 V.

respect. In 1593, for instance, he was warned that his *Politica* was to be put on the papal Index unless he rewrote the book, which he did with the help of some friends in Rome and Louvain. Fortunately, the new Index was postponed. The corrected text of the *Politica* was finally sanctioned by Roberto Bellarmino, who, although not yet a cardinal, was already influential in Rome. The revised version appeared in print from 1596 onwards, but was challenged again by the Vatican in 1601.[33]

No less significant, though, is the development of his political views in those years, as far as these can be gauged from his correspondence. Political and military news is mentioned from time to time in his letters, but pertinent political statements are scarce; maybe even scarcer than they were in Lipsius's correspondence from Leiden.[34] A constant theme, though, was the lamentable state of European politics. The deeper cause of it was religious strife, as he remarked in 1592. The fact that the Spanish king had considerably increased his power by conquering Portugal and a number of overseas dominions was viewed as a positive development, but it was obvious that more changes were necessary, especially in Spain itself and in France.[35] In the summer of 1593 Lipsius wrote about great hopes – hopes he hardly shared, however – concerning the conclusion of a truce between Henry IV of France and the French Catholic League. In the same letter, addressed to his old friend the geographer Abraham Ortelius in Antwerp, he pointedly referred to the Dutch army under Maurice of Nassau as 'enemy' forces, as would be expected of him now that he lived in the Southern Netherlands. The capture of Geertruidenberg by Maurice prompted Lipsius to air the view that now the Dutch would reject any peace proposals even more readily than before.[36] Nevertheless he continued to admire the stadholder because of his genuine interest in Roman military practice.[37] When Lipsius was still

---

[33] Lipsius, *Politica*, ed. Waszink, 120–124; *ILE*, VI, 93 02 10 B; 93 03 18; 93 05 13; 93 05 30 BEL; 93 05 30 BEN; 93 06 14 DE; 93 07 09; 93 07 18 D; 93 07 31 BA; 93 07 31 BEL; 93 07 31 BEN; 93 08 14 BE; 93 08 20; *ILE*, VII, 94 03 27 B; 94 09 12 M; 94 10 10 M.

[34] Lipsius sometimes even refused to discuss politics, cf. for instance *ILE*, VI, [93] 06 14 R.

[35] *ILE*, V, 92 11 29; 92 09 23 B; *ILE*, VI, 93 03 04 S.

[36] *ILE*, VI, 93 06 09; 9 07 22 C. Cf. also *ILE*, V, 92 01 15 A and *ILE*, VIII, 95 11 05.

[37] *ILE*, VIII, 95 09 13 BU.

in Liège expecting the appointment to a chair in Louvain, he had addressed a long letter about the current political situation to Cornelis Aerssens, who was at the time clerk of the States General. Lipsius stressed the need for peace negotiations, although personally he was not in a position to judge the situation. However, Emperor Rudolf II and some other important politicians of the Empire were advocating peace talks, and the king of Spain might have had good reasons for entering into them, too. So it would be prudent for the Dutch not to dismiss the idea of peace: it could be either now or never.[38]

His pessimistic mood clearly speaks from a short letter about politics to an Antwerp merchant, Franciscus Sweertius. Although he rejoiced at the news about the crushing defeat inflicted in June 1593 on the Turks by the imperial army near Sisak on the border between Croatia and Bosnia, he worried about the deplorable state of Europe in general and the Southern Netherlands in particular. The king of Spain, Lipsius wrote, powerful though he is, and certainly favoured by God and Fortune, is sometimes let down by others, and he is very slow in making decisions. However, Lipsius emphasized that he did not want to criticize Philip II, because kings were taking higher and remoter matters into account than normal mortals, who were only concerned with affairs that related to themselves.[39] We have seen that Lipsius would return to the pressing problem of the slowness of the royal decision-making processes in his letter to Esteban de Ibarra, secretary of State and War of the Southern Netherlands, in January 1595.

The news of the appointment of Archduke Ernest of Austria as the new governor, and his arrival in January 1594, filled Lipsius with fresh hope. Especially the mutinous, badly paid and ineffective army of the Southern Netherlands might profit from his strong hand. He was of course aware of the fact that Archduke Ernest, though deemed capable, might not be able to remedy every evil at once, but he was hoping for the best.[40] He even copied the text of the laudatory poem with which the Genoese merchants of Antwerp welcomed the

---

[38] *ILE*, V, 92 01 05 A.
[39] *Ibid.*, 93 08 06 S.
[40] *Ibid.*, 93 08 25; [93] 09 22 H; 93 12 21; *ILE*, VII, 94 02 03; 94 02 05 J; 94 02 05 M; 94 06 21 OU.

governor and sent it to an acquaintance in that town.[41] Lipsius had discussed with friends the possibility of dedicating his new book *De militia romana* (published in June 1595) to the archduke, but this idea was dropped following Ernest's sudden death in February 1595.[42] The chance for a lasting peace with the Dutch was much on Lipsius's mind during the whole year 1594. On the whole he took a pessimistic view, blaming the Dutch for their unwillingness to put an end to a conflict that Lipsius still chose to regard as a civil war.[43] He was not alone in this view. In contemporary news pamphlets from the Southern Netherlands the war with the North was often depicted as an unfortunate civil war between a loyalist and a rebellious part of what was basically one country, of which the inhabitants shared a common fatherland and perhaps even a common national identity.[44] Pieces of news, especially concerning anti-Roman Catholic measures, for instance that the Dutch threatened to forbid students to attend Catholic universities such as Louvain, were understandably upsetting to Lipsius.[45] Philip II, however, was blamed as well, because he was seen to pay more attention to other matters – maybe Lipsius was hinting at the king's costly military interventions in France – than to the welfare of the Southern Netherlands.[46] Lipsius also sharply condemned the troubled situation in the Southern Netherlands itself, where ineptitude and confusion in political life together with regular cases of mutiny in the army were now the rule.[47]

It seems safe to assume that especially in the period immediately prior to writing his letter to San Víctores on 2 January 1595 Lipsius became more and more worried about the political and military situation in his homeland. Archduke Ernest evidently had not been able to provide the panacea that would cure all the ills of the Southern

---

[41] *ILE*, VII, 94 03 11.

[42] *Ibid.*, 94 06 05; 94 06 21 OU; 94 12 06; 94 12 18; 94 12 21 C; *ILE*, VIII, 95 02 22 B. Lipsius dedicated *De militia romana* to Crown Prince Philip of Spain, cf. 95 04 21 B and the dedicatory letter: [95 04 21] P.

[43] *Ibid.*, VII, 94 07 01 B; 94 07 01 R²; 94 07 20 B; 94 07 29 A; 94 11 14 A.

[44] V. van Zuilen, 'The Politics of Dividing the Nation? News Pamphlets as a Vehicle of Ideology and National Consciousness in the Habsburg Netherlands (1585–1609)', in J.W. Koopmans, ed., *News and Politics in Early Modern Europe (1500–1800)*, Groningen Studies in Cultural Change 13 (Louvain, 2005).

[45] *ILE*, VIII, 95 09 18.

[46] *Ibid.*, VII, 94 09 24 H.

[47] *Ibid.*, 94 10 17.

Netherlands, Philip II was otherwise occupied, and peace with the Dutch seemed further away than ever. This heightened awareness of a crisis overwhelming Europe in general and his native country in particular might have been an incentive to Lipsius to put on paper certain thoughts he normally reserved for himself and his closest friends: his ideas about Spanish foreign policy and the respective merits of war, peace or a truce. Lipsius had spent the year 1594 working on his book *De militia romana*, in which he contrasted Roman military practice and the near-perfect organization and high morale of the Roman army with the sorry picture of the undisciplined soldiery of his own time.[48] He must have feared that the Spanish king would never be able to win any war with such armies, not even a just war against the Dutch rebels.[49]

His worries are also expressed in a few of his many letters from the year 1595 about his possible move to Bologna, where the university had offered him the most important chair in the Faculty of Arts, the professorship of Literature. It is a moot point whether Lipsius ever was serious about accepting this prestigious position at one of Europe's oldest and most famous universities. He certainly considered it carefully, using the tempting offer to negotiate with the authorities in his own country, such as the Estates of Brabant and representatives of the king of Spain, to raise his salary, or at least to get it paid more regularly, and generally to improve his position.[50] Nevertheless, some of his complaints vented in his letters about Bologna's offer have the ring of sincerity about them. The state of affairs in his native country is now very unstable, he wrote to Christophe d'Assonleville, a member of the Council of State; Bologna is attractive because it is a more peaceful place than Louvain, he

---

[48] J. de Landtsheer, 'Justus Lipsius's *De Militia Romana*: Polybius Revived or How an Ancient Historian was Turned into a Manual of Early Modern Warfare', in K. Enenkel, J.L. de Jong and J. de Landtsheer, eds., *Recreating Ancient History. Episodes from the Greek and Roman Past in the Arts and Literature of the Early Modern Period*, Intersections 1 (Leiden, 2001), 114–115. Lipsius occasionally refers to mutinies in his correspondence, cf. for example *ILE*, VIII, 95 06 01 K.

[49] For Lipsius's ideas about a just war cf. his *Politica*, ed. Waszink, 540–551; J. Papy, 'An Unpublished Dialogue by Justus Lipsius on Military Prudence and the Causes of War: the *Monita et Exempla Politica de Re Militari* (1605)', *Bibliothèque d'Humanisme et Renaissance* 65 (2003), 135–148.

[50] Cf. letters from the first six months of the year 1595 in *ILE*, VIII, a crass example of Lipsius threatening to leave for Italy unless he gets a higher and more regular remuneration is 95 06 20 RI.

told his old friend Nicolaas Oudaert.[51] And if Louvain would become unsafe because of the war with the Dutch, he certainly would consider emigrating to a foreign country, Germany or Italy for instance.[52] In short, the old fearfulness about having to live in times of war and other troubles, feelings that obsessed Lipsius so much when he was living in Leiden, had not left him after his arrival in Louvain. He had reason to be concerned, too; while on his way to Spa in the summer of 1595 he had a narrow escape from Dutch cavalrymen who had captured Franchimont. In a very detailed letter in elegant Latin, embellished with a Greek quotation or two, Lipsius described how he and his companion, the Jesuit Leonardus Lessius, had to jump over a hedge and flee over rough terrain to reach safety.[53]

After 1595 Lipsius took care not to write any more letters about politics that were in danger of becoming public, as his letter to San Víctores had done. But he did not quite succeed in this. In July 1596 he replied to a letter of Philip de Croy, count of Solre, governor of Tournai, again dealing with the question of whether war or peace was preferable to Philip II. Although Lipsius expressly requested Croy not to give the letter to others, both manuscript and printed copies appeared. Lipsius's tone was now quite militant: a great king such as Philip II should strive to vanquish his enemies, especially because he has God and the law on his side. The conclusion of a peace or a truce could nevertheless be useful to him. Contrary to his ideas expressed in his letter to San Víctores, Lipsius was now averse to peace with either France or England. Concluding a lasting peace with France seemed impossible to Lipsius: although civil war had weakened the country, it was only waiting for an opportunity to start another war with Spain. Winning the war against Elizabeth I of England (Lipsius referred to her as 'that woman') would be a very good thing: it would lead to Spanish rule of the sea and end English support of the Dutch rebels. Again, Lipsius showed himself in favour of peace or at least a truce with the Dutch, but only in theory. He described the general mood in the Northern Netherlands as especially militant: politicians, the military, as well as

---

[51] *ILE*, VIII, 95 02 25; 95 03 09 O.
[52] *Ibid.*, 95 02 12 BUY.
[53] *Ibid.*, 95 07 04.

the influential exiles from the Southern Netherlands were all in favour of the continuation of the war against Spain. His advice was that the new governor of the Southern Netherlands, Archduke Albert of Austria, should step up his war efforts in order to terrorize the common people in the North. Maybe that would make the Dutch more peace-minded. But even then Lipsius considered the chance for the conclusion of a truce minimal, as the Dutch would undoubtedly stick to their heretical beliefs and to their foreign allies.[54]

In January 1604 Lipsius sent a last letter about European politics to a nobleman in Brussels. By then, the situation had changed totally. By concluding peace with France in 1598 Philip III had recognized his inability to fight three wars simultaneously. In June and in August 1603 respectively, the Archdukes Albert and Isabella, and Philip III, had sent embassies to London to congratulate the new King James I as well as to put out feelers for peace. In May 1604 an embassy was sent to London to negotiate the peace. Lipsius's acquaintances Charles de Ligne, prince-count of Arenberg, and Jean Richardot (president of the Privy Council), represented the Brussels government, together with the audiencier Louis Vereycken. On the Spanish side the chief negotiator was the constable of Castile, Juan Fernández de Velasco, duke of Frías, although he only arrived at the peace conference in Somerset House on 10 August 1604, nine days before the Treaty of London was formally concluded. As the only complete version of Lipsius's letter was found in the archives of the dukes of Frías in the castle of Montemayor near Córdoba, it seems likely that Velasco was the addressee, the more so as he was in Brussels during the winter 1603–04.[55]

Now that peace with France was a fact and peace with England was within reach, Lipsius's main worry was the continuing war with the Dutch. Therefore he concentrated his arguments in the letter of

---

[54] I wish to thank Dr Jeanine de Landtsheer for putting her edition of the letter at my disposal before publication.

[55] P. Croft, 'Brussels and London: the Archdukes, Robert Cecil and James I', in W. Thomas and L. Duerloo, eds., *Albert & Isabella 1598–1621. Essays* (Brussels and Louvain, 1998), 79–86. I wish to thank Dr Jeanine de Landtsheer for putting her edition of the letter at my disposal before publication, and also for sending me photocopies of the partial edition of the letter in A. Ramírez, *Epistolario de Justo Lipsio y los españoles (1577–1606)* (Madrid, 1966), 416–417, as well as of the full transcription of the letter by the Duque de Frías, 'Una carta inédita de Justo Lipsio', *Archivum. Revista de la Facultad de Filosofía y Letras* 16 (1966), 91–107.

1604 on the English negotiations and the possibility of reaching peace with the Dutch. According to Lipsius the fate of Europe depended on the developments in the Netherlands, and the Spanish should be aware of it. He expressed the hope that peace negotiations with the English would be successful, although he saw difficulties: the difference in religion and the position of English and Scottish Roman Catholics for instance, and the continuing English support for the Dutch rebels. In Lipsius's view the war with the Dutch was much more difficult to end, because it was a civil war. But even a civil war could be ended, for instance by following the example of Augustus, who concluded a peace with Pompey, after which Pompey's men defected to him en masse. Lipsius had used the same example in his letter to San Víctores in January 1595.[56] It would be good, he thought, if James I would compel the Dutch to make peace. But unfortunately, Lipsius was convinced that the Dutch politicians feared peace more than war, so he advised, as he had done in 1596, to continue the war against the Dutch after reorganizing the army and banning corruption, in the hope that, in the end, the king of Spain would triumph over his rebellious subjects. Apparently, only this kind of peace would satisfy Lipsius.

Humanists like Lipsius seem to show us two very different facets: the unworldly scholar in search of highly-placed patrons or a good job at a renowned university in order to have financial security, social prestige and as few daily worries as possible, and, on the other hand, the sure-footed political philosopher, adviser of rulers or arbiter in political questions, who was in touch with the political realities of his day and possibly influenced – or at least was meant to influence – the course of events. These facets mirror the old problem which had occupied the mind of many a humanist since Petrarch: the choice between a *vita contemplativa* and a *vita activa*: life as a scholar far from the madding crowd, or as a man immersed in political life. It remains a moot point how many humanists ever effectively influenced the political decisions, big or small, of the rulers they served with their advice. Usually they just delivered the materials for princely propaganda at their patron's bidding, or offered him their publications in the hope of remuneration.[57] Humanist political philosophers north

---

[56] *ILE*, VIII, 95 01 02 S, 102–110.
[57] Grafton, 'Humanism and Political Theory', 9–10; M.E.H.N. Mout, *De volmaakte redenaar. De macht van het woord in de Renaissance* (Leiden, 1995), 14–18.

of the Alps, such as Lipsius, held in common a particular perception of the human condition, assuming that the wisdom of ancient
political values contrasted strongly with the folly and uncertainty of
current political practice. Mankind required a fitting political system
together with a degree of flexibility in the process of political decision-making, and here, the humanists could help out. They had
access to the best minds of antiquity and, moreover, deemed themselves able to present the ideas found there in a rhetorically com-
pelling and systematic way to the rulers of their own time. Humanists
such as Lipsius were able to reconcile and combine these ancient
ideas with Christian morality and practical politics, making sure that
their counsels fitted contemporary conditions and that society as a
whole profited from them.[58] A public letter, such as Lipsius wrote
in 1595, was a suitable rhetorical form for just such well-argued
advice to the king of Spain. He would have agreed with Erasmus:
who else but the humanist should show the prince the way to per-
fect rule, advising him about all aspects of government, including
questions of war and peace?[59]

---

[58] B. Bradshaw, 'Transalpine Humanism', in J.H. Burns and M. Goldie, eds.,
The Cambridge History of Political Thought 1450–1700 (Cambridge, 1991), 106–109,
114.
[59] Desiderius Erasmus, *The Education of a Christian Prince*, transl. N.M. Cheshire
and M.J. Heath; ed. L. Jardine (Cambridge, 1997), 2.

CHAPTER NINE

MEDIUM AND MESSAGE.
POLITICAL PRINTS IN THE DUTCH REPUBLIC, 1568–1632

Andrew Sawyer

Given the quantity of artworks produced in the Dutch Republic, its citizens must have been unusually sensitized to imagery – found most famously in paintings, but also in many other media, for example ceramics, textiles, stained glass, numismatics, and civic events such as the tableaux and ceremonial arches of the *Joyeuse Entrée*.[1] The creators could exploit a rich iconography which itself drew upon a medieval inheritance, an extensive knowledge of the Bible (as befits a state with large Calvinist and sectarian populations), and Renaissance classicism (popular especially among artists at the dawn of the Golden Age).

This high level of image literacy was exploited politically. For example, it has been argued that one of the finest expressions of Dutch political thought on freedom of conscience is not a text, but the stained glass window of the Janskerk in Gouda. 'Freedom of conscience' is portrayed as a carriage in which there are two female figures representing freedom of conscience and freedom of religion. This carriage is being pulled by female depictions of the virtues of love, justice, fidelity, concord and constancy. The carriage and its attendants are able to crush tyranny, which is depicted lying on the ground with a broken sword and spear.[2]

[1] G. Luijten *et al.*, eds., *Dawn of the Golden Age. Northern Netherlandish Art 1580–1620* (Amsterdam, 1993); M. Westermann, *The Art of the Dutch Republic, 1585–1718* (London, 1996), 184–187, and M. North, *Art and Commerce in the Dutch Golden Age*, trans. C. Hill (New Haven and London, 1997), provide good introductions.

[2] M. van Gelderen, *The Political Thought of the Dutch Revolt 1555–1590* (Cambridge, 1992), 264. See C.L. Janson, 'Preserving the Word: Wtewael's Freedom of Conscience Window at Gouda', *Kunsthistorisk Tidskrift* 57 (1988), 19–29.

Prints and engravings also bore political messages, overt, or implicit in historical or allegorical scenes.[3] Their pictorial nature offered a powerful set of building blocks which could be used, like pamphlets, to define the nature of political problems in a particular manner. The famous adoption of the term 'Beggar' (at a party given by Count Brederode in April 1566) also gave birth to its own imagery – two clasped hands holding a beggar's bag – which rapidly spread in a range of media. It did not so much illustrate, as help to create, a dissident political culture.[4]

Politics and power in the Republic was more easily portrayed than described: arguably 'the complexity of human affairs is always a complexity of multiple interacting relationships; and pictures are a better medium than linear prose for expressing relationships. Pictures can be taken in as a whole and help to encourage holistic rather than reductionist thinking about a situation'.[5] And it is usually real situations, and not theory, which are portrayed so dynamically in the prints. The rebel state had not only exploited its pictorial literacy to create a dissident political culture. It had then utilized it in the negotiations and the pragmatic *Realpolitik* of decision making in a state that was engaged in a war for survival over several generations, with the enemy always at the gates.[6]

---

[3] The prints referred to here are the satirical prints catalogued by nineteenth-century collectors: F. Muller, *De Nederlandsche geschiedenis in platen, beredeneerde beschrijving van Nederlandsche historieplaten, zinneprenten en historische kaarten*, 4 vols. (Amsterdam, 1863–82; repr. 1970) [hereafter abbreviated as FM], and G. van Rijn, *Atlas van Stolk. Katalogus der historie – spot – en zinneprenten betrekkelijk de geschiedenis van Nederland*, 10 vols. (Amsterdam, 1895–1933) [hereafter abbreviated as AvS], or the collection at Simon van Gijn – Museum aan huis [hereafter abbreviated as SvG]. They can be seen, together with transcripts of the texts, in D. Horst's well-illustrated book, *De Opstand in zwart–wit. Propagandaprenten uit de Nederlandse Opstand 1566–1584* (Zutphen, 2003). In this essay 'print' is taken to include woodcuts and engravings.

[4] Van Gelderen, *Political Thought*, 6; H.F.K. van Nierop, 'A Beggars' Banquet. The Compromise of the Nobility and the Politics of Inversion', *European History Quarterly* 21 (1991), 420–421. For the spectacular take up of Beggar imagery, see Duke, 'Dissident Propaganda', 122–123.

[5] P. Checkland, *Systems Thinking, Systems Practice* (Chichester, 1993), A16. My thanks to R. Day for drawing my attention to the importance of pictures in analysing political systems.

[6] A.Th. van Deursen, 'Holland's Experience of War during the Revolt of the Netherlands', in A.C. Duke and C.A. Tamse, *War and Society. Papers Delivered to the Sixth Anglo-Dutch Historical Conference*, Britain and the Netherlands 6 (The Hague, 1977), 19–53, there 19.

It should be noted that there seems to have been very little dissident visual propaganda before the crisis of the mid 1560s, after which there was a marked increase, and it was to remain a feature of the Republic's politics when the rebels had established their new state.[7] Moreover, the topoi they used were constantly evolving: for example, in the initial crisis, the appearance of the *pijlbundel* [bundle of arrows] was seen by some at least as a harbinger of civil war, then with the establishment of the Republic it became a popular sign of unity.[8] Prints became ubiquitous in this period, they were visible to everyone. They were found in all types of household, although expensive prints might only be found in wealthy homes (where servants and visitors would see them). Cheaper prints were fixed to buildings and furniture, coloured and given to children, or used as badges. A proportion of these would have been political images.[9] Can the message derived from such pictures contribute to the knowledge gained from pamphlet literature, such as that examined by Van Gelderen for the period 1555–90?[10] This essay intends to analyse whether the major themes identified in the pamphlets can be traced in the hundred or so images from 1568 to 1632.[11]

---

[7] Duke, 'Posters, Pamphlets and Prints', 32; *idem*, 'Dissident Propaganda', 126, and *Reformation and Revolt*, 105–106.

[8] Duke, 'Dissident Propaganda', 118.

[9] For households, see J.M. Montias, *Artists and Artisans in Delft. A Socio-Economic Study of the Seventeenth Century* (Princeton, NJ, 1982), 228. For the distribution of cheaper prints, see paintings such as those by Pieter Breughel the Elder (1525/30–69), for example *The Battle Between Carnival and Lent* (Kunsthistorisches Museum, Vienna: 1559), where an illustrated document is fixed to the church door, and for cheap woodcuts, see K. van Mander, *The Lives of the Illustrious Netherlandish and German Painters*, trans. H. Miedema (Amsterdam, 1603; Doornspijk, 1994), 121, and D. Landau and P. Parshall, *The Renaissance Print, 1470–1550* (London, 1994), 359–360. See J.M. Montias, 'Works of Art in Seventeenth-Century Amsterdam', in D. Freedberg and J. de Vries, eds., *Art in History, History in Art* (Santa Monica, CA, 1991), 331–372, there 354, where he estimated 7.8 per cent of prints were political. This figure was based on finer prints found in inventories and the proportion could be much higher if cheap prints were included.

[10] Van Gelderen, *Political Thought*. Perhaps the most useful catalogue of pamphlets for the period covered by this essay is W.P. Knuttel, *Catalogus van de pamflettenverzameling berustende in de Koninklijke Bibliotheek*, 10 vols. (The Hague, 1899–1920; repr. 1978).

[11] A complete list of the specific images from which this article was drawn can be found in A.C. Sawyer, 'Pictures, Power and the Polity. A Vision of the Political Images of the Early Dutch Republic', unpublished Ph.D. thesis (University of Southampton, 2000), based on a computer aided analysis of 103 images, the dates ranging from 1568 to 1632; 86 were prints, the remainder being painted and numismatic evidence, since the focus was on concepts and themes, not genre. In referring to specific prints, the titles quoted are those on the images themselves, or

The majority of the images under discussion are prints. They range from expensive, finely engraved images by gifted designers, skilled engravers and expert press-men, and produced on an intaglio press, to the coarsest of woodcuts requiring little in the way of expertise or technology to publish.[12] Whilst the existence of major catalogues of prints may imply that they form a distinct genre, in fact they are an eclectic, miscellaneous collection, resistant to classification.[13] Moreover they have some similarities to pamphlets: both media are produced using a similar technology which allowed them to be produced in large quantities. Both were intended for the popular market, and appear to have circulated widely. Indeed, pamphlets bearing illustrations, and prints with significant elements of text show a blurring of boundaries between the two media, and although the analysis of pictorial data can be problematic, the material here often has texts or captions within the image which can assist.[14]

Van Gelderen focused his study on the issues raised in the period before 1581, such as views on authority, what might be regarded as 'good government' (especially sovereignty and the relationship between government and ecclesiastical authority), and the relationship of Dutch political ideology to mainstream European thinking. In his view, there is a marked dichotomy in the historical background between what he regards as a 'theocratic, descending' view of authority in tune with monarchical power, and a 'communal, federative and constitutional model cherished by towns and provinces'.[15] Van Gelderen argues that an ideology developed during the Revolt that lauded the notion of liberty, and that 'in the Low Countries freedom was pro-

---

conventionally assigned to well known images. In a few cases I have assigned titles. Dates quoted are normally the earliest quoted in FM and AvS.

[12] For an introduction to prints in this period, including information on production, see Landau and Parshall, *The Renaissance Print*.

[13] 'Popular prints as an acknowledged category of images is primarily a creation of the eighteenth century': Landau and Parshall, *The Renaissance Print*, 219.

[14] See Van Gelderen, *Political Thought*, 288–290, on assumptions about genre and pamphlets. See J.-C. Schmitt, 'Images and the Historian', in A. Bolvig and P. Lindley, eds., *History and Images. Towards a New Iconology* (Turnhout, 2003), 19–44, and G. Jaritz and B. Schuh, 'Describing the Indescribable', in M. Thaller, ed., *Images and Manuscripts in Historical Computing* (St. Katharinen, 1992), 143–153, for the analysis of images. Note that accompanying texts do not always relate directly to the image: *Spaensche tiranni*, printed in 1613, bears an image from a much older plate. See FM, I, 159.

[15] Van Gelderen, *Political Thought*, 30.

tected by a political framework which was based on the notion of popular sovereignty and functioned through fundamental constitutional guarantees, and representative institutions and virtuous citizens who were the guardians of liberty'.[16] He charts the emergence of four main, and inter-related, themes: liberty (the political virtue *par excellence*), privileges, and the States, which had a particular role in preserving and administering the fourth concept, popular sovereignty. Other significant themes in the pamphlets were the nature of military power, the importance of civic virtue and the place of religion.[17]

To what extent does the evidence from prints support this contention? The first task of the artists was to set the political themes in a context, and to relate the image to the Netherlands. They used a range of motifs to signify the Republic: cows, ships, and the 'Dutch Maiden' in her garden are well-known examples.[18] However, these depictions were not isolated representations of the state but are usually deployed in more complex scenes. For example, we find cows being stolen, or ships ploughing through seas populated by specific 'enemies', or the Dutch Maiden's garden being defended by Orangist nobles, as in *Spaensche tiranni* (*c.* 1575?) [fig. 9.1].[19] Thus the state is not personified, as in dynastic art, as bound up with the person of the monarch, but situated in the hurly-burly of real events.

The *Leo Belgicus* is a particularly well-known representation of the Republic, which appeared in cartographic depictions of the Netherlands, but was also a significant emblem in prints.[20] The lion had a symbolic place in both classical and Christian iconography, and its significance evolved during the course of the Revolt to become more than a heraldic device; this can be charted through pamphlets and

---

[16] *Ibid.*, 262–263.

[17] *Ibid.*, 265.

[18] For ships, see for example *Powerless Thundering* (fig. 4), which shows a ship (on wheels), drawn by lions, accompanied by allegorical virtues and rolling over Tyranny, and *Idea Belgicarum provinciarum*, of 1620, showing a ship sailing past struggling Jesuits. There are countless images of the Dutch Maid in her garden: the genesis of this topos has been traced to the fourteenth century, see P.J. van Winter, 'De Hollandse tuin', *Nederlandse Kunsthistorisch Jaarboek* 8 (1975), 19–122.

[19] This print, FM no. 1288, exists as the cover of *S. Castellio, opera*... about the rising crisis in religion, published in 1613, but it is undoubtedly a much older image – perhaps a woodcut – from the previous century.

[20] In the sample images there are around seventy Dutch Lions. On the cartographic depiction of lions, see Paul Regan's essay in this volume.

Fig. 9.1. The Dutch Republic as a maid in a garden. *Spaensche tiranni* (reproduced
by kind permission of the Rijksmuseum, Amsterdam).

popular prints, as well as medals and coins.[21] One of the earliest
prints to illustrate this development is in *Den slapende leeu* [The Sleeping
Lion] (1579?), where the beast slumbers whilst the Netherlands are
increasingly oppressed by the Spanish. The implication is that the
leaders of the Netherlands have allowed the country to be despoiled
rather than choosing to act.[22] In later prints, the lion is active,
deployed both more freely (i.e. in a variety of stances and actions)
and in a more sophisticated manner (indicating a wider range of
meaning), and this utility, perhaps, is another reason for its popularity with designers when depicting the new state.

As an example of this versatility, *St. Andries* (1600) [fig. 9.2], a
print celebrating the capture of Fort St. Andries by Maurice, shows
a rampant lion, aided by patriotic bees and frogs, who fight off

---

[21] B. Kempers, 'Assemblage van de Nederlandse leeuw: politieke symboliek in
heraldiek en verhalende prenten uit de zestiende eeuw', in *idem*, ed., *Openbaring en
bedrog. De afbeelding als historische bron in de Lage Landen* (Amsterdam, 1995), 61, 62,
68–69.
[22] *Den slapende leeu* is FM no. 524a; J. Tanis and D. Horst, *Images of Discord* (Grand
Rapids, Mich., 1993), 45.

Fig. 9.2. The *Leo Belgicus*, detail from *St. Andries* (reproduced by kind permission of the Rijksmuseum, Amsterdam).

attacks by Papist locusts and Spanish swine.[23] The lion wears a cap marked 'liberty'. Another image depicting the Lion astride a globe and a fish, is accompanied by a text:

> See how Holland growls; with the Sceptre of power [. . .]
> Now the tail of the Lion of Holland is [evident?] through all the World
> And God's good hand directs Neptune . . .

Alternatively, the lion could be depicted together with the Dutch Garden, or it could be shown in diagrams of power which clearly

---

[23] FM no. S1126A.

define what lies 'within' and 'without' the Republic, in both geo-graphical and ideological terms. In *Spaensche tiranni* wolves carry off sheep, and even break into the garden, which the Dutch Lion defends with his scimitar, at the same time aiding the Prince (William of Orange), who is abroad destroying the Inquisition.

Liberty is the first of the key themes identified in the pamphlets: how significant is its portrayal in prints? Traditionally Liberty is shown as a maiden with a Phrygian cap, sometimes bearing a scep-tre, but such figures are rare in the prints, and the identification is not always clear. The scarcity of free-standing representations, and doubt about the identification of some of them, may seem surpris-ing.[24] Liberty is usually depicted as an attribute of other characters. Typically in *T' Arminiaens testament* (1618) [fig. 9.3], for example, it is present in the form of a 'liberty bonnet' or cap on a lance – firmly grasped by the Dutch Lions on the twin towers, and closely associated with the House of Orange.[25]

In a very fine and complex engraving celebrating the Twelve Years' Truce in the form of a fountain – *The Fountain of Peace* (1609) – liberty is a cap mounted on a lance, held by a noble (a senior mem-ber of the Nassau family, perhaps William of Orange), but cast into shadow.[26] Similarly, in *Elenchus rerum, Deo auspice, a confoederatis Belgis praeclaere gestarum* (*c.* 1600) [fig. 9.4], the lance and hat are held by the Dutch Lion.[27]

Variations on this depiction of liberty can be identified in further prints. In a *Picture of the Prosperity of the Independent Provinces of the Netherlands* (1608),[28] the lion wields two lances with caps, represent-ing *Libertas Conscientiae* [Freedom of Conscience] and *Libertas Patriae* [Freedom of the Fatherland] set over the motto of Orange. Twenty years later, another print portrayed Frederick Henry holding the lance, topped with a hat marked *Vryheyt* [Freedom].[29] In a print

---

[24] There are around 200 different distinct allegorical figures in the prints exam-ined, ranging from personifications of well-known civic vices and virtues, Envy for example, with six or seven examples, to Neptune (three) and the weather (twice), as against Liberty (six); the Liberty Bonnet or Cap appears on twelve occasions.

[25] FM nos. 1330, 1329a.

[26] FM no. 1256.

[27] FM no. 1152.

[28] FM no. 1415, see also FM no. 1255.

[29] *Ob debellatos hostes, civesque servatos* (1629), FM no. 1649.

Fig. 9.3. *T' Arminiaens Testament* (reproduced by kind permission from Atlas van Stolk, Rotterdam).

Fig. 9.4. The *Leo Belgicus* bearing a lance and liberty cap. Detail from *Elenchus rerum, Deo auspice, a confoederatis Belgis praeclare gestarum* (reproduced by kind permission of the Rijksmuseum, Amsterdam).

showing the Habsburg and Independent Netherlands as two lions, *St. Andries* [fig. 9.2], the lion representing the Republic wears the cap of liberty, garnished with two knives.[30]

Besides being portrayed in the hands of allegorical or identifiable figures, the lance and cap were also shown in the context of mar-

---

[30] The cap with two knives refers to republican action against tyrants: it first appeared on a coin from republican Rome, issued by Brutus in 43–42 BC, commemorating the assassination of Caesar in 44 BC. It was copied by Lorenzo de' Medici in a medal in 1537 after the assassination of his cousin, Alexander (who had been declared a hereditary duke in 1530 and thus was open to charges of tyranny), and by Henry II of France in 1552. The Roman coin was extant in Renaissance collections and the link with republicanism recognized by contemporaries, see J. Sleidan, *The General History of the Reformation of the Church from the Errors and Corruptions of the Church of Rome*, trans. E. Bohun (London, 1689), 554.

Fig. 9.5. The Republic as a ship, bearing a liberty bonnet. Detail from *Powerless Thundering of the Hellish Hound* (reproduced by kind permission of Simon van Gijn – Museum aan huis).

itime imagery. In an extraordinary allegorical ship seen in *Powerless Thundering of the Hellish Hound* (1585) [fig. 9.5], the lance and cap are mounted on the bowsprit.[31] A finer and more conventional ship of state, showing the happy condition of the Netherlands, may be seen in *Idea Belgicarum provinciarum confaederatarum* (1620), where again the lion clutches a lance and cap in its left claw, with a *pijlbundel* representing unity.[32]

The notable absence of free-standing depictions of liberty, and its close association with other elements such as the Dutch Lion and the Nassau dynasty, suggest a rather careful deployment of the theme. The princes of Orange, or lions representing the state, normally grasp it firmly, almost as if they are a guarantee of liberty. Given that even in the darkest days of the Revolt, Reformed Protestant authors for example had played down the political role of the individual subject, this is not surprising.[33] Furthermore, the Dutch Lion also often represented the military capacity of the Republic, suggesting that independence from Habsburg domination was equated

---

[31] SvG no. 1008, see also FM no. 433 and FM no. S1304B.
[32] FM no. 1416.
[33] Van Gelderen, *Political Thought*, 104, 107.

with liberty. Victory, and above all Justice, also appear in this context.[34]

The second major theme identified in the pamphlet literature concerned was that of privileges, but these are rarely surveyed in the images. Privileges were particularly important in the propaganda of the early years of the Revolt; they are admittedly an essential ingredient of depictions of the *Tyranny of Alba* [fig. 9.6], and are usually shown torn at his feet.[35] However, they do not appear elsewhere in the sample, and, furthermore, their appearance in later versions may be simply convention; by the later 1580s and beyond, Alba's regime was slipping from memory to history, and by the time of Van de Venne's version of the *Tyranny of Alba* (1622), the privileges have perhaps only historical rather than contemporary significance.[36] In the early years of the Revolt, the defence of the privileges was a major theme (and indeed they appear in earlier images).

The defence of privileges was closely linked to the role of the States, the third principal theme in the literature, by prominent pamphleteers such as Jacob van Wesenbeke. Similarly the role of the States, and the provincial States, are also rarely depicted in the prints. The urban patriciate, who might be regarded as a personification of the States, do not often appear in the prints, and when they do, it is not clear whether they are magistrates, i.e. office-holders, or simply merchants, although sometimes a distinctive motif is provided by showing figures in *tabbaards*, long, dark, fur collared robes. The existence of divisions among the elite is indicated in later versions of a popular composition, the *Tyranny of Alba* [fig. 9.6] (which first appeared in 1568),[37] and is also suggested in the *Elenchus rerum* [fig. 9.4], where some figures are dressed as magistrates. Here, in what is a partisan picture, they are cast entirely into shadow by the victory wagon of Maurice, whilst their gestures convey their confusion and that they have been surprised by Maurice's success. A rare, favourable depiction of the magistrates may be seen in the happy ship of state in *Idea Belgicarum provinciarum*. This scarcity contrasts with the flourishing

---

[34] Justice appears on seventeen occasions, and Victory around fifteen times.
[35] Van Gelderen, *Political Thought*, 117–118.
[36] FM no. 514.
[37] Also known as the *Throne of Alba*. For a summary of the development of the several prints and more than twenty paintings depicting this subject, see A.C. Sawyer, 'The *Tyranny of Alva*. The Creation and Development of a Dutch Patriotic Image', *De zeventiende eeuw* 19 (2003), 181–211.

Fig. 9.6. *The Tyranny of Alba*, 1568 (reproduced by kind permission from the Atlas van Stolk, Rotterdam).

of civic portraiture in the Netherlands and it may be that, like the unauthorized pamphleteers, these illustrators were wary of depicting the civic authorities for fear of punishment.[38] In contrast, depictions of the stadholders themselves appear frequently enough, and are almost always positive, if (in the case of Maurice) not always very reverent.

Research has revealed one particular representation of the States General, published in 1600, in the form of a print engraved by Christoffel van Sichem, but this is somewhat problematic.[39] In its

---

[38] C.E. Harline, *Pamphlets, Printing and Political Culture in the Early Dutch Republic* (Dordrecht, 1987), 111–117, 127.

[39] This image appeared as an illustration in J.F. Le Petit, *La Grande Chronique ancienne et moderne, de Hollande, Zélande, [. . .] jusques à la fin de l'an 1600*, 2 vols. (Dordrecht, 1601). It was available separately as *De gouverneurs en gourvernanten van de Nederlanden* in 1603 and as an illustration in E. Grimeston, *A Generall Historie of the Netherlands* (London, 1627).

context (as one of a series showing rulers of the Netherlands), the picture is startling, since it is part of a sequence which begins with feudal lords, and then progresses to Governors General, all in the form of portraits of the individuals concerned. Attuned to this depiction of personalized power, the reader is then 'bounced', with no warning, into a confrontation with a radically different scene [fig. 9.7]. Here, in a formalized council chamber, is the central figure of the rampant Dutch Lion, with symbols of unity and military power (the *pijlbundel* and scimitar), in front of, rather than seated upon, a throne. Perhaps the lion is one of the ways in which unity could be emphasized in connection with 'national' issues (which, in a dynastic, sovereign state might be thought the preserve of the prince and his court). At the front, two heraldic figures symbolize the Provinces represented in the chamber. Between are two rows of empty seats, upon which lie the cushions on which deputies sat.

Van Sichem is not depicting a particular council chamber. The motif comes from an earlier age and was popular beyond the Netherlands, appearing, for example, in an altarpiece by Niklas Strobl, dated to 1478.[40] The composition was adopted as part of the panoply of the Order of the Golden Fleece, adorning the documents associated with investiture as a member; an example exists showing Charles the Bold seated at the apex of the chamber as Master of the Order.[41] This 'diagram' of authority is therefore more suggestive of the medieval visualization of the state than to the depiction of the monarchic state by Bodin and, later on, Hobbes.[42]

---

[40] Now in the Stadtmuseum, Graz, Austria, showing the same pattern of seating in the Kingdom of Heaven, with Christ flanked by the apostles, replicated in an earthly scene below. It is illustrated on the cover of G. Jaritz, ed., *Disziplinierung im alltag des Mittelalters und der Frühen Neuzeit*, Veröffentlichungen des Instituts für Realienkunde des Mittelalters und der Frühen Neuzeit 17 (Vienna, 1999).

[41] See Ms. 187 of the Fitzwilliam Museum, Cambridge, reproduced in A. Arnould and J.M. Massing, *Splendors of Flanders* (Cambridge, 1993), 147, 177. My thanks to D. Freemantle for drawing my attention to this image. For another example of the theme, showing Charles the Bold and Guillaume Fillastre, the Chancellor of the Order, see W. Prevenier and W. Blockmans, *The Burgundian Netherlands* (Cambridge, 1986), 340, pl. 308.

[42] Van Sichem's illustration forms an interesting contrast with the frontispiece of Hobbes *Leviathan* which shows a crowned figure towering over his kingdom, composed of many smaller figures. It has been argued that Hobbes supervised the design of the image, see M. Corbett and R. Lightbown, *The Comely Frontispiece. The Emblematic Title Page in England 1550–1660* (London, 1979), 219–224.

Fig. 9.7. The States General

Given the empty seats in this print, where are the rulers? Perhaps the empty chamber indicates the abstract nature of power, vested in the assembly and not in individuals. Or, if we maintain that power can be encapsulated, it may refer to the representative nature of the States General, and the constraints of *ruggespraak*: the deputies present were instructed on what to say and how to vote on specific issues by the civic communities they represented – they did not speak and vote as a Parliamentary body. Dynamic, effective power was therefore to be found not in a sovereign head or even perhaps a collegiate body, but outside the chamber: in civic government, certainly, but also perhaps in less formal settings.

How does this illustration of the States General (and other prints) relate to the final key theme, that of the significance of popular sovereignty? There are no explicit references in the prints to this theoretical term – or at least, it is hard to reference such abstract concepts – but even in the pamphlets, it appears to some extent by implication.[43] Some aspects of imagery, whilst difficult to analyse systematically across numerous sources, may prove significant. First, individuals are often shown with meaningful poses and gestures, sometimes emphasized by gaze and eye contact which can form a web or network within the picture.[44] Secondly, the composition or structure of the images may reflect the nature of sovereignty in the Republic.

An example of significant eye contact and gesture is in the original version of the *Tyranny of Alba*, [fig. 9.6].[45] The magistrates, gazing at the political action in the scene, and depicted as herms with their hands on their lips, seem guilty of inaction – an interpretation confirmed by the text, which notes that they have 'been transformed

---

[43] Van Gelderen, *Political Thought*, 162–163, suggests it is implicit rather than explicit – the States were the leading sovereign powers in Dutch politics, and since they were to some degree representative, popular sovereignty can be implied.

[44] For an introduction to the significance of gesture and gaze, see E.H. Gombrich, 'Action and Expression in Western Art', in R.A. Hinde, ed., *Non-Verbal Communication* (Cambridge, 1972); M. Barasch, *Giotto and the Language of Gesture* (Cambridge, 1987), esp. 5 and 13, demonstrates that Giotto did not paint gestures 'realistically', but according to a well-known code which flourished in court and church. For an example of historians using gesture, and the transmission of meaning thereby, see J. Spicer, 'The Renaissance Elbow', in J. Bremmer and H. Roodenburg, eds., *A Cultural History of Gesture* (Cambridge, 1991), 84–128, who correlates the depiction of gestures of figures in Dutch art with the level of external threat to the Republic.

[45] FM no. 518.

into stone pillars, they have become deaf and weak: they dare not speak for fear of losing [their] possessions'. Clearly the author felt that they had some responsibility for governance of the state – and that he could illustrate the connection between their physical and political stances.

A political text requires the commitment and engagement of a reader, whereas the cognitive impact of an image, and to some extent its message, is more instantaneous – to be confronted by an image meant to be 'caught in the trammels of an implicit line of argumentation addressed to the eye of the imagination'.[46] A political print on a trader's stall or in a relatively public room was seen by everyone, rather than just those who took the money and time to buy and read a text. Moreover political prints normally depicted real events and disputes. In that sense, prints, as a 'popular' medium, represented political issues to the whole community, though decision-making was shown to be restricted to the social elites.

Since the prints often illustrate pastoral or commercial scenes, and occasionally warfare, a large number of labourers and soldiers are depicted – naturally these are 'invisible' in texts about political theory, but the nature of graphic representation is such that designers were almost obliged to include them in some scenes. Again, looking at the stance and gesture of many of the figures, it can be seen that labourers are usually shown at work, with no clear eye contact with any other person, and no self-conscious pose. By contrast, most elite figures are depicted with a specific stance, gesture, and often with an identifiable gaze or eye contact. If these images are diagrams about power, the active components are the gentry or regents, and a large proportion of the population appear to have little to say about politics.[47]

Yet, 'top down', dynastic compositions are also rare in the prints, which either emphasize networks, relationships, the lack of a focal point, and a wealth of detail. For example, few prints show a central, enthroned figure or an equestrian portrait or a large, prominent

---

[46] C. Johaud, 'Readability and Persuasion: Political Handbills', in R. Chartier, ed., *The Culture of Print. Power and the Uses of Print in Early Modern Europe*, trans. L. Cochrane (Cambridge, 1989), 235–260, there 258; Duke, 'Dissident Propaganda', 126.

[47] Civic government took care to make it so, see R. Dekker, 'Labour Conflicts and Working-Class Culture in Early Modern Holland', *International Review of Social History* 35 (1990), 377–420, there 384. For Oldenbarnevelt's horror of 'popular' involvement, see J. Den Tex, *Oldenbarnevelt*, 4 vols. (Haarlem, 1960–72), I, 133.

building or architectural motif. From 1590 obelisks appear in prints, but only as vehicles for satire. See for example *Piramide Papistique* (*c.* 1590), and *Rendez voi knapsack* (1615), where there is a collapsing pyramid or obelisk.[48] Such use of obelisks to vilify rather than exalt may be a response to Domenico Fontana's renowned achievement in erecting a 360 ton obelisk in the centre of St. Peter's Square in 1586, which was commemorated in *Della transportione dell'obelisco vaticano*, published in 1590. As with networks of gaze and gesture, systematically demonstrating and referencing this contrast across a wide range of images is problematic; but taken together, this evidence suggests that contemporaries did not see the state in terms of sovereignty, at least as understood by Bodin, Hobbes and their successors.[49]

Whilst in the pamphlets there is some support, in theory at least, for princely government, such support is almost entirely absent from the imagery.[50] With very few exceptions, symbols such as crowns and thrones, which speak of monarchy, have very negative connotations.[51] One exception, in the form of a medal, *Deo optimo maximo Laus*... (1587), reveals Elizabeth of England in an exalted role, trampling the beast of the Apocalypse, and with the provinces kneeling at her feet, as naked youths.[52] As depictions of the provinces as naked and kneeling are usually an indication of misfortune, this medal may not have been a successful effort at political propaganda.[53] The image

---

[48] FM no. 437. The distinction between obelisks and pyramids was not always clear at this period: FM no. 1297. The title is a war-cry of the time: see FM, I, 161.

[49] For a conventional definition of sovereignty, see F.H. Hinsley, *Sovereignty* (London 1966), and more recently A. Heywood, *Political Ideas and Concepts* (Basingstoke, 1994).

[50] See Van Gelderen, *Political Thought*, ch. 5, and 208–209.

[51] The only significant exceptions among the sample are *The Plague of Alba's Tyranny in the Low Countries* (*c.* 1573), FM no. RPK518A, showing William of Orange and Alba enthroned opposite one another, with the 'free' Provinces inclining to William and the rest, blindfolded and naked, driven to Alba's feet, and a fine equestrian portrait of Frederick Henry, *The Invincible Frederick Hendrik*... (1630), FM no. 1629, which includes a crown – practically invisible, but present in a heavenly scene – and is possibly referring to King David.

[52] E. Hawkins, A.W. Franks and H.A. Grueber, *Medallic Illustrations of the History of Great Britain and Ireland to the Death of George II*, 2 vols. (London, 1885), I, 139, no. 99.

[53] The medal does not bear any attribution, but see G. van Loon, *Beschryving der Nederlandsche Historipenningen*, 4 vols. (The Hague, 1726–31), I, 369; H.E. Greve, *De tijd van den Tachtigjarigen oorlog in beeld* (Amsterdam, 1908), 67, and R.C. Strong and J.A. van Dorsten, *Leicester''s Triumph* (London, 1964), facing p. 24, who all assume it was produced by Leicester's faction. See also Hawkins, Franks and Grueber, *Medallic Illustrations*, I, 139–140, who claim that the style of the medal is consistent with those produced by the States General at this period, suggesting an official

probably relates to the heated exchange of pamphlets between the supporters of Leicester and the States on the subject of sovereignty.[54] In 1587, a pamphlet by Thomas Wilkes deployed the novel theories of Bodin on sovereignty, in support of Leicester's claims. In response François Vranck presented what has been seen as a reliable overview of the workings of the new polity, and a logical conclusion to developments during the Revolt.[55]

Inferring abstract concepts such as popular sovereignty from pictorial data is difficult and is one area where illustrative material is less effective than the written word. Whilst pamphlets, as a medium, allowed authors to make a series of arguments and can employ words for complex abstract terms such as sovereignty, by their nature the prints could not so easily reference such terms. But perhaps other factors can also explain its absence. In the early stages of the Revolt, it seems that some of the leaders thought the term 'sovereignty' was to be avoided, whilst perhaps there were in any case too many practical crises to allow much time for theory.[56] Certainly the prints are almost all concerned with actual situations, and not theoretical justifications. In addition, the political thinking of the Republic appears to have contributed little to modern state theory.[57]

The tension between top-down 'sovereign' rule and representative power found in pamphlets is absent from the imagery. Though this tension had perhaps abated by the 1580s, when the issue of resistance

---

sanction. The only other reference I know of, which describes the provinces as male (for in all the prints I have seen they are female), is in another English source, Spencer's *Faerie Queene* (1590), where he refers to Belgica's 'Sons'. Certainly Leicester's allies were well aware of the importance of imagery (Strong and Van Dorsten note they put on tableaux at many towns). Among the medal's features are many showing a strong 'Reformed' flavour: the reverse shows seven Roman ecclesiastics (the pope, losing his grip on a chalice, a cardinal, two monks, two bishops, and a further cleric, possibly a Jesuit). The somewhat apolcalyptic theme is enhanced by a text from II Thessalonians 2, 8.

[54] Van Gelderen, *Political Thought*, 200.

[55] See E.H. Kossmann and A.F. Mellink, *Texts Concerning the Revolt of the Netherlands* (Cambridge, 1974), 49.

[56] E.H. Kossman, 'Popular Sovereignty at the Beginning of the Dutch Ancien Régime', *Acta Historiae Neerlandica* 14 (1981), 1–28, there 11; G. de Bruin, *Geheimhouding en verraad: de geheimhouding van staatszaken ten tijde van de Republiek (1600–1750)* (The Hague, 1991), 120; see also E.J. Dijksterhuis, *Simon Stevin* (The Hague, 1970), 123. Stevin (*c.* 1548–1620) was dismissive of theoretical questions about the legitimacy of power.

[57] M.E.H.N. Mout, 'Van arm vaderland tot eendrachtige republiek: de rol van politieke theorieën in de Nederlandse Opstand', *BMGN* 101 (1986), 345–365, there 348.

to tyranny within political debate was subsiding,[58] a negative portrayal of monarchic power continues to pervade the images (moderated slightly in propaganda associated with Frederick Henry). This suggests a deep-rooted hostility to monarchic rule and distaste for centralized sovereignty, as befits a society where the landscape itself, in the north at least, had prevented feudalism from flourishing, and undermined the establishment of centralized power.[59]

Three other significant political issues are identified in the pamphlets, that is the military effectiveness of the Republic (or rather, those attitudes and changes in practice which provided an effective army), the role of civic virtues, and religion. The authors of the pamphlets stressed the importance of a disciplined, virtuous standing army.[60] Realistic depictions of warfare are uncommon in the prints (though marching troops and burning cities do sometimes provide a sinister backdrop), but allegories of military action abound: a fascinating example can be seen in *Een pasquil tot verwijt der Holland. gemackt . . .* (1615) where a lion represents the Republic at war.[61] Eschewing a heraldic past, it storms across the page to assault the Habsburg eagle. Armed with a scimitar called *Eendracht Heeft macht* [Unity is might], it has sliced the orb of world dominion in half and lopped off one of the eagle's heads.[62]

Another embattled lion can be seen in *Rendez voi knapsack*, in this case with a scimitar called *Beschermer des vaderlants* [Protector of the Fatherland] wielded against *Landt bespringer* [Invader of the Country]. Again, in *Vreemden handel* [fig. 8] (*c.* 1615), the lion attacks Spain, in the role of a monster, directed by a figure who may be Maurits.[63] Here, there is a close association between the lion, clutching the *pijl-*

---

[58] Van Gelderen, *Political Thought*, 160.
[59] See J. de Vries and A. van der Woude, *The First Modern Economy. Success, Failure and Perseverance of the Dutch Economy, 1500–1815* (Cambridge, 1997), 17, and also ch. 5.
[60] Van Gelderen, *Political Thought*, 182, 197–199. See also G. Oestreich, *Neostoicism and the Early Modern State*, ed. B. Oestreich and H.G. Koenigsberger, trans. D. McLintock (Cambridge, 1982).
[61] FM no. 1302.
[62] The text confirms the bellicose message of the image, though here the sword is called Unity. The lion's wings are not explained (though the text notes that the lion has 'a new Brandenburg cloak', a reference to the conversion of John Sigismund of Brandenburg to Calvinism at Christmas 1613). Perhaps here, 'Unity' raises issues of sovereignty, in as much as the Republic had to be able to manage its armed forces coherently.
[63] FM no. 1298.

Fig. 9.8. *Vreemden Handel, c.* 1615 (reproduced by kind permission from the Atlas van Stolk, Rotterdam).

bundel of seven arrows indicating the unity of the Provinces, and the Republic's military might. Whilst the lion itself could represent the wider state, the scimitar it wields emphasizes the significance of war-like activity. Another example of the scimitar, *Patria Defensio* [Defence of the Fatherland], appears in *Elenchus rerum* [fig. 9.4].[64] Often the scimitar is actively employed against the enemies of the Republic, for example in *St. Andries* [fig. 9.2]. Thus the scimitar often appears to indicate the armed might of the Republic. The choice of a scimitar, rather then a sword, was presumably to differentiate it from the sword of justice.

The ability to deploy force in defence of the Republic is exploited in several images. Some lions fiercely defend the Dutch Maid in her garden, for example in *Maechts Antwoort tegen op en aen de aenspraek van een courtisaen* ... [Maiden's reply to the claims of a courtesan] (*c.* 1617?),[65] where, rather than a scimitar, the lion brandishes the

---

[64] Holland in *Desideratæ pacis* has a scimitar labelled B. Unfortunately the print lacks a key but clearly the weapon has an independent meaning within the ensemble. FM no. 1232.

[65] FM no. S1315A.

fasces, the symbol of unity. In another, *Handelinge van Trefues* [The Truce Negotiations] (1609),[66] the *Vryen Nederlantschen Leeu* [Free Dutch Lion] is beset by Johan Ney, Spinola, the pope, a cardinal, a Jesuit, and several Spaniards.

By the early seventeenth century, with the rise of the Remonstrant crisis, Orangists closely associated the army with Maurice, for example in *T' Arminiaens Testament*, [fig. 9.3] where lions stand atop the twin towers on the left, and are described as 'the exalted alliance of the Netherlands and the Orange tower shooting its powerful arrows against the writings and works of slanderous lies'. The same image with another lion is set among items depicting fundamental aspects of the state – Liberty, Unity, and the House of Orange – at the foot of the page: the lion is grasping the *Orangje Bandt* or *Bandt der vryevereende Nederland* [Orange Band or Band of the Free Netherlands].[67]

Another concern of the pamphlets which is emphasized in the prints is the role of civic virtue.[68] In particular, concord and unity were regarded as indispensable for the defence of liberty, and the pictorial evidence, by associating unity with the lion, echoes the pamphlets. Additionally, the printmakers illustrated a profusion of other virtues and vices. Not all can be easily identified, though a number have captions to prevent misunderstandings, which can aid identification of others. Justice and Liberty appear, but in addition there is a large cast of minor characters, representing diligence, discipline, fidelity, fortitude, hope and so on through to vigilance and watchfulness. Virtues could be contrasted with vices, and early in the Revolt these were applied crudely to William of Orange and Alba – the justice, peace and piety ascribed to William being contrasted with injustice, war and blasphemy on the part of Alba.[69] By making Orange and Alba vehicles for civic virtues (and vices) such propaganda indicates theoretical political preference.

A more sophisticated deployment can be illustrated by the vice of Envy, often depicted with snakes in her hair, and gnawing her heart. Her role in *T' Arminiaens Testament* is emphasized with a trowel – she is one of the builders of the Arminian folly: in *Amnistia ofte vergatel- heyd, vermanende d'inwoonders* . . . [Amnesty or Forgetfulness admonishing

---

[66] FM no. S1259a.
[67] FM nos. 1330, 1329a.
[68] Van Gelderen, *Political Thought*, 263–264.
[69] See Tanis and Horst, *Images of Discord*, 25–27.

the inhabitants] (1623),[70] along with *Tweedracht* [Disunity] and *Ongeoorlofde staetsucht* [Improper Ambition], she is chased away by a Patriot; whilst in *Pyramis pacifica* (1609),[71] she is chained, with Mars, to an obelisk celebrating the Peace; in *Idea Belgicarum provinciarum*, she is about to be run down by the Republic, in the form of a ship; in *Het groot balet* (1632), [The Great Ballet],[72] she is scattering apples of discord; and she is depicted in the company of Tyranny and other sinister figures in *Romsche hemel uaert* [Romish Ascent to Heaven] (*c.* 1621).[73]

A range of civic virtues could be combined in one print; in *Elenchus rerum*, besides Liberty and Freedom a significant role is given to Prudence with her mirror and candle, whilst Victory holds a trophy from the defeat of the Spanish at Turnhout.[74] From 1629, there is a fine example, *Victori-waeghen vanden doorluchtige Prince van Orangien . . .* [fig. 9], showing a 'Victory Wagon' bearing Frederik Hendrik and accompanied by Liberty and other virtues.[75] The plethora of vices and virtues shown in the prints, even if in many cases they provided the 'background music' to the main events shown, indicates their significance to the political theory of the day, and clearly echoes the pamphlet writers' concerns.

Turning finally to the significance of religion in the Republic, Van Gelderen suggested that between 1572 and 1590 – as the Reformed church was constructing itself – the Dutch had to address questions of politics and religion. By the 1590s, it was clear the government would have a say in Reformed church affairs, though of course sects such as the Anabaptists, who recognized civil authority, nonetheless rejected any role for civil government in the Church and argued against Christians holding political office. For Van Gelderen, the relationship between religion and the state was fundamentally important in the development of Dutch political thought. This could be seen in contemporary debates where unity and concord were the 'stay and foundation' of countries and towns, whilst 'discord or

---

[70] FM no. 1502.
[71] FM no. 1270.
[72] FM no. 1708a.
[73] FM no. 1433.
[74] The print celebrates a bitter defeat for the Spanish, referring to January 1597 when Habsburg forces were caught in disarray at Turnhout and badly mauled, whilst Maurits's campaign of that year resulted in a string of victories.
[75] FM no. 1647.

Fig. 9.9. Liberty and other virtues. Detail from *Victori-waeghen vanden doorluchtige Prince van Orangien* (reproduced by kind permission of the Rijksmuseum, Amsterdam).

dissension' were the causes of 'all adversity, total ruin, spoilation and desolation'; therefore some form of religious peace was essential.[76]

Religion rarely plays a prominent role in the prints, though there are non-partisan images which show a studied lack of confessional precision, perhaps reflecting the apparent religious equivocation of the emergent Republic. On other occasions, and by contrast, some prints bitterly attack religious enemies, particularly the Roman Catholic Church. Though Catholic practice is rarely attacked, the religious personnel – monks, bishops, cardinals and especially Jesuits – are almost always shown as deeply sinister figures.

A more measured depiction of religion is found in *Elenchus rerum* [fig. 4], which does echo some of the aspects found in the pamphlets. Here the lion grasps a lance, and the caption informs us that

---

[76] Van Gelderen, *Political Thought*, 217, 219.

he holds the deadly lance of Spain (on which FREEDOM is the Cap of Liberty that is your emblem) and the gleaming sword of LIBERTY: by this sword is meant DEFENCE OF THE FATHERLAND and by liberty is meant RELIGION, which things are protected by the Lion's zeal.

On the lion's wreathed shield, the *pijlbundel*, labelled Unity, are held in clasped hands. The lion rests his paw on a book which – labelled 'Religion' – is just visible in the shadows.

In conclusion, while some of the themes that can be identified in the print culture of the Dutch Revolt were clearly present in the visual sources – most notably Liberty, albeit often accompanied with Justice – other themes such as the States or popular sovereignty are less visible. This may be in part a reflection of the difficulty of portraying abstract concepts, although in some instances subtle references are made through the use of gesture and gaze. Furthermore while prints – often showing specific crises or strains in the polity – were themselves a vehicle for the exploration of and debate about political issues, this might itself perhaps indicate an aspect of popular sovereignty. The scarcity of depictions of the privileges may be explained by their declining importance once the Republic was established. The ability of the Republic to resist Habsburg attacks, with a 'virtuous' and disciplined army, and the prominence of the Dutch Lion as a vehicle for this aspect of the state are notable – the ability to wage war aggressively, energetically and effectively is portrayed as an integral feature of the new state. As for religion, it is often downplayed, but where it does appear the emphasis is upon those aspects of the Roman Catholic Church which are perceived as especially dangerous – the Jesuits in particular. The role of civic virtue stressed in the pamphlets is clearly affirmed in the prints, as an essential element for the continuing success of the Republic.

Political prints do confirm an almost violent antipathy to dynastic, hierarchic deployment of power as expressed in the language of monarchy, and stress the negotiated, dispersed, oligarchic power structures of the Republic. To the designers, the theoretical justification for advocating a different kind of state was perhaps less crucial than making that antipathy clear.

CHAPTER TEN

PUBLIC OPINION OR RITUAL CELEBRATION OF CONCORD? POLITICS, RELIGION AND SOCIETY IN COMPETITION BETWEEN THE CHAMBERS OF RHETORIC AT VLAARDINGEN IN 1616

Joke Spaans

In the summer of 1616 fifteen chambers of rhetoric – lay societies which composed and performed erudite vernacular plays on formal occasions – met for a festival in Vlaardingen, a port and fishing town on the Meuse just west of Rotterdam. The Vlaardingen chamber, The Oaktree (*De Akerboom*), had invited sister-chambers from a number of towns and villages to come and compete in a rhetorical display. The occasion lasted for several days. It began with the formal reception of the visiting chambers, who processed in, wearing their stage-costumes. They presented their hosts with ornamental shields emblazoned with their coat of arms, accompanied with appropriate poetic greetings, which were answered with a similar form of welcome by the brothers of The Oaktree. Over the next few days the chambers staged morality plays and held contests in the recitation of poems, both prepared and extempore, developing a theme set by their host. A jury awarded prizes for various aspects of performance, presentation and content, and the festival was concluded by a formal closing ceremony.

Festivals of this kind were obviously not only a literary competition but also an occasion for public festivity. The Reformed Church was highly critical of these public performances and put pressure on secular authorities to prohibit them altogether. The plays usually had a moral content, expressed in religious terms sometimes drawing upon Bible stories for their subject matter. The Church resented this use of theologically sensitive material, as the popular format of a morality play almost inevitably led to deviations from established orthodoxy. Moreover, the Church condemned performing on Sundays, the travesty of male players impersonating female characters and the general incitement to frivolity that the theatre represented. Even the activities of the rhetoricians in the privacy of their chambers were deeply mistrusted, as they provided a forum where Reformed and non-Reformed exchanged playful verses on matters of political, social and moral relevance over drinks and tobacco.[1]

Recent research, however, has convincingly shown that the activities of the chambers of rhetoric also had more serious aspects. Besides venues for male conviviality they functioned as popular academies, providing adult men with a formalized education in vernacular linguistic skills, both written and oral, that were necessary for all those aspiring to public office.[2] These skills were honed in the regular meetings of the chambers under the patronage of local magistrates and in the more controversial locally performed public plays and supra-local festivals. Until well into the eighteenth century the chambers of rhetoric provided this educational role, despite the misgivings of the Church. Recently they have even been credited with preparing the way for a modern public sphere, in forming public opinion, both among the members of the chamber and in the audience. It has been claimed that the plays presented a variety of possible points of view on often controversial issues and intended to offer the audience food for thought and for further discussion.

This view had recently been advocated by Arjan van Dixhoorn. His thesis has demonstrated that the founding of new chambers and supra-local festivals noticeably coincided with periods of heightened tension, such as the penetration of Protestant thought into the Netherlands, the Revolt, the discussions on humanist reforms in poor relief and the Twelve Years' Truce.[3] Dixhoorn's view is in line with the recent work of Willem Frijhoff and Marijke Spies, who coined the term 'discussion culture' to describe the cultural formation of the Republic. Its decentralized political structure, with an abundance of corporate bodies on all levels of government and administration, demanded constant rounds of consultation and the building of con-

---

[1] A previous version of this chapter was published as Joke Spaans, 'Politiek, religie en samenleving in *Vlaerdings redenrijck-bergh*' in: B. Ramakers (ed.), *Op de Hollandse Parnas. De Vlaardingse rederijkers wedstrijd van 1616* (Zwolle, 2006). F.C. van Boheemen and T.C.J. van der Heijden, *De Hollandse rederijkers vanaf de middeleeuwen tot het begin van de achttiende eeuw. Bronnen en bronnenstudies* (Delft, 1999).

[2] Above all A. van Dixhoorn, *Lustige geesten, Rederijkers en hun kamers in het publieke leven van de Noordelijke Nederlanden in de vijftiende, zestiende en zeventiende eeuw* (n.p., 2004).

[3] Van Dixhoorn, *Lustige geesten*, 366–388.

sensus.[4] Specialists on Dutch Renaissance theatre, moreover, identify specific partisan positions in individual plays or festivals.[5]

The Vlaardingen chamber invited participants in the 1616 festival to present a morality play on the question 'What necessary measures should be taken for the common good of the people and the country?' Beside plays, poems had to be delivered on what seems to be an unrelated and uncontroversial topic: 'He who raises his children well and properly, what do they, once grown up, owe him in return?' At first sight the theme for the plays does indeed fit Van Dixhoorn's thesis. The year 1616 was one of mounting tension. The performances might be expected to reflect the political and religious opinions of their various authors and/or the elites of their home cities, presenting the audience with a range of arguments that lent themselves to further discussion and in relation to which each person could formulate a position of his or her own. The published scripts of the plays, however, raise serious questions about these assumptions. The scripts are ambiguous at best, and can hardly be credited with the viewpoints that, with hindsight, we know characterized the opposing parties.[6]

This article will analyse the published texts on three related questions. The first concerns the representation of the political and religious problems that confronted the Dutch Republic in 1616. These cluster around the relative merits of war and peace, the rivalry between stadholder Maurice and the *landsadvocaat* Oldenbarnevelt, and the associated religious controversies. Secondly, the article will consider the perception of an ideal society that emerges from these plays and poems. Finally it will question the assertion made in recent studies that plays like these contributed to a public debate, or even to the formation of a climate of public opinion.

---

[4] W. Frijhoff and M. Spies, *1650. Bevochten eendracht* (The Hague, 1999), 218–224.

[5] M. Spies, 'Rederijkers in beroering: religie en politiek bij de Hollandse rederijkers in de eerste decennia van de zeventiende eeuw', in F. de Bree, M. Spies and R. Zemel, eds., *'Teeckenrijcke Woorden' voor Henk Duits. Opstellen over literatuur, toneel, kunst en religie, meest uit de zestiende en zeventiende eeuw* (Amsterdam and Münster, 2002); M.B. Smits-Veldt, 'Menenius Agrippa op het rederijkerstoneel in Vlaardingen en Amsterdam', in K. Porteman and K.E. Schöndorf, eds., *Liber amicorum prof. dr. Kåre Langvik-Johannessen* (Leuven, 1989).

[6] *Vlaerdings redenryck-bergh, met middelen beplant, die noodigh sijn 't Gemeen, en vorderlijck het landt* (Amsterdam, 1617).

The Twelve Years' Truce: Half a Peace and Uneven Profits

By 1616 there was increasing tension in the Dutch Republic over
the political and religious controversies, which would bring the
country to the brink of civil war. First, the Twelve Years' Truce
(1609–21) in the protracted war against Spain brought to the fore
the question of the precise relationship between the provincial States
and the States General, which was poorly defined, while the position of the stadholder remained ambiguous. Who was to decide
whether to resume the war after 1621 or to look for lasting peace?
This was a complicated issue as the provinces that constituted the
Republic, and the powerful cities that dominated the States of Holland
in particular, had diverging views on this matter.

The economic arguments that had led to the Truce in the first
place were still as valid in 1616 as they had been in 1609. The war
had bled the economies of both protagonists. Spanish trade embar-
goes hampered trade between the Baltic and the Iberian Peninsula,
which was the mainstay of Dutch overseas commerce. The lucrative
colonial venture of the Dutch East India Company clashed with
Spanish interests in the East, as did plans to form a Dutch West
Indian Company in the Caribbean. The *landsadvocaat* of Holland,
Johan van Oldenbarnevelt, through patient but determined diplomacy, agreed with Spain on a truce for twelve years, for a very low
price. The Truce lifted the embargo on the north-south route.
Moreover it offered respite to the land-provinces, which had suffered
most heavily from war damage inflicted upon the land and its population by battles and sieges, the passage of armies and marauding
soldiers. In return, the Republic merely promised not to expand its
trade activities in the East and West Indies, denying the wishes of
the king of Spain for concessions towards improving the position of
the Catholic Church in the Republic. A continuation of the war
would have been to the advantage of Zeeland and some Holland
towns, but the Truce benefited all those involved in colonial trade,
and the land-provinces.

The stadholder, Count Maurice of Nassau, supported by his cousin
Louis of Nassau, stadholder of the northern provinces, had always
advocated a continuation of the war which aligned the Republic
with England. This policy met with increasing support from the
States General. The *landsadvocaat*, on the other hand, supported by
a powerful party in the States of Holland, favoured the conclusion
of peace and an alliance with France as the most favoured European

power. For all parties the Truce was a halfway solution, although none could deny that it brought the Republic considerable advantages in the short term. The Republic had gained international prestige because it had bought the Truce from its formidable enemy for such a low price. Prosperity returned, although its benefits were unevenly divided.[7]

The plays reflect all these dilemmas. For most of them, the Revolt against Spain is the backdrop of the action. In some form they all comment on the contemporary political and economic situation of the country, and the relative advantages and disadvantages of peace, truce or war. The first half of the play performed by representatives from Kethel, for example, presents a dialogue between Monarchy, representing the king of Spain, with his advisers Tyranny, Force, Deceit and Dishonest Inquiry. Monarchy brags about his world-wide dominion, marred only by his failure to subdue the Republic. He describes how this irksome little nation robs him of the profit in colonial trade which he so sorely needs to pay his armies, utterly frustrating his hopes of eventual victory. The advisers counsel their king to agree to a Truce, with the deceitful intent to attack when the Dutch are off their guard.

The second half of Kethel's play shows Freedom of the Land, representing the Republic, in conference with her councillors Constant Prudence and Vigilance. The proposed Truce is here decried as a mere semblance of peace, which offers no guarantee against the treachery of a vengeful enemy. How to choose between a ruinous war or a partial peace, which moreover will incite all sorts of sectaries to divide the population? She briefly considers the benefits of open war, but is moved by advisers, with allegorical names like Profound Wisdom, Common Weal, True Teaching and Fear of God, to pursue lasting peace. This can be attained, concludes the chamber of Kethel, when a prudent regime, under a unified government, faithfully guides a godfearing people.[8]

Not all chambers envisioned such a peaceful solution to the Republic's problems. Amsterdam's The Sweet-Briar (*De Egelantier*) rejects any compromise with the enemy which limits industry and the freedom of trade. It sings an unabashed panegyric of war: true

---

[7] Israel, *Dutch Republic*, 399–477. The perspective of the main protagonists in J.J. den Tex, *Oldenbarnevelt*, 5 vols. (Haarlem, 1960–72), II and III, and A.Th. van Deursen, *Maurits van Nassau. De winnaar die faalde* (Amsterdam, 2000), 201–278.

[8] *Redenryck-bergh*, fol. Ee2v Ff1v, Ff3v–4ʳ.

Batavians are in their element when the drum rolls, the trumpet rings out, the horses are bridled and soldiers march as far as the eye can see. According to the Amsterdam chamber, what was best for people and country was to pray for divine blessing while preparing for war. Even so, a precondition for success was concord on the home front.[9]

The protagonist of this play is Ruler, who is counselled by a succession of advisers on good government. They argue that a good prince abhors tyranny and venality, protects religion, is virtuous and just, capable and a man of his word. He shows self-restraint, and prevents discord among the ruled arising from deceit, hatred or distrust of government. Most importantly, he must have the courage to be firm. At the same time he can never afford to lose his subjects' love towards him. The entire play never even mentions the war against Spain, the Truce or its approaching end. The message of the play remains ambiguous: it could be read as an argument in favour of resuming the war against Spain with God's blessing, or as the truism that a good prince should not hesitate to take up arms where needed – leaving open the question of whether this was such a moment of need.

The play of the chamber of Gorcum is equally ambiguous about the merits of war, but applies its reflections more directly to current affairs. Here a spectacular part is reserved for the war god Mars. When the main character, Nation, complains it is tired of war, Vigilance and Suspicion recall the excellent services of Mars in the war against Spain. They advise Nation to call in the help of Mars again, now that tensions are mounting in the country itself, which are rendered more dangerous as Spain's armies are mobilized just across the border for an intervention in the contested succession of Jülich and Cleves.[10]

At the same time, however, the god of war is courted by Conceited Mind and Unrest. In what must have been a spectacular scene, these two shady characters make Mars perform a magic ritual to conjure up Discord from the deepest regions of Hell.[11] Good Government promptly sends Vigilance to remind Mars of his long-standing friendship with Nation, to persuade him to preserve the country against

---

[9] *Ibid.*, fols. M3v–4r.
[10] *Ibid.*, fol. Tt2v, cf. Israel, *Dutch Republic*, 407.
[11] *Redenryck-bergh*, fol. Tt4r–v.

external and internal enemies, and to restrain him from unleashing civil war. High Authority and Good Government symbolically avert these dangers by disarming Mars and tying one of his arms behind his back, leaving the other one free to protect Nation.[12] In this way the Gorcum chamber, like the Amsterdam Sweet-Briar, avoids pleading openly for resumption of the war. At the same time it declares that war against an external enemy has its proper use, and calls for concord on the home front.

The chamber from the port of Rotterdam also emphasized the positive sides of war. Where wars usually only bring destruction, by God's grace it has made the Dutch Republic flourish, and has increased both its wealth and its international standing. The Rotterdam Chamber praised the prosperity, military strength, and world-wide trade networks of the Republic, that together made it a world power, despite the war. The one blemish on this splendid performance was the recent discord that augured no good in view of the dangers inherent in its current position. A truce, after all, was only half a peace, and the god of war (shown sleeping on the stage) remained anything but harmless.[13]

The Amsterdam chamber, The White Lavender (*Het Wit Lavendel*), specified some economic aspects of this internal discord. Its play depicts a dethroned and somewhat grumpy Mars. He blames the king of Spain, who, despite his otherwise admirable bloodthirstiness, has let the Dutch get away with a truce, which will not profit either side: both have struck a bad deal. In a series of sketches, a farmer, a burgher of independent means, and a group of city dwellers comment on its mixed blessings. The farmer and the man of means prosper, but the city dwellers suffer from a decline in manufacture. They have a hard time making ends meet. Moreover, there is division in the Church – represented on stage by the Devil sowing the seeds of discord, while the people are asleep.[14] For all their astute diagnosis, the brothers of The White Lavender propose a remarkably apolitical solution to the question posed by their hosts. They counsel concord, peace and love in accordance with God's will.[15]

---

[12] *Ibid.*, fol. Xx2v.
[13] *Ibid.*, fols. Hh3v, Kk1r–v.
[14] *Ibid.*, fols. O1r, O2r and O3v–V1r.
[15] *Ibid.*, fol. Q2r.

On the whole these five chambers each show considerable ambi-
guity about the relative merits of war or the Truce and most of
them do not even draw upon this theme. Delft, Gouda and Nootdorp
straightforwardly plead for love and concord. Delft compares the
Republic with the ancient Greeks, who through concord, piety and
other republican virtues succeeded in beating off the Persian invasion under the mighty King Xerxes. The play by the chamber of
Gouda asserts that God will continue the support he has shown the
Republic in the war against Spain as long as concord is not broken. Nootdorp does not even need to make an explicit reference to
the political situation to deliver a comparable message. The chambers represented at the Vlaardingen festival in 1616 overwhelmingly
answer the political question of The Oaktree in the sense that restoration of love and harmony are the most necessary measures to be
taken on behalf of people and country.

The Portrayal of Maurice and landsadvocaat Oldenbarnevelt in the Plays

In their emphasis on the virtues of peace and concord the chambers actually conformed to official state policy. In 1616 no official
decision had yet been taken about what to do after the Truce
expired – and in fact this remained an open question even in 1621.[16]
It was no secret that the stadholder and the *landsadvocaat* had their
differences of opinion on constitutional matters and foreign policy.
Both had, however, so far avoided open confrontation, and presented
a united front. Provincial States and city magistrates might have their
preferences for one or the other, but most kept their own counsel.[17]

Two chambers at the Vlaardingen contest allowed their preferences to show in the plays they staged. The character *Lands' Advocaat*
appears in the play performed by Maasland, where together with
Nobility, Knights and Cities, he provides advice to the character
Country, a representation of the States of Holland. Country is riven
by discord. Pro-Spanish Counsel proposes to return to the obedience of the king of Spain, as only a monarchy can wield the power
needed to enforce strict laws and regulations, and so restore tran-

---

[16] J.J. Poelhekke, *Tuytgaen van den Trêves. Spanje en de Nederlanden in 1621* (Groningen,
1960).
[17] S. Groenveld, *Evidente factiën in den staet. Sociaal-politieke verhoudingen in de 17e-
eeuwse Republiek der Verenigde Nederlanden* (Hilversum, 1990), 14–32.

quility. When Country shows some susceptibility to these arguments, *Land's Advocaat* forcefully rejects them. Force has proven to be totally counter-productive, and has led to revolt and war in the first place.[18] In this play *Lands' Advocaat* is the only figure with a strong and convincing position, squarely defending the constitution of the Republic, whereas Nobility, Knights and Cities seem to waver and Country is desperate. The stadholder is not mentioned at all. The answer that it finally formulated on the Vlaardingen theme, however, gave pride of place, not to statesmen, but to Fear of God – not a religious party, but 'the beginning of all wisdom' – which will lead the people to obedience to those set in authority above them and to love of their neighbours.[19]

The chamber of Gorcum briefly mentioned Oldenbarnevelt as the architect of the Truce, this half-peace. In contrast, it presents the princes of Orange as the true shepherds of the country. Lamentably William the Silent was treacherously murdered, but his House has produced a new hero, a splendid war leader, who with God's help leads the Republic to victories that are lauded all over the world. The character High Authority symbolically offers him a sword with which to quell the internal dissension, and exhorts him to extend impartial judgment over rich and poor.[20] The play thus echoes sentiments that would recur in periodic Orangist opposition movements against the power of the urban regent factions. The latter were perceived as only looking after their own profit, to the exclusion of all others, whereas only the stadholders were in a position to protect the common interests of all inhabitants. Unlike Maasland, Gorcum seems to advocate a sovereignty vested in the States General, represented in the play by High Authority, and the stadholder as their executive arm, bypassing the claims of the Provincial States.

Most chambers do not mention the rivalry between statesmen or the high colleges of State at all. The White Carnations (De Witte Angieren) of Haarlem advocates harmonious collaboration between stadholder and States, as they are both bound by oath to maintain its laws and privileges. Others limited themselves to a more general plea that each should do his duty in the positions to which they had been called.[21]

---

[18] *Redenryck-bergh*, fol. D1v.
[19] *Ibid.*, fol. E1r.
[20] *Ibid.*, fol. Tt3v, Vv3r, Vv4r.
[21] Cf. the section below: 'The Ideal Society'.

Remonstrants and Counter-Remonstrants

The discussion over the constitution and the political future of the
Republic was exacerbated by growing dissension in the public Church
over the interpretation of its Reformed confession of faith. The Dutch
Reformation had been a political Reformation. The new regime that
had established itself in the wake of the Revolt relied heavily on
groups that had rallied to a Reformed style of Protestantism. Consequently, the Reformed Church was established as the public Church
in each of the United Provinces.[22] Theologically this Reformed heritage had initially been somewhat fluid.[23] The first generation of
Reformed ministers had focused on the differences between Protestantism and Roman Catholicism and the organization of a new
Church. The generation that graduated from the Dutch universities
around the turn of the seventeenth century had ambitions to develop
Reformed doctrine and define it more sharply. These younger men
were the products of an academic culture of formalized disputation,
which had taught them to examine and defend the tenets of their
faith in the light of biblical testimony. Inevitably this led to discussions that touched on the foundations of Reformed theology.

The theological controversies not only added to a given conflict
of interests, but are often seen as the most explosive issue. They centred on election and reprobation.[24] Standard Reformed doctrine states
that God is both merciful and just. Although, as a consequence of
Adam's sin, the entire human race is tainted, in His mercy God
delivers from eternal damnation all those He elects to save in Jesus
Christ, irrespective of their merits. Justly, He leaves others to the
eternal punishment they deserve because of their sins.[25] In the seven-

---

[22] J. Spaans, 'Catholicism and Resistance to the Reformation in the Northern
Netherlands', in Benedict *et al.*, eds., *Reformation, Revolution and Civil War*, 149–163.
[23] W. Nijenhuis, 'De publieke kerk, veelkleurig en verdeeld, bevoorrecht en onvrij',
in D.P. Blok *et al.*, eds., *Algemene geschiedenis der Nederlanden*, 15 vols. (Haarlem, 1977–
83), VI.
[24] Cf. I. Schöffer, 'De crisis van de jonge Republiek 1609–1625', in J.A. van
Houtte *et al.*, eds., *Algemene geschiedenis der Nederlanden*, 13 vols. (Antwerp, 1949–58),
VI; A.Th. van Deursen, *Bavianen en slijkgeuzen. Kerk en kerkvolk ten tijde van Maurits en
Oldenbarnevelt* (Assen, 1974); W. van 't Spijker *et al.*, eds., *De synode van Dordrecht in
1618 en 1619* (Houten, 1987), 38–48.
[25] J.N. Bakhuizen van den Brink, *De Nederlandsche belijdenisgeschriften* (Amsterdam,
1940), 89.

teenth century theological inquiry could and did push further, asking why, if man's will is unfree and God is merciful, He elects some but rejects others. In his *Institutes of the Christian Religion*, Calvin himself defended the freedom of academic theological speculation, but warned against vain curiosity, moving beyond what is biblically defensible on this topic. For him, digging deeper than what God has seen fit to reveal in Scripture amounted to blasphemy.[26] Following these guidelines, around 1600, both in the Republic and abroad, Reformed theologians speculated on the logical sequence in God's eternal decrees.

The resulting theological opinions can be broadly divided into three main streams. The so-called infralapsarian position stated that God had foreseen Adam's fall before Creation, had then decided to elect some and reject others, without taking account of their acts, and finally decided to let His Son atone for the sins of the elect on the Cross. The somewhat sterner supralapsarian argument held that God had first and foremost decreed to elect some and declare others as reprobate. Only subsequently would he have decided to allow Adam to fall and to let Christ atone for the sins of the elect.[27] Both these varieties of Reformed teaching leave the initiative entirely with God and deny that Christ died for *all* of humanity.

Considering that ultimately these views could be construed in ways that made God the 'author of sin', a third option developed, which would become the Remonstrant position. Here it was argued that God, again from eternity, had foreseen the Fall and decreed the atonement of Christ. Unlike the previous options, this one held that God had foreseen that some would accept the saving grace he offered to all in Christ, and others would not. Based on this foreknowledge, God decreed redemption for the former and damnation for the latter. In this way predestination and the impossibility for man to work towards his own salvation were maintained, as his eternal fate had been preordained before Creation. For stricter Calvinists, however,

---

[26] John Calvin, *Institutes*, book III, chapter 21; cf. E.P. Meijering, *Calvin wider die Neugierde. Ein Beitrag zum Vergleich zwischen reformatorischem und patristischem Denken* (Nieuwkoop, 1980).

[27] H.I.J. Groenewegen, ed., *De Remonstrantie op haren driehonderdsten gedenkdag, 1610–14 januari 1910, in de oorspronkelijke vorm uitgegeven, afgebeeld en toegelicht* (Leiden, 1910), 4–10; also in C. Augustijn *et al.*, eds., *Reformatorica. Teksten uit de geschiedenis van het Nederlandse protestantisme* (Zoetermeer, 1996), 120–122.

this was unacceptable, as judgment was based on *foreseen* merit, and so did not completely deny human agency.[28]

Around the turn of the century this third option had been considered by Jacobus Arminius, professor of theology at Leiden University. During his lifetime, Arminius had been suspected of unorthodox views, but he had managed to avoid any open confrontation and official censure. After his death, however, his followers faced a hardening opposition. In 1610 sixteen of them presented a petition, or *Remonstrance*, to the States of Holland, in which they articulated the opposing views. They explained their doubts about the supralapsarian position, protested their adherence to the Reformed tradition and complained about their harassment by theological adversaries. They petitioned the States either to decree toleration of divergent interpretations of the Dutch Confession of Faith, or to convene a National Synod for the purpose of examining and clarifying Reformed doctrine on the points under discussion.

Revision of the Confession had been a long-standing desideratum in the Dutch Reformed Church, but for political reasons the States of Holland had always opposed convening a National Synod. Especially in Holland the Reformed Church and the political authorities were at odds about the church order, specifically on the procedures for the nomination and election of ministers and members of local consistories. Established practice allowed local magistrates, wielding formal or informal powers of patronage, and often through being themselves members of the consistories, to have considerable influence in this field. Synods insisted on more autonomy for the Church, but time and again they saw their efforts frustrated by the States. In Holland, as in a number of provinces, the Dutch Reformed Church did not have a church order approved both by the Church and the Provincial States, and where provincial church orders were in place, they maintained the prerogatives of secular powers.[29]

The opponents of the signatories of the *Remonstrance*, who came to be known as Counter-Remonstrants, submitted in response a petition of their own, in which they accused the Arminians of misrepresentation, not only in the *Remonstrance*, but above all in the popular

---

[28] Cf. Groenewegen, *De Remonstrantie*; P. van Rooden, 'De Synode van Dordrecht', in N.C.F. van Sas, ed., *Waar de blanke top der duinen* (Amsterdam and Antwerp, 1995).
[29] Schöffer, 'Crisis', 12.

polemics that had by this time started to appear. These popular pamphlets concentrated on two counter-intuitive final consequences of the doctrine of unconditional election. The first of these was that innocent infants could be predestined for damnation, and the second that the elect could sin with impunity. The defenders of unconditional election emphatically denied ever teaching any of this from their pulpits. On the contrary, they held that a strictly rational analysis of the key tenets of the faith, such as the doctrines on predestination – but also the Trinity, the dual nature of Christ and salvation – would inevitably yield absurdities. They protested that their adversaries concentrated their attacks on a caricature of their theology.[30]

Remonstrants and Counter-Remonstrants had by this time become party labels in what was no longer an academic dispute. Both sides drew support from factions in government circles, which increasingly coalesced into parties around the persons of stadholder Maurice and *landsadvocaat* Johan van Oldenbarnevelt. Although these factions differed on national defense and foreign policy as much as on theology, political action to quell the divisions mainly focused on the religious controversies.[31] In 1614 the States of Holland promulgated a *Resolution towards the Peace of the Church*, formulating the theological common ground of human impotence to attain salvation. Both parties held that God elects those who, by His saving grace, believe and persevere in the faith. Theologians were forbidden to go beyond this point in their biblical exegesis and interpretations of the Confession.[32] The *Resolution* could not prevent, however, the hardening of the Counter-Remonstrant opposition to the Arminianism which had become dominant in high government circles in Holland, thereby rejecting further compromise. In March 1616 the States of Holland insisted on the election of ministers by committees in which the magistrates and consistory were represented in equal numbers, in an attempt to break the consolidation of the Counter-Remonstrant party.[33]

[30] *Schriftelicke conferentie, gehouden in 's-Gravenhage inden jare 1611, tusschen sommighe kerckendienaren, aengaende de godlicke praedestinatie metten aencleven vandien* (The Hague, 1612), 20–23, also in Augustijn, *Reformatorica*, 122–124.

[31] Schöffer, 'Crisis', 30–35 and *passim*; Van Deursen, *Maurits*, 234–251.

[32] Israel, *Dutch Republic*, 430–432; Van Deursen, *Bavianen en slijkgeuzen*, 260–263; Den Tex, *Oldenbarnevelt*, III, 298–301.

[33] Van Deursen, *Bavianen en slijkgeuzen*, 263–268.

Landsadvocaat Oldenbarnevelt was the prime mover in this policy
of confrontation which sought to prevent a schism in the public
Reformed Church and the body politic. The controversies during
the Truce increasingly became centred on the *landsadvocaat* and a
close circle of his supporters in high places. When in July 1617 stadholder Maurice ostentatiously attended a Counter-Remonstrant church
service in The Hague, he thereby formally distanced himself from
this policy. The so-called *Sharp Resolution* of the States of Holland,
authorizing city magistrates to recruit armed militias, was a step
towards further escalation. The stadholder's *coup* in 1618, when he
replaced the magistrates of cities dominated by Oldenbarnevelt's partisans, and the following trial and execution of the *landsadvocaat* himself ended the conflict before it could erupt into civil war. After that,
the National Synod convened at Dordrecht in 1618–19 condemned
Arminianism and formulated its doctrine on election and grace in
the famous Canons of Dordrecht, which together with the Dutch
Confession and the Heidelberg Catechism would henceforth form
the credal statements of the Dutch Reformed Church.[34]

Reverend Rhetoricians?

In the summer of 1616, when the chambers of rhetoric convened
in Vlaardingen, both the *landsadvocaat* and the stadholder still kept
aloof from the controversies that troubled the Church. Oldenbarnevelt's
policy was to prevent schism, and the stadholder concurred.[35] The
theological gist of the controversies was highly arcane and the conflicts
surrounding the church order may not have been a matter of popular concern. How then did the rhetoricians tackle these matters?

Most outspoken are the plays of Rotterdam and, again, Gorcum.
The chamber of Rotterdam has the character United Country deliver
a lengthy monologue on Dutch religious diversity, a topic not found
in any of the other plays. She relates how the tolerated churches
are at peace, they obey the authorities which protect them and duti-
fully pay their taxes. Diversity is thus not the reason for the religious strife that disturbs her. On the contrary, it is the public Church

[34] W. van 't Spijker *et al.*, eds., *Synode van Dordrecht*.
[35] Israel, *Dutch Republic*, 433–434.

that foments discord. Wise Council and True Minister tell the audience how human curiosity and intellectual pride have tempted theologians to search the divine mysteries. This has led them away from true Christianity, which consists in wholeheartedly loving God and one's neighbour. Consequently, instead of keeping the peace and edifying the people, they incite hatred. Ultimately, however, the divisions in the Church derive from ambition, greed and worldly favours, unbecoming in ministers of Christ.[36] The chamber of Rotterdam seems to allude here to the patronage involved in ecclesiastical careers, which intimately connected the clergy to a political elite increasingly riddled by factionalism.

While Rotterdam and Gouda see it as a responsibility of the ministers to restore and maintain peace, the chamber of Gorcum states that these are so hopelessly divided that secular authorities need to step in. In a snappy dialogue the character True Minister convinces Suspicion and Vigilance, the watchdogs of High Authority and Good Government representing the States General and the stadholder, that secular authorities do not overstep their jurisdiction in taking ecclesiastical matters in hand. On the contrary, when the ministers of the Church are at odds, High Authority is beholden, even by divine precepts, to restore order. With remarkable foresight, the brothers of Gorcum make True Minister plead for a national Synod to decide the doctrinal conflict.[37]

On the whole, however, the plays are very reticent in their treatment of the theological and ecclesiological controversies. Unlike today, theology and church government apparently were not topics fit for free public discussion. The only aspects touched upon, and then very lightly, are the pragmatic question of whether political power can be used to end the conflict, and the use of the general factionalism of this period to further ecclesiastical careers. There is no attempt to discredit either one theological position or the other, and even the caricatures drawn in popular polemics are completely lacking.

The chambers of Maasland, Kethel and Nootdorp hardly mention the theological controversies at all, and limit themselves to the political and economic ambiguities inherent in the Truce. All other plays do mention the division in the Church, but only in the most

---

[36] *Redenryck-bergh*, fols. Hh4r–Ii2v.
[37] *Ibid.*, fol. Vv2v.

general of terms. Even more so than in the case of the respective
merits of peace, truce or war, they simply extol the virtue of concord.
Love of God and love of one's country should go hand in hand. In
its most outspoken form this sentiment is expressed by The Sweet-
Briar of Amsterdam. Here the character Wisdom exhorts the play's
protagonist Ruler to protect religion, as the springhead of all human
societies and the principal bond of harmony in any commonwealth.[38]

The Ideal Society

Besides arguments on the benefits of peace or war, sporadic acclaim
for either the stadholder or the *landsadvocaat*, and reflections on religion as the principal element of social cohesion, the plays at this
festival express conceptions of the ideal society. These usually surface at the end of the plays, in the elaboration on the answer of
each Chamber on the question posed by their hosts. The ideal society
is hierarchically structured and derives its legitimacy from God. Rights
and duties are sharply defined according to rank and status.[39]

The play of Gouda presents a Disunited People that has lost its
Five Senses. Through the good offices of Theologian, it is converted
into a sensible United People. At the end of the play High Authority,
Lawful magistrate and Theologian conclude the argument presented
by the chamber: Godly Government creates Harmony, and together
they protect the People. Examples of this can be found in biblical
history, in Gideon with his trusted band, Joshua, David and the
Maccabees. The four classical virtues Justice, Moderation, Prudence
and Fortitude concur that without Harmony they are powerless.
Once this is clear, Fear of Perdition is dispelled and Happiness
evoked in its stead. The order of appearance of the allegorical personages suggests a structure in which Godly Government, itself hierarchically composed of High Authority, Lawful Magistrate and
Theologian, is placed above the People, which in turn is supported
by the four virtues.[40]

---

[38] *Ibid.*, fol. M1r.
[39] Cf. W. Doyle, *The Ancien Régime* (Basingstoke and London, 1986).
[40] *Redenryck-bergh*, fols. Nn3v–Oo2r.

All chambers except those of Zoetermeer, Nootdorp and Dordrecht, Haarlem's White Carnations and Amsterdam's White Lavender, included the personification of secular government in their casts, either as one character, or in a number of hierarchically ordered characters representing separate ranks or aspects of government. Their prime responsibility is the well-being of the people and the prosperity of the country. In comparison, clergy is far less prominent. Most plays, although they sing the praise of true religion as the cement of society, do not present the ministry as part of the ideal social order. The play of Dordrecht even contains two allegorical figures, Erudite Conceit and Boundless Zeal, who represent the divisive aspects of religion by arguing in favour of religious coercion and the persecution of heresy. Eventually they turn out to be Catholic theologians 'from Louvain' advocating the exact opposite of what true ministers should preach, that is: God's goodness, contrition and redemption.[41]

Only the chambers of Rotterdam, Gouda and Gorcum cast a Reformed minister or theologian. In Gouda's play, Theologian, as part of the ruling elite, has a major role as a mediator between government and people. The character True Minister is less prominent in Rotterdam's performance. As the curtain rose for the the last act, the audience saw the populace sitting on the stage. True Minister ranked first among them, before the people and the civic virtues.[42] The hierarchical sequence here is the same as in Gouda's play: government – clergy – people – virtues, only here the minister is not part of government, but simply a paid civil servant, and thus a subject.

The plays thus mirror the social hierarchies of the Ancien Régime, but for all that they do not simply affirm a top-down power structure. Some plays allude to the biblical metaphor of society as a body made up of many members, some honourable and others less so, but each necessary for the well-being of the whole. Most outspoken was the chamber of Rotterdam, which blamed the current discord on vain curiosity towards the divine mysteries as well as on the endemic factional rivalry whereby powerful families gathered power and wealth for themselves and their clients, to the exclusion of all

---

[41] *Ibid.*, fols. Eee1r–Eee4r, Fff2r.
[42] *Ibid.*, fol. Kk1r.

others. Such rivalry is harmful for the body of society. By contrast,
the chamber sketches an ideal society in which the rich support the
poor, as fellow members of one body, for the common good.[43]

This motif is also found in the plays of Nootdorp and the Schiedam
chamber, The Fig Tree (*De Vijgeboom*). Both elaborate on the body
metaphor to denounce greed for wealth and power, but also to warn
of the dangers of discord and the revolt of the lower orders against
those set in authority over them. In both plays the stomach's greed
which consumes all the food and drink, without having to work for
it, is resented by the other members: the head which has all the
worry, the legs that carry the body, and the hands that do all the
work. Self-involved dissent among the members, however, will inevitably
destroy the body. The body cannot revolt against the stomach. All
members are equally necessary and have to support each other. Only
by providing the stomach with food can the health of the body as
a whole be maintained, and this in turn is the proper task of the
stomach.[44]

Whereas in most histories of the Twelve Years' Truce, the theological controversies take pride of place, these plays seem far more
concerned with a just division of the economic benefits that the sus-
pension of open warfare had brought. The use of the body metaphor in
the plays of Schiedam and Nootdorp echoes the dialogue between the
farmer, the man of independent means and the city-dwellers in the
play of the Amsterdam chamber, The White Lavender, in which
the former two could boast increasing prosperity, whereas the latter
had fallen on hard times through lack of work. Recently Jonathan
Israel has argued that industrial centres, among which Schiedam can
be counted, experienced an economic slump during the Truce, suggesting that disaffected masses of the working poor played a prominent part in the tide of popular unrest during the years 1617 and
1618.[45]

The concept of an ideal, hierarchically ordered society, with mutual
obligations between higher and lower ranks all contributing towards
the common good, seamlessly meshes with the topics addressed in
the poems (*refereinen*) which the chambers had to present on the question: 'What do children, once grown up, owe a parent who has

---

[43] *Ibid.*, fols. Ii2v–Ii3r.
[44] *Ibid.*, fols. Pp4v, Iii4v–Kkk1r.
[45] Israel, *Dutch Republic*, 437.

raised them properly?' The answers of the various chambers are virtually united and relatively predictable. Children owe a conscientious
parent respect, obedience, gratitude, and, above all, love.

Limited as it is, the answers do show some variation. Most chambers emphasize the religious nature of these childish virtues, and
adduce biblical examples of filial respect, obedience, gratitude and
love. Some use models from classical literature and from nature
alongside biblical material. Some of the poems, however, broaden
the scope of the question beyond the relationship between parents
and their offspring, to a more general treatment of hierarchical relations. The White Carnations from Haarlem liken proper parental
guidance to God's providence towards humanity: a loving form of
discipline, neither cruel nor soft. The chamber of Delft and Schiedam's
The Fig-Tree compare the loving obedience of children towards their
parents to the duties of subjects to secular authorities.[46] In line with
the overall scant representation of clergy only one chamber, that of
Zoetermeer, mentions ministers among those in authority.[47]

Conclusion

How are the political and religious choices that confronted the Dutch
Republic in 1616 represented in these plays and poems? Political
and religious controversies are commented upon, although mostly in
very general terms. Of the fifteen plays presented, several elaborate
on the ambiguities inherent in the Truce. Only two, those of Maasland
and Gorcum, explicitly name the political protagonists in the troubles, praising them as great men. The religious controversy is addressed
only in veiled terms. It is generally lamented, as religion should be
the cement of society, but neither the disputed points nor even the
names of the contesting parties are mentioned. Some plays show
concern about factional power politics and the uneven distribution
of increasing economic prosperity.

None of the chambers presumes to have any practical proposal
to offer other than making a plea for concord. The image of a well-
ordered society, in which good government maintains discipline in
ways that command respect and love from those governed, most

---

[46] *Redenryck-bergh*, fols. Z2r, Kkk3r.
[47] *Ibid.*, fol. Cc4r.

pointedly presented in the use of the body metaphor and the poems on filial duty, supports this general message. This is the context in which the political, economic and religious controversies have their place. They are mentioned, but none of the plays shows much interest in the main protagonists of the developing conflicts, nor in their actual programmes. There is no actual discussion.

How then, does all this fit the functions of the Chambers of Rhetoric, as recent scholarship presents it? Can plays like these be said to be a contribution to a public debate, or even the formation of a climate of public opinion? On the basis of the printed texts, it is hard to fathom what impression the series of performances made on the audience. We cannot even be certain who were in this audience. The plays were staged in the open air, in a public place, but would a rhetorician's festival attract the average Vlaardingen inhabitant? The literary style is stilted, the message highly conventional. Decorations and costume, the rhetorical quality of delivery and gesture certainly must have had entertainment value. Prizes were awarded for all these aspects.

As for the reception of the message, we can only look to the prizes for the morality plays. First and second prizes went to the chambers of Gorcum and Maasland, which explicitly praised either the stadholder or the *landsadvocaat*. This outspokenness may have been valued, even though praise for one political leader did not amount to blame for the other. Third and fourth prize fell to the plays of Zoetermeer and Dordrecht. These do not clearly relate their message to actual political, economic or religious questions, but voice a general criticism of the hedonism and self-centredness of their contemporaries. Both give the same pious answer to the question posed by their hosts: what the country needs is ardent prayer, refraining from sin and a simple Christian life.

On the whole it is hard to see how the brothers could have invited public discussion through their performances. The plays certainly show concern for public affairs, but they studiously avoid taking a clear position. They fall considerably short of Van Dixhoorn's description; they do not seem to have provided the audience with arguments for further discussion, or towards individual points of view. They do not elaborate or even mention the possible options, let alone compare alternatives. Discord is blamed on the greed of ruling factions for wealth and power, and the loosely related factionalism in the Church. Their criticism is, however, thickly veiled in metaphor. The plays do not contribute to a public debate in the current or any other meaning of that term. Perhaps a public sphere, or even the embryonic beginnings of one, should not really be expected in the early seventeenth century. As mild as censorship may have been in the Dutch Republic, compared with the European situation in general, open and free criticism of the political elite and/or the public Church by commoners was suppressed.[48]

The rhetoricians' plays and festivals rather resemble rituals, meant to create and celebrate concord. The rhetorical mastery aspired to in the chambers of rhetoric, and demonstrated in the morality plays, was directed precisely at this ritual function. Van Dixhoorn and others have convincingly argued that the chambers were schools of vernacular rhetoric, offering an education in the skills needed for a variety of public functions.[49] Whereas academic theological and legal training taught the formulation and defense of adversarial positions, the vernacular rhetorical skills polished in the chambers may well have aimed at a totally different goal.

The backbone of the 'culture of discussion' in the multifarious councils, boards and committees of early modern Dutch society, as described by Marijke Spies and Willem Frijhoff, was building and reaching consensus.[50] Problems had to be addressed and decisions formulated, in terms that could satisfy all involved and that enabled them to present a unified front to the outside world. This was not a public process, but it took place behind the closed doors of these various councils, boards and committees. To teach this balancing act, getting things done without undue antagonism, conjuring up harmony and concord with the magic of word and gesture, if possible in a playful mood, even, or especially, in times of sharp discord, was the core business of the chambers of rhetoric.

---

[48] S. Groenveld, 'The Mecca of Authors? States Assemblies and Censorship in the Seventeenth-Century Dutch Republic', in A.C. Duke and C.A. Tamse, eds., *Too Mighty to Be Free Censorship and the Press in Britain and The Netherlands*, Britain and the Netherlands 9 (Zutphen, 1987), 63–86.

[49] Van der Heijden and Van Boheemen, *Met minnen versaemt*; Van Dixhoorn, *Lustige geesten*.

[50] Frijhoff and Spies, *1650*, 218–219.

CHAPTER ELEVEN

'BRABANTERS DO FAIRLY RESEMBLE SPANIARDS AFTER ALL'. MEMORY, PROPAGANDA AND IDENTITY IN THE TWELVE YEARS' TRUCE

Judith Pollmann

'This city's *magnafique*, but what a grubby folk!'[1]

With this judgment on the city of Amsterdam, the rake Jerolimo, protagonist of Gerbrant Bredero's *Spaanschen Brabander*, in 1617, opens one of the most famous, and most puzzling plays of the Dutch Golden Age. Reworking the third chapter of the anonymous Spanish novel *Lazarillo de Tormes* (1554), Bredero introduced his Dutch audience to the adventures of Robbeknol, the Dutch Lazarillo, and of his master Jerolimo, a 'Spanish Brabanter', who had left the city of Antwerp to come to Amsterdam in search of innocents to fleece.[2]

The plot could not be simpler. To escape his debts in Antwerp, Jerolimo has come to Amsterdam. Presenting himself as a proud and prosperous gentleman from the Southern Netherlands, he hires the hapless Robbeknol to be his servant. Soon, Robbeknol discovers that his new master is virtually penniless, but feeling sorry for him, he does not leave him but begs for food for them both. When Jerolimo is at last found out by his creditors and has to flee the city, he leaves Robbeknol to face the music. It is only with the help of some female neighbours that Robbeknol escapes punishment; he, and Jerolimo's Amsterdam creditors, have learned the hard way that 'the eye can well behold a man and know him not at all'.[3]

---

[1] For this and other quotations, I rely on the English translation, G.A. Bredero, *The Spanish Brabanter. A Seventeenth-Century Dutch Social Satire in Five Acts*, ed. and transl. H.D. Brumble III, Medieval and Renaissance Texts and Studies 2 (Binghamton, NY, 1982), here verse 1. Otherwise I have used G.A. Bredero, 'Spaanschen Brabander', in idem, *Moortje en Spaanschen Brabander*, ed. E.K. Grootes (Amsterdam, 1999).

[2] *Het leven van Lazarillo de Tormes en zijn voorspoed en tegenslagen/La vida de Lazarillo de Tormes y de sus fortunas y adversidades*, Spanish text with parallel Dutch translation by Sophie Brinkman (Groningen, 1988).

[3] Bredero, *Spanish Brabanter*, verse 2223.

Bredero, a member of the *Nederduitse Academie*, and a specialist in farces, upholstered this thin plot by a series of memorable scenes in which Amsterdammers discuss life in their town, and each other's vices. Two hussies describe what brought them to prostitution, three men discuss the legislation on begging and the many alien poor who flock to the city, three spinsters talk of religion and of charity, a group of boys banter and exchange insults during a game of marbles. While the main protagonists do not mingle in all of these scenes, they certainly have their own thrilling tales to tell. Young Robbeknol is a northerner – the child of an Alkmaar mother and a fraudulent father from Friesland, who has died in Spanish service. Jerolimo is from Brabant, and proud of it:

> In Brabant we're all quite exquisite
> In dress and bearing – in the Spanish mode –
> Like lesser kings, gods visible on earth
> O imperial Antwerp, great and rich!
> In all the sun's wide range there's nowhere else
> Such abundance of slime, and comely fields
> Triumphant churches, cloisters most devout
> And stately buildings, lofty ramparts
> And overarching trees along the piers
> And quays where flows the mighty Scheldt.[4]

Much of the play's entertainment derives from Jerolimo's Brabantine loquaciousness, and the many Gallicisms in his Dutch. Sweet girls are to him *cordiale princessen*, and pleasure is *recreatie*. Jerolimo's one regret about Robbeknol is that the boy is not of Brabant descent. The Hollanders, to Jerolimo, are *botmuylen* (blockheads) who express themselves crudely, who have no respect for titles and rank, and who know nothing of honour and *politesse*, or of elegance. While Jerolimo saves on food to spend money on his apparel, in Holland even the rich dress in black, and do not display their wealth.[5]

Critics have often seen the play as a reflection of current issues in 1617 Amsterdam, and especially of debates about the roles of immigrants in the booming city. In the early seventeenth century, nearly half the bridegrooms in Amsterdam had not been born there, and there is evidence that the role of newcomers was the subject of

---

[4] *Ibid.*, verses 2–11.
[5] Bredero, 'Spaanschen Brabander', ed. Grootes, verses 43, 174–228, 840–866.

lively debate.[6] Many Amsterdammers voiced resentment about the pressure that poor Germans, especially, placed on urban resources.[7] Rich immigrants did not escape censure either; the thousands of Flemings and Brabanters who had fled north in the 1580s had brought with them a level of education and sophistication that was thought by some to corrupt the 'simple', traditional culture of Holland. Although he had many personal friends among the exiles and their descendants, Bredero personally campaigned against the many Gallicisms and other Brabantine oddities that were creeping into honest Holland speech. In this context, Bredero's description of Jerolimo, with his fanciful language, his finery, and his exaggerated notions of honour, has often been interpreted as a critique of the prominent part Brabanters were playing in Golden Age Amsterdam.[8] In this paper I propose that such a view is mistaken; while the play indeed sought to warn Bredero's contemporaries, it was not about the Brabant exiles living in their midst. Rather, Bredero's aim was to point to the dangerous consequences of making peace with the 'Spanish' Brabanters in the Southern Netherlands.

There are several reasons to question the notion that Brabantine exiles were the main target of the *Spaanschen Brabander*. Jerolimo seems hardly typical for the Brabantine immigrants in 1617 Amsterdam, who were mostly Protestant, and long-time residents of the city.[9] Moreover, as René van Stipriaan has emphasized, the play is not actually up front about its contemporary relevance. It is set in the

---

[6] S. Hart, 'Geschrift en getal. Onderzoek naar de samenstelling van de bevolking van Amsterdam in de 17de en 18e eeuw, op grond van gegevens over migratie, huwelijk, beroep en alfabetisme', in idem, *Geschrift en getal. Een keur uit de demografisch-, economisch- en sociaal-historische studieën op gron van Amsterdamse en Zaanse archivalia, 1600–1800* (Dordrecht, 1976), 144.

[7] Like the *onnutte bedelaar*, the sturdy beggar in Abraham de Koning, *'t Spel van Sinne, vertoont op de tweede lotery van d'arme oude mannen en vrouwen gast-huys* (Amsterdam, 1616). See also M.B. Smits-Veldt, 'Het Brabantse gezicht van de Amsterdamse rederijkerskamer "Het Wit Lavendel"', *De zeventiende eeuw* 8 (1992), 160–166.

[8] J.C.G.A. Briels, 'Brabantse blaaskaak en Hollandse botmuil. Cultuurontwikkelingen in Holland in het begin van de Gouden Eeuw', *De zeventiende eeuw* 1 (1985), 12–36. On this tradition in the histioriography, see R. van Stipriaan, 'Historische distantie in de Spaanschen Brabander', *Nederlandse letterkunde* 2 (1997), 103–127, and E.K. Grootes, 'Bredero's personages spreekbuis van de dichter?', *Jaarboek van de maatschappij der Nederlandse letterkunde te Leiden, 1998–1999* (Leiden, 2000), 3–17.

[9] Although some new immigrants continued to arrive. See O. Gelderblom, *Zuid-Nederlandse kooplieden en de opkomst van de Amsterdamse stapelmarkt (1578–1630)* (Hilversum, 2000), 194–195, 264–266.

past, in an ill-defined world of 'forty years ago', which takes us back to the 1570s and the early phases of the Dutch Revolt, light-years away from the boomtown that was Amsterdam during the Twelve Years' Truce. Bredero explained that he had opted for this setting, 'so that my readers will think less of making connections in the present, just as I myself was little concerned with such correspondences', and some scholars have chosen to believe him.[10] Yet he seems to offer rather too many pointers to the 'pastness' of the situation he is describing for us to feel that we can simply ignore its historical dimensions. For one thing, the Amsterdam of the play is clearly still a Catholic town. Jerolimo goes off to hear Mass at the altar of the confraternity of Our Lady in the city's Oude Kerk, and convents are still functioning.[11] When the sherrif is called out by Jerolimo's creditors, he claims he has his hands full with breaking up heretical conventicles and with catching the printers who are selling the *Geuzenliedboek*, a famous collection of songs by the Dutch rebels.[12] Moreover, the duke of Alba is in the country. We learn that Robbeknol's father served the Spanish soldiers and that his mother had a 'Moorish' child with Alba's groom; Jerolimo brings out a ditty that he claims to have received from the duke himself.[13] Nevertheless, the exact historical setting remains frustratingly vague. The signature to a decree on begging points to 1567, reference to a flood suggests a date of 1570, mention of the plague might point to 1575, while Robbeknol's personal history suggests that the war against the Spanish has been ongoing for some time, so that a date in the late 1570s seems more likely.[14]

While dating the *Spaanschen Brabander* has made for a nice scholarly parlour-game, it seems more sensible to accept that to try and date the action is futile. There is no reason to believe that Bredero or his audience possessed an extensive knowledge of the city's history in the 1570s; the playwright himself was born in 1585, and while some general histories of the Revolt had appeared by 1617,

---

[10] Bredero, *Spanish Brabanter*, introduction to the readers, 41.
[11] Bredero, 'Spaanschen Brabander', ed. Grootes, verses 240, 281.
[12] *Ibid.*, verses 1984–1999.
[13] *Ibid.*, verses 80–90, 663.
[14] Discussions of these dating issues in G.A. Bredero, *Spaanschen Brabander*, ed. C.F.P. Stutterheim (Culemborg, 1974), 18–24, and Van Stipriaan, 'Historische distantie'.

none of them offered a particularly detailed account of what had happened in Amsterdam. The work of Pieter Christiaensz Bor, who had been commissioned by the States to write the official history of the Revolt, was still very much in progress, and as yet only ran to 1573.[15] And while the city's local historian, Johannes Isacius Pontanus, had published his history of the city in 1611, he had actually done little to elucidate the history of the town during the Revolt. As Henk van Nierop has highlighted, Amsterdam's historians were embarrassed by the fact that the city had chosen the 'wrong' side in the Revolt; alone among the major Holland towns, it had supported the king until the 'Satisfactie' and the 'Alteratie', the regime change of 1578, had finally brought the city on the side of the rebels. Pontanus therefore had a delicate mission on his hands, which he met by not being very specific about what had happened in the 1570s, and by blaming the support for the Crown on the many clerical refugees who had made their way to Amsterdam when the Revolt erupted in the rest of Holland.[16]

Bredero did not try to offer a more precise or critical account than Pontanus. There are no references in the *Spaanschen Brabander* to the Revolt that had broken out in Holland in 1572, the ensuing war and the city's isolation, while the suggestion in the play that Amsterdam attracted refugees 'for Scripture's sake' in this period is clearly ludicrous. Neither was he concerned about anachronisms; one of the spinsters is asked whether she is 'Mennonite, Papist, Arminian or *geus*', but of course no one knew anything of Arminianism in the 1570s. Jerolimo, in one of his moments of grand delusion, offers to

---

[15] See on the early historiography of the Revolt, J. Romein, 'Spieghel historiael van de Tachtigjarige oorlog', in J. Romein, B.W. Schaper [pseud. of J. Presser], A.J.C. De Vrankrijker, eds., *De tachtigjarige oorlog* (Amsterdam, 1941); A.E.M. Janssen, 'A Trias Historica on the Revolt of the Netherlands. Emanuel van Meteren, Pieter Bor and Everhard van Reyd as Exponents of Contemporary Historiography', in Duke and Tamse, eds., *Clio's Mirror*.

[16] Johannes Isacius Pontanus, *Rerum et urbis Amstelodamensium historia. In qua Hollandiae primum atque inde Amstelandiae, oppidique, natales, exordia, progressus, privilegia, statuta eventaque mirabilia cum novis urbis incrementis commercijsque ac navigationibus longinquis, aliaque ad politiam spectantia, additis suo loco tabulis aeri incisis, ad haec usque tempora, observata annorum serie accurate omnia deducuntur* (Amsterdam, 1611). A Dutch translation appeared in 1614; see H. van Nierop, *Het foute Amsterdam*, inaugural lecture at the University of Amsterdam (Amsterdam, 2000). Various manuscript sources about the Revolt in Amsterdam also circulated in the town, but there is no evidence that Bredero had read them.

pay for the reclamation of the Haarlemmermeer, which was very topical in 1617 but hardly in the 1570s.[17]

If the point was not to offer an exact historical setting, why set the play in this vague context of the early phases of the Revolt at all? René van Stipriaan has recently offered a new answer to this question. He points out that for all the criticism of foreigners, the Amsterdammers themselves do not come off lightly in this play. Not only are they taken in by a crook like Jerolimo; many of them are themselves greedy, deceitful and lascivious. Van Stipriaan suggests that Bredero set the play in ill-defined 'bad old days' to mock the sentimental complaints about the demise of the virtues of ancient Holland, that were made by contemporaries such as burgomaster C.P. Hooft.[18] Still, this explanation poses problems of its own. If it was Bredero's intention to ridicule the Amsterdammers of the 1570s, it seems odd he made so little reference to their support for the king. Moreover, as Eddy Grootes has pointed out, we may not have to give so much weight to the moral flaws of the Amsterdam characters, since contradictions between actual behaviour and the moral message of protagonists are not unusual in Renaissance theatre.[19] Yet even if Bredero's point was not to ridicule his contemporaries' nostalgia for the good old days, Van Stipriaan must be right that the historical dimension of the play is significant and requires a proper explanation. I hope to show that such an explanation may emerge if we read the play in the context of the social memory of the Revolt among Bredero and his Amsterdam contemporaries, and consider the role that the history of the Revolt played in the political debates of the Truce years.

While, by 1617, concrete knowledge about the details of the Dutch Revolt was still surprisingly hard to come by, the 'social memory' of the rebellion was nevertheless playing a key role in the newly emerging culture of the Republic.[20] Social memory, the collective engagement with and redeployment of the past, can be shaped and maintained in a myriad of ways: through markers in the landscape and *lieux de mémoire*, through commemoration and ritual, and through

---

[17] Bredero, 'Spaanschen Brabander', ed. Grootes, verses 1315, 1383.
[18] Especially in Van Stipriaan, 'Historische distantie'.
[19] Grootes, 'Bredero's personages'.
[20] See on this concept, J. Fentress and C. Wickham, *Social Memory* (Oxford, 1992).

books and homilies, but in its most elementary form it is fed by storytelling. People in the late sixteenth- and seventeenth-century Netherlands frequently connected the past of their own families to key moments in the Reformation and the Revolt, and liked to tell and retell these tales. The descendants of the Protestant martyrs prided themselves on the blood their ancestors had shed for the faith.[21] The Calvinist descendants of the radical martyr Anneken Jans, for instance, cherished the connection, and the moment when, on her way to the scaffold, she entrusted her son Esaiah into the care of a baker.[22] The tales of war victims, too, were passed on to future generations; sometimes in the diaries and memoirs of the war that were circulating in manuscript, but most often orally. Thus historian Pieter Cornelisz Hooft could base his account of the Spanish Fury in Antwerp on the experiences of his wife's grandmother, that were remembered in the family.[23] At the same time, such tales and memories were themselves shaped by core texts and images that symbolised the war and its *raison d'être*. Key among these, for instance, was the *Geuzenliedboek* (1574) that Bredero mentions in the play, a collection of songs that had first emerged in the Revolt itself and that was constantly being extended and reprinted.

There is evidence that the Dutch appropriated images of their personal past from such propaganda literature. The Utrecht chronicler Arnoldus Buchelius recalled in around 1590 how a Spanish soldier had been billetted at his family home twenty years earlier, when Buchelius was six years old:

> He used to say that all the Netherlands had been found guilty of *lèse majesté* and had been granted as booty to the Spanish soldiers. He wanted the best of everything to be given to him and proclaimed that we ought to obey him (he, who had probably been drawn from a goosepen or a Marrano stable) as slaves do their masters. And in this he went so far, first with flattery and then with threats, as to second me as his armour-bearer. Mother resisted him with the greatest force, clamouring with all her might. But this had no effect, nor did

---

[21] For examples of such stories, see e.g. Pieter Joossen, 'De kroniek van Pieter Joossen, Altijt Recht Hout', ed. R. Fruin, *Archief. Mededeelingen van het Koninklijk Zeeuwsch Genootschap der Wetenschappen* (1909), 67–95; J. Pollmann, *Religious Choice in the Dutch Republic. The Reformation of Arnoldus Buchelius (1565–1641)* (Manchester, 1999), 161–162.

[22] H. ten Boom, *De Reformatie in Rotterdam, 1530–1585*, Hollandse historische reeks 7 (Amsterdam, 1987), 91–92.

[23] A. Romein-Verschoor, *P.C. Hooft, 1581–1647* (Amsterdam, 1947), 63–64.

violence from my stepfather. In the end, by the captain's orders, he
was forced to desist and to move somewhere else.[24]

This recollection was undoubtedly roughly correct, but the soldier's
claim that 'the Netherlands had been found guilty of *lèse majesté*' came
straight from the propaganda pamphlets of the rebels. In many variations these had presented the alleged 'advices' and 'decrees' in which
Cardinal Granvelle, the Spanish Inquisition or the duke of Alba had
condemned all Dutch to slavery.[25]

Buchelius's suggestion that the soldier was acting the gentleman,
but really came from a *marrano* stable or a goosepen, also derived
from a motif in the pamphlet literature and the rebel songbooks. In
the *Geuzenliedboek* we find many examples of people with pretensions
that are similar to those of this soldier – and of Jerolimo. Several
of the songs refer to 'Spanish gents' in 'ragged pants', who at home
were 'knitting nets, herding donkeys and cows', before they had come
to lord it over the Netherlands. In a song describing the fall of the
Vredenburg Castle in Utrecht, 'Spanish whores', Dutch women who
had taken up with the Spanish soldiers, said their farewells to 'Seignior
Ragpants':

> You came from Spain with valour
> With your elbow showing through your sleeves
> And your toes peeping out of your shoes.[26]

The theme was derived from an older anti-Spanish tradition that
dated back to the Italian wars but was rapidly being developed during the Dutch Revolt. This complex of ideas, known as the 'Black
Legend', focused on Spanishness as a cultural and even racial propen-
sity to pride, cruelty, deceitfulness and lust for power that had already
made many victims, for instance in Italy and the New World, before
it was the turn of The Netherlands. It drew upon a number of
sources, some of which were actually Spanish. The Jewish and Moorish
'blood' of the Spanish was often cited as an explanation for their

---

[24] Cited in Pollmann, *Religious Choice in the Dutch Republic*, 36.

[25] E.g. *Het besluyt des officium teghen het volck van de Nederlanden* (n.p., 1570); *Het Aviis,
der Inquisicie van Spaegnien bewijsingghe dat in alle de Nederlanden geen papist of catholijcke
persoonen en sijn na het geluyt ders selver inquisicy van Spaengien* (n.p., 1571); *Copie van den
puncten en articulen ghesloten bij den hertoghe van Alba en synene nieuwen raet van twelven* (n.p.,
1568).

[26] *Het Geuzenliedboek*, ed. E.T. Kuiper and P. Leendertsz, 2 vols. (Zutphen, 1924),
I, no. 127. See also I, nos. 84 and 123.

wickedness – an unforeseen byproduct of the anxiety about the new Christians and *limpieza de sangre* in Spain itself – while Spanish works like those of Bartolomé de las Casas were frequently used as evidence for Spanish misdeeds.[27] Spanish novels and plays, however popular, were in the Dutch Republic simultaneously presented as yet more evidence of 'Spanish' iniquities. Thus, the full title of the Dutch translation of *Lazarillo*, Bredero's source, that appeared in 1579 and was reprinted in 1609, read 'The enjoyable and amusing tales of Lazarus of Tormes from Spain, in which one can get to know the manners, condition, speech and cunning of the Spanish'.[28]

Anti-Hispanicism was more than an accidental byproduct of the Revolt. One of the main challenges for the rebel propagandists had been to define a common cause with which all Netherlanders could identify. In many ways, the Reformed religion was an unsuitable banner, since it was Catholics, in particular, who had to be won over. The Low Countries were a recent political creation and the provinces had not very much in common. Although, as Alastair Duke has shown, some sense of Netherlandish identity had been developing, it was not very deep, and in some respects it was also closely bound up with the Habsburg regime.[29] Anti-Hispanicism emerged, therefore, not only because of the experiences with Spanish soldiers, real and gruesome as these were, but also because the threat of a common alien and semi-heathen enemy could be used to unite the otherwise so disparate Netherlands.[30] As the war continued, the anti-Spanish

---

[27] S. Arnoldsson, *La Leyenda Negra. Estudios sobre sus orígines*, Acta Universitatis Gothoburgensis 66, 3 (Göteborg, 1960). On the Black Legend in the Netherlands, see K.W. Swart, 'The Black Legend during the Eighty Years War', in J.S. Bromley and E.H. Kossmann, eds., *Some Political Mythologies. Papers Delivered to the 5th Anglo-Dutch Conference*, Britain and the Netherlands 5 (The Hague, 1975), and on the European origins of the Dutch Black Legend, see J. Pollmann, 'Eine natürliche Feindschaft. Ursrpung und Funktion der schwarzen Legende über Spanien in den Niederlanden, 1560–1581', in F. Bosbach, ed., *Feindbilder. Die Darstellung des Gegners in der politischen Publizistik des Mittelalters und der Neuzeit* (Cologne, 1992). On German connections, see A. Duke, 'A Legend in the Making. News of the "Spanish Inquisition" of the Low Countries in German Evangelical Pamphlets, 1546–1550', *Nederlands archief voor kerkgeschiedenis* 77 (1997), 124–144.

[28] *De ghenuechlijcke ende cluchtighe histories van Lazarus van Tormes, wt Spaignen. In de welcke, ghy eensdeels meucht sien en leeren kennen, de manieren, condicien, reden ende schalckheyt der Spaignaerden* (Delft, 1579), cited in G.A. Bredero, *Spaanschen Brabander*, ed. Stutterheim, 9–10.

[29] Duke, 'The Elusive Netherlands'.

[30] Duke, 'From King and Country to King or Country?'; Swart, 'The Black Legend'; Pollmann, 'Eine natürliche Feindschaft'. See also H.A. Enno van Gelder, 'Het streven van prins Willem van Oranje, 1568–1572', *De Gids* 97 (1933), 153–189.

discourse did not lose its attractions – quite the opposite. From around 1600, and throughout the Truce, there was a strong revival of interest in the early phases of the Revolt, especially among Flemish and Brabant exiles and their children. This was partly because there were fears that younger generations were forgetting what their ancestors had been through. In 1611, the refugee merchant Peter Pels wrote to his contemporary Anthoine L'Empereur about the difference between their experiences in the 1560s and 1570s, and those of their children:

> But as you say about yourself, in the loss of your father and amidst the flames of sorrow, God shows us his great benevolence, as He does to all His people. . . . But our children, who have never seen and known such plights, do not know what it is, and think that through God's mercy all should come to pass as they desire.[31]

Johannes Gysius, originally from Ostend, noted in 1616 that there were still 'several old people who have lived through all these miseries, who have seen all this . . . inhuman cruelty and many of whom experienced it in some way or other, who say of the same that it's been so enormous that it can barely be told by human tongues, or be believed, once told'. Yet 'since these old folks are dying off daily', he was now collecting the tale of their woes, so that 'these miseries and Spanish cruelties will always remain fresh in the memory of us Netherlanders'.[32]

Even more so than had been the case in the propaganda of the 1570s and 1580s, the early seventeenth-century popular histories, plays and poems that evoked the Revolt did not recognize grey areas. The Revolt had not been a civil war, in which many people had had to make uncomfortable decisions; in the image of the past that the Dutch created for themselves, a choice for Revolt was the only option open to a people doomed to perennial slavery under a Spanish regime. The reason for this was that efforts to keep the memories of the Revolt alive were not inspired by the personal need for remem-

---

[31] Cited in P.T. van Rooden, *Theology, Biblical Scholarship and Rabbinical Studies in the Seventeenth Century. Constantijn L'Empereur (1591–1648), Professor of Hebrew and Theology at Leiden*, transl. J.C. Grayson (Leiden, 1989), 17.

[32] [Johannes Gysius], *Oorsprong en voortgang der Neder-landtscher beroerten ende ellendicheden.: Waerin vertoont worden, de voornaemste tyrannÿen, moorderÿen, ende andere onmenschelÿcke wreetheden, die onder het ghebiedt van Philips II . . . door zÿne stad-houders in 't werck ghestelt zÿn, gheduyrende dese Nederlantsche troublen ende oorlogen* (n.p., 1616), introduction.

brance alone. The emphasis on a common Netherlandish struggle helped to integrate the Flemish and Brabant exiles into the host population, for instance; as fellow-Netherlanders, they had suffered the same plight as Hollanders and Zeelanders. In a play written in 1616 to raise funds for the Amsterdam poor houses, Abraham de Koning drew a sharp contrast between the sturdy beggars from Germany and the grateful refugees from Flanders, like his own family, who had lost hearth and home through Spanish tyranny.[33]

But the interest was also closely bound up with the political situation, and especially with the burning issue of peace negotiations with the Spanish. During the peace negotiations of 1607–09 it had become clear that the character of the war had changed. The impediments to peace lay in the trade interests of the new Republic, and the war was to be continued in 1621 as a trade war as much as one about territory. Yet the legitimation of the conflict and the debate about the desirability of peace continued to play on older themes – the Spanish tyranny, pride and lack of faith that the Dutch had experienced in the 1570s. 'Could one really trust the Spanish?', asked one patriot after another. Should not the Republic continue to fight for the liberation of the South? Such fears did not abate once the Truce had come into force. As Joke Spaans shows in her chapter in this volume, the need for unity and the fear of Spanish deceit figured prominently in the plays produced for the rhetoricians' contest in Vlaardingen in 1616. When several of the Amsterdammers in the *Spaanschen Brabander* lamented the lack of unity, the civil strife and divisions in the Church, they did so because 'if the frog and the mouse stand bickering thus, the fox may well surprise them'.[34] Playwright Jan Kolm claimed that his *Nederlants Treur-Spel* of 1616, the first play about the Revolt, would offer food for thought to *Bataefssche lant-lievers*, in these 'dangerous, wild and quarrelsome days' and warned them of the 'amnesia' of the House of Burgundy, that was prone to breaking its oaths.[35] In the same year, Johannes Gysius hoped that his history of the struggle would teach the people in the Free Netherlands:

---

[33] De Koning, *'s Spel van Sinne*.
[34] Bredero, *Spanish Brabanter*, verses 1010–1011.
[35] I.S. Kolm, *Nederlants treur-spel inhoudende den oorspronck der Nederlandsche beroerten, 't scheyden der ed'len, 't sterven der graven van Egmont, Hoorn ende der Batenborgers* (Amsterdam, 1616), introduction.

what is to be expected of the Spanish and the Spanish regime, so that
we learn from this that, once being rid of this evil (however pretty
and sweet the tunes they may be whistling to tempt us), we should
not allow ourselves to be brought back into our former slavery, and
bear the punishment for our foolishness.[36]

By the time Bredero wrote the *Spaanschen Brabander*, calls to remember the Revolt were thus routinely bound up with contemporary
political questions; this alone makes it likely that Amsterdammers
would have understood the play in a contemporary context. Jerolimo,
the Spanish Brabander, is very reminiscent of the Spanish *sinjoren*
that Bredero and his contemporaries knew so well from the tales of
the Revolt. That was probably the reason why Bredero chose this
part of Lazarillo de Tormes for his reworking of the tale. It also
made the 1570s a creditable setting for Jerolimo's appearance, since
that had been the time when Spanish would-be seigneurs had been
swarming all over the Netherlands.

But why did Bredero not turn Jerolimo into a real Spaniard?
Jerolimo is a mongrel. He probably has a Spanish father; sired by
any one of the genteel military customers to which his Brabant
mother delivered pastry and marzipan, Jerolimo is mighty proud of
this illegitimate connection.[37] His name is almost Spanish, and he is
lacing his conversations with pseudo-Spanish expletives such as 'par
Dio sante' and 'je lo bassa la man'; Bredero's audience would have
been familiar with such comic use of Spanish phrases from the *gueux*
songs.[38]

Jerolimo's mongrel status is of real significance. In the course of
the Revolt, there had developed a stereotype of the 'hispanicised'
Netherlander. When embellishing their own version of the Black
Legend, Netherlandish propagandists were following closely in the
footsteps of the German Protestants and French Huguenots. In
Huguenot propaganda there had emerged the 'franc espagnol', the
Frenchman who had been 'hispanicized' and so lost his claims to
Frenchness; in the Revolt a similar phenomenon soon became appar-
ent.[39] The Netherlandish 'peace lovers' who opposed Antwerp's

---

[36] [Gysius], *Oorsprong*, introduction.
[37] Bredero, *Spaanschen Brabander*, ed. Grootes, verses 1602–1610.
[38] E.g. *ibid.*, verses 210, 713.
[39] As in *Declaration et protestation de ceux de la religion reformée de Rochelle* (La Rochelle,
1568), cited in D.R. Kelley, *The Beginning of Ideology. Consciousness and Society in the*

Calvinist regime in the early 1580s were denounced as 'Spanish' in propaganda pamphlets.[40] Farmer Abel Eppens in Groningen described the citizens of Catholic Groningen and the 'neutralists' of the surrounding countryside as *spannisierten*.[41] Archduke Albert, said the patriotic historian Johannes Gysius in 1616, might be of Germanic blood, but he was a 'gespagniolisierden Duyts' (a hispanicized German).[42]

What had begun as an attractive strategy to turn opponents of the Dutch Revolt into 'traitors' soon acquired a useful additional function; within the Republic it helped to supercede religious differences, and to obscure the fact that the Revolt in its early decades had been a real civil war. In his sermons the Haarlem minister Samuel Ampzing did not hesitate to point to the dangers of popery, yet in his *Lof van Haarlem*, his eulogy about the city, he chose not to describe quite how divided the Haarlemmers had been in 1572–73 or to shift the blame onto Catholics. He could not avoid references to the opposition to the Revolt, but blamed that just on a few 'gespanjoliseerden'.[43] By denouncing Netherlandish opponents of the Revolt as 'aliens', who had transformed themselves into foreigners, the Dutch had thus found a very effective way of stressing that true lovers of the *patria* had chosen to support the Revolt. This was important especially because it offered an opportunity to include Catholics. One of the most sympathetic characters in the *Spaanschen Brabander*, for instance, is a Catholic. The simple spinster Trijn is delighted when Robbeknol offers to read her an *evangelytje*, a bit of Scripture; naively she tells him that her priest only speaks Latin, which even he does not understand; she would prefer her priests to teach 'simply and directly'.[44]

While the contrast between true lovers of the patria and the 'Spanishness' of their opponents thus served to unify the Republic, it should be noted that from the early seventeenth century onwards

---

French Reformation (Cambridge, 1981). See also M. Yardeni, *La Conscience nationale en France pendant les guerres de religion 1559–1598* (Louvain and Paris, 1971), and Van Gelder, 'Het streven van Prins Willem van Oranje', 170.

[40] As in *Dialogus of 't samensprekinghe tusschen eenen Spaensch-gesinden Peysmakere ende eenen goeden Patriot ofte liefhebber des vaderlants* (Antwerp, 1584).

[41] W. Bergsma, *De wereld volgens Abel Eppens. Een Ommelander boer uit de zestiende eeuw* (Groningen, 1988), 114, 122.

[42] [Gysius], *Oorsprong*, 406.

[43] H. van Nierop, 'How to Honour One's City. Samuel Ampzing's "Vision of the History of Haarlem"', *Theoretische geschiedenis* 20 (1993), 268–282, there 279.

[44] Bredero, 'Spaanschen Brabander', ed. Grootes, verses 1349–1369.

it was also used to 'other' the Netherlanders south of the Republic's border. While the propagandists in the north drew ever more gruesome pictures of life under the Spanish yoke, and assumed that the brethren in the south were pining for the moment of liberation, from 1600 political realities had begun to impose a strain on this neat image. When preparing for the Flemish campaign in 1600, deputies from the States General had genuinely believed that the Flemish would be keen to pay 'contributions' to the Dutch war effort. Yet once in Flanders, Maurice and his army discovered that Flemish peasants were seeing them not as their liberators but as their bitter enemies.[45] Every inch of Flemish and Brabant land would have to be fought for.

Yet how could one explain that southerners apparently accepted the Spanish mantle, and proved unwilling to see themselves as victims of tyranny? Many northerners assumed that people in the south were simply 'asleep'.[46] In his dialogue *Morgenwecker* (Wake-up call) of 1610, the Flemish exile Willem Baudartius had a 'free' Netherlander 'awaken' a *gespanioliseerden Nederlander* with a potted history of the past forty years of tyranny and broken promises.[47] In 1602 an unknown poet admonished the cities of Antwerp and Brussels:

> Antwerp rich and powerful, Brussels *gentil* and pleasant
> Do you want to remain in slavery for ever
> To a people barbaric, ugly, deformed and tanned,
> Who throughout the world commit their tyranny?
> Wake up, 't is now the time, wake up, offer resistance
> Take courage, like men, take courage, and don't behave like women
> Follow the noble Batavians, don't let yourself be dishonoured
> By the domination of such an evil monster.[48]

---

[45] A.Th. van Deursen, *Maurits van Nassau. De winnaar die faalde* (Amsterdam, 2000), 91; Anthonis Duyck, *De slag bij Nieuwpoort. Journaal van de tocht naar Vlaanderen in 1600*, ed. W. Uitterhoeve, transl. V. Roeper (Nijmegen, 2000), 11–13, 35–40.

[46] E.g. the Enkhuizen publisher Jan Arentsz Chaallon in his introductory sonnet to *El Paternostro de gli Spagnioli ofte rhijm-gedicht, so in Duytsch als Italiaens vervaetende 't goe-leven van de Spaignaerden ende haar comportementen ter plaetsen dat sij meyster zijn. Mitsgaders Los Dies Mandamentos de los Theatinos, wesende de Thien Gheboden der Jesuiten, originelijck in Spaensch ende paraphrastice in Duytsche ghedicht overgheset door een beminder der Nederlandtsche vrijheijt* (Enkhuizen, 1602), n.p. His name suggests that he himself originated from the south.

[47] [Willem Baudartius], *Morgen wecker der vrije Nederlantsche provintien ofte een cort verhael vande bloedighe vervolghinghen ende wreetheden door de de Spaenjaerden ende hare Adherenten . . .* (Danzig, 1610).

[48] *El Paternostro.*

Others were less forgiving. In 1601 the Amsterdam physician Jacobus Viverius published *Den spieghel der Spaensche tyrannie* (The Mirror of Spanish Tyranny). Viverius, himself born in Flanders, targeted his pamphlet against the peace proposals that had been initiated in the south, and against those in Flanders who considered living under a Spanish regime acceptable. Stanza by stanza, he described the atrocities the Spanish had committed first in the New World and subsequently in the Netherlands, before making short shrift of collaborating Southerners. It pained him, he said, to see how in the 'sweet land of Flanders', people were ready to shake hands with the 'cruel Spaniards', and he warned them that those who 'feed the tyrants will have to put up with tyranny'. Like so many of the songs in the *Geuzenliedboek*, Viverius made ample use of the motif of the 'Spanish whores', the Netherlandish women who took up with the Spanish, and so got infected with the 'Spanish pocks', syphilis:

> Yes, kiss your Spanish swain, and get the Spanish disease
> Drive Christ and his people from the dwellings of your court
> Thou wilt see the day (if ever blind folk have eyes)
> That he in whom you are now placing so much faith
> Will betray you. To choose alien swains
> Means to choose a fire that freezes wondrously fast
> . . . That's what thou doest, Flanders and Brabant, to your shame
> He who kindles the fire, will necessarily burn.[49]

Viverius's message was clear; the Netherlandish brethren and sisters in the south who chose to fraternize with the Spanish were sleeping with the enemy, and so losing their patriotic virtues and their birthright.

Bredero's Jerolimo is a prime exponent of Southerners of this type. His noble pretensions derive from the adultery of his Brabant mother with a Spanish *sinjoor*, he acts like a Spanish gent, prides himself on good relations with the duke of Alba and the Infanta Isabella, and flirts with everything that is Spanish and alien, from his finery to his religion to his language. Haughty and unreliable, he even somewhat resembles the duke of Alba who, as Van Stipriaan has pointed out, had also left Amsterdam without paying his debts.[50] But the

---

[49] Jacobus Viverius, *Den spieghel van de Spaensche tyrannie: waer by ghevoegt is eene vreughdighe vieringhe over het veroveren van de stede Rijnberck: waer in verhaelt wordt den ondergangh vande Spaensche Tyrannie of bloedt-dorst* (Amsterdam, 1601), stanzas LXI and LXII, see also LXVII.

[50] Van Stipriaan, 'Historische distantie', 115–116.

point about Jerolimo is not that he is a figure of the past: the message of the *Spaanschen Brabander* is precisely that he is an enemy of
the present; 'Brabanters do fairly resemble Spaniards after all', Bredero
said, and this was the central message of his play.[51]

Twenty years earlier such a statement would have been unthinkable. Yet in the run up to the Truce, but also in the years of the
Truce itself, when the borders had opened, and frequent visits had
become possible, it had become very evident that Southerners were
but a poor fit for the Netherlandish self-image that had developed
in the Republic. Southerners were not suffering under a Spanish
yoke but were increasingly proud of themselves, of their religion,
and of their archdukes; no longer, it could seem therefore, were they
willing to be Netherlanders. Moreover, it was becoming less convenient for Northerners to think of Southerners only as victims.
Amsterdam had been deeply opposed to the Truce, mainly for economic reasons. Interpretations of the play have sometimes assumed
that Antwerp, by 1617, was just a shadow of its former self, yet that
notion is no longer supported by the findings of economic historians. Antwerp had rallied, and revived as a centre for manufacturing and trade.[52] The city no longer functioned as an *entrepôt* for the
international market, but it might do so again; hence the fact that
the blockade of the Scheldt had become non-negotiable for the
Northerners, the Amsterdammers included. It seems significant that
Jerolimo, for all his noble pretensions, is priding himself on his role
in trade, in buying indigo and cochineal, but also trading in Guinea
on the West Coast of Africa. Bredero's audience was being warned,
in a language and imagery shaped by decades of patriotic propaganda, not to be taken in by the Southerners or their Spanish masters, and that was a message Amsterdammers were willing to hear.

Vincent van Zuilen has shown that in southern Netherlandish propaganda there existed a tension between the desire to see the
Northerners as Netherlanders, with whom people in the south hoped
to be reunited, and the simultaneous need to define the enemy as

---

[51] Bredero, *The Spanish Brabanter*, 44.
[52] E.g. Bredero, *Spaanschen Brabander*, ed. Stutterheim, 26. See H. van der Wee
and J. Materné, 'De Antwerpese wereldmarkt tijdens de 16de en 17de eeuw', in
J. van der Stock, ed., *Antwerpen, verhaal van een metropool* (Antwerp, 1993), 19–35.

the 'other'.[53] From 1585 loyalist propagandists in the Southern Netherlands therefore drew a sharp distinction between the majority of their fellow Netherlanders and the headstrong minority of rebels, whom they described as 'Hollanders' and '*gueux*'.[54] As I hope to have shown, the *Spaanschen Brabander* was the product of a parallel development in the Republic. Like the Netherlanders in the south, the Dutch maintained the fiction of a united Netherlands, which was expressed, for instance, in the image of the *Leo Belgicus* that is discussed by Paul Regan in this volume. But once the Dutch had become committed to the fictions of their own propaganda, it became ever more difficult to recognize the kinship between themselves and the people of the south. It is ironic that it was especially the exiles from Brabant and Flanders, who were keener than anyone else to continue the Revolt until the Spanish Netherlands were 'liberated', who simultaneously did most to define and articulate the cultural parting of the ways between the Dutch and the Netherlanders south of the border. Rather than to reflect conflicts between native Amsterdammers and the refugees from the south, then, the *Spaanschen Brabander* shows how important the Southerners had become in defining the shape of Dutch identity.

---

[53] V. van Zuilen, 'The Politics of Dividing the Nation. News Pamphlets as a Vehicle of Ideology and National Consciousness in the Habsburg Netherlands (1585–1609)', in J.W. Koopmans, ed., *News and Politics in Early Modern Europe (1500–1800)*, Groningen Studies in Cultural Change 13 (Leuven, 2005), 62.

[54] J. Andriessen, *De Jezuïeten en het samenhorigheidsbesef der Nederlanden, 1585–1648* (Antwerpen, 1957), 164–165.

CHAPTER TWELVE

'CONCORDIA RES PARVAE CRESCUNT'.
REGIONAL HISTORIES AND THE DUTCH REPUBLIC IN THE SEVENTEENTH CENTURY

Raingard Esser

The Eighty Years' War between what would emerge as the Dutch Republic and the Spanish Netherlands under Habsburg rule was certainly one of the first propaganda wars in history. Countless prints, woodcuts, engravings and pamphlets called for the readers' solidarity and support for their respective cause. In the north, the appeal for unity and strength against an over-mighty, seemingly ruthless enemy formed the heart of these publications.[1] Here the rebellious provinces were frequently depicted as a sheaf of arrows tied about the middle to symbolize strength through unity. This call for a united front against the Spanish was not only essential for the uprising in its various stages, but remained a recurring theme during the later stages of the war and well beyond the Peace of Westphalia, with which the Dutch Republic was officially recognized as an independent political unit.[2] This unit, however, was never as strong as described in the political propaganda of the time and it was never regarded as a natural union of seven provinces with one single aim, the preservation of their traditional rights and freedom, and one common enemy, the tyranny of Spain.

The earlier history of the Low Countries had been rather chequered. As Alastair Duke has recently reminded us, the Netherlandish provinces before the outbreak of the war in 1572 had only been

---

[1] For a discussion of pamphlets and prints in the Dutch Revolt, see Duke, 'Posters, Pamphlets and Prints'; *idem*, 'Dissident Propaganda'; J. Tanis and D. Horst, eds., *Images of Discord. A Graphic Interpretation of the Opening Decades of the Eighty Years' War* (Philadelphia, Penn., 1993); D. Horst, *De Opstand in zwart-wit* (Zutphen, 2003).

[2] As late as 1660, for instance, the Provincial States of Utrecht adorned their local militia's headquarter with the motto *'Concordia res parvae crescunt'*, which is still visible on the front of the building in Utrecht's city centre. The motto derived from Sallust, *Bellum Jughurtinum*, 10.6.

united under the Habsburg overlords for a relatively short time and
had fought aggressive wars against each other through most of the
Middle Ages and during the Burgundian and early Habsburg period.[3]
Moreover, the provinces themselves had different political relations
with their overlords in Brussels and, thus, more or less room for
manoeuvre at the outbreak of hostilities.[4] And even during the Eighty
Years' War, dividing lines between the members of the Union of
Utrecht and the southern provinces under the Habsburgs were often
blurred and changed over the course of the armed struggle. These
divisions did not disappear with the Twelve Years' Truce (or even
with the Peace of Westphalia). Politicians and intellectuals in the new
Dutch Republic were well aware of the historical, economic and
social differences within the United Provinces and frequently addressed
the issue of an 'ever greater union' in their writings. Reflecting upon
the Truce in 1609 Pieter Cornelisz Hooft, for instance, regarded the
ensuing twelve years as an opportunity 'for the provinces, and particularly the mightiest and most distrusting to bind themselves together
in a strong bond . . . and that all adjoining members through the
declaration of their difficulties and advantages could come so close
to each other that the seams of this emergent body might gradually
disappear'.[5] The Dutch Republic remained intact as a more or less
stable political union well after fighting resumed in the 1620s, but
their members certainly retained their own, regional identity, which
found its expression in the political and historical writings of the
time. However, as Sandra Langereis has recently pointed out, in the
seventeenth century this regional identity was always defined with
an eye to the larger political union of the Dutch Republic, be it by
incorporating or challenging the master narrative of the United

---

[3] Duke, 'The Elusive Netherlands'. The research project 'Centralization or
Particularism? The Development of National Identities in the Low Countries
(1250–1585)', currently undertaken by Wim Blockmans, Robert Stein, A.G. Noordzij
and S. Bijker at Leiden University, addresses questions of regional identity in the
medieval Netherlands through case studies of medieval Gelderland and Brabant.

[4] The non-patrimonial, distant province of Friesland, for instance, preserved a
greater measure of autonomy from Brussels than the core provinces of Brabant or
Flanders.

[5] 'De landen, sonderling de machtigste en mistrouwenste t'samenvlechten door
crachtige verbonden . . . ende alle de aeneenclevende leden door verclaringe van
onderlinge noot en nut, soo diep elckanderen inlijven, dat de naeden van't samenge-
groeijde lichaem metter tijt verduisteren': *De briefwisseling van Pieter Corneliszoon Hooft*,
ed. H.W. van Tricht, 3 vols. (Culemborg, 1976–79), I, 114.

Provinces' political (and economic) success-story as presented by eminent historians such as Emmanuel van Meteren or Pieter Christaensz Bor, which were frequently cited in these works.[6] Historians of the Dutch Republic have generally tended to emphasize the role of Holland as the culturally, politically and economically dominant province of the republic, which could gradually impose its own version of national identity on the other members of the union.[7] It might be argued that this is a result of the historiographical interest in state formation as the dominant paradigm in early modern history in the 1970s and 1980s.[8] This has resulted in a focus on the great 'national' texts of the period and a neglect of histories which were written from a distinctly provincial perspective. It is important, however, to shed further light on the other six provinces' particular perception of themselves, their own past and their relation to the new political entity of the Dutch Republic. The intention of this article is to argue that the idea of an emerging national identity dominated by Holland's master narrative provides an oversimplified account of identity formation in the Northern Netherlands in the seventeenth century, which underestimates the historical traditions and contesting identities provided by artists, historians, and politicians in the other provinces of the Dutch Republic.

The essay addresses the issue of contesting identities in the Dutch Republic through a study of the historiography of two very different provinces – Gelderland and Zeeland – in the mid-seventeenth century. The examples were chosen because they provide two particular, very different historiographical traditions. Moreover, both provinces

---

[6] S. Langereis, *Geschiedenis als ambacht. Oudheidkunde in de Gouden Eeuw. Arnoldus Buchelius en Petrus Scriverius* (Hilversum, 2001), 20. Examples of contemporary master narratives of the Dutch Revolt are Emmanuel van Meteren, *Belgische ofte Nederlantsche historie van onze tijden* (1st Dutch ed., Delft, 1599, rev. ed., 1612); Pieter Christiansz Bor, *Oorspronck, begin ende aenvang der Nederlantscher oorlogen, beroerten ende borgerlijcke oneenicheyden. Waarachtighe ende historische beschrijvinge* (Utrecht, 1595, rev. ed. The Hague, 1603). See also Everhard van Reyd, *Voornaemste geschiedenissen in de Nederlanden ende elders* (Arnhem, 1626); *idem, Oorspronck ende voortganck vande Nederlantsche oorloghen* (Arnhem, 1633).

[7] For traditional interpretations of Holland's dominance see, for instance, E.H. Kossmann, 'The Dutch Case: a National or a Regional Culture?', *Transactions of the Royal Historical Society* 29 (1979), 155–168.

[8] See, for instance, H.G. Koenigsberger, *Dominium regale or Dominium politicum et regale. Monarchies and Parliaments in Early Modern Europe* (London, 1975), and his, *Monarchies, States Generals and Parliaments. The Netherlands in the Fifteenth and Sixteenth Centuries* (Cambridge, 2001).

had a distinctly different relationship to Holland, which is clearly
reflected in their histories. They demonstrate that the story of the
Dutch Revolt was only one factor in the shaping and re-shaping of
regional identity in the seventeenth century and that alliances with
neighbouring territories and their changes played an equally important part in this process.

During the years of the Truce of 1609–21, and after 1648, when
external enemies did not pose an imminent threat to the United
Provinces, internal rivalries and competing histories, which had been
muffled during the Revolt and the Eighty Years' War, re-emerged.
Regional authorities as well as city and town magistrates now commissioned historical works that should help to define the new identity of the towns or provinces, which formed part of the new republic.
Chorographies, topographical-historical descriptions, formed an essential part of this new 'patriotic' scripture. Chorographies witnessed a
steep rise in popularity and production in the Dutch Republic during the seventeenth century. It is probably no coincidence that the
genre boomed particularly during the Twelve Years' Truce and then
again after the Peace of Westphalia. Chorographies derived from an
interest in antiquarianism and were often based on the use of archaeological evidence, geographical surveys and histories (which were seen
as a different genre). They usually followed a distinctive pattern,
which was both innovative and traditional. Earlier descriptions of
Renaissance authors such as Flavio Biondo and Leonardo Bruni
served as models for the presentation of a specific urban or regional
history and topography.[9] Typically, a chorography started with the
etymological explanation of a town's or region's name, which often
discussed legendary foundation myths. It then provided a geographical survey of the area and offered, often clearly outlined as a second part, a history of the region with their leading families and
political alliances. This format was generally kept throughout the
seventeenth century. Style and interpretation, however, changed deci-
sively. Dutch chorographers had a distinct regional or local agenda.
In many cases they were not professional historians, but certainly
belonged to the intellectual elite of the Netherlands, who shared their

---

[9] Flavio Biondo, *Romae Instauratae* (1471) and his *Italia illustrata* (1474); Leonardo
Bruni, *Historiarum Florentini populi libri XII* (Florence, 1473).

interests through a lively exchange of letters, mutual visits, poems dedicated to each others' work and the circulation of manuscripts and ideas for comments and discussions.[10]

So, not surprisingly, the two works in the centre of this discussion were written by two men who had much in common. Their approach to the writing of chorographies was similar, their academic background comparable. Arend van Slichtenhorst, the author of the *Geldersse Geschiedenissen* (published in 1654), had been a student and later a friend of the older Marcus Zuerius Boxhorn, who presented a massive chorographical survey of Zeeland in 1644. Although they pursued different careers, both men saw themselves as part of a circle of Calvinist intellectuals, whose members were interested in the history of their country, be it on a regional, urban or national level. Although they applied the same scholarly and methodological tools to their studies and shared a distinct academic perspective on history in general and on the writing of history, these two accounts offer a very different interpretation of the Dutch Republic's past and can shed light on the alternative regional agendas that informed the interpretation of the provinces' history.

Arend van Slichtenhorst was born into a family of lawyers from Nijkerk in Gelderland in 1616. In 1630 he attended the 'Gymnasium Illustre' in Harderwijk (which received university status in 1648), where his family was then living. Here, he met the eminent historian and professor of Philosophy and Languages Johannes Isacius Pontanus, who had been working on an official history of Gelderland, commissioned by the provincial States, since 1621. His *Historia Gelrica* eventually appeared in Latin in 1639. The voluminous work largely comprised of a collection of earlier chronicles outlining the medieval history of the earls and dukes of Gelderland. Within three years Van Slichtenhorst, who had probably read law in Leiden and was then working as a clerk for the States of Gelderland, began a translation of Pontanus's compendium, which he completed in 1645. He not only provided a Dutch version of Pontanus's text, but added and re-edited parts of the book. Van Slichtenhorst's story was eventually published in Arnhem in 1654.

---

[10] An example for the early seventeenth-century Republic of Letters in Langereis, *Geschiedenis als ambacht*, where she discusses the intellectual world of Arnoldus Buchelius and Peter Scriverius.

The history of Gelderland certainly did not fit easily into the master-narrative of the Dutch Revolt. The dukedom had a chequered
history of opposition first against the Burgundians and then against
their Habsburg overlords. The dukes of Gelderland, who came from
the house of Egmond, played a prominent role as the leading political figure in the Northeastern Netherlands. In the first decades of
the sixteenth century Duke Karel van Egmond had pursued an
expansionist policy, waged war against Holland and invaded neighbouring Drenthe, Overijssel and Utrecht. In 1543 Charles V rein-
tegrated the dukedom into the Spanish Habsburg's territory and
claimed the ducal title for himself. Gelderland was then centrally
governed from the Habsburg-dominated *Hof* in Arnhem, while the
smaller territorial lords in the country maintained their traditionally
close links with the Holy Roman Empire. In 1576 the province
joined the Revolt on the side of Holland and Zeeland, but its support remained uncertain throughout the conflict due to the differing
political allegiances of the towns and the gentry, who supported the
Revolt, and the higher nobility, who remained largely loyal to the
royalist cause and welcomed the Spanish invasions from neighbouring German territories. In the peace treaty of 1648 the south-east-
ern part of the territory, the so-called *Over-quartier* with Roermond
as its regional centre, was officially integrated into the German dukedom of Berg, while the rest of Gelderland remained a member state
of the Dutch Republic.[11] The links between Gelderland and the Holy
Roman Empire had always been an essential part of the province's
identity, and this was clearly reflected in medieval and early modern regional historiography.[12] The other great theme that had preoccupied Gelderland's historians since the late Middle Ages was the
search for the origins of ancient Batavia and their inhabitants, who
were seen as the founding fathers of an idealized Dutch society with
its core values. The identification of the Batavian homeland based

---

[11] For a history of Gelderland in the late middle ages see, for instance, G. Nijsten
et al., *In the Shadow of Burgundy. The Court of Guelders in the Late Middle Ages* (Cambridge,
2003).

[12] See, for instance, A.J. de Mooij, ed., *De Geldersse kroniek van Willem van Berchem*
(Arnhem, 1950), first published in 1480; Gerard Geldenhouwer, *Lugubatiuncula de
Batavorum insula* (1520) and his *Historia Batavica* (1530). For a brief overview on
Gelderland's late medieval historiography, see K. Tilmans, 'De ontwikkeling van
een vaderland-begrip in de laat-middeleeuwse en vroeg-moderne geschiedschrijving
van de Nederlanden', in N.C.F. van Sas, ed., *Vaderland. Een geschiedenis van de vijftiende eeuw tot 1940* (Amsterdam, 1999), 36–38.

on evidence from Tacitus' 'Germania' was a key historiographical issue throughout the early years of the Dutch Republic with both Holland and Gelderland claiming Batavia for their own territories, but the discussion clearly predated the uprising and the patriotic pro-paganda of the United Provinces.[13] Gelderland's relations with the Holy Roman Empire and its Batavian origins were dealt with exten-sively in Van Slichtenhorst's book and formed the backbone of his description of the dukedom. Both issues featured prominently in the creation of a distinct Gelderland identity, which was clearly predi-cated in contrast and competition with the mightiest Dutch province, which had emerged as the political and economic powerhouse of the new republic, Holland. The competition between both provinces was certainly not new; the Batavian issue had already given rise to a controversial interpretation of the past and polemical exchanges between the scholars involved, which Van Slichtenhorst acknowl-edged in his work.[14] In the light of the new political unit that had emerged from the uprising and that formed the umbrella under which both provinces now had to operate – both in practice and ideologically – old divisions had to be presented in a new, less con-troversial light. Moreover, the new interpretation of Gelderland's history went hand in hand with the application of new methods of historical analysis which moved away from the humanist tradition of the sixteenth century and emphasized a study which depended more on antiquarian methods of research and on the interpretation of artefacts and other non-written sources. Van Slichtenhorst's strat-egy certainly paid tribute to these new historiographical standards. He also used the structure of his text for his interpretation of Gelderland's history. For him, the 'Imperial' perspective on Gelderland's past featured more prominently than the debate on the Batavian ori-gins. Characteristically, his survey, which is dedicated to the States of Gelderland, begins with an appraisal of the province's status as the most noble member of the union and as its oldest earldom.

---

[13] For an overview on contemporary historiography on the Batavians see, for instance, E.O.G. Haitsma Mulier, 'De Bataafse mythe opnieuw bekeken', *BMGN* 111 (1996), 344–367, and for the pre-Revolt historiography, István Bejczy, 'Drie humanisten en een mythe. De betekenis van Erasmus, Aurelius en Geldenhouwer voor de Bataafse kwestie', *TvG* 109 (1996), 467–484. See also Tilmans, 'De ontwik-keling van een vaderland-begrip'.

[14] See, for instance, K. Tilmans, *Historiography and Humanism in Holland in the Age of Erasmus, Aurelius and the Divisiekroniek of 1517* (Nieuwkoop, 1992), esp. 254 ff.

Moreover, he outlined in detail Gelderland's elevation to the status
of a dukedom, the only one within the Union, by the Emperor
Ludwig in 1339.[15] The extent of Gelderland's power and prestige
during the fourteenth century was emphasized by reference to the
first duke's wife, Eleonore, daughter of the English king, Edward III,
which demonstrated the international standing of the ruling house.
Clearly, good relations with the Holy Roman Empire in the medieval,
pre-Burgundian past seemed more important for Van Slichtenhorst's
view on his home territory than the reference to earlier, Roman
times and the Batavians, who only enter his account four pages
later.[16] Here, Tacitus is cited as the authoritative source for Gelderland's
Batavian history and particularly for the city of Nijmegen, which is
identified as the ancient stronghold of the Batavians. With reference
to earlier historiographical controversies, Van Slichtenhorst ridicules
claims by historians such as Cornelius Aurelius, who had identified
his native Holland as the homeland of the Batavians.[17] However,
even Aurelius's contemporary adversary, Gerard Geldenhouwer from
Nijmegen, who had positioned the Batavians in Gelderland, does not
escape Van Slichtenhorst's criticism. His version of a myth relating
to Batavian origins, dating back to a legendary Bato as their royal
founding father, is equally dismissed as an old wives' tale.[18] In contrast, Van Slichtenhorst offers his own interpretation of the Batavian
past, which is based not only on references to classical authors, but
also on archaeological evidence aiming at the deconstruction of the
Bato-legend as a folk-tale without historical basis.[19] Even more bit-
ing criticism is directed against the Catholic histories of Gelderland
and their use of pious legends such as the origin myth of the town
of Gelre, which is associated with a dragon slain by the bishop of
Paderborn. These stories, the author claims, are clearly fabrications
of the former Catholic establishment.[20]

---

[15] Arend van Slichtenhorst, *XIV boeken van de Geldersse geschiedenissen* (Arnhem,
1654), 2.
[16] *Ibid.*, 6.
[17] Van Slichtenhorst also criticized later authors with a Holland perspective such
as Hadrianus Junius, *ibid.*, 7–8.
[18] *Ibid.*, 8. Geldenhouwer reappeared at a later stage the text as an eminent son
of the city of Nijmegen, who, although not equipped with as much reason as other
Nijmegenaers – including the Catholic Peter Canisius! – should be honoured by
the city as her leading historian.
[19] *Ibid.*
[20] *Ibid.*, 21.

Of Gelderland's towns and cities, which are described in great detail, Nijmegen stands out. Not only is it the ancient home of the Batavians; what is more important for Van Slichtenhorst is that her history was firmly embedded in the history of the Holy Roman Empire and its first and most prominent representative, Charlemagne. Not only did Van Slichtenhorst claim the city as the place of Charlemagne's coronation as king of the Franks, he also emphasized her status as an imperial free city within the empire and her favoured position as the main residence of the Frankish kings and Holy Roman Emperors, who had adorned her with a number of eminent buildings such as the *Valkhof*, a smaller imitation of the imperial cathedral in Aachen.[21] Although Van Slichtenhorst mentions Nijmegen's loss of her imperial status during the tumultuous mid-thirteenth century, when Count William of Holland donated the city to Count Otho II of Gelderland in exchange for his support for Count William's imperial ambitions, the episode is clearly played down.[22] Nijmegen's position as a *de facto* imperial free city, which was confirmed by Charles V in 1549, is further underlined by a discussion of artefacts and coins found in and around the city as well as inscriptions and buildings within the city walls. These material remains are clearly favoured as pieces of evidence which could reveal a more authentic picture of the past than histories and chronicles. In his description of prominent places within Nijmegen, churches, schools and government buildings stand out, and here again Van Slichtenhorst emphasizes the links with the Holy Roman Empire as in the description of Charlemagne's statue in the town hall and his coat-of-arms, as well as the black double-headed imperial eagle, which adorns the exterior of the building.[23] In Nijmegen's main church, the St. Stevenskerk, the grave of Catharina of Bourbon, wife to Duke Adolf van Egmond (1439–77), is singled out for particular comment; the detailed description of the tomb serves as a reminder of Gelderland's international status in pre-Burgundian times.[24] Its noble houses of Nassau, Jülich, and Egmond are praised while the Valois Dukes and their Habsburg successors are dismissed as 'the envious Burgundians

---

[21] *Ibid.*, 35.
[22] *Ibid.*, 94.
[23] *Ibid.*, 36–37.
[24] *Ibid.*, 36.

and greedy Austrians', who were eventually driven out of the country.[25] The 'imperial' theme is continued in the second part of the book, which provides a narrative account, organized by reigns, of the Merovingian and Carolingian kings and Holy Roman Emperors and covers much of the history of the Holy Roman Empire. In this account Charles V is thus succeeded by Ferdinand I and not, as might have been expected, by Philip II, who was, after all, duke of Gelderland until the Act of Abjuration in 1581.

The Dutch Revolt features prominently in this story, but it receives a distinct Gelderland 'spin' with particular emphasis on the eastern theatre such as the War of Cologne (1583–88). The relationship between the Low Countries and their mighty eastern neighbour, the Holy Roman Empire, remains a prominent feature in the story, with Van Slichtenhorst discussing the possibilities of an alliance with the German princes, although he dismisses this option due to the familial link between the emperor and Philip II.[26] Van Slichtenhorst's war is very much a war of the nobility, where the leading actors were the members of the most powerful aristocratic houses in the Northern Netherlands such as Willem, Count van den Bergh, who joined the Revolt early in 1572, and his contemporary Karel van Brunen, stadholder of Gelderland, who planned a coup against the duke of Alba, but died before 'this raging beast' could be lured to Nijmegen for the imminent assault.[27] Although Van Slichtenhorst touches on the key events in the story of the Revolt such as the sieges of Leiden, Zutphen, Naarden and Haarlem, and praises the princes of Orange as the champions of the uprising, he uses every opportunity to smear the reputation of Holland and its role in the war. He mentions, for instance, the duke of Alba's welcome in Amsterdam after the siege of Haarlem in 1574, when the city gave material support to him and his troops and even built a ship, characteristically called the 'Inquisitie', for the arch-enemy of the Dutch cause.[28] Other criticisms include sniping remarks on Holland's selfish politics and even a critique on the weather in the province, which is, clearly, much less healthy than Gelderland's climate and much too wet.[29]

---

[25] *Ibid.*, 554: 'nydighen Burgondier en gulsighe Oostenrijkers'.
[26] *Ibid.*, 522.
[27] *Ibid.*
[28] *Ibid.*, 527.
[29] *Ibid.*, 526 and 2.

However, these rivalries are forgotten in the final chapter of the text, which deals with the Act of Abjuration. Here, the unity of the provinces is proclaimed and references are made to the Batavian example, which is now firmly embedded both in Gelderland's and in Holland's past.[30] The princes of Orange are the leading figures, the heroes of the uprising, who are compared to the legendary Batavian rulers Civilis Claudius and his brother Julius Paulus. Their political activities are carefully described so as to impress on the readers that the nobles, not 'the people', rose against first and foremost the evil representatives of the king rather than Philip himself. The account culminates in the assurance that the current king of Spain, Philip IV, eventually accepted the independence of the seven united provinces in the Treaty of Westphalia.[31]

A very different story of the Dutch uprising and earlier events in the Netherlands emerged from the work of Marcus Zuerius Boxhorn in his *Chroniick van Zeelandt*. Boxhorn was born at Bergen-op-Zoom, on the border of Zeeland, and was the son of a Calvinist minister. He studied in Leiden, became professor of eloquence in 1633 and director of the 'Collegium oratorum' four years later. In 1648 he was also awarded a chair in history. He died in 1653 and left a substantial *oeuvre* of Latin prose and poetry, discourses on language and literature and histories and chorographies of several Dutch provinces and towns. His interest in the history of Zeeland was kindled partly by his close friend Adriaen Hoffer, mayor of Zierikzee, and partly by the family of his wife Susanna Duvelaer, daughter of the mayor of Middelburg. Boxhorn asked Hoffer to lobby for his

---

[30] *Ibid.*, 551–555.
[31] Van Slichtenhorst was not the only seventeenth-century historian of Gelderland to emphasize the province's traditionally close relations to the Holy Roman Empire. Nijmegen's eminent historians, Johannes Smetius senior (a disciple and friend of Johannes Pontanus) and junior, both focus on the imperial connections of the city as well as on her position as the base for the ancient Batavians: Johannes Smetius, *Oppidum Batavorum, seu Noviomagum* (Amsterdam, 1644); a Dutch annotated translation in Johannes Smetius, *Nijmegen, stad der Bataven*, ed. and trans. A.A.R. Bastiaensen, S. Langereis and L.G.J. Nelissen, 2 vols. (Nijmegen, 1999); Johannes Smetius junior, *Chronyck van de oude stadt der Batavieren. Waer in (nevens de beschryvinge van Nymegen) de eerste orspronck van dese landen, de achtbaere oudtheyt van dese stadt, de voortreflickheyt van haere privilegien, en de oornaemste geschiedenissen van de voorige eeuwen kortelick vertoont worden* (Nijmegen, 1660). Slichtenhorst made frequent references to the works of Smetius senior. Smetius junior listed Van Slichtenhorst as one of the sources that he used for his own study.

commission as the official historian of Zeeland (which also explains the dedication of his work to the States of Zeeland), but the sudden death of his father-in-law stopped further ambitions in this direction. Like Van Slichtenhorst, Boxhorn used an older work on the province as a starting point for his chorographical survey on Zeeland. *Dye Chronyck van Zeeland* by the Catholic Johan Reygersbergen or Reygersberch, a native of Kortgene on the peninsula of Walcheren, had originally been published in Antwerp in 1551. This volume had been the first chronicle of Zeeland, which in earlier works had always been overshadowed by her more powerful neighbours – Flanders in the south and Holland in the north.[32] They not only cast their shadows on Zeeland's historiography, but also on the political composition of the province which largely comprised of islands and peninsulas located between the rivers Maas and Scheldt. Culturally, economically and politically Zeeland had acted as an intermediary between the north and the mighty and prosperous province of Flanders. From 1428 onwards both Holland and Zeeland came under Burgundian and then Habsburg rule, which they formally challenged in the Union of 1575–76. Politics in Zeeland was dominated by the House of Orange whose members were the most powerful players both in governmental institutions such as the *Gecommitteerde Raad* and in military matters.

Like Van Slichtenhorst, Boxhorn re-edited and updated Reygerbergen's original and commented extensively on his predecessor's interpretations of Zeeland's past. These comments, which are clearly marked in the text, offer an excellent opportunity to compare historiographical conventions and their changes over a period of slightly less than one hundred years. These comparisons can also shed light on the portrayal of provincial identity by historians, and how it changed as a result of war and partition. Boxhorn's book falls into two parts. Part one is a chorographical description of the province with details on its topography, its main towns and regions, an etymological outline of their origins and the nature of their inhabitants. The second part is a chronological narrative of the counts of Zeeland

---

[32] Gerard Geldenhouwer, *Epistola de situ Zelandiae* (Leuven, 1514), was written in reaction to Chrysostomus's appraisal of Holland. His contemporary Hadrianus Barlandus mentioned Zeeland towns alongside those in Holland in his *Hollandiae comitu historia et icones*, 1519.

until 1581, when Philip II lost his power over the province. For
Zeeland's more recent history Boxhorn refers the reader to a future
volume, which would pick up the story from the Act of Abjuration
to his own time.[33] Unlike Van Slichtenhorst for Gelderland, Boxhorn
could not claim any noble origins for the establishment of Zeeland.
The many small islands, he argues, were ruled by individual smaller
lords with little power outside their territories. He ridicules Reygersbergen's version of Zeeland's origins, which are linked to the legendary founding fathers Walachrius (for Walcheren) and Zalandius
(for Zeeland in general).[34] These references to noble origins might
be understandable, he comments, but were completely unfounded in
history. Neither great heroes nor even heroic peoples such as the
Batavians play a part in the foundation of the province. The closest that the Zeelanders come to having noble ancestry is their labelling
as 'Vriesen', Frisians, which Boxhorn introduces during his comment
on the region's early christianization.[35] However, the reader is informed
that this is a bit of a misnomer by earlier historians, who tended to
describe both Hollanders, Zeelanders and Vrieslanders under this
heading. There are no references to 'Frisian liberties' and Frisian
virtues such as courage, pride and a sense of order, which play a
prominent part in the identity of the north-eastern provinces of the
Netherlands.[36] Instead, Boxhorn uses the contemporary phrase 'Zeelanders' and leaves Reygersbergen's description of a peace-loving,
industrious, but quite simple folk in place.[37]

As in Gelderland, key events for Zeeland's history are linked to
Charlemagne. His greatest achievement from the province's perspective was his crusade against the Danes and Goths, who had been
oppressing Zeeland's population since the early Middle Ages and
thereby brought civilization and political order to the region.[38] Unlike
Van Slichtenhorst's Gelderland, however, Zeeland always remained

---

[33] Marcus Zuerius Boxhorn, *Chroniick van Zeelandt*, 2 vols. (Middelburg, 1644), II,
604.
[34] *Ibid.*, I, 1, 19–20; II, 4–5.
[35] *Ibid.*, I, 26–27.
[36] See, for instance, Johan Picardt, *Annales Drenthiae ofte een provisioneel ontwerp en
beginsel van seekere antiquiteten, en beschrijvinghe sommigher ghedenckwaerdige geschiedenissen, die
in de landtschap Drent ghepassert zijn, vande geboorte Christi af tot op desen tijdt* (Amsterdam,
1659); idem, *Korte Beschryvinge van eenige vergetene en verborgene antiquiteten der provintien en
landen, gelegen tusschen de Noord-Zee, de Yssel, Emse en Lippe* (Amsterdam, 1660).
[37] Boxhorn, *Chroniick*, I, 21.
[38] *Ibid.*, II, 3.

a weak and remote junior partner in Charlemagne's political plans
and a side show with little importance in imperial policy-making.
Further support against foreign invaders was granted by his son,
Emperor Ludwig, during his stay in Nijmegen, eventually driving
the Danes out of the country with his German troops. What follows
is a long and meticulous description of the establishment of the first
count of both Holland and Zeeland by either Ludwig's son Charles,
or, as other historians claimed, by the latter's brother Lothar. Boxhorn
discusses this claim with reference to original documents, which are
cited in their entirety, and with a detailed examination of the relevant secondary literature, but leaves the final conclusion to the
reader.[39]

The Burgundian period is covered extensively in a special appen-
dix. Here, Zeeland eventually enters high politics as an active player
rather than the passive victim of raids and invasions. Through the
province's overlord, the dukes of Burgundy, Zeeland became involved
in international politics, in particular with England, Scotland and
Scandinavia. Generally, Zeeland's history remains intertwined with
the history of its northern neighbour Holland. While occasionally
references are also made to the southern neighbour and rival, Flanders,
other provinces in Burgundian possession are scarcely mentioned for
this period. There are some references to Gelderland and its opposition against Maximilian and Philip. Here, the sympathies of the
author are undoubtedly on the side of the Burgundians, who get
support from Zeeland's finest men during their campaign against the
unruly Duke Karel van Egmond.[40] Unlike Gelderland, Zeeland profited
from the Burgundian rule, which saw the rise of cities such as Middelburg, which became one of the centres of the herring industry and
traded extensively with England and Scotland, as did the smaller
towns of Veere, Goes and Vlissingen.

While most of the earlier history of the counts is written in the
shadow of the mightier neighbour Holland, Zeeland itself could shine
in the Dutch Revolt, which Boxhorn covers extensively both in the
descriptions of towns and regions and in the second, narrative section. In his description it is this period that clearly formed a distinct
Zeelandic identity, and which was a source of regional pride. In

---

[39] *Ibid.*, II, 6–8.
[40] *Ibid.*, Korte Summatie, 366, 389.

Boxhorn's edition, 'Dutch liberty' overshadows Reygersbergen's main theme: the draining of the land and the province's heroic struggle against the sea. Although land reclamation and dike building are still included in the story, the emphasis has now shifted towards the fight against the Spanish. Although the princes of Orange are the heroes of his story, Boxhorn focuses on the urban theatre of war, where the citizens of Zeeland's towns become active participants in the struggle against Habsburg tyranny.[41] 'The liberty of the United Netherlands' motivated the citizens of towns such as Middelburg to shake off the 'the unbearable yoke of Spanish tyranny' – a story which is told in great detail.[42] In his account, it is both Philip's religious fanaticism and his oppression of trade which caused the towns to rise, and Zeeland's towns were in the forefront of the rebellion. Boxhorn thus feeds into one of the most prominent features of the public memory of the Eighty Years' War in the north: the leading role of the cities and their burghers in the Dutch Revolt. Civic unrest had been particularly strong in Zeeland with its strategic places such as Vlissingen and Veere.[43] The memory of what historians have described as the 'great' and the 'small' tradition of urban resistance against princely centralization and against overpowering oligarchical governments supported the revolt and also fed into the historiography of the events of the Dutch Revolt thus creating and emphasizing a tradition of resistance against an unjust regime.[44]

During his account of the revolt, Boxhorn repeatedly mentions 'der verbonden Nederlanden' (the united Netherlands), but special emphasis is again placed on the union between Zeeland and Holland.[45] His narrative of events remains strictly focused on Zeeland. Thus, the reader is not presented with the master narrative of the Dutch

[41] *Ibid.*, II, 534.

[42] *Ibid.*, I, 150.

[43] Vlissingen and Veere opened their gates for the Sea Beggars at the beginning of the armed struggle in 1572. Middelburg was held by Spanish troops until 1574. The garrison was besieged by Dutch forces for twenty months and eventually surrendered in February 1574.

[44] W.P. Blockmans, 'Alternatives to Monarchical Centralization. The Great Tradition of Revolt in Flanders and Brabant', in H.G. Koenigsberger, ed., *Republiken und Republikanismus im Europa der frühen Neuzeit* (Munich, 1988); M. Boone and M. Prak, 'Rulers, Patricians and Burghers.The Great and the Little Traditions of Urban Revolt in the Low Countries', in K. Davids and J. Lucassen, eds., *A Miracle Mirrored. The Dutch Republic in European Perspective* (Cambridge, 1995).

[45] Boxhorn, *Chroniick*, Dedicatie; II, 561.

Revolt with its key elements such as the heroic sieges of Naarden, Leiden or Haarlem, but is referred to the works of Pieter Bor, Holland's leading historian of the Revolt, for an account of the wider picture. Boxhorn's war concentrates on the west, and events at other theatres are not even mentioned. Extensive references to the great narratives of the Revolt were, therefore, not necessary to boost the regional as well as the national pride of Boxhorn's readership. By the mid-seventeenth century Zeeland's identity had been reshaped by the Dutch Revolt. Reygersbergen's regional master-narrative of the heroic struggle of Zeeland's men and women against the sea and their efforts in dike building and land-reclamation were replaced by Boxhorn's story of the uprising, in which the Zeelanders fought with equal zeal and determination against a human enemy: the Spanish oppressors. Zeeland's involvement in the Revolt provided enough material that had already become part of the national mythology of the war. Like Van Slichtenhorst's story, however, Boxhorn's book ends in a call for the unity of the Dutch Republic and an invocation of God's grace and protection for the Union, which had risen from humble origins to the blessed and prosperous state that it had become in his time.[46] Post-Habsburg relations with the Holy Roman Empire are carefully written out of Boxhorn's story. Even after the Peace of Westphalia the political nature of the links between the Empire and the United Provinces were far from clear. Boxhorn himself was well aware of the judicial debates about the emperor's alleged sovereignty over the Netherlands and contributed to discussions of protocol and nomenclature that had arisen during the international conferences at the end of the Thirty Years' War with his treaties *Disquisitiones politicae*.[47] By avoiding references to the eastern neighbour, Boxhorn not only remained in line with his account of Zeeland's earlier history; he also avoided the complicated question of legal (if not factual) sovereignty, which Van Slichtenhorst still identified with the Holy Roman Empire. Boxhorn's *Chroniick* remained the most

---

[46] *Ibid.*, II, 604.

[47] Marcus Boxhorn, *Disquisitiones politicae* (The Hague, 1655). For the political relations between the Dutch Republic and the Holy Roman Empire, see J. Arndt, *Das Heilige Römische Reich und die Niederlande 1566 bis 1648. Politisch-konfessionelle Verflechtungen und Publizistik im 80-jährigen Krieg* (Cologne, 1998), esp. 85f., and H. Gabel and V. Jarren, *Kaufleute und Fürsten. Außenpolitik und politisch-kulturelle Perzeption im Spiegel niederländisch-deutscher Beziehungen 1648–1748* (Münster, 1998), 447 f.

comprehensive topographical-historical work on Zeeland in the seventeenth century. His own *Chronycke van Hollandt, Zeelandt ende Westvriesland* (Leiden, 1650) presented another annotated re-edition of an earlier work (Johannes Veldernaer's *Chronyck van Hollandt, Zeelandt, ende Westvrieslandt*), whose historical survey ended with the reign of Emperor Maximilian and, thus, ignored the Habsburg period and ensuing Revolt.[48]

In both works the ideological framework and the rhetoric of a 'fatherland' remained carefully limited to the respective region. In his dedication Van Slichtenhorst praised the political elite of Gelderland as 'the true *patres patriae*'[49] and although Boxhorn does not explicitly use the term 'vaderland' his narrative is, as we have seen, unambiguously focused on Zeeland. Both authors, however, also emphasize strongly the role of the 'vereenighde landschappen' and the 'Staten van de vereenighde Nederlanden' for the prosperity and well-being of their own particular province and invoke God's help to protect peace and prosperity in the Republic.[50] This somewhat ambivalent and vague use of a patriotic rhetoric can be described as a typical feature of the regional and urban histories of the mid-seventeenth century and later.[51] Sandra Langereis's observations on the links between regional historiography and the wider political world of the Dutch Republic are reflected in the use of a 'vaderland' vocabulary for the provinces and the appeal to a wider political unit at key moments in the republic's past (such as the Act of Abjuration). It is only in the eighteenth century that a clearer association of the 'vaderland' with the whole of the Dutch Republic emerges. Not

---

[48] Jacob van Oudenhoven, *Oude ende nieuwe beschryvinge van Holland, Zeeland en Vriesland* (The Hague, 1662), offered a translation of Petrus Scriverius's *Batavia illustrata* (1609). Mattheus Smallegang, *Nieuwe chronyck van Zeeland* (Middelburg, 1696), a compilation of the works of Johannes Eyndius, Johannes Reygersbergen and Marcus Boxhorn, provided a topographical survey, but not an historical account of the province. Smallegang died before the completion of his work in 1710. His unfinished study is seen as the last Dutch chorography. See P.J. Verkruijssse, *Mattheus Smallegang (1624–1710), Zeeuws historicus, genealoog en vertaler* (Nieuwkoop, 1983).

[49] Van Slichtenhorst, *Geldersse geschiedenissen*, Dedicatie.

[50] *Ibid.*, 554; Boxhorn, *Chroniick*, 604. Here Boxhorn again refers to one of the key topoi in the early republic's rhetoric, the miraculous rise of the Dutch Republic from small beginnings to a mighty political and economic power.

[51] This and the following observations are discussed in E.O.G. Haitsma Mulier, 'Het begrip "vaderland" in de Nederlandse geschiedschrijving van de late zestiende eeuw tot de eerste helft van de achttiende', in Van Sas, ed., *Vaderland*.

surprisingly, the renewed interest in histories – as opposed to chorographies – of the Netherlands and the marked decline in the publication of regional and town histories and topographical descriptions
corresponds to this trend. The 'vaderland' of eighteenth-century
authors such as Jan Wagenaar, Frans van Mieris and Gerard van
Loon, however, was clearly seen through the lens of the mighty
province, Holland.

While the political scenario thus differed in the two regional narratives, religion, the second great theme of the Dutch Revolt, is
treated in a very similar way. Both authors clearly identify themselves as staunch Calvinists, who present the Revolt as a success for
the Protestant cause against the oppressive powers of Catholicism.
Boxhorn's praise for the princes of Orange as Zeeland's champions
of Protestantism in his preface and conclusion is complemented by
his account of the motivation behind Spanish politics.[52] In Boxhorn's
topographical description religious houses, monasteries and churches
in Zeeland are described in great detail, but it is their architectural
beauty and artwork and their political role in the province, rather
than their religious function, which are praised. Middelburg Abbey,
for instance, an impressive and influential Premonstratensian monastery, is presented for its role as a mighty power-broker in the region,
which raised the political profile of the town and surrounding Walcheren. On a more critical note, Boxhorn describes the expulsion of
the Canons Regular from the abbey, who had to leave due to alleged
misbehaviour.[53] Equally dismissive are Van Slichtenhorst's comments
on Catholicism. Like Boxhorn, he firmly identifies Catholic priests
as conspirators siding with the Spanish tyranny as in the siege of
Zutphen, where 'a blood-thirsty Franciscan monk and a native of
the town' persuaded Alba to order the atrocities for which the episode
became notorious.[54] The reference to God's guidance and support
for the Protestant cause was, of course, part of the master narrative
of the Dutch Revolt from a northern perspective.[55] It was also incor-

---

[52] Boxhorn, *Chroniick*, Dedicatie; II, 604.
[53] *Ibid.*, 152–156.
[54] Van Slichtenhorst, *Geldersse geschiedenissen*, II, 524: 'bloed-gierigh Franciscaner
Moninck wt de Stad geboortigh'.
[55] Emmanuel van Meteren, for instance, outlined 'the freedom of the [Dutch]
nation and the reformed religion' as a key theme of his work in the preface to the
1599 edition of the *Commentarien*, see A.E.M. Janssen, 'A "Trias Historica" on the
Revolt of the Netherlands: Emmanuel van Meteren, Pieter Bor and Everhard van
Reyd as Exponents of Contemporary Historiography', in Duke and Tamse, eds.,

porated in many of the regional and urban chorographies of the time.[56] In Van Slichtenhorst's and Boxhorn's works, this strong Protestant message resonated in the confessional realities in the region under review. Although some Catholic strongholds remained in and around Goes in Zeeland and in South Beveland, of all the Dutch provinces Zeeland and Gelderland had by far the lowest percentage of resident Catholics in the mid-seventeenth century.[57] The triumphant tone of the authors, therefore, would probably not have met with too much opposition in their respective regions.[58] However, it is significant that both works concluded with the Act of Abjuration and left the more recent history unwritten. The controversies between Remonstrants and Counter-Remonstrants in the first decades of the seventeenth century had been a very testing time for the unity of the Republic and had left deep scars in the political, religious and social composition of the United Provinces (and, particularly, in Gelderland, whose population had been deeply divided over the issue). These controversies were difficult to discuss even as late as 1644 or 1654. Both historians must have found it easier to terminate their books on a high note of unity, even in the light of the provinces' struggle to come to a more or less unanimous conclusion. It certainly mirrored the struggles of the Republic itself throughout most of its turbulent early history. Unity was certainly (and still is) an important theme in the propaganda and self-representation of the Dutch Republic. The debate over the key elements of this unity – the common fight against Spanish suppression, the bond of the Calvinist faith, and an enterprising "burgher" society – was dominated by its most vocal contributors: the citizens of Holland's towns and cities who commissioned histories, art works and architecture which praised what they perceived as distinctive Dutch values.

Clio's Mirror, 16. The reference to the 'vaderland' and Protestantism also frequently appeared in pamphlets of the time. See G. de Bruin, 'Het begrip "vaderland" in de pamfletliteratuur ten tijde van de Republiek, 1600–1700', in Van Sas, ed., *Vaderland*, 146.

[56] See, for instance, Jacob van Oudenhoven, *Beschryvinge der stadt ende meyerye van 's Hertogen-Bossche* (Amsterdam, 1649), introduction; Johannes Isacius Pontanus, *Historische beschrijvinghe der seer wijt beroemde coopstadt Amsterdam* (Amsterdam, 1614), introduction, 34.

[57] For more details, see Israel, *Dutch Republic*, 389, 642.

[58] Other chorographers, such as Adriaen Haverman in his *Kort Begrip en Bericht van de Historie van Brabant* (Leiden, 1652), were much more guarded and could not afford to engage in an all too open anti-Catholic rhetoric.

Historians have largely accepted Holland's dominance in this creation of a new nation. Only recently have studies of both the rhetoric
of difference (in its various guises) and the contributions of other
regions to a Dutch master narrative, started to appear.[59] This article is a contribution to this literature, which tries to shed light on
the complicated interplay between regional and national identity in
the Dutch Republic during the seventeenth century through an analysis of the different layers of affiliation and loyalty as expressed in
the construction and de-constructions of traditions and histories in
Gelderland and Zeeland.

---

[59] The establishment of museums with a distinctly regional agenda such as
Nijmegen's Het Valkhof (opened in 1999) and Venlo's Limburgs Museum (opened
in 2000) also reflect this new interest.

CHAPTER THIRTEEN

'SO MANY PAINTED JEZEBELS'.
STAINED GLASS WINDOWS AND THE FORMATION
OF AN URBAN IDENTITY IN THE DUTCH REPUBLIC

Andrew Spicer

English travellers to the Dutch Republic during the seventeenth century were fascinated by the religious diversity that they found in the towns. They took the opportunity to observe the religious practices of different sects and creeds, while in Amsterdam the Jewish community and their worship at the synagogues held a particular interest for them.[1] Yet these travellers also visited the major urban churches used by the Reformed Church, observing not only the services being held, but also the appearance and furnishing of these buildings. Churches such as the Bavokerk in Haarlem, the Oude Kerk in Amsterdam or the Nieuwe Kerk in Delft, were included on a number of travel itineraries. In these churches, they saw not only the liturgical arrangement of Reformed worship, but also funerary monuments to the leaders of the Revolt – William of Orange and Maurice of Nassau – and the naval heroes of the Republic, as well as references to the civic mythology and the history of each particular town. Although Dutch parish churches had always engendered a degree of civic pride, during the early seventeenth century, they had become an increasingly important vehicle for expressing urban identity. This was a development that was reflected in the prominent role that these buildings assumed in the chorographies of particular cities.

There was, however, one medium for portraying this urban iconography – stained glass windows – that was regarded as incongruous

---

[1] See for example, William Brereton, *My Travels into Holland and the United Provinces, England, Scotland and Ireland*, ed. E. Hawkins, Chetham Society 1 (s.l., 1844), 60–61, 64, 65, 67–68; Peter Mundy, *The Travels of Peter Mundy in Europe and Asia, 1608–1667*, ed. R. Carnac Temple, 5 vols., Hakluyt Society 17, 35, 45, 55, 78 (Cambridge, 1907–36), IV, 68; John Evelyn, *The Diary of John Evelyn*, ed. E.S. de Beer, 6 vols. (Oxford, 1955), II, 42, 44.

by a number of English visitors. Sir William Brereton, who was later to serve as a Parliamentary general, visited Amsterdam in 1634 where he particularly admired the recently completed Lutheran church. Here he noted with obvious pleasure that 'the greater number of [the Lutherans] will not allow the use of images in any sense, the rest only for ornament, not for adoration: herein I was the rather confirmed because no images at all extant in their church and windows'. His delight that there were 'no pictures in their windows' can be compared with his comment on the Zuiderkerk, where he found 'in the windows of this church . . . the pictures of the arms of companies of every trade'. Brereton's somewhat terse comments reflected his strong belief that clear glass was more appropriate for a Reformed place of worship.[2]

Brereton was relatively silent about the actual windows he did see, but a number of other English visitors, particularly in the wake of the Civil War, did make more detailed observations. The nobleman William Lord FitzWilliam spent several months during 1663 touring the provinces and commented on the iconography of some of the windows. At the Oude Kerk in Amsterdam, he described the stained glass that had only recently been installed in the church:

> Upon the windows you will find many old pieces of painting of Philip the Good and his wife, Christ's nativity, and Mary's and Elizabeth's salutation. Behind the choir is a new piece which represents King Philip of Spain's coronation [sic] and his signing with his own hands the peace with the Seven United Provinces.

He continued to the Nieuwe Kerk, where he observed:

> The windows above two doors are finely painted; one represents Earl William [sic] giving the city of Amsterdam a new coat of arms, the other Maximilian, King of the Romans, crowning them with an imperial crown.

In his description of the Bavokerk at Haarlem, he noted that 'upon one of the windows you will see painted the sedition of the Casembroots'.[3] FitzWilliam's comments should not be regarded as

---

[2] Brereton, *My Travels into Holland*, 63–64, 67.

[3] K. van Strien, *Touring the Low Countries. Accounts of British Travellers, 1660–1720* (Amsterdam, 1998), 30, 181. FitzWilliam was mistaken in believing the new window in the Oude Kerk at Amsterdam referred to the coronation of Philip IV. The window in fact depicted the crowned king in a symbolic setting which commemo-

exceptional; other English visitors, such as Thomas Penson, left similar accounts of the 'delicate glass painting' they saw in these churches and which he regarded as 'the finest in the world'.[4]

Although FitzWilliam's itinerary did not include a visit to Gouda, the fame of the stained glass windows at the Janskerk had attracted a number of other tourists to the town by the end of the seventeenth century.[5] One of the most detailed accounts of such a visit is provided by the clergyman John Leake in 1712. He found in the Janskerk 'one and thirty windows adorned with historical painting both profane and sacred, done by the best hands of their several times'. Leake went on to reflect:

> I could not forbear reflecting upon the different tempers of the foreign Calvinists from those of that stamp in our island. Here they ... permit stories of the Old and New Testament and the figures of some several deliverances that themselves have received at the hands of Providence to look them in their faces in the places of their religious worship without dread of idolatry and fears of Popery ... Now it is well-known our Reformation-reformers managed after a quite different rate when they usurped the administration of affairs amongst us. Then the churches that were most beautified were sure to be the greatest sufferers. All the historical paintings in their windows were so many painted Jezebels, and therefore to be thrown down and destroyed ... whatever was decent and tended to advance the beauty of holiness was nicknamed superstition and the trappings of the whore of Babylon, and therefore to be hewed to pieces as Samuel did Agag, etc. May latest posterity never see the second part of this Holy Farce acted amongst us. And may those who are fondest of bringing us to correspondence with Dutch models learn so much sense and religion of our neighbours as to conclude that slovenliness and inharmoniousness are far from being agreeable in places where divine service is performed.[6]

---

rated the Peace of Munster and the conclusion of the Revolt. The Haarlem window was dedicated to the memory of Nicolaas van Ruyven, who was murdered in 1492 while trying to maintain order in the face of the revolt by inhabitants from North Holland and Alkmaar – the 'Cheese and Bread Folk' (*Kaas en Brood Volk*). The duke of Saxony required the people of Haarlem, Alkmaar, and villages in the Kennemerland and West Friesland to pay over two hundred guilders to the Van Ruyven family for two windows to be erected in the churches of Alkmaar and Haarlem. M.M. Mochizuki, 'The Reformation of Devotional Art and the Great Church in Haarlem', unpublished Ph.D. thesis, 2 vols. (Yale University, 2001), I, 138.

[4] Van Strien, *Touring the Low Countries*, 40, 169.
[5] *Ibid.*, 169, 171, 172–173.
[6] *Ibid.*, 172–173.

These English observers were surprised by the presence of stained glass in places of worship because it seemed to be so completely at odds with the traditional teachings of the Reformed Church concerning religious imagery and the dangers of idolatry. For some visitors, such as Leake, the tolerance shown by the Dutch towards these windows and other furnishings, in particular, organs, was in marked contrast to their experience at home during the Commonwealth. In 1641, John Evelyn had commented: 'Generaly, there are in all the Churches in Holland Organs, Lamps, Monuments &c: carefully preserved from the fury, and impiety of popular reformers, whose zeale has foolishly transported them in other places rather to act like madmen, then religious'.[7] In English parish churches, stained glass was one of the principal surviving decorative features from before the Reformation, but it was condemned by more radical Protestants as evidence of idolatry. A month after the entry in Evelyn's diary, the House of Commons ordered the removal of altars and other Laudian innovations from parish churches. In some instances this also resulted in the taking down of stained glass windows. A series of iconoclastic ordinances was passed the following year, which included the appointment of a commissioner for each county to oversee the removal of stained glass. Exceptionally, for the eastern counties, a special commission was established under William Dowsing, which systematically purged over two hundred and fifty churches across Cambridgeshire and Suffolk of their remaining religious imagery, including a number of stained glass windows.[8] Even the consistory of the Dutch Church in London received a complaint from a member of its congregation that 'in some windows we find these idolatrous inscriptions "The Temple of our Lord Jesus Christ" and in others "Jesus Temple"'.[9]

Just as in England, the fate of stained glass in the Netherlands in fact reflected the course of the Dutch Reformation. Although considerable damage had been done to churches across the Netherlands during the course of the Iconoclastic Fury and after the seizure of

---

[7] Evelyn, *The Diary of John Evelyn*, II, 49.

[8] J. Spraggon, *Puritan Iconoclasm during the English Civil War* (Woodbridge, 2003), 64–65, 71, 101; William Dowsing, *The Journal of William Dowsing. Iconoclasm in East Anglia during the English Civil War*, ed. T. Cooper (Woodbridge, 2001), 91–93.

[9] J.H. Hessels, ed., *Ecclesiae Londino-Batavae archivum. Epistulae et Tractatus*, 3 vols. (Cambridge, 1887–97), III, Pt 2, 1928.

Den Briel and Vlissingen by the Sea Beggars, as Alastair Duke has shown, in many towns the removal of religious images and of the trappings of Catholicism had been a more orderly process than has been suggested by a historiography coloured by the accounts of wanton destruction at Antwerp and in Flanders. In the north, the magistrates at Breda and Oudenaarde were able to remove some of the church treasures in advance of the iconoclasts, and the intervention of the magistrates also spared the furnishings of the Nieuwe Kerk in Delft. At The Hague, the local authorities co-operated with the Reformed Church and paid for the removal of images and other furnishings associated with the mass.[10] There was also a willingness to re-use and adapt certain fittings such as pews and pulpits for Reformed worship. At 's-Hertogenbosch, the pulpit was retained as well as an altar for the Lord's Supper, while at Elburg in Gelderland, 'the font, pulpit and the pews where the women sat were spared'.[11] Similarly in the Pieterskerk in Leiden, the pulpit and the new choir stalls were adapted for Reformed use, while in Utrecht the choir stalls from the demolished Buurkerk were retrieved and re-erected in the cathedral.[12] The extent to which some of these pre-Reformation decorations and furnishings survived can easily be seen in the depictions of church interiors sketched during the seventeenth century by Pieter Saenredam and other artists.

Although Frans Hogenberg's depiction of the iconoclasm in Antwerp shows a man taking a hammer to the windows of the church, paintings – and the handful of surviving windows – show that stained glass still remained in a number of the major churches into the seventeenth century. Glass certainly served a very important and obvious function in keeping out the elements and in making the church habitable or suitable for worship.[13] Furthermore, the Reformed Church

---

[10] Duke, *Reformation and Revolt*, 131–134, 205–206; J.D. Bangs, *Church Art and Architecture in the Low Countries before 1566*, Sixteenth Century Essays & Studies 37 (Kirksville, Miss., 1997), 10, 11.

[11] A.C. Duke, 'De Calvisten en de "Paapse beeldendienst". De denkwereld van de beeldenstormers in 1566', in M. Bruggeman *et al.*, eds., *Mensen van de Nieuwe Tijd. Een liber amicorum voor A.Th. van Deursen* (Amsterdam, 1996).

[12] Bangs, *Church Art and Architecture*, 18, 33–34, 42; A. de Groot, 'Internal Arrangements in the Utrecht Cathedral before and after the Reformation', in E. de Bièvre, ed., *Utrecht, Britain and the Continent. Archaeology, Art and Architecture*, British Archaeological Association Conference Transactions 18 (London, 1996), 259.

[13] In Scotland, specific instructions were given to those adapting the cathedral at Dunkeld for Reformed worship not to damage the windows: J. Sinclair, ed., *The Statistical Account of Scotland*, 21 vols. (Edinburgh, 1791–99), XX, 422.

seems to have had an initially ambiguous position regarding stained
glass, and to have permitted some decoration in the form of texts
to appear in their windows. The temple erected at Ghent in 1566
was lit by numerous windows that 'were all glazed with plain glass,
except for the lower windows which bore inscriptions from the Ten
Commandments of God and from other passages of Scripture'.[14] At
the same time, windows were donated by wealthy individuals for the
new temple at Gorcum, although there are no details about whether
this was decorative glass or emblazoned with coats of arms as can
be seen in the depiction of the contemporary temple at Lyons.[15] The
Count of Culemborg did, however, decide to install new windows
bearing his own coats of arms when he converted some outbuild-
ings into a temple at his residence in June 1566.[16]

The secular authorities were also prepared to reuse stained glass.
At Gouda, the convent of the Regulars was demolished between
1576 and 1580, but in selling the building materials from the site,
the town corporation stipulated that the windows were to become
the property of the municipality. The seven windows, which were
contemporary with those of the Janskerk, were transferred and remod-
elled into two windows so as to the complete the reglazing of the
ambulatory of the parish church. The subject matter of these windows fitted with, and completed, the existing iconographical scheme
for the ambulatory which already depicted scenes from the lives of
Christ and St. John the Baptist. Nonetheless the new use of these
windows was commemorated with the following inscription which
was painted on the glass:

> These two windows standing present here
> Were first intended for the Convent of the Regulars
> And when the monastery lay in ruins
> Were placed and put to good use here.[17]

[14] A. Duke, G. Lewis and A. Pettegree, eds., *Calvinism in Europe 1540–1610. A
Collection of Documents* (Manchester, 1992), 153.
[15] Duke, *Reformation and Revolt*, 139. On coats of arms in the windows of Huguenot
temples, see R.A. Mentzer, 'The Reformed Churches of France and the Visual
Arts', in P. Corby Finney, ed., *Seeing Beyond the Word. Visual Arts and the Calvinist
Tradition* (Grand Rapids, Mich., 1999), 217–218, plate 21.
[16] O.J. de Jong, *De Reformatie in Culemborg* (Assen, 1957), 102–104. I am grateful
to Alastair Duke for this reference.
[17] H. van Harten-Boers, Z. van Ruyven-Zeman *et al.*, *The Stained-Glass Windows
in the Sint Janskerk in Gouda*, 3 vols. (Amsterdam, 1997, 2000, 2002), I, 103–117.

The survival of stained or painted glass windows in the Netherlands was not without criticism; some windows were damaged during the Revolt and the adaptation of the churches for Reformed worship. Typical was the window in the Grote Kerk at Alkmaar, in which the depiction of God the Father had been vandalized and had to be repaired by the Haarlem glassmaker Willem Tybaut in 1572.[18] It was the attempts to encapsulate the godhead within these windows that caused the most offence to the Calvinists, and steps were taken during the later sixteenth century to remove portrayals of God the Father, Son and Holy Spirit as well as the Trinity or references to the mass. It was for this reason that the authorities in Haarlem decided in 1595 to take down the window donated by Bishop Joris van Egmond, which portrayed him praying before the Holy Trinity.[19] Similarly at the Oude Kerk in Amsterdam, a window depicting the 'Adoration of the Shepherds' was modified with the coat of arms of the town, perhaps to replace a depiction of the local cult of the 'Miraculous Host'.[20]

The Reformed Church also issued several ordinances about the unsuitability of stained glass in some churches. Ironically, in 1595, at the same time as the reglazing programme was being completed in the Janskerk, the provincial synod of South Holland ruled against what they regarded as unseemly paintings in church glass, such as crucifixes and other profane images, although this ruling had to be repeated in 1596 and 1597. During the early seventeenth century, the classis of Leiden ordered that measures should be taken against an idolatrous window at Benthuizen in 1607, while following a visitation of the church at 's-Gravenmoer, the *kerkmeesters* were ordered by the classis of Dordrecht to remove an image of the Holy Trinity from a church window.[21]

---

[18] P.J. Glasz, 'Voormalige glasschilderingen zoo te Alkmaar als door Alkmaar elders geschonken', *Oud Holland* 26 (1908), 10–90, 79. On Calvinism and the donation of windows in general, see L. Noordegraaf, 'Religie, mecenaat en gebrandschilderd glas in Noord-Nederlandse gereformeerde kerken gedurende de zestiende en zeventiende eeuw', *Bulletin van de Stichting Oude Hollandse Kerken* 51 (2000), 3–22.

[19] Van Harten-Boers, *The Stained-Glass Windows*, III, 142, 163 n. 20.

[20] Noordegraaf, 'Religie, mecenaat en gebrandschilderd glas', 5–6.

[21] J. Reitsma and S.D. van Veen, eds., *Acta der provinciale en particuliere synoden, gehouden in de Noordelijke Nederlanden gedurende de jaren 1572–1620*, 8 vols. (Groningen, 1892–99), III, 43–44, 66–67, 80; J. Roelevink, ed., *Classicale Acta 1573–1620. V Provinciale synode Zuid-Holland, Classis Leiden 1585–1620, Classis Woerden 1617–1620*, Rijks Geschiedkundige Publicatiën, Kleine Serie 88 (The Hague, 1996), 195–196;

The success of the Counter-Remonstrants in 1618 led to calls for a *nadere reformatie* or Further Reformation of the church, which focused not on theology but on actual religious practice. The main direction of these calls for reform concerned issues of personal morality and behaviour, as well as what they regarded as superstitious practices.[22]

In November 1621, the consistory at Gouda complained to the magistrates about the idolatrous images in the church windows. The Counter-Remonstrants were in the political ascendancy amongst the magistracy of the town, and in 1622 they sanctioned the removal of depictions of the Trinity and God the Father from three windows in the Janskerk.[23] This included another window donated by Joris van Egmond depicting the 'Baptism of Christ', at the head of which was a portrayal of 'God the Father', which was replaced with yellow glass.[24]

The stained glass at the Janskerk in Gouda is the most well-known and complete series of early modern stained glass windows in the Northern Netherlands. They reflect the widespread patronage for stained glass windows during the early sixteenth century, some of which also survives in the Southern Netherlands, at Brussels Cathedral for example. In the north, some pre-Reformation windows do remain, such as in the Jacobskerk in The Hague and the Oude Kerk in Amsterdam, but others have been lost not solely due to iconoclasm, but through damage, and wear and tear over the subsequent centuries.[25]

The Gouda windows are unusual because they include windows that were commissioned both before and after adaptation of the church for Calvinist worship. The church had undergone major building work in the later fifteenth century, which had included the construction of a new choir and ambulatory. Between 1530 and

---

J. Roelevink, ed., *Classicale Acta 1573–1620. II Particuliere synode Zuid-Holland, Classis Dordrecht 1601–1620, Classis Breda 1616–1620*, Rijks Geschiedkundige Publicatiën, Kleine Serie 86 (The Hague, 1991), 678.

[22] For a summary on the *nadere reformatie*, see J. Israel, *The Dutch Republic. Its Rise, Greatness and Fall, 1477–1806* (Oxford, 1995), 474–477.

[23] A.A.J. Rijksen, 'Veranderingen in de zeventiende eeuw krachtens gereformeerde opvattingen in drie van de Goudse Glazen gedeeltelijk hersteld in de twintigste eeuw', *Zuid-Hollandse Studiën* 1 (1950), 40–52.

[24] Van Harten-Boers, *The Stained-Glass Windows*, II, 67.

[25] See Bangs, *Church Art and Architecture*, 125–134; A. van der Boom, *Monumentale glasschilderkunst in Nederland* (The Hague, 1940).

1550, a series of windows depicting the apostles were installed in the clerestory. These windows fortunately survived a fire in the church in 1552 after which the church authorities undertook an extensive programme of re-glazing, concentrating in particular on the ambulatory of the choir and the nave.[26] The church authorities approached a number of prominent figures in the Netherlands to act as sponsors for these windows; the designs were the result of negotiations between the artist and the church authorities rather than with the donor. Religious leaders such as the Provost of Utrecht Cathedral, the Commander of the Catharijne-convent in Utrecht, the abbess of Rijnsburg, the Commander of the Hospital of St. Jan in Haarlem, the canons of St. Mary's Utrecht all sponsored windows which were installed in the ambulatory, while in the transepts and nave the secular sponsors included Philip II of Spain and Mary Tudor, Margaret of Parma, William of Orange, Duke Erich of Brunswick, Duke Philip de Ligne and Count Jean de Ligne and his wife.[27] The windows formed a coherent iconographic scheme with those in the choir depicting John the Baptist as the forerunner of Christ, while in the transepts and nave the windows reflect the relationship between the Old and the New Testaments.[28] There is a certain irony in that one of the last pre-Reformation windows installed, in 1566, was that sponsored by William of Orange, which depicted 'The Cleansing of the Temple of Jerusalem'.

Construction on the Janskerk resumed in 1590, presumably completing an earlier building scheme, whereby the height of the nave was raised to match that of the choir. The earlier glazing campaign had also been left unfinished with the outbreak of the Revolt and was therefore resumed by the town authorities. Between 1594 and 1603, windows were donated by the towns of Amsterdam, Delft, Dordrecht, Haarlem, Leiden and Rotterdam as well as by the States of Holland and the Board of the Polders of the Rijnland.[29] One significant difference in the completion of the glazing programme at the Janskerk was a change in the management of the project. Following the Revolt, the property of the Church had been taken into lay administration during the early 1570s and by 1580 Catholic worship

---

[26] Van Harten-Boers, *The Stained-Glass Windows, 1556–1604*, I, 15–16.
[27] *Ibid.*, I, 16–17, II, 21–23.
[28] *Ibid.*, II, 23–46.
[29] *Ibid.*, I, 17–18, III, 145–46.

had been outlawed throughout the northern provinces – although this had been achieved earlier in provinces such as Holland. While the Reformed Church was recognized as the public church, responsibility for the church fabric remained with the parish rather than the congregation which only represented a minority of the urban population. Furthermore there was no legal requirement until the mid-seventeenth century for these 'civic' officials, the *kerkmeesters*, to be members of the Reformed Church.[30]

In urban areas the magistrates had been actively involved in the maintenance and beautification of their parish churches prior to the Reformation. Patrician families and the major office-holders were amongst the donors to the churches; their names were recorded in the bead rolls and memorial lists, they were portrayed within the altarpieces or stained glass windows they donated, or were physically present or recorded in their tombs or memorials.[31] While donations were intended to benefit the souls of their donors and while their iconography may have reflected personal aspirations, it is also important to remember that the church served as a focal point for urban patronage. At times of civic prosperity or in exceptional circumstances, boards of church masters drawn from the local patriciate commissioned new building projects. Expenditure on the refurbishment and enhancement of churches continued until the eve of the Revolt. At Leiden the refurbishment of the Pieterskerk was on-going during the early 1560s with the magistrates providing a substantial loan for the new choir stalls in 1565. The last window of the pre-Reformation re-glazing programme at the Janskerk in Gouda was not installed until February 1567.

The example of Gouda might suggest that the Revolt meant a dramatic change in window donations and a shift of patronage away from individuals, towards towns and other political institutions.

[30] Duke, *Reformation and Revolt*, 259; A.Th. Van Deursen, 'Kerk of parochie? De kerkmeesters en de dood ten tijde van de Republiek', *TvG* 89 (1976), 531–537; A.Th. van Deursen, *Bavianen en slijkgeuzen. Kerk en kerkvolk ten tijde van Maurits en Oldenbarnevelt* (Assen, 1974), 22, 107; H. Schilling, 'Religion and Society in the Northern Netherlands. "Public Church" and Secularization, Marriage and Midwives, Presbyteries and Participation', in his *Religion, Political Culture and the Emergence of Early Modern Society. Essays in German and Dutch History* (Leiden, 1992), 360–363.

[31] Bangs, *Church Art and Architecture*, 125; L. Noordegraaf, 'Macht en Mecenaat. Gebrandschilderd glas in Hollandse kerken (16de–18de eeuw)', in M. Bruggeman et al., eds., *Mensen van de Nieuwe Tijd. Een liber amicorum voor A.Th. van Deursen* (Amsterdam, 1996), 310–311.

A more wide-ranging survey of the patronage of windows has illustrated that there was no such clear-cut division in donations.[32] More representative is the example of another church that underwent a reglazing programme before the Revolt, a decade before the Janskerk, and that was also completed after the Revolt. The Jacobskerk in The Hague had been damaged by fire in 1539 and work had begun on installing new windows during the early 1540s. Windows were donated by the Emperor Charles V and leading members of the nobility such as Maximilian van Egmond, René of Châlon and the Count of Hoogstraten as well as the canons of the Royal Chapel and the bishop of Utrecht. Yet the Holland towns, too, donated windows to the Jacobskerk. Three windows were given by the magistracies of Leiden, Haarlem and Amsterdam in 1541 and a further nine windows were donated by the other towns of Holland. The scheme was completed in the 1590s with windows donated by the States of Holland, Maurice of Nassau and the *kerkmeesters*.[33]

In other pre-Reformation churches, too, patronage was not confined to individuals or religious institutions. Three windows were, for example, donated by Haarlem in the early sixteenth century. The Amsterdam magistrates gave a window to the church at Sloten in 1557 and two years later to the church at Medemblik, which also received windows from Alkmaar and Haarlem at this time.[34] The donation of windows virtually ceased during the conflicts of the later sixteenth century, although the church of Oudewater was the notable exception to this with windows being given in 1579 and 1580 by Alkmaar, Amsterdam, Gouda, Haarlem, Leiden, and Rotterdam.[35]

---

[32] See L. Noordegraaf, 'Mecenaat vóór en na de Opstand. Gebrandschilderde glazen in Hollandse kerken gedurende de late Middeleeuwen en vroegmoderne tijd', *Holland* 33 (2001), 17–37.

[33] H.E. van Gelder, 'De zestiende-eeuwsche glasschilderingen in de Haagsche Sint-Jacobskerk', *Oud Holland* 36 (1918), 1–41, 29–31, 33–34; Van der Boom, *Monumentale Glasschilderkunst in Nederland*, 138–50.

[34] E. van Biema, 'Nalezing van de stadsrekeningen van Amsterdam vanaf het jaar 1531', *Oud Holland* 25 (1905), 150–162, 238–2; 26 (1906), 45–62, 109–128, 171–192, 242–248, there 160; C.J. Gonnet, 'Haarlemsche glasschrijvers', in C. Hofstede de Groot, ed., *Feest-bundel Dr Abraham Bredius aangeboden den achttienden April 1915* (Amsterdam, 1915), 73; Glasz, 'Voormalige glasschilderingen zoo te Alkmaar', 70; Noordegraaf, 'Mecenaat vóór en na de Opstand', 25.

[35] Van Biema, 'Nalezing van de stadsrekeningen van Amsterdam', 48; Gonnet, 'Haarlemsche glasschrijvers', 74; Glasz, 'Voormalige glasschilderingen', 70–71; Bangs, *Church Art and Architecture*, 214; F.D.O. Obreen, *Archief voor Nederlandse kunstgeschiedenis*, 7 vols. (Rotterdam, 1877–90), II, 235, III, 29.

It was not only the towns that donated windows before the Revolt; institutions such as the *Hoogheemsraadschap* also provided windows for various churches.[36] Similarly, there were also individual donors of windows, as again could be seen in The Hague, after the Revolt.[37]

Although relatively little of the actual stained glass survives, numerous local studies have demonstrated the importance of the culture of donating windows in the Dutch Republic. As a rule, these have tended to concentrate either on the glazing schemes of particular churches such as at Gouda, Edam, Schermerhorn or De Rijp,[38] for example, or drawing upon published extracts from the archives, have looked at the windows donated by a certain town or the work of a particular artist. The records for Amsterdam are incomplete, as they do not mention the donation of a window to the Janskerk at Gouda, but they nonetheless show that tweny-three payments were made for church windows between 1591 and 1656. At Alkmaar, forty-five donations were made between 1594 and 1673 and Haarlem made fifty-seven between 1595 and 1684. Archival studies for shorter periods have similarly demonstrated the importance of this tradition of window donations. Twelve windows were donated by Leiden between 1594 and 1620, fifteen by Gouda between 1579 and 1639, five by The Hague from 1598 to 1623, while twenty-five were given by Hoorn to the North Holland churches between 1624 and 1669. At Dordrecht, the magistrates employed the glass painter Gerrit Gerritsz Cuyp to provide seven windows for different churches between 1597 and 1639.[39] Such studies have tended to concentrate on the custom of donating windows within the province of Holland, which as the most urbanized and prosperous state within the Republic is perhaps

---

[36] Noordegraaf, 'Mecenaat vóór en na de Opstand', 25–26.

[37] *Ibid.*, 30–32. One remarkable donation was the window that is unfortunately no longer extant, installed in the Hooglandse kerk, Leiden, by Floris Hey, a Roman Catholic canon of the church. Bangs, *Church Art and Architecture*, 214.

[38] See Z. van Ruyven-Zeman *et al.*, eds., *Kleurrijk Verleden. Edam, De Glazen van de Grote Kerk. Monument van Kunst en Geschiedenis* (Edam, 1994); C.C.M. Kampf-Rekelhof, *De Grote Kerk van Schermerhorn* (Schermerhorn, 1998); P. Mens, *De Rijper glazen* (De Rijp, 2000). A list of seventeenth-century stained glass can be found in W. Bogtman, *Nederlandsche glasschilders* (Amsterdam, 1944).

[39] Van Biema, 'Nalezing van de stadsrekeningen van Amsterdam', *passim*; Gonnet, 'Haarlemsche glasschrijvers', *passim*; Glasz, 'Voormalige glasschilderingen', *passim*; Bangs, *Church Art and Architecture*, 214; S. Groenveld, *Haarlemse glasraamschenkingen. Stedelof tussen domine, regent en koopman* (Gouda, 1998), 16, 31; Van Ruyven-Zeman, *The Stained-Glass Windows*, III, 149, 151; Obreen, *Archief voor Nederlandse Kunstgeschiedenis*, II, 115, 117, 124, 129, III, 29, 41, 45, 46, 47, 51, 52, 53, 61, 62, 63, 64.

not surprising. Nonetheless the tradition of towns presenting windows to churches in other communities can also be seen elsewhere within the United Provinces.[40] Looking slightly further afield to Friesland, twenty-four churches received stained glass windows in the late sixteenth century and 154 during the following century.[41] While there is now plentiful evidence for local donations, it is only recently that the work of Simon Groenveld and Leo Noordegraaf has started to place this form of patronage in a broader context. The intention of the remainder of this essay is to consider why this system of patronage survived after the Revolt and to consider what it reveals about civic identity in the Dutch Republic.

One particularly significant factor is that the patronage of windows allowed the donating magistrates to establish and publicize their own urban identity within the public sphere. The subject matter of these windows enabled them to deploy a particular iconography that reflected the importance of the donor. Any such survey of these windows is inevitably restricted by what glass has survived from the early modern period, and the extent to which there are references in the archives to their content or – in exceptional circumstances – surviving drawings or cartons of the design. The range of the subjects illustrated in the windows donated to the Janskerk is particularly informative of the range of imagery deployed and can be divided into three distinct categories. Firstly there are the windows that referred to historical events and in particular those related to the Revolt. Amongst these should be included the windows given by the States of Holland which represented the themes of 'King David and the Christian Knight' and 'The Triumph of Freedom of Conscience'.[42] Of the urban donations, Delft's window depicted the 'Relief of the Siege of Leiden', whereas the Biblical image depicted in the window financed by Leiden was an allegorical reference to the same

---

[40] Utrecht donated three windows between 1635 and 1639, for example. Obreen, *Archief voor Nederlandse Kunstgeschiedenis*, II, 254, 256.
[41] S. ten Hoeve, 'Geschilderde glazen in Friese kerken in het bijzonder uit de 18de eeuw', *Stichting Alde Fryske Tsjerken* 1 (1973), 121.
[42] See C. Janson, 'Warfare with the Spirit's Sword. The *Christian Knight* Window at Gouda', *SCJ* 21 (1990), 235–257; C.L. Janson, 'Preserving the Word. Wtewael's Freedom of Conscience Window at Gouda', *Konsthistorisk Tidskrift* 57 (1988), 18–29; Van Harten-Boers, *The Stained-Glass Windows*, III, 192–194, 199.

event.[43] This showed 'The Relief of Samaria' where God's miraculous intervention resulted in the flight of the enemy, thereby allowing the Leiden authorities to make an analogy with the providential relief of their own city from the Spanish forces in 1574.[44] These windows sought to memorialize aspects of the Revolt and the associations that were forged between towns during the conflict, in the same way as war relics were maintained in churches.[45] The use of windows to commemorate national events was reflected in other donations made during the seventeenth century. The Dutch naval battle at Gibraltar was commemorated in three windows, including one in the Oude Kerk in Amsterdam (1607) and as a cartouche in a transept window donated by the Admiraliteit van West-Friesland to the church at Hoorn in 1630.[46] The magistrates in Amsterdam decided in 1655 to mark the conclusion of the Eighty Years' War with Spain with a window in the Oude Kerk depicting Philip IV signing the Treaty of Westphalia.[47]

Some towns that made donations to Gouda decided to illustrate aspects of their own civic mythology in the windows. Haarlem chose the siege of Damietta as its subject while Dordrecht portrayed the 'The Maiden of Dordrecht in the Garden of Holland'. The 'Taking of Damietta' had become an important element in the civic iconography of Haarlem during the sixteenth century. According to legend, a ship from Haarlem had played a crucial role in the conquest of the Egyptian city of Damietta during the fifth crusade in 1219, for which the city was rewarded by the Holy Roman Emperor with the inclusion of a sword in their coat of arms. Although apocryphal,

---

[43] *Ibid.*, III, 232–233.

[44] *Ibid.*, III, 222–223. Delft also donated a window on the 'Relief of Leiden' to the Hooglandsche kerk in Leiden in 1603, W.J.J.C. Bijleveld, 'Leidsche kerkglazen', *Oud Holland* 45 (1928), 198–199, there 198.

[45] C. Janson, 'Public Places, Private Lives. The Impact of the Dutch Revolt on the Reformed Churches in Holland', in A.K. Wheelock and A. Seeff, eds., *The Public and Private in Dutch Culture of the Golden Age* (Newark, 2000), 194–195, 197. I am grateful to Dr Janson for sending me a copy of her essay.

[46] Bogtman, *Nederlandsche glasschilders* (Amsterdam, 1944), 68; A. van der Boom, 'Monumentale glasschilderkunst in den Nederlanden in de zeventiende eeuw', in H.E. van Gelder *et al.*, eds., *Kunstgeschiedenis der Nederlanden*, 11 vols. (Zeist, 1963–65), VI, 1165; C.A. van Swigchem, T. Brouwer and W. van Os, *Een huis voor het Woord. Het protestantse kerkinterieur in Nederland tot 1900* (The Hague, 1984), 291.

[47] A. de Groot, 'Het Vredeglas in de Oude Kerk te Amsterdam', *Bulletin van de Stichting Oude Hollandse Kerken* 47 (1998), 21–25.

the story was an important part of the city's history and political
iconography, and one which found particular favour after the Revolt
as a means of uniting the disparate elements in the town's population. The story was recorded in prints and, within the Bavokerk,
there were also 'trophies' on display, as well as reminders of the
siege that included a bell and model ships; they were commented
on by Brereton, Evelyn and FitzWilliam.[48] The Damietta theme was
used as early as 1522 when the town commissioned Willem Dircxz
Tybaut to produce stained glass windows for the churches at
Purmerend and Enkhuizen.[49] In 1595 the artist Willem Willemsz
Tybaut was commissioned to work on the window for the Janskerk
and also on a replacement west window for the Bavokerk at Haarlem
on the same theme. The latter window, which was removed in the
mid-eighteenth century to make way for an organ, is known to us
through the paintings of the church by Pieter Saenredam and Job
Berckheyde. The window depicted the Emperor Frederick II, in the
presence of the Patriarch of Jerusalem, adding the sword to the coat
of arms of Haarlem.[50] The same subject was chosen for the window
donated to the Janskerk at Gouda [fig. 13.1], although the actual
imagery portrayed was different. The Gouda window depicted the
siege of Damietta itself, with a view across the sea to the besieged
city and the Haarlem ship, so prominently placed that it is almost
equal in height to the city tower [fig. 13.1b] A version of this design,
only slightly modified, was employed in 1606 in the window donated
to the church at Edam.[51] The depiction of the Damietta story continued to be employed in windows donated by the city to the churches
at Egmond aan den Hoef in 1633, the window – now lost – at
Schermerhorn in 1642 and at De Rijp in 1655 [fig. 13.2]. The latter

[48] Van Harten-Boers, *The Stained-Glass Windows*, III, 209–211; Janson, 'Public
Places, Private Lives', 197–201; Groenveld, *Haarlemse glassraamschenkingen*, 3–4, 32–40;
Evelyn, *Diary of John Evelyn*, II, 51; Brereton, *My Travels into Holland*, 51; Van Strien,
Touring the Low Countries, 181.
[49] Gonnet, 'Haarlemsche glasschrijvers', 73.
[50] Janson, 'Public Places, Private Lives', 201; *Dutch Church Painters. Saenredam's
Great Church at Haarlem in context* (Edinburgh, 1984), 22–23; G. Schwartz and
M.J. Bok, *Pieter Saenredam. The Painter and His Time* (New York, 1990), 116, 207;
J. Giltaij and G. Jansen, eds., *Perspectives. Saenredam and the Architectural Painters of the
17th Century* (Rotterdam, 1991), 274–275.
[51] Van Harten-Boers, *The Stained-Glass Windows*, III, 209–11; Van Ruyven-Zeman,
Edam. De Glazen van de Grote Kerk, 58–61.

Fig. 13.1. 'The Seige of Damietta' window in the Janskerk, Gouda
(Stichting Fonds Goudse Glazen).

Fig. 13.1b. Detail from the 'The Seige of Damietta' window
(Stichting Fonds Goudse Glazen).

two windows represented a much simpler version of the Damietta legend with the arms of Haarlem surmounting an image of a ship at sea in the centre of the painting, while the city itself is placed off centre.[52]

Dordrecht chose as the theme for the window at Gouda a motif that symbolized the pre-eminence of the town within the province and reflected its position as the most senior of the six great towns in the province, as well as the place where Counts of Holland were invested. The imagery of the 'Maiden of Dordrecht' [fig. 13.3] had developed during the sixteenth century and the image surmounted the Groothoofdpoort which had been erected in 1549. During the course of the Revolt, the guardianship of the town by the Virgin Mary metamorphosed into the Maiden of Dordrecht, reflecting the fact that the town remained inviolate as it had never been besieged during the conflict with Spain. Furthermore its primacy within the province was enhanced because the first meeting of the States General of the rebel provinces took place there in 1572. The image used in the windows represents a variation on this earlier architectural depiction. This motif portrayed a seated woman within a fenced enclosure, symbolizing Holland, placed underneath a classical arch on which were the coats of arms of the fifteen lesser towns of the province. The depiction of 'The Maiden of Dordrecht in the Garden of Holland' was an image which was repeated in the window donated to the Grote Kerk at Edam in 1606.[53] As with Haarlem's Damietta motif, this was a theme that was repeated in a number of other windows donated by the town during the early seventeenth century.

The Amsterdam authorities do not seem to have used the donation of windows as a vehicle for elaborate depictions of their own history or mythology. Their donation to Gouda was marked by the inclusion of their coat of arms at the base of the window, and more subtly was integrated into the design itself by having the Roman soldiers carrying banners bearing the city's arms.[54] Closer to home

---

[52] For a detailed assessment, see Groenveld, *Haalemse glasraamschenkingen*, 32–40.

[53] Van Ruyven-Zeman, *Edam. De Glazen van de Grote Kerk*, 57–59; Van Harten-Boers, *The Stained-Glass Windows*, III, 149, 202–203; W. Veerman, 'Gerrit Gerritsz. Cuyp', *Spiegel Historiael* 8 (1973), 106–114; W. Veerman, 'De "Maagd van Dordrecht" staat er weer gekleurd op', *Kwartaal en Teken van Dordrecht* 1 (1975), 10–13; W. Veerman, 'Een traditie? Het schenken van gebrandschilderde ramen', *Kwartaal en Teken van Dordrecht* 3 (1977), 1–6.

[54] Van Harten-Boers, *The Stained-Glass Windows*, III, 215–217.

Fig. 13.2. Window donated by Haarlem to the church at De Rijp
(Rijksdienst Monumentenzorg Zeist).

Fig. 13.3. 'The Maiden of Dordrecht' window in the Janskerk, Gouda
(Stichting Fonds Goudse Glazen).

the city was prepared to commemorate its past in glass. In 1651 the magistrates paid Jacob van Bronckhorst 12,400 gulden for the installation of a window in the Nieuwe Kerk and three other smaller windows.[55] The principal window in the north transept showed the granting of the new coat of arms to the town by Count William IV in 1342. A second window of the same date, in the south transept, depicted the imperial crown being added to the city's arms by the Emperor Maximilian in 1488 [fig. 13.4].[56]

These historical and mythological representations of the towns were generally less common than displaying a coat of arms in the window that had been donated. In many of the entries recording the financing of a church window, reference is made to the incorporation of a coat of arms. This was often a cheaper means of projecting the image of a particular corporation within these churches. What can not be so easily gleaned from the sparse entries in the archives is the way in which these arms were displayed. The evidence of some of the surviving stained glass shows that some of these heraldic displays could be part of a much more elaborate window as well as having an equally significant meaning.

The magistrates at Gouda did not contribute one of the major windows in the completion of the glazing progamme at the Janskerk, but they did pay for the town's arms to appear in the church in no less than twelve locations [fig. 13.5]. Even a simple coat of arms provided an opportunity for further symbolism and the chance to project a particular message. The cartouche bearing their arms was encircled by a wreath of leaves of either an olive tree or an *oranjeboom*, the former symbolizing wisdom and the latter a clear reference to the House of Orange, Gouda being the first of the six towns to declare for the prince in 1572.[57]

The example of the donations made by Alkmaar provides an illustration of this heraldic form of civic iconography. Alkmaar was not one of the six 'great' towns of Holland and only became a member of States during the course of the Revolt. Although Alkmaar was not amongst the donors to the Janskerk, the windows it donated to the churches at Edam, Egmond aan den Hoef, Schermerhorn

---

[55] Van Biema, 'Nalezing van de stadsrekeningen van Amsterdam', 174.
[56] Bogtman, *Nederlandsche glasschilders*, 77–78.
[57] Van Harten-Boers, *The Stained-Glass Windows*, III, 183–185.

Fig. 13.4. Cartoon by Jacob van Bronckhorst depicting Maximilian adding the imperial crown to the arms of Amsterdam (Amsterdam City Archive).

Fig. 13.5. Window depicting the coat of arms of Gouda in the Janskerk
(Stichting Fonds Goudse Glazen).

and De Rijp still survive. The iconography of these windows is much simpler than the 'Taking of Damietta' and 'Maiden of Dordrecht' motifs, and in fact probably represents the form employed by the principal towns in the less prestigious churches to which they donated windows. Central to these Alkmaar windows is the depiction of the coat of arms of the town. The arms displayed in the Grote Kerk in Edam represent a relatively simple rendition of the shield with its supporters and crest, above a cartouche with the name of the town and the date, 1606. This may have been part of a more decorative scheme which has now been lost.[58] The window donated to the church at De Rijp in 1657 [fig. 13.6] shows the arms of the town in an elaborate form with swags of leaves and fruit surrounding it, but in the lower section of the window, an attractive view is also seen of a town amidst the windmills and waterways (teeming with ships) of Holland. The design of this window, minus the landscape, was similar to that employed in the window commissioned for Schermerhorn in 1635.[59]

Not all of the towns used civic iconography or coats of arms in window donations as vehicles for affirming their identity. A third genre of subject matter can also be identified in the early seventeenth century, the representation of popular biblical themes. At Gouda this can be seen in the windows donated by Amsterdam ('The Pharisee and the Publican'), Rotterdam ('Christ and the Woman Taken in Adultery') and technically in the 'Relief of Samaria' donated by Leiden, although as has been seen this could also be read as an allegory.[60] A similar choice of subject matter can also be identified in two of the contemporary windows – now lost – given to the Hooglandse kerk in Leiden between 1596 and 1603. Leiden's window depicted the 'Relief of Samaria' and Amsterdam's 'The Pharisees and the Publican'. These two windows may in fact have replicated the Gouda design as they were both completed at the same time and Leiden's window was the work of the same painter, Cornelius Corneliusz Clock, and designer, Isaac Claesz Swanenburg.[61] A different

---

[58] Van Ruyven-Zeman, *Edam. De glazen van de Grote Kerk*, 65, 70.

[59] Mens, *De Rijper glazen*, 78–81; Kampf-Rekelhof, *De Grote Kerk van Schermerhorn*, 51–53.

[60] Van Harten-Boers, *The Stained-Glass Windows*, III, 215–217, 222–223, 227–229.

[61] Bijleveld, 'Leidsche kerkglazen', 198; Van Harten-Boers, *The Stained-Glass Windows*, III, 149–151.

Fig. 13.6. Window depicting the coat of arms of Alkmaar at De Rijp.

theme was depicted by Swanenburg in the window donated in 1611 by the Leiden authorities to the church at Valkenburg, where he portrayed the 'Conversion of Saul'.[62] The choice of biblical imagery for municipal donations to other churches seems to have been confined to the early seventeenth century. While none of the windows at Edam had a biblical theme, thirty years later the local magistrates at Schermerhorn paid for a window of the 'Judgment of Solomon', and the 'First Meeting of the Apostles' was donated by the Dijkgraaf en Hoogheemraden of Kennemerland and West-Friesland. Similarly at De Rijp, biblical themes were paid for by the local elite; the 'Building of the Temple' was financed by the *kerkmeesters*, for example.[63]

While the glazing of the Janskerk, the principal church of the sixth great town of Holland, was a major project, the use of heraldic devices, rather than elaborate glass paintings, equally served to convey the importance and identity of the donor in a less prestigious building. Whether it was in terms of historical, mythological or allegorical representations of the town or more simply in the use of heraldic devices, the iconography selected served to propagate a recognizable urban identity for the donating magistracy in other communities. This growing interest in the portrayal of urban identity was no doubt in part due to the closer involvement of the donors in the design of their windows in the later sixteenth century. Before the Revolt, the sponsors approached by the church authorities at Gouda were not consulted about the themes of their windows. Although the local magistrates acted as intermediaries for the States of Holland and the Rhineland polder board, the donors were more actively involved in the commissioning of the windows which completed the programme after the Revolt. They were also more closely involved in their execution. Is it any coincidence, for instance, that the two Gouda windows that depicted civic iconography were both commissioned from natives of Dordrecht and Haarlem? The creator of the windows donated by Leiden and Delft, Isaac Claesz Swanenburg, was actually one of the Leiden magistrates, and all of the windows

---

[62] E. Pelinck, 'Het Leidsche glas in de kerk te Valkenburg', *Leidsch Jaarboekje* (1944), 201–206.
[63] Mens, *De Rijper glazen*, 110–113; Kampf-Rekelhof, *De Grote Kerk van Schermerhorn*, 34–36, 39–41.

he designed were municipal or institutional gifts.[64] Hendrik de Keyser was on the payroll of the Amsterdam authorities when their window was designed for Gouda.[65] Such close links inevitably ensured the projection of an urban identity which may not have been feasible before the Revolt.

Besides establishing a recognizable urban identity through the medium of church windows, the custom of donating stained glass also served to confirm and consolidate the existing links between the towns. The most important of these were their commercial ties. As early as 1518, the Haarlem authorities responded to a request from the authorities in Edam to provide a window because of the quantity of their beer that was drunk there.[66] The significance of these economic factors in explaining the pattern of donations made by the Haarlem magistrates has been examined by Simon Groenveld. He demonstrated that there was a close correlation between the donation of windows and the economic interests of the town. Plotting the donations made by the town shows that they were mainly concentrated in the area north of the river IJ, the area which coincided with the town's main economic influence in the province of Holland, and the main market for Haarlem beer. But equally striking are the donations that were made towards the south, which reflected the growing influence of Haarlem's textile industry. The economic and political importance of Haarlem also partly explains why the windows were donated to churches much further afield such as to Leeuwarden in Friesland, for example. Unfortunately a similar study of the geographical extent of donations by Amsterdam is lacking and might show an even greater range. Interestingly, although Alkmaar was also a major donor of windows, reflecting the relative prosperity of the town in the early seventeenth century, the geographical range of these gifts was much more circumscribed than those given by Haarlem. This is also true of the windows financed by Hoorn in this period.[67]

The whole tradition of donating windows also provides some interesting insights into urban identity within the emerging Dutch Republic.

---

[64] Van Harten-Boers, *The Stained-Glass Windows*, III, 153–155, 225, 235–36.
[65] The attribution to Hendrik de Keyser is conjectural as it can not be confirmed in the archives: Van Harten-Boers, *The Stained-Glass Windows*, III, 155, 219–220.
[66] Gonnert, 'Haarlemsche glasschrijvers', 72.
[67] Groenveld, *Haarlemse glasraamschenkingen*, 28–32, 41, 45, 47.

Although it represented the continuance of a pre-Revolt custom, it developed into a vehicle to project urban iconography and to acknowledge the economic ties that connected the different towns. But it also provided a means of demonstrating the relative importance of these communities within the emergent state. Importantly, the placing of the windows within the building would have reinforced for contemporaries the hierarchical importance of the donors within the Dutch Republic. Traditionally the north side of the church was regarded as the more prestigious, so that when the glazing programme of the Jacobskerk in The Hague was concluded, the window donated by Maurice of Nassau in 1596 was given precedence over that of the States of Holland.[68] Similarly at Gouda, there were only eleven empty windows but two equally prestigious sites had to be made available to the States of Holland at the west end of the north and south aisles. The positioning of the remaining windows donated by the towns also reflected their status within the hierarchy of the province of Holland, so that Dordrecht and Haarlem were in the north aisle, while moving from the east end of the south aisle were the towns of Delft, Leiden, Amsterdam and Rotterdam. One of the coats of arms financed by the Gouda magistrates was located in a highly visible place over the west door, the main entrance to the church, and therefore between – and hence associated with – the 'Freedom of Conscience' and 'Christian Knight' windows donated by the States of Holland.[69] Even in a less prestigious building such as at De Rijp, this hierarchy can be noted. At the liturgical centre of the church, the States of Holland and Haarlem had their windows placed in the north transept and those of Amsterdam and the Gecommitteerde Raden of the Noorderkwartier in the south transept, whereas the windows donated by the lesser towns of Holland (Medemblik, Edam, Hoorn, Alkmaar, Enkhuizen, Monnickendam and Purmerend) are all at the east end.[70] This convention was not always maintained, as can be seen at Edam. Although the window provided by the States of Holland was erected in the north transept and that of the Admiraliteit of West-Friesland and the Noorderkwartier facing it in the south transept, those paid for by the towns were not

[68] Van Gelder, 'De zestiende-eeuwsche glasschilderingen in de Haagsche Sint-Jacobskerk', 33–34.
[69] Van Harten-Boers, *The Stained-Glass Windows*, III, 145–146.
[70] Mens, *De Rijper glazen*, 32.

placed according to their rank within the urban hierarchy of the province.[71]

In spite of this conscious hierarchical placement of the windows, the custom of donating windows also reflected the close links that existed between the towns in the Dutch Republic. This certainly contrasts with the rivalry that existed at a political level because of the differing economic interests of the commercial and manufacturing towns within Holland. In the early seventeenth century such divisions came to a head over the issue of the Twelve Years' Truce with Spain; opposition to its renewal has been seen to be linked in some towns to the rise of the Counter-Remonstrants. Besides this broad urban rivalry, there were a range of other specific issues and disputes which caused conflict between particular towns.[72] Yet in contrast to the divisive impression resulting from such tensions and rivalry, the donation of windows suggests an underlying sense of communal identity and friendship with the United Provinces. All of the six great towns contributed windows to complete the glazing of the Janskerk in Gouda, while in the more major glazing scheme at Edam, all of the major and the lesser towns of Holland contributed. The decision of Rotterdam to donate a window came in spite of the tense relations between the two communities, who were at odds over conflicting interests concerning inland navigation.[73] Even when the major towns did not contribute en bloc to the glazing schemes of some of the smaller communities, there is clear evidence of regional loyalties and friendship. The donations at Schermerhorn and De Rijp, for example, came from the nearby towns of North Holland.[74] One remarkable example of enduring urban connections relates to the reglazing of Roermond, which lay outside the Republic, in 1616. A series of eight windows were commissioned with scenes of the life of the Virgin Mary, but the scheme also included the arms of Nijmegen, Arnhem and Zutphen, which had presumably

---

[71] Van Ruyven-Zeman, *Edam. De glazen van de Grote Kerk*, 40–41, 47.

[72] J.L. Price, *Holland and the Dutch Republic in the Seventeenth Century. The Politics of Particularism* (Oxford, 1994), 172–182.

[73] Van Harten-Boers, *The Stained-Glass Windows*, III, 229.

[74] Schermerhorn received windows from Medemblik, Edam, Hoorn, Alkmaar, Enkhuizen and Monnikendam. Windows were donated by Amsterdam, Purmerend, Monnickendam, Enkhuizen, Alkmaar, Hoorn, Edam, Medemblik and Haarlem to the church at De Rijp: Kampf-Rekelhof, *De Grote Kerk van Schermerhorn*, 44–57; Mens, *De Rijper glazen*, 50–53, 66–93, 102–105.

contributed to the programme.[75] Probably more than the regional associations evident in Holland, the involvement of the other towns of Gelderland in the reglazing at Roermond reflects a continued sense of provincial identity in a province that had been politically divided by the Revolt.

The medium of glass therefore provided a means through which the towns of the Dutch Republic could affirm and consolidate provincial and inter-regional loyalties and ties, even sometimes against the background of urban rivalry and political division. In so doing they reflected the complex nature of the Dutch Republic, in which the states were able to work together but expressed their own individual and strong urban identity. With the proscription of Catholic worship during the course of the Revolt, religious buildings increasingly became a vehicle for urban patronage and the display of civic iconography, either in the form of complex motifs or coats of arms. It was the remarkable relationship between Church and state in the northern provinces that meant that these decorative windows, that were so strikingly at odds with the Calvinist condemnation of idolatry, nevertheless appeared in a Reformed place of worship. Certainly, what the English tourists regarded as incongruous, and as a further example of the tolerance of the Dutch, showed that it was easier to forge an urban identity than to achieve religious consensus.

---

[75] Obreen, *Archief voor Nederlandse kunstgeschiedenis*, I, 168–170.

CHAPTER FOURTEEN

GROUP IDENTITY AND OPINION AMONG THE HUGUENOT DIASPORA AND THE CHALLENGE OF PIERRE BAYLE'S TOLERATION THEORY (1685–1706)

Jonathan Israel

Europe having suffered severely from religious warfare and violence during the age of the Thirty Years' War, it is scarcely surprising that the late seventeenth century and the early eighteenth witnessed a debate on public toleration on a scale never before seen in the West. By the 1680s, toleration was being widely and frequently discussed in sermons, books, learned periodicals, academic disputations, ecclesiastical councils and in political assemblies. Yet, it is also striking that one particular religious and cultural community, the Huguenot diaspora, exiled from France following the Revocation of the Edict of Nantes (1685), displayed a quite exceptional preoccupation with this question far beyond that of all the rest, turning it into a matter of public concern, to a greater extent and in a more emphatic manner than any other sector of European society.

Given that no other community of comparable size suffered anything like as much displacement and disruption, as well as psychological trauma, during the latter part of the seventeenth century (in western Europe), as did the Huguenot population of France, owing to Louis XIV's intolerant policies, this is scarcely surprising. It is obvious enough why the question of toleration became a central concern of all sections of the Huguenot diaspora outside of France; and not least of that part of the Huguenot diaspora, congregating in the Netherlands where the majority of the exiled preachers, publishers, and teachers, Pierre Bayle among them, settled.

On one level toleration was a theme which bound together the Huguenot public everywhere as practically nothing else could, in a sense even more than the Reformed faith. For a by no means insignificant fringe of the Huguenot population in exile, including a proportion of its preachers, were not convinced Calvinists but openly or semi-covertly adhered to Arminian, Socinian, Deistic and other

currents of theological opinion which set them at odds with the
Calvinist views and the beliefs of the main body of their group.
Theologically, the Huguenots by the late seventeenth century were
in fact a deeply divided community. On the other hand, resentment
at the way Louis XIV had treated them, and abhorrence of persecution (at any rate of the French Reformed Churches) united more
or less all Huguenots. The pain of a shared experience, which had
caused such a deeply felt wrench, led to something like a shared
commitment to the principle of toleration which historically proved
to be one of the most decisive new cultural phenomena of the age.
It was also one which had an immediate practical point to it despite
the remoteness of any prospect of a return to France. For there was
a distinct question mark over the status of the Huguenot churches
in England prior to the Toleration Act of 1689, whilst in much of
Germany, including the great commercial metropolis of Hamburg
where hundreds of Huguenots settled,[1] and the Scandinavian lands,
Lutheran intolerance long continued to block the way to formal permission for the French Reformed to maintain their own public
churches, and educational and welfare institutions.

A modicum of toleration seemed a desirable thing to practically
all Huguenots, but it soon proved to be the case not just that toleration could take very different forms and come in very different
varieties but that, intellectually, toleration was such a problematic
issue that it was even capable of becoming a whole fresh source of
division and recrimination in itself. Even if most of those who made
up what might be termed Huguenot intellectual circles saw toleration as a positive good and the great bulk of the Huguenot public
readily conformed to this view, it is remarkable and ironic that even
in the Netherlands, still perhaps relatively the most tolerant country
in Europe, toleration rapidly developed into a deeply troubling and
destabilizing philosophical battle-ground. Difficulties arose because of
the widely perceived need to discredit and marginalize the more
comprehensive varieties of toleration theory, in particular that propagated by the most eloquent and forceful of all the Huguenot writers
of the time – Pierre Bayle.

---

[1] On the difficulties of the Huguenots owing to local intolerance in Hamburg,
see Joachim Whaley, *Religious Toleration and Social Change in Hamburg, 1529–1819*
(Cambridge, 1985), 112–113, 123–124, 136–141.

One should not be misled by the fact that one or two Huguenot preachers in Holland were long prepared to give Bayle the benefit of the doubt, to take his adamant professions of orthodoxy and submission to ecclesiastical authority at face value, and to accept his professed conformity to the doctrines of the French Reformed churches. For even such long-standing loyal friends of his as Jacques Basnage, over many years minister of the Huguenot congregation at The Hague, and David Durand (*c.* 1680–1763), who moved to England, eventually came to feel, as the full implications of Bayle's post-*Dictionnaire* books sank in, that they had been duped by him.

In fact, during the years both immediately before and after Bayle's death, in December 1706, nearly all Dutch and Dutch Huguenot commentators came to see his thought in general and his toleration theory in particular as something dangerously subversive even from the most liberal Christian, let alone orthodox Calvinist, viewpoint. By 1706 hardly any French (or Dutch) Calvinist minister was willing to give Bayle's writings and attitudes any kind of seal of approval. Yet, no matter how strongly most Huguenot preachers disapproved of his writings, it was undeniable that Bayle had propounded what was perhaps the clearest and most sophisticated defence of toleration of the early Enlightenment era. There can be little doubt, moreover, that his use of an ostensibly fideist stance to perplex his intellectual opponents, combined with an incisive critical-historical perspective furthering what was basically a radical philosophical position, proved a highly effective method of promoting the cause of toleration, as well as promoting a new, purely secular conception of morality and politics.[2]

Secular moral arguments were indeed crucial to Bayle's toleration thesis. For his strongest card was the unresolved character of religious conflict in Europe since the Reformation. 'Bayle's reciprocity argument for religious toleration', as one scholar has aptly put it, 'turns on the frightful results of the Wars of Religion'.[3] By showing that religious persecution and efforts to impose religious uniformity

---

[2] J.I. Israel, 'Pierre Bayle's Political Thought', in A. McKenna and G. Paganini, eds., *Pierre Bayle dans la République des Lettres. Philosophie, religion, critique* (Paris, 2004).

[3] J. Kilcullen, *Sincerity and Truth. Essays on Arnauld, Bayle and Toleration* (Oxford, 1988), 110–111; T.M. Lennon, 'Bayle, Locke and the Metaphysics of Toleration', in M.A. Stewart, ed., *Studies in Seventeenth-Century European Philosophy* (Oxford, 1997), 188.

by force wreak dreadful havoc to life and property, he persuades
the reader that religious persecution and intolerance are highly destruc-
tive and hence fundamentally wrong morally, and can not therefore
be advocated by God, Christ or, justifiably, by any Church. The
words of the Apostle Luke (14, 23), '*contrains-les d'entrer*', as Bayle
expresses them in his *Commentaire philosophique* of 1686, could be
uncompromisingly taken up by any of the Churches so that, were
this admonition to be taken seriously, all Christian sects would be
equally entitled to persecute and try to exterminate the rest, resulting
in a manifestly irrational state of violence, insecurity, and mayhem.[4]

Bayle's theory of toleration is grounded on what might be termed
the 'pseudo-fideist' theologico-philosophical claim that there is no
way of knowing, via reason, which is the true faith – or whether
there is a true faith. In a true Baylean paradox, he simultaneously
declares the primacy and yet, at the same time, the virtual irra-
tionality of faith. Were one to take his fideism seriously – which, on
the whole, modern scholars, in contrast to Bayle's contemporaries,
have tended to do – it would mean that what is most important in
human life is wholly indistinguishable from both 'superstition' and
unjust persecution, both of which Bayle clearly detested and considered unmitigated curses and plagues. Such a position is manifestly
highly paradoxical and unstable especially in combination with Bayle's
doctrine of the overriding validity of individual conscience in matters of morality. Adherents of religions believe they follow the true
faith, and faith is the chief guide in this world; but as there is no
way of demonstrating, rationally, that one's faith is the truth to someone who believes otherwise, everybody's faith is for the interim (even
if not ultimately) proclaimed equally valid.[5]

This argument provides the basis of Bayle's famous doctrine of
the '*conscience errante*'.[6] Since one can not know or prove, through
reason, the truth or falsity of any particular religion, or the legitimacy
or illegitimacy of any particular heresy or sect, there is no rational

---

[4] Pierre Bayle, *Commentaire philosophique*, introd. J.-M. Gros (Paris, 1992), 130–131,
256–257; G. Mori, *Bayle philosophe* (Paris, 1999), 274–275, 279.

[5] M. Paradis, 'Les Fondements de la tolérance universelle chez Bayle', in E. Groffier
and M. Paradis, eds., *Tolerance and Human Rights. Essays in Honour of Raymond Klibansky*
(Montreal, 1991), 25, 27–28.

[6] Bayle, *Commentaire philosophique*, 300–303, 307, 309–310; J.-M. Gros, 'Introduction'
to Bayle, *Commentaire philosophique*, 28–29.

means of convincing someone addicted to erroneous doctrines, or even wholly ridiculous superstitions, that their beliefs are false. Hence, the only reasonable course is to grant the same freedom of conscience, and of religious practice, to all dissenting minorities as one accords to believers in what most consider the true faith.[7] Therefore, according to Bayle, it is not via the force of any theological argument, however irenicist, but rather through examining history and moral philosophy that we discover that reason can never justify persecution and that intolerance, to cite the heading of the second chapter of the *Commentaire philosophique*, is incontestably 'contraire aux plus distinctes idées de la lumière naturelle'.[8] In fact, in Bayle, it is never Christian forbearance and charity which condemn persecution but solely the intrinsic injustice, rationally determined, of oppressing the innocent. Toleration in Bayle rests on the exclusive principles of equity and reciprocity which, he argues, are obvious enough to us through the dictates of natural reason even though usually negated or obscured by zeal and the dictates of religious doctrine.[9]

While it can not have been Christ's intention, holds Bayle, that his Church should persecute, all established Churches have in practice engaged in persecution and been intolerant. Remarkably boldly, even by his radical standards, he argues in his *Supplément* that his contention that 'l'esprit de persécution a plus régné parmi les orthodoxes, généralement parlant, depuis Constantin, que parmi les hérétiques' applies not only to Greek Orthodox, Catholic, Lutheran and Anglican orthodoxy but also to the Reformed Church. It was, avows Bayle, a scandalous thing that those who wished to reform the Church after its perversion by the papacy 'n'aient point compris les immunités sacrées et inviolables de la conscience', but rather adhered to 'le dogme de la contrainte'; and that at Geneva, the birth-place of the Reformed Church, the Calvinists in the year 1535 suppressed Catholicism, expelling everyone refusing to abandon the old Church.[10]

---

[7] Mori, *Bayle philosophe*, 276; M. Marilli, 'Cartesianesimo e tolleranza. Il *Commentaire philosophque* di Pierre Bayle', *Rivista di storia della filosofia* 3 (1963), 555–579, here 562–563, 566; Kilcullen, *Sincerity and Truth*, 66–68.

[8] Bayle, *Commentaire philosophique*, 97–98.

[9] *Ibid.*, 89–91; Pierre Bayle, *Réponse aux questions d'un provincial*, 5 vols. (Rotterdam, 1704–07), IV, 276, 289–290, 436, 456; Marilli, 'Cartesianesimo e tolleranza', 566.

[10] Pierre Bayle, *Supplément du Commentaire philosophique* (1688), ed. M. Pécharman, in Y.C. Zarka, F. Lessay and J. Rogers, eds., *Les Fondements philosophiques de la tolérance*, 3 vols. (Paris, 2002), II, 239, 254–256.

Only the Socinians and Arminians, affirms Bayle, were free of this intolerance; but these were both tiny, fringe churches: 'ainsi, le dogme de la tolérance n'est reconnu pour vrai que dans quelques petits recoins du Christianisme qui ne font aucune figure, pendant que celui de l'intolérance va partout la tête levée'.[11] It is typical of Bayle's elaborately convoluted but devastatingly effective style of argument that he relentlessly assails the Socinians for being theologically muddled and inconsistent, confusing reason with faith (which, in Bayle's view, must be kept totally separate), while simultaneously applauding them for being morally more just and upright (as well as tolerant) than others.

Central to Bayle's thought is his idea that established Churches possess no more, and frequently – or perhaps even usually – less moral validity, in terms of rational moral criteria such as equity and tolerance, than do fringe churches.[12] Hence, his toleration, unlike Locke's, has nothing to do with exemption from powerful church structures which otherwise retain an overriding validity. Bayle's was, in fact, less a theory of toleration – given that he recognized no established or public Church in his schema – than a universal freedom of conscience entailing mutual Christian, Muslim, Jewish and pagan forbearance, Catholic acceptance of Protestants, and vice versa, and all major Churches accepting as equals the lesser dissenting Churches.[13] Nor was it only Socinians, Jews, Muslims and pagans who could, within Bayle's framework, claim rights of conscience and hence benefit from this proposed freedom, but equally Deist freethinkers and, in principle, atheists. There is, it is true, a weak and perfunctory disavowal where he claims his philosophy is not a charter for atheists, since if secular authority considers 'atheism' incompatible with their laws they can always ban it. But such a ban has no inherent place or justification in Bayle's moral, political and social theory and is purely extraneous to it.[14] In principle, under Bayle's theory of tol-

---

[11] *Ibid.*, 228; see also B.S. Tinsley, *Pierre Bayle's Reformation. Conscience and Criticism on the Eve of the Enlightenment* (Selinsgrove, 2001), 251, 270, 304–320.

[12] Paradis, 'Fondements', 32; J.-M. Gros, 'Bayle. De la Tolérance à la liberté de conscience', in Zarka *et al.*, eds., *Les Fondements*, I, 296, 304.

[13] *Ibid.*, I, 295–296, 308–309.

[14] Pierre Bayle, *Pensées diverses sur la comète*, ed. A. Prat, 2 vols. (Paris, 1994), II, 5–8; Bayle, *Commentaire philosophique*, 272–276, 312–313; Lennon, 'Bayle, Locke', 187, 193.

eration there is no way for agnostics, *indifférents*, Spinozists, Confucianists or any kind of philosophical atheists to be denied toleration.[15]

In this respect, of course, Bayle was preceded by Spinoza; but this, of course, was no recommendation in the Huguenot world of the early Enlightenment. Moreover, he was emulated in his comprehensive toleration theory only by such radical writers as Toland, Collins, Lau, Radicati, Jean-Frédéric Bernard, Johann Lorenz Schmidt, and Diderot who, indeed, was a much warmer admirer of Bayle than were, for example, Voltaire or Hume. In fact, no-one in the moderate mainstream could or would subscribe to such a view of toleration and morality as that propagated by Bayle. If, like Bernard Mandeville (1670–1733), an openly anti-clerical republican and in moral philosophy a Spinozist, as well as a writer deeply influenced by Bayle, an early eighteenth-century writer does clearly endorse his views on toleration, then one can be fairly sure that that writer adhered to a general radical stance himself.[16]

Bayle's formulations plainly implied that the Dutch States General's general decree prohibiting Socinian and other anti-Trinitarian opinion was socially and morally unjust, philosophically (as well as theologically) unjustifiable, and ultimately untenable.[17] Not surprisingly, Bayle found an ardent supporter in the French Socinian exiled to Holland, Noel Aubert de Versé, who, in his *Traité de la liberté de conscience* (1687), echoes many of Bayle's key points, restating whole phrases which Bayle uses in his *Commentaire*.[18] It is also true that the Remonstrant Jean Le Clerc (1657–1737), the leading francophone giant of the republic of letters in Amsterdam, being himself an ardent champion of toleration also, initially endorsed Bayle's theory of the '*conscience errante*', though later, as his relationship with Bayle soured, and he grew more aware of the real implications of Bayle's philosophical system, he became very much more guarded and less sympathetic towards Bayle's toleration theory.

---

[15] L. Bianchi, 'Religione e tolleranza in Montesquieu', *Rivista critica di storia della filosofia* 49 (1994), 49–71, here 68; M. Wielema, *Filosofen aan de Maas* (Baarn, 1991), 66; J.B. Schneewind, *The Invention of Autonomy. A History of Modern Moral Philosophy* (Cambridge, 1998), 279–282.

[16] See E.D. James, 'Faith, Sincerity and Morality: Mandeville and Bayle', in I. Primer, ed., *Mandeville Studies* (The Hague, 1975), 43–65.

[17] Bianchi, 'Religione e tolleranza', 68–69; Mori, *Bayle philosophe*, 289.

[18] *Ibid.*, 287.

In the public debate about toleration among the French Reformed community, in and outside the Netherlands, Bayle was vigorously opposed, among many others, by Le Clerc, Élie Saurin (1639–1703), Jacques Saurin (1677–1731), Isaac Jaquelot (1647–1708), Jacques Bernard (1658–1718), David Durand, Élie Benoit (1640–1728), Jean la Placette (1629–1718), Jean-Pierre de Crousaz (d. 1750) and Jean Barbeyrac (1674–1744). When unremitting, open antagonism erupted early in the new century between Bayle and the so-called *rationaux*, that is those Huguenot thinkers who urged that Enlightenment must be based on 'rational religion', and a balanced junction of reason and faith, especially Le Clerc, Jaquelot and Jacques Bernard, toleration emerged as one of the key points of dispute. Le Clerc angrily reacted to Bayle's charge that (behind a rhetorical show of tolerance) he was really a practitioner of intolerance, in a way which shows that in a sense Bayle was right. Openly questioning Bayle's claims to be a Christian thinker in his later writings, Le Clerc professed never to have 'taken issue with theologians who denounce those who attack divine providence, who ridicule religion, who excuse atheism and who propound matters that overthrow all religion, as he [Bayle] did'.[19]

Le Clerc continually reaffirmed the position he shared with Locke, a thinker to whom he felt much closer than he did to Bayle, concerning toleration, as well as on other issues, arguing that toleration of atheism is wholly unacceptable since it fundamentally damages civil society, one of the chief foundations of which is belief in 'un Dieu saint et bienfaisant'. It was all very well for Bayle to call him an 'Inquisiteur', but if Bayle thought toleration ought to extend to permitting men to attack 'la providence d'un Dieu bon et saint', then Le Clerc was willing publicly to condemn his toleration and all who embraced it. Such persons, in Le Clerc's opinion, have no conscience, nor any right to complain when they are forbidden to express their views ('quand on leur défend de parler').[20] Bayle, complained Le Clerc, in 1706, continually harped on about the contra-

---

[19] Bayle, *Réponse aux questions*, IV, part 2, 5–16: 'trouvé mauvais que les théologiens criassent contre ceux qui attaquent le Providence de Dieu, qui tournent la religion en ridicule, qui font l'apologie des athées, et qui débitent des choses qui détruisent toute religion, comme il [i.e. Bayle] fait'; [Jean Le Clerc], *Bibliothèque Choisie* 10 (1706), 392.

[20] *Ibid.*, 393.

diction he professed to see between Scripture and reason, his insidious purpose being to drive reason and faith apart, render faith suspect and the Bible redundant. What, he enquired sarcastically, does the philosopher of Rotterdam propose to put in Scripture's place? 'Seroit-ce cette Societé d'athées, qui devient tous les jours plus célèbre par les écrits de M. Bayle?'[21]

By the time of Bayle's death, in 1706, even the most liberal Huguenot Calvinist ministers had responded to Bayle's late (i.e. post-*Dictionnaire*) published writings with deep consternation, construing his stance, rightly I would argue, as an extremely subversive pseudo-fideism, a feigned orthodoxy leading directly to the loss of established status for the largest Churches, elimination of ecclesiastical authority in society, full separation of morality from theology, and a purely philosophical stance of strict neutrality not just as between religions but, worse still, as between religion, philosophical Deism and atheism. It was bad enough, complained Jaquelot, that Bayle argues that 'reason finds itself always contrary and opposed to decisions of faith, and that it is obliged to relinquish its clearest ideas and most distinct notions in order to submit blindly, and as it were against itself, to faith' something that 'appears in all his works', being 'the main object that he always aims for, and the fixed point in his spirit that he never loses sight of';[22] but on top of this he had evidently made it his life's work to plead the cause of the atheists, 'et de faire leur apologie', his great ability and vast erudition being put to work 'pour faire lever l'arrêt que le public a prononcé contre eux'.[23] The effort to maintain that public wall of condemnation and rejection by refuting Bayle's arguments, answering his baffling paradoxes, denouncing his separation of morality and religion and blocking the sweeping 'freedom of conscience' he introduces, was to pervade the subsequent toleration debate in Europe for decades.[24]

---

[21] [Jean Le Clerc], *Bibliothèque Choisie* 9 (1706), 168–169.

[22] [Isaac Jaquelot], *Conformité de la foi avec la raison, ou defense de la religion* (Amsterdam, 1705), 280: 'la raison se trouve toujours contraire et opposée aux décisions de la foi, et qu'elle est obligée de renoncer à ses idées les plus claires et à ses notions les plus distinctes pour se soumettre aveuglement, et comme malgré elle, à la foi', something that 'paroît dans tous ses ouvrages', being 'le grand but où il vise toujours, et le point fixe dans son esprit qu'il ne perd jamais de vue'.

[23] [Isaac Jaquelot], *Examen de la théologie de Mr. Bayle* (Amsterdam, 1706), 15.

[24] Bianchi, 'Religione e tolleranza', 52–53, 60–61.

The prime objection to Bayle's toleration, then, was its comprehensiveness and its reduction of all Churches and religions to equal status. Nothing could consistently be excluded from it, not even atheism or Spinozism or idolatry which everyone considered the rankest superstition. One of the most prominent Huguenot advocates of toleration who joined in the attack on Bayle's toleration was Jacques Bernard (1658–1718), a former pupil of Le Clerc, who in his own life had suffered first Catholic intolerance in his native France and then Calvinist persecution in Switzerland. Bernard had found employment in Holland, first as a Reformed minister to the French congregation at Gouda, then teaching philosophy and afterwards, in succession to his mentor, Le Clerc, as editor, in the early 1690s, of six volumes of the *Bibliothèque Universelle*. By 1699, he ranked among the foremost *érudits* in the United Provinces and, ironically, had become editor of the *Nouvelles de la Republique des Lettres* at the head of which he remained until 1710, turning this major instrument of Huguenot public consciousness into a vehicle for criticizing its original editor, Pierre Bayle.

Urging, against Spinoza and Bayle, the essential compatibility of Christianity and 'reason', Bernard moved philosophically from orthodox Cartesianism to the conviction, to which he was converted by Le Clerc, that Locke and English empiricism afforded the best solution to the acute intellectual problem of how to stabilize the relationship between philosophy and theology. Persuaded that for reconciling religion and science on a truly 'enlightened' basis 'la méthode des philosophes anglois étoit la plus sûre',[25] at Leiden Bernard proved, as the curators had hoped, as staunch an ally of Le Clerc's 'English' strategy as he was unremitting an antagonist of Spinoza and Bayle's insistence on separating faith and reason.

Bernard's 'fort longue dispute avec Mr Bayle' revolved essentially around two main questions: first, the issue of whether 'le consentement de toutes les nations à croire une Divinité' is a valid proof of God's existence, which Bayle, almost alone among the prominent Huguenot intellectual figures of the age, adamantly denied; and secondly, Bayle's deeply seditious pretension that atheism is not a worse evil than idolatry and the implications of this for toleration.[26] While

---

[25] *L'Europe Savante*, July 1718, 154; P. Hazard, *The European Mind, 1680–1715* (Harmondsworth, 1964), 288.
[26] Pierre Bayle, *Continuation des pensées diverses sur la Comète*, 2 vols. (Rotterdam,

the first was philosophically the more complex, the second, with its far-reaching moral implications, was religiously and socially the more emotive. For, as Bernard notes, Bayle's contention that atheism was not worse than pagan idolatry excited many against him, and greatly disconcerted others, given that in Huguenot and Dutch society, as for most people in the rest of Europe at the beginning of the eighteenth century, atheism was considered 'la plus pernicieuse disposition d'esprit et de coeur' to be found among men.[27]

Society simply can not subsist, held Bernard, 'sans la pratique de ces devoirs', and hence 'atheism', in the sense of denial of a Creator and divine providence as well as Revelation, violates society's most precious concerns far more than idolatry or paganism, indeed entails 'la destruction totale des societez'.[28] Bayle, however, totally disagreed. Some religions, in his view, had nothing edifying to offer. Contradicting Bernard, he stressed the frightful consequences of the bigotry, cruelty, and credulity he deemed typical of Graeco-Roman pagan religion. Claiming the pagan Greek cults inculcated dread of wholly immoral divinities driven mainly by base, unrestrained and violent passions, he held that anyone raised on such beliefs would be quite incapable of seeing that pride, greed, ambition, lasciviousness, love of luxury, violence and vengeance are immoral or sinful. Nor would they learn to admire positive moral qualities. For what the Graeco-Roman gods demanded of men, and their worshippers called piety, was really just subservience, adoration and flattery. Hence Graeco-Roman pagan religion, held Bayle, could not help establish a moral framework of equity, justice and integrity supportive of human needs and aspirations. Greek pagan cults, in other words, amounted to 'la renversement de la morale', which is why, he alleges, Socrates felt called upon to take his stand against them and was persecuted and put to death.[29]

1705), II, 364; Jacques Georges Chaufepié, *Nouveau Dictionnaire historique et critique pour servir de supplémen ou de continuation au Dictionnaire de* [. . .] *Pierre Bayle*, 4 vols. (Amsterdam and The Hague, 1750), I, 253–235; Mori, *Bayle philosophe*, 186, 209, 307; S. Brogi, *Teologia senza verità. Bayle contro i 'rationaux'* (Milan, 1998), 24, 97–100, 117–119.

[27] Chaufepié, *Nouveau Dictionnaire*, I, 256; H.T. Mason, 'Voltaire devant Bayle', in A. Mckenna and G. Paganini, eds., *Pierre Bayle dans la Republique des Lettres* (Paris, 2004), 448–449.

[28] Bayle, *Réponse aux questions*, IV, 267; Jacques Bernard, *De l'Excellence de la religion* (Amsterdam, 1714), 352–353.

[29] Bayle, *Continuation*, II, 560, 610–620, 630–631, 643, 658.

More disturbing, though, from the *rationaux*'s, as from Locke's, perspective, than his claiming that pagan idolatry was worse than 'atheism', was the uncompromising manner in which he demoted the Churches from their traditional status as the undisputed chief guide to moral truth. His sweeping liberty of conscience was based on a formula which dramatically reversed the age-old procedure in human judgements about values. Instead of churchmen pronouncing on what is right and wrong, universal moral principles based purely on reason, and secular criteria, were laid down and made the judge of every religious doctrine, and every sect, and the universal commentator on church history.[30]

This profound clash between Bayle's toleration and that of the Huguenot *rationaux* who opposed him led the latter to coin a new tolerationist terminology to express the antagonism between the two rival conceptions. Élie Saurin, minister of the Utrecht French Reformed congregation for over thirty years, and a fervent advocate of toleration, vehemently repudiated Bayle's system as something wholly incompatible with a Christian outlook. Where Bayle, in his *Commentaire philosophique*, maintains that every individual should act according to his private conscience whether inspired by true religion, or in error, and that no prince can justifiably coerce individual conscience – except where political sedition directly issues from heterodox belief – so that the individual is equally entitled to embrace Sadduceeism, Socinianism, Hinduism, Islam, Judaism, Deism or atheism, as any variant of Christianity, the Utrecht preacher rejected this as altogether libertine and invalid, a scandalous example of irreligious indifferentism. In works such as his *Réflections sur les droits de la conscience* of 1697, Saurin emphatically distances himself from Bayle, striving instead to locate the liberal Calvinist conscience midway between what he considered the bigoted 'intolérance' of Pierre Jurieu which he, like Le Clerc, Jaquelot, Bernard (and Bayle) despised, and the – in his eyes – equally, or still more, pernicious 'indifférence des religions, et l'impiété du *Commentaire philosophique*'.[31] For Saurin, irrespective of whether one believes Bayle's fideist avowals or not, Baylean

---

[30] *Ibid.*, 306–307; Paradis, 'Fondements', 29–31.
[31] M. Turchetti, 'Élie Saurin (1639–1703) et ses *Réflexions sur les droits de Conscience*', in C. Berkevens-Stevelinck, J.I. Israel and G.H.M. Posthumus Meyjes, eds., *The Emergence of Tolerance in the Dutch Republic* (Leiden, 1997), 176; Tinsley, *Pierre Bayle's Reformation*, 316; Mori, *Bayle philosophe*, 288.

toleration remains altogether devoid of Christian content, ruinous for religion and morality alike.

Bayle was a palpable threat to the entire community. Saurin drew reassurance, though, from the fact that among the Huguenot congregations in the Netherlands both Jurieu's adherents, 'les intolérants', and Bayle's, 'les indifférents', remained numerically insignificant fringes: 'la multitude et la foule des Réformés', he confidently (and surely rightly) maintained, 'tient le milieu entre l'intolérance et l'indifférence'.[32] If hard-line Calvinists such as the unbending Jurieu absurdly lumped liberal Calvinists like Saurin and Basnage together with 'indifférents' like Bayle, Saurin countered by pointing out that his own toleration theory – like Locke's, essentially liberty of conscience for all Christians accepting the Christian *fundamenta*: the 'Arminian' approach, in other words – increasingly favoured by liberal Calvinists generally, both manifests Christian charity (unlike Jurieu's steely dogmatism) and uncompromisingly rejects Bayle's unrestricted freedom of belief, thought and conscience.

This unbridgeable gulf between two irreconcilable conceptions of toleration and individual freedom subsequently reappeared in the controversies of the mid-eighteenth century, when toleration theorists hostile to what they saw as the illegitimate comprehensive freedom of thought and conscience proposed by Bayle and Spinoza, and determined to segregate it from true and legitimate Christian toleration, again contrasted the two in dramatic terms. The Abbé Pluche, in France, for example, carefully distinguishes between what he calls 'la Tolerance et le Tolérantisme', the latter signifying a generalized indifference to confessional status and differences such as was taken to be typical of the *esprits forts* and of Bayle: thus the respectable Enlightenment, Catholic and Protestant, invariably repudiated, and had to repudiate this as wrong, harmful and sinful.[33] In the 1780s it continued to be a characteristic feature of the European intellectual arena to contrast 'la tolérance chrétienne' with what a pamphlet published at Fribourg in 1785 called 'le tolérantisme philosophique'.[34]

---

[32] Quoted in Turchetti, 'Elie Saurin', 177.

[33] H. Bots, 'Le Plaidoyer des journalistes de Hollande pour la tolérance (1684–1750)', in M. Magdalaine *et al.*, eds., *De l'Humanisme aux lumières. Bayle et le protestantisme. Mélanges en l'honneur d'Elisabeth Labrousse* (Paris, 1996), 557–558.

[34] *La Tolérance chrétienne opposée au tolérantisme philosophique* (new edn., Fribourg, 1785).

Toleration, purification and rationalization – that was the agenda of the moderate mainstream Enlightenment. The leading theorists of the liberal Protestant middle ground, such as Le Clerc, Locke, Jaquelot, Bernard, Van Limborch, Turretini, and Leibniz, all converged in judging theological polemics over secondary and unnecessary issues to be not just pointless obfuscation but a serious and constant threat to true Christianity along with superfluous dogma, age-old schisms, and fabricated 'miracles'. Such reprehensible 'priestcraft', while particularly disfiguring the Catholic and Greek confessions, in their view, marred all the churches in varying degrees while serving no useful purpose other than to clog the path to Christian reunification and overly inflate ecclesiastical authority.

On one level, their programme was coherent and clear. However, the protagonists of rational Christianity faced a serious dilemma where and whenever they sought to further their agenda. For insofar as they sought to discredit 'superstition', false 'miracles', superfluous theology and excessive ecclesiastical power, they appeared to attack the very same outer bastions of tradition and ecclesiastical authority as the Deists and Spinozists. The fact that they, unlike their more radical rivals, wished to leave the inner citadel wholly intact was not necessarily obvious to the defenders within. Their problem, then, was not how to segregate themselves intellectually from the radicals but rather how to avoid appearing to endorse and assist the *esprits forts* and freethinkers in their combined push for toleration and assault on what the latter considered unmitigated 'superstition'. The situation, as Le Clerc saw in battling with Bayle, Locke discovered in fending off Toland, and Christian Thomasius found in disentangling himself from the Baltic Spinozist Theodor Ludwig Lau (1670–1740),[35] was one which forced the moderate mainstream into the highly uncomfortable predicament of a two-front war. Theirs was an often uncomfortable and risky strategy requiring a whole armoury of new theological arguments.

Liberal Calvinists and Huguenots in northern Europe during the early Enlightenment generally adhered to a limited toleration, carefully distancing themselves from the ideas of Bayle no less than of Spinoza.[36] Bayle's equal rights for the individual conscience whether

---

[35] See J.I. Israel, *Radical Enlightenment. Philosophy and the Making of Modernity, 1650–1750* (Oxford, 2001), 652–654.
[36] W. Frijhoff, 'Religious Toleration in the United Provinces. From "Case" to

Christian or non-Christian – since 'le droit de la conscience errante de bonne foi [involontaire et invincible] est tout le même que celui de la conscience orthodoxe'[37] – everywhere aroused the profoundest misgivings. Bayle's failure to assert that it is self-evidently true that Christianity is the true faith sharply segregates his conception of tolerance from that of the Arminians (including Episcopius, Le Clerc and Locke), and those of Basnage, Bernard, Saurin and Jaquelot, and like so much of his philosophy when carefully examined seemed inexorably to call into question the sincerity of his allegiance to the Reformed faith.

"Model"', in R. Po-Chia Hsia and H.F.K. van Nierop, eds., *Calvinism and Religious Toleration in the Dutch Golden Age* (Cambridge, 2002), 36–38.
    [37] Turchetti, 'Élie Saurin', 187; Bayle, *Commentaire philosophique*, 300; Gros, 'Introduction', 29.

INDEX

STUDIES IN MEDIEVAL AND REFORMATION TRADITIONS

(Formerly Studies in Medieval and Reformation Thought)

Founded by Heiko A. Oberman†
Edited by Andrew Colin Gow

1. DOUGLASS, E.J.D. *Justification in Late Medieval Preaching.* 2nd ed. 1989
2. WILLIS, E.D. *Calvin's Catholic Christology.* 1966 *out of print*
3. POST, R.R. *The Modern Devotion.* 1968 *out of print*
4. STEINMETZ, D.C. *Misericordia Dei.* The Theology of Johannes von Staupitz. 1968 *out of print*
5. O'MALLEY, J.W. *Giles of Viterbo on Church and Reform.* 1968 *out of print*
6. OZMENT, S.E. *Homo Spiritualis.* The Anthropology of Tauler, Gerson and Luther. 1969
7. PASCOE, L.B. *Jean Gerson: Principles of Church Reform.* 1973 *out of print*
8. HENDRIX, S.H. *Ecclesia in Via.* Medieval Psalms Exegesis and the *Dictata super Psalterium* (1513-1515) of Martin Luther. 1974
9. TREXLER, R.C. *The Spiritual Power.* Republican Florence under Interdict. 1974
10. TRINKAUS, Ch. with OBERMAN, H.A. (eds.). *The Pursuit of Holiness.* 1974 *out of print*
11. SIDER, R.J. *Andreas Bodenstein von Karlstadt.* 1974
12. HAGEN, K. *A Theology of Testament in the Young Luther.* 1974
13. MOORE, Jr., W.L. *Annotatiunculae D. Iohanne Eckio Praelectore.* 1976
14. OBERMAN, H.A. with BRADY, Jr., Th.A. (eds.). *Itinerarium Italicum.* Dedicated to Paul Oskar Kristeller. 1975
15. KEMPFF, D. *A Bibliography of Calviniana.* 1959-1974. 1975 *out of print*
16. WINDHORST, C. *Täuferisches Taufverständnis.* 1976
17. KITTELSON, J.M. *Wolfgang Capito.* 1975
18. DONNELLY, J.P. *Calvinism and Scholasticism in Vermigli's Doctrine of Man and Grace.* 1976
19. LAMPING, A.J. *Ulrichus Velenus (Oldřich Velenský) and his Treatise against the Papacy.* 1976
20. BAYLOR, M.G. *Action and Person.* Conscience in Late Scholasticism and the Young Luther. 1977
21. COURTENAY, W.J. *Adam Wodeham.* 1978
22. BRADY, Jr., Th.A. *Ruling Class, Regime and Reformation at Strasbourg, 1520-1555.* 1978
23. KLAASSEN, W. *Michael Gaismair.* 1978
24. BERNSTEIN, A.E. *Pierre d'Ailly and the Blanchard Affair.* 1978
25. BUCER, M. *Correspondance.* Tome I (Jusqu'en 1524). Publié par J. Rott. 1979
26. POSTHUMUS MEYJES, G.H.M. *Jean Gerson et l'Assemblée de Vincennes (1329).* 1978
27. VIVES, J.L. *In Pseudodialecticos.* Ed. by Ch. Fantazzi. 1979
28. BORNERT, R. *La Réforme Protestante du Culte à Strasbourg au XVIe siècle (1523-1598).* 1981
29. CASTELLIO, S. *De Arte Dubitandi.* Ed. by E. Feist Hirsch. 1981
30. BUCER, M. *Opera Latina.* Vol I. Publié par C. Augustijn, P. Fraenkel, M. Lienhard. 1982
31. BÜSSER, F. *Wurzeln der Reformation in Zürich.* 1985 *out of print*
32. FARGE, J.K. *Orthodoxy and Reform in Early Reformation France.* 1985
33. 34. BUCER, M. *Etudes sur les relations de Bucer avec les Pays-Bas.* I. Etudes; II. Documents. Par J.V. Pollet. 1985
35. HELLER, H. *The Conquest of Poverty.* The Calvinist Revolt in Sixteenth Century France. 1986

36. MEERHOFF, K. *Rhétorique et poétique au XVIᵉ siècle en France.* 1986
37. GERRITS, G. H. *Inter timorem et spem.* Gerard Zerbolt of Zutphen. 1986
38. POLIZIANO, A. *Lamia.* Ed. by A. Wesseling. 1986
39. BRAW, C. *Bücher im Staube.* Die Theologie Johann Arndts in ihrem Verhältnis zur Mystik. 1986
40. BUCER, M. *Opera Latina.* Vol. II. Enarratio in Evangelion Iohannis (1528, 1530, 1536). Publié par I. Backus. 1988
41. BUCER, M. *Opera Latina.* Vol. III. Martin Bucer and Matthew Parker: Flori-legium Patristicum. Edition critique. Publié par P. Fraenkel. 1988
42. BUCER, M. *Opera Latina.* Vol. IV. Consilium Theologicum Privatim Conscriptum. Publié par P. Fraenkel. 1988
43. BUCER, M. *Correspondance.* Tome II (1524-1526). Publié par J. Rott. 1989
44. RASMUSSEN, T. *Inimici Ecclesiae.* Das ekklesiologische Feindbild in Luthers "Dictata super Psalterium" (1513-1515) im Horizont der theologischen Tradition. 1989
45. POLLET, J. *Julius Pflug et la crise religieuse dans l'Allemagne du XVIᵉ siècle.* Essai de synthèse biographique et théologique. 1990
46. BUBENHEIMER, U. *Thomas Müntzer.* Herkunft und Bildung. 1989
47. BAUMAN, C. *The Spiritual Legacy of Hans Denck.* Interpretation and Translation of Key Texts. 1991
48. OBERMAN, H.A. and JAMES, F.A., III (eds.). in cooperation with SAAK, E.L. *Via Augustini.* Augustine in the Later Middle Ages, Renaissance and Reformation: Essays in Honor of Damasus Trapp. 1991 *out of print*
49. SEIDEL MENCHI, S. *Erasmus als Ketzer.* Reformation und Inquisition im Italien des 16. Jahrhunderts. 1993
50. SCHILLING, H. *Religion, Political Culture, and the Emergence of Early Modern Society.* Essays in German and Dutch History. 1992
51. DYKEMA, P.A. and OBERMAN, H.A. (eds.). *Anticlericalism in Late Medieval and Early Modern Europe.* 2nd ed. 1994
52. 53. KRIEGER, Chr. and LIENHARD, M. (eds.). *Martin Bucer and Sixteenth Century Europe.* Actes du colloque de Strasbourg (28-31 août 1991). 1993
54. SCREECH, M.A. *Clément Marot: A Renaissance Poet discovers the World.* Lutheranism, Fabrism and Calvinism in the Royal Courts of France and of Navarre and in the Ducal Court of Ferrara. 1994
55. GOW, A.C. *The Red Jews: Antisemitism in an Apocalyptic Age, 1200-1600.* 1995
56. BUCER, M. *Correspondance.* Tome III (1527-1529). Publié par Chr. Krieger et J. Rott. 1989
57. SPIJKER, W. VAN 'T. *The Ecclesiastical Offices in the Thought of Martin Bucer.* Translated by J. Vriend (text) and L.D. Bierma (notes). 1996
58. GRAHAM, M.F. *The Uses of Reform.* 'Godly Discipline' and Popular Behavior in Scotland and Beyond, 1560-1610. 1996
59. AUGUSTIJN, C. *Erasmus. Der Humanist als Theologe und Kirchenreformer.* 1996
60. McCOOG S J, T.M. *The Society of Jesus in Ireland, Scotland, and England 1541-1588.* 'Our Way of Proceeding?' 1996
61. FISCHER, N. und KOBELT-GROCH, M. (Hrsg.). *Außenseiter zwischen Mittelalter und Neuzeit.* Festschrift für Hans-Jürgen Goertz zum 60. Geburtstag. 1997
62. NIEDEN, M. *Organum Deitatis.* Die Christologie des Thomas de Vio Cajetan. 1997
63. BAST, R.J. *Honor Your Fathers.* Catechisms and the Emergence of a Patriarchal Ideology in Germany, 1400-1600. 1997
64. ROBBINS, K.C. *City on the Ocean Sea: La Rochelle, 1530-1650.* Urban Society, Religion, and Politics on the French Atlantic Frontier. 1997
65. BLICKLE, P. *From the Communal Reformation to the Revolution of the Common Man.* 1998
66. FELMBERG, B.A.R. *Die Ablaßtheorie Kardinal Cajetans (1469-1534).* 1998

67. CUNEO, P.F. *Art and Politics in Early Modern Germany.* Jörg Breu the Elder and the Fashioning of Political Identity, ca. 1475-1536. 1998
68. BRADY, Jr., Th.A. *Communities, Politics, and Reformation in Early Modern Europe.* 1998
69. McKEE, E.A. *The Writings of Katharina Schütz Zell.* 1. The Life and Thought of a Sixteenth-Century Reformer. 2. A Critical Edition. 1998
70. BOSTICK, C.V. *The Antichrist and the Lollards.* Apocalyticism in Late Medieval and Reformation England. 1998
71. BOYLE, M. O'ROURKE. *Senses of Touch.* Human Dignity and Deformity from Michelangelo to Calvin. 1998
72. TYLER, J.J. *Lord of the Sacred City.* The *Episcopus Exclusus* in Late Medieval and Early Modern Germany. 1999
74. WITT, R.G. *'In the Footsteps of the Ancients'.* The Origins of Humanism from Lovato to Bruni. 2000
77. TAYLOR, L.J. *Heresy and Orthodoxy in Sixteenth-Century Paris.* François le Picart and the Beginnings of the Catholic Reformation. 1999
78. BUCER, M. *Briefwechsel/Correspondance.* Band IV (Januar-September 1530). Herausgegeben und bearbeitet von R. Friedrich, B. Hamm und A. Puchta. 2000
79. MANETSCH, S.M. *Theodore Beza and the Quest for Peace in France, 1572-1598.* 2000
80. GODMAN, P. *The Saint as Censor.* Robert Bellarmine between Inquisition and Index. 2000
81. SCRIBNER, R.W. *Religion and Culture in Germany (1400-1800).* Ed. L. Roper. 2001
82. KOOI, C. *Liberty and Religion.* Church and State in Leiden's Reformation, 1572-1620. 2000
83. BUCER, M. *Opera Latina.* Vol. V. Defensio adversus axioma catholicum id est criminationem R.P. Roberti Episcopi Abrincensis (1534). Ed. W.I.P. Hazlett. 2000
84. BOER, W. DE. *The Conquest of the Soul.* Confession, Discipline, and Public Order in Counter-Reformation Milan. 2001
85. EHRSTINE, G. *Theater, culture, and community in Reformation Bern, 1523-1555.* 2001
86. CATTERALL, D. *Community Without Borders.* Scot Migrants and the Changing Face of Power in the Dutch Republic, c. 1600-1700. 2002
87. BOWD, S.D. *Reform Before the Reformation.* Vincenzo Querini and the Religious Renaissance in Italy. 2002
88. PELC, M. *Illustrium Imagines.* Das Porträtbuch der Renaissance. 2002
89. SAAK, E.L. *High Way to Heaven.* The Augustinian Platform between Reform and Reformation, 1292-1524. 2002
90. WITTNEBEN, E.L. *Bonagratia von Bergamo,* Franziskanerjurist und Wortführer seines Ordens im Streit mit Papst Johannes XXII. 2003
91. ZIKA, C. *Exorcising our Demons,* Magic, Witchcraft and Visual Culture in Early Modern Europe. 2002
92. MATTOX, M.L. *"Defender of the Most Holy Matriarchs",* Martin Luther's Interpretation of the Women of Genesis in the *Enarrationes in Genesin,* 1535-45. 2003
93. LANGHOLM, O. *The Merchant in the Confessional,* Trade and Price in the Pre-Reformation Penitential Handbooks. 2003
94. BACKUS, I. *Historical Method and Confessional Identity in the Era of the Reformation (1378-1615).* 2003
95. FOGGIE, J.P. *Renaissance Religion in Urban Scotland.* The Dominican Order, 1450-1560. 2003
96. LÖWE, J.A. *Richard Smyth and the Language of Orthodoxy.* Re-imagining Tudor Catholic Polemicism. 2003
97. HERWAARDEN, J. VAN. *Between Saint James and Erasmus.* Studies in Late-Medieval Religious Life: Devotion and Pilgrimage in The Netherlands. 2003
98. PETRY, Y. *Gender, Kabbalah and the Reformation.* The Mystical Theology of Guillaume Postel (1510–1581). 2004

99. EISERMANN, F., SCHLOTHEUBER, E. und HONEMANN, V. *Studien und Texte zur literarischen und materiellen Kultur der Frauenklöster im späten Mittelalter.* Ergebnisse eines Arbeitsgesprächs in der Herzog August Bibliothek Wolfenbüttel, 24.-26. Febr. 1999. 2004

100. WITCOMBE, C.L.C.E. *Copyright in the Renaissance.* Prints and the *Privilegio* in Sixteenth-Century Venice and Rome. 2004

101. BUCER, M. *Briefwechsel/Correspondance.* Band V (September 1530-Mai 1531). Herausgegeben und bearbeitet von R. Friedrich, B. Hamm, A. Puchta und R. Liebenberg. 2004

102. MALONE, C.M. *Façade as Spectacle: Ritual and Ideology at Wells Cathedral.* 2004

103. KAUFHOLD, M. (ed.) *Politische Reflexion in der Welt des späten Mittelalters / Political Thought in the Age of Scholasticism.* Essays in Honour of Jürgen Miethke. 2004

104. BLICK, S. and TEKIPPE, R. (eds.). *Art and Architecture of Late Medieval Pilgrimage in Northern Europe and the British Isles.* 2004

105. PASCOE, L.B., S.J. *Church and Reform.* Bishops, Theologians, and Canon Lawyers in the Thought of Pierre d'Ailly (1351-1420). 2005

106. SCOTT, T. *Town, Country, and Regions in Reformation Germany.* 2005

107. GROSJEAN, A.N.L. and MURDOCH, S. (eds.). *Scottish Communities Abroad in the Early Modern Period.* 2005

108. POSSET, F. *Renaissance Monks.* Monastic Humanism in Six Biographical Sketches. 2005

109. IHALAINEN, P. *Protestant Nations Redefined.* Changing Perceptions of National Identity in the Rhetoric of the English, Dutch and Swedish Public Churches, 1685-1772. 2005

110. FURDELL, E. (ed.) *Textual Healing: Essays on Medieval and Early Modern Medicine.* 2005

111. ESTES, J.M. *Peace, Order and the Glory of God.* Secular Authority and the Church in the Thought of Luther and Melanchthon, 1518-1559. 2005

112. MÄKINEN, V. (ed.) *Lutheran Reformation and the Law.* 2006

113. STILLMAN, R.E. (ed.) *Spectacle and Public Performance in the Late Middle Ages and the Renaissance.* 2006

114. OCKER, C. *Church Robbers and Reformers in Germany, 1525-1547.* Confiscation and Religious Purpose in the Holy Roman Empire. 2006

115. ROECK, B. *Civic Culture and Everyday Life in Early Modern Germany.* 2006

116. BLACK, C. *Pico's* Heptaplus *and Biblical Hermeneutics.* 2006

117. BLAŽEK, P. *Die mittelalterliche Rezeption der aristotelischen Philosophie der Ehe.* Von Robert Grosseteste bis Bartholomäus von Brügge (1246/1247-1309). 2007

118. AUDISIO, G. *Preachers by Night.* The Waldensian Barbes (15th-16th Centuries). 2007

119. SPRUYT, B.J. *Cornelius Henrici Hoen (Honius) and his Epistle on the Eucharist (1525).* 2006

120. BUCER, M. *Briefwechsel/Correspondance.* Band VI (Mai-Oktober 1531). Herausgegeben und bearbeitet von R. Friedrich, B. Hamm, W. Simon und M. Arnold. 2006

121. POLLMANN, J. and SPICER, A. (eds.). *Public Opinion and Changing Identities in the Early Modern Netherlands.* Essays in Honour of Alastair Duke. 2007